The Joy of Clojure

The Joy of Clojure

MICHAEL FOGUS
CHRIS HOUSER

MANNING

Greenwich
(74° w. long.)

Manning Publications Co.   Development editor: Susan Harkins
180 Broad St.   Copyeditor: Benjamin Berg
Suite 1323   Typesetter: Dottie Marsico
Stamford, CT 06901   Cover designer: Marija Tudor

ISBN 978-1-935182-64-1
Printed in the United States of America
1 2 3 4 5 6 7 8 9 10 – MAL – 16 15 14 13 12 11

The Joy of Clojure ... *wherein we teach you the joys of Clojure programming.*

We have written this book for you, the adventurous programmer with prior experience in Java or functional programming languages—especially Lisp. Our aim is to enhance your programming knowledge in general, and your understanding of Clojure in particular, by exploring the philosophy, motivations, and semantics of the Clojure programming language.

brief contents

contents

foreword

The authors of this book have taken an ambitious and aggressive approach to teaching Clojure. You know how everyone loves to say they teach using the "drinking from a fire hydrant" method? Well, at times it feels like these guys are trying to shove that fire hydrant right up... let's just say it's a place where you don't normally put a fire hydrant. This isn't intended as a first book on programming, and it may not be an ideal first book on Clojure either. The authors assume you're fearless and, importantly, equipped with a search engine. You'll want to have Google handy as you go through the examples. The authors blaze through many of the classics of both functional programming and industry programming in a whirlwind tour of Clojure that feels at times more like a class-five tropical storm. You'll learn fast!

Our industry, the global programming community, is fashion-driven to a degree that would embarrass haute couture designers from New York to Paris. We're slaves to fashion. Fashion dictates the programming languages people study in school, the languages employers hire for, the languages that get to be in books on shelves. A naive outsider might wonder if the quality of a language matters a little, just a teeny bit at least, but in the real world fashion trumps all.

So nobody could be more surprised than I that a Lisp dialect has suddenly become fashionable again. Clojure has only been out for three years, but it's gaining momentum at a rate that we haven't seen in a new language in decades. And it doesn't even have a "killer app" yet, in the way that browsers pushed JavaScript into the spotlight, or Rails propelled Ruby. Or maybe the killer app for Clojure is the JVM itself. Everyone's fed up with the Java language, but understandably we don't want to abandon our investment in the Java Virtual Machine and its capabilities: the libraries, the configuration, the monitoring, and all the other entirely valid reasons we still use it.

For those of us using the JVM or .NET, Clojure feels like a minor miracle. It's an astoundingly high-quality language, sure—in fact, I'm beginning to think it's the best I've ever seen—yet somehow it has still managed to be fashionable. That's quite a trick. It gives me renewed hope for the overall future of productivity in our industry. We might just dig ourselves out of this hole we're in and get back to where every project feels like a legacy-free startup, just like it was in the early days of Java.

There are still open questions about Clojure's suitability for production shops, especially around the toolchain. That's normal and expected for a new language. But Clojure shows so much promise, such beautiful and practical design principles, that everyone seems to be jumping in with both feet anyway. I certainly am. I haven't had this much fun with a new language since Java arrived on the scene 15 years ago. There have been plenty of pretenders to the JVM throne, languages that promised to take the Java platform to unprecedented new levels. But until now, none of them had the right mix of expressiveness, industrial strength, performance, and just plain fun.

I think maybe it's the "fun" part that's helped make Clojure fashionable.

In some sense, all this was inevitable, I think. Lisp—the notion of writing your code directly in tree form—is an idea that's discovered time and again. People have tried all sorts of crazy alternatives, writing code in XML or in opaque binary formats or using cumbersome code generators. But their artificial Byzantine empires always fall into disrepair or crush themselves into collapse while Lisp, the road that wanders through time, remains simple, elegant, and pure. All we needed to get back on that road was a modern approach, and Rich Hickey has given it to us in Clojure.

The Joy of Clojure just might help make Clojure as fun for you as it is for us.

STEVE YEGGE
GOOGLE
steve-yegge.blogspot.com

preface

To fully appreciate Clojure, we hearken back to Paul Graham's essay "Beating the Averages," an interesting look at the inner workings of his company Viaweb during the years prior to being bought by Yahoo! Inc. in 1998. Though interesting as survey of startup culture, the truly memorable part of the essay was the description of how Viaweb used the programming language Lisp as an advantage over its competition. How could a programming language more than 50 years old provide *any* market advantage over Viaweb's competitors, who were surely using modern enterprise technologies? Without repeating the exact terms of the essay, Graham makes a compelling case for the capability of Lisp to facilitate a more agile programming environment.

Clojure is a dialect of Lisp directly supporting concurrent software development using functional programming techniques, and like the Lisp described in "Beating the Averages," provides an environment conducive to agility. Clojure fosters agility in ways that many popular programming languages can't. Many programming languages are bewitched with most or all of the following:

- Verbosity
- Unavoidable boilerplate
- A long thought-code-feedback loop
- Incidental complexity
- Difficulties in extension
- Deficiencies in supporting crucial programming paradigms

In contrast, Clojure provides a mixture of power and practicality fostering rapid development cycles. But the benefits of Clojure don't stop with its agile nature—as the clarion call declares, "Multicore is the new hot topic" (Mache Creeger in *ACM Queue*, vol. 3, no. 7).

Though the idea of multicore processors isn't in itself new, its importance is becoming increasingly focused. Until recently, you could avoid concurrent and parallel programming techniques and instead ride the ever-quickening processor wave to better performance. Well, that ride is slowing to a stop, and Clojure is here to help.

Clojure provides a unique mix of functional programming and *host symbiosis*—an embrace of and direct support for its host platform, in this case the Java Virtual Machine. Additionally, the simplification and often elimination of the complexities involved in coordinated state change have positioned Clojure as an important language moving forward. All software developers must eventually address these problems as a matter of course, and the study, understanding, and eventual utilization of Clojure is an essential path toward conquering them. From topics such as software transactional memory to laziness to immutability, this book will guide you on your way to understanding the "why" of Clojure, in addition to the "how."

We'll be your guides into a thoughtful understanding of the joyfulness in Clojure, for we believe its art is prelude to a new age of software development.

acknowledgments

The authors would like to jointly thank Rich Hickey, the creator of Clojure, for his thoughtful creation, furthering the state of the art in language design. Without his hard work, devotion, and vision, this book would never have been.

We'd also like to thank the brilliant members of the young Clojure community, including but not limited to: Stuart Halloway, David Edgar Liebke, Christophe Grand, Chas Emerick, Meikel Brandmeyer, Brian Carper, Bradford Cross, Sean Devlin, Tom Faulhaber, Stephen Gilardi, Phil Hagelberg, Konrad Hinsen, George Jahad, David Miller, David Nolen, Laurent Petit, and Stuart Sierra. Finally, we'd like to thank a few early adopters who took the time to provide thoughtful feedback, including Jürgen Hötzel, Robert "Uncle Bob" Martin, Grant Michaels, Mangala Sadhu Sangeet Singh Khalsa, and Sam Aaron. And finally, we would like to thank Steve Yegge for agreeing to write the foreword and for inspiring us over the years.

Manning sent out the manuscript for peer review at different stages of its development and we would like to thank the following reviewers for their invaluable feedback: Art Gittleman, Stuart Caborn, Jeff Sapp, Josh Heyer, Dave Pawson, Andrew Oswald, Federico Tomassetti, Matt Revelle, Rob Friesel, David Liebke, Pratik Patel, Phil Hagelberg, Rich Hickey, Andy Dingley, Baishampayan Ghose, Chas Emerick, John D'Emic, and Philipp K. Janert.

Thanks also to the team at Manning for their guidance and support, starting with publisher Marjan Bace, associate publisher Michael Stephens, our development editor Susan Harkins, and the production team of Nicholas Chase, Benjamin Berg, Katie Tennant, Dottie Marsico, and Mary Piergies. And again to Christophe Grand for a final technical review of the mansucript during production.

FOGUS

I'd like to thank my beautiful wife Yuki for her unwavering patience during the writing of this book. Without her I would've never made it through. I also owe a great debt to Chris Houser, my coauthor and friend, for teaching me more about Clojure than I ever would've thought possible. I'd also like to thank Dr. Larry Albright for introducing me to Lisp and the late Dr. Russel E. Kacher for inspiring in me a passion for learning, curiosity, and reflection. Additionally, I'd like to thank the organizers of the National Capital Area Clojure Users Group—Matthew Courtney, Russ Olsen, and Gray Herter—for providing a place for others in the DC area to discover Clojure. Finally, I'd like to thank my boys Keita and Shota for teaching me the true meaning of love and that it's not always about me.

CHOUSER

My most grateful thanks go to God, the source of all good things. To my parents, thanks for your love and support—your spirit of exploration launched me on a life of wonderful adventure. To my brother Bill, thanks for my earliest introduction to computers and the joys and challenges of programming. To my wife Heather, thanks for your constant encouragement from the very first moments of this book project to the last. To my friend and coauthor Michael Fogus, thanks for the brilliant inspiration and stunning breadth of knowledge you've brought to these pages.

about this book

Why learn Clojure?

The only difference between Shakespeare and you was the size of his idiom list—not the size of his vocabulary.

—Alan Perlis

When this book was conceived, our first instinct was to create a comprehensive comparison between Clojure and its host language, Java. After further reflection, we reached the conclusion that such an approach would be disingenuous at best, and disastrous at worst. Granted, some points of comparison can't be avoided, but Java is very different from Clojure and to try and distort one to explain the other would respect neither. Therefore, we decided that a better approach would be to focus on "The Clojure Way" of writing code.

When we become familiar with a programming language, the idioms and constructs of that language serve to define the way we think about and solve programming tasks. It's therefore natural that when faced with an entirely new language, we find comfort in mentally mapping the new language onto the familiar old. But we plead with you to leave all of your baggage behind; be you from Java, Lisp, Scheme, C#, or Befunge, we ask you to bear in mind that Clojure is its own language and begs an adherence to its own set of idioms. You'll discover concepts that you can connect between Clojure and languages you already know, but don't assume that similar things are entirely the same.

We'll work hard to guide you through the features and semantics of Clojure to help you build the mental model needed to use the language effectively. Most of the samples in this book are designed to be run in Clojure's interactive programming environment, commonly known as the *Read-Eval-Print Loop*, or *REPL*, an extremely powerful environment for experimentation and rapid prototyping.

By the time you're done with this book, the Clojure way of thinking about and solving problems will be another comfortable tool in your toolbox. If we succeed, then not only will you be a better Clojure programmer, but you'll also start seeing your programming language of choice—be it Java, C#, Python, Ruby, J, or Haskell—in an entirely different light. This reassessment of topics that we often take for granted is essential for personal growth.

Who should read this book?

> *Paths are made by walking.*
> —Franz Kafka

This book isn't a beginner's guide to Clojure. We start fast and don't devote much space to establishing a running Clojure environment, although we do provide some guidance on page xxix. Additionally, this isn't a book about Clojure's implementation details, but instead one about its semantical details. This is also not a "cookbook" for Clojure, but instead a thorough investigation into the ingredients that Clojure provides for creating beautiful software. Often we'll explain how these ingredients mix and why they make a great match, but you won't find complete recipes for systems. Our examples directly address the discussion at hand and at times leave exposed wiring for you to extend and thus further your own knowledge. It wouldn't serve us, you, or Clojure to try to awkwardly mold a comprehensive lesson into the guise of a book-length project. Often, language books spend valuable time halfheartedly explaining "real-world" matters totally unrelated to the language itself, and we wish to avoid this trap. We strongly feel that if we show you the "why" of the language, then you'll be better prepared to take that knowledge and apply it to your real-world problems. In short, if you're looking for a book amenable to neophytes that will also show you how to migrate Clojure into existing codebases, connect to NoSQL databases, and explore other "real-world" topics, then we recommend the book *Clojure in Action* by Amit Rathore (Manning, 2011).

Having said all of that, we do provide a short introduction to the language and feel that for those of you willing to work hard to understand Clojure, this is indeed the book for you. Additionally, if you already have a background in Lisp programming, then much of the introductory material will be familiar, thus making this book ideal for you. Though by no means perfect, Clojure has a nice combination of features that fit together into a coherent system for solving programming problems. The way Clojure encourages you to think about problems may be different than you're used to, requiring a bit of work to "get." But once you cross that threshold, you too may experience a kind of euphoria, and in this book we'll help you get there. These are exciting times, and Clojure is the language we hope you'll agree is an essential tool for navigating into the future.

Roadmap

We're going to take you on a journey. Perhaps you've started on this journey yourself by exploring Clojure beforehand. Perhaps you're a seasoned Java or Lisp veteran and are coming to Clojure for the first time. Perhaps you're coming into this book from an entirely different background. In any case, we're talking to you. This is a self-styled book for the adventurous and will require that you leave your baggage behind and approach the enclosed topics with an open mind. In many ways, Clojure will change the way you view programming, and in other ways it'll obliterate your preconceived notions. The language has a lot to say about how software should be designed and implemented, and we'll touch on these topics one by one throughout this book.

FOUNDATIONS

Every so often, a programming language comes along that can be considered foundational. Occasionally a language is invented that shakes the foundations of the software industry and dispels the collective preconceived notions of "good software practices." These foundational programming languages always introduce a novel approach to software development, alleviating if not eliminating the difficult problems of their time. Any list of foundational languages inevitably raises the ire of language proponents who feel their preferences shouldn't be ignored. But we're willing to take this risk and therefore list the following programming languages in this category.

Foundational programming languages

Year	Language	Inventor(s)	Interesting reading
1957	Fortran	John Backus	John Backus, "The History of Fortran I, II, and III," *IEEE Annals of the History of Computing* 20, no. 4 (1998).
1958	Lisp	John McCarthy	Richard P. Gabriel and Guy L. Steele Jr., "The Evolution of Lisp" (1992), www.dreamsongs.com/Files/HOPL2-Uncut.pdf.
1959	COBOL	Design by committee	Edsger Dijkstra, "EWD 498: How Do We Tell Truths That Might Hurt?" in *Selected Writings on Computing: A Personal Perspective* (New York: Springer-Verlag, 1982).
1968	Smalltalk	Alan Kay	Adele Goldberg, *Smalltalk-80: The Language and Its Implementation* (Reading, MA: Addison-Wesley, 1983).
1972	C	Dennis Ritchie	Brian W. Kernighan and Dennis M. Ritchie, *The C Programming Language* (Englewood Cliffs, NJ: Prentice Hall, 1988).
1972	Prolog	Alain Colmerauer	Ivan Bratko, *PROLOG: Programming for Artificial Intelligence* (New York: Addison-Wesley, 2000).
1975	Scheme	Guy Steele and Gerald Sussman	Guy Steele and Gerald Sussman, the "Lambda Papers," mng.bz/sU33.

Foundational programming languages *(continued)*

Year	Language	Inventor(s)	Interesting reading
1983	C++	Bjarne Stroustrup	Bjarne Stroustrup, *The Design and Evolution of C++* (Reading, MA: Addison-Wesley, 1994).
1986	Erlang	Telefonaktiebolaget L. M. Ericsson	Joe Armstrong, "A History of Erlang," *Proceedings of the Third ACM SIGPLAN Conference on History of Programming Languages* (2007).
1987	Perl	Larry Wall	Larry Wall, Tom Christiansen, and Jon Orwant, *Programming Perl* (Cambridge, MA: O'Reilly, 2000).
1990	Haskell	Simon Peyton Jones	Miran Lipovača, "Learn You a Haskell for Great Good!" http://learnyouahaskell.com/.
1995	Java	Sun Microsystems	David Bank, "The Java Saga," *Wired* 3.12 (1995).
2007	Clojure?	Rich Hickey	You're reading it.

Like them or not, there's little dispute that the listed programming languages have greatly influenced the way that software is constructed. Whether Clojure should be included in this category remains to be seen, but Clojure does borrow heavily from many of the foundational languages and also from other influential programming languages to boot.

Chapter 1 starts our journey and provides some of the core concepts embraced by Clojure. These concepts should be well understood by the time you've finished the chapter. Along the way, we'll show illustrative code samples highlighting the concepts at hand (and sometimes even pretty pictures). Much of what's contained in chapter 1 can be deemed "The Clojure Philosophy," so if you've ever wondered what inspired and constitutes Clojure, we'll provide that for you.

Chapter 2 provides a fast introduction to specific features and syntax of Clojure.

Chapter 3 will address general Clojure programming idioms that aren't easily categorized. From matters of truthiness and style to considerations of packaging and nil, chapter 3 is a mixed bag. All of the topics are important in their own right, and to understand them is in many ways a start to understanding a large portion of idiomatic Clojure source code.

DATA TYPES

The discussion on scalar data types in chapter 4 will be relatively familiar to most programmers, but some important points beg our attention, arising from Clojure's interesting nature as a functional programming language hosted on the Java Virtual Machine. Java programmers reading this book will recognize the points made concerning numerical precision (section 4.1), and Lisp programmers will recognize the discussion on Lisp-1 versus Lisp-2 (section 4.4). Programmers will appreciate the practical inclusion of regular expressions as first-class syntactical elements (section 4.5). Finally, long-time Clojure programmers may find that the discussion of rationals and keywords (sections 4.2 and 4.3, respectively) sheds new light on these seemingly innocent types.

Regardless of your background, chapter 4 will provide crucial information in understanding the nature of Clojure's underappreciated scalar types.

Clojure's novel persistent data structures will be covered in chapter 5; this should be enlightening to anyone wishing to look more deeply into them. Persistent data structures lie at the heart of Clojure's programming philosophy and *must* be understood to fully grasp the implications of Clojure's design decisions. We'll only touch briefly on the implementation details of these persistent structures, because they're less important than understanding why and how to use them.

FUNCTIONAL PROGRAMMING

Chapter 6 will deal with the nebulous notions of immutability, persistence, and laziness. We'll explore Clojure's use of immutability as the key element in supporting concurrent programming. We'll likewise show how, in the presence of immutability, many of the problems associated with coordinated state change disappear. Regarding laziness, we'll explore the ways that Clojure leverages it to reduce the memory footprint and speed execution times. Finally, we'll cover the interplay between immutability and laziness. For programmers coming from languages that allow unconstrained mutation and strict evaluation of expressions, chapter 6 may prove to be an initially mind-bending experience. But with this mind-bending comes enlightenment, and you'll likely never view your preferred programming languages in the same light.

Chapter 7 will tackle Clojure's approach to functional programming full-on. For those of you coming from a functional programming background, much of the chapter will be familiar, although Clojure will present its own unique blend. But like every programming language dubbed "functional," Clojure's implementation will provide a different lens by which to view your previous experience. For those of you wholly unfamiliar with functional programming techniques, chapter 7 will likely be mind-bending. In coming from a language that centers on object hierarchies and imperative programming techniques, the notion of functional programming seems alien. But we believe Clojure's decision to base its programming model in the functional paradigm to be the correct one, and we hope that you'll agree.

LARGE-SCALE DESIGN

Clojure can be used as the primary language for any application scale, and the discussion of macros in chapter 8 might change your ideas regarding how to develop software. Clojure as a Lisp embraces macros, and we'll lead you through the process of understanding them and realizing that with great power comes great responsibility.

In chapter 9, we'll guide you through the use of Clojure's built-in mechanisms for combining and relating code and data. From namespaces to multimethods to types and protocols, we'll explain how Clojure fosters the design and implementation of large-scale applications.

Clojure is a symbiotic programming language, meaning that it's intended to run atop a host environment. For now, the host of choice is the Java Virtual Machine, but the future bodes well for Clojure becoming host-agnostic. In any case, Clojure provides top-notch functions and macros for interacting directly with the host platform.

In chapter 10, we'll discuss the ways that Clojure interoperates with its host, focusing on the JVM throughout.

Clojure is built to foster the sane management of program state, which in turn facilitates concurrent programming, as you'll see in chapter 11. Clojure's simple yet powerful state model alleviates most of the headaches involved in such complicated tasks, and we'll show you how and why to use each. Additionally, we'll address the matters not directly solved by Clojure, such as how to identify and reduce those elements that should be protected using Clojure's reference types.

TANGENTIAL CONSIDERATIONS

The final part of this book will discuss topics that are equally important: the design and development of your application viewed through the lens of the Clojure Philosophy. In chapter 12, we'll discuss ways to improve your application's performance in single-threaded applications. Clojure provides many mechanisms for improving performance, and we'll delve into each, including their usage and caveats where applicable. And to wrap up our book, in chapter 13, we'll address the ways that Clojure changes the ways that you look at tangential development activities, such as the definition of your application domain language, testing, error-handling, and debugging.

Code conventions

The source code used throughout this book is formatted in a straightforward and pragmatic fashion. Any source code listings inlined within the text, for example (:lemonade :fugu), will be formatted using a fixed-width font and highlighted. Source code snippets outlined as blocks of code will be offset from the left margin, formatted in a fixed-width font, and highlighted to stand out:

```
(def population {::zombies 2700 ::humans 9})
(def per-capita (/ (population ::zombies) (population ::humans)))
(println per-capita "zombies for every human!")
```

Whenever a source code snippet indicates the result of an expression, the result will be prefixed by the characters ;=>. This particular sequence serves a threefold purpose:

- It helps the result stand out from the code expressions.
- It indicates a Clojure comment.
- Because of this, whole code blocks can be easily copied from an EBook or PDF version of this book and pasted into a running Clojure REPL:

```
(def population {::zombies 2700 ::humans 9})
(/ (population ::zombies) (population ::humans))
;=> 300
```

Additionally, any expected display in the REPL that's not a returned value (such as exceptions or printouts) will be denoted with a leading ; prior to the actual return value:

```
(println population)
; {:user/zombies 2700, :user/humans 9}
;=> nil
```

In the previous example, the map displayed as {:user/zombies 2700, :user/humans 9} is the printed value, whereas nil denotes the returned value from the println function. If no return value is shown after an expression, then you can assume that it's either nil or negligible to the example at hand.

> **READING CLOJURE CODE** When reading Clojure code, skim it when reading left-to-right, paying just enough attention to note important bits of context (defn, binding, let, and so on). When reading from the inside out, pay careful attention to what each expression returns to be passed to the next outer function. This is much easier than trying to remember the whole outer context when reading the innermost expressions.

All code formatted as either inline or block-level is intended to be typed or pasted exactly as written into Clojure source files or a REPL. We generally won't show the Clojure prompt user> because it'll cause copy/paste to fail. Finally, we'll at times use the ellipsis . . . to indicate an elided result or printout.

Code annotations accompany many of the listings, highlighting important concepts. In some cases, numbered bullets link to explanations that follow the listing.

Getting Clojure

If you don't currently have Clojure, then we recommend you retrieve the Clojure REPL package (Cljr) created by David Edgar Liebke, located at http://joyofclojure.com/cljr and installing it via the following instructions.

PREREQUISITES

- Java version 1.6 and later
- An Internet connection

INSTRUCTIONS

Run the following from your operating system's console:

```
java -jar cljr-installer.jar
```

If your chosen download method appended a .zip file extension to the Cljr package, then the following is fine:

```
java -jar cljr-installer.jar.zip
```

You'll see output from Cljr indicating its installation and package download progress. Once it has completed, you'll see instructions for running Clj similar to the following:

```
Cljr has been successfully installed. Add $HOME/.cljr/bin to your PATH:

    $ export PATH=$HOME/.cljr/bin:$PATH

Run 'cljr help' for a list of available commands.
```

Following the steps displayed, run Cljr.

REPL

The Cljr package runs a Clojure REPL (Read/Eval/Print Loop) for version 1.2.0—the same version corresponding to this book. When you launch the Cljr program, you'll see the window shown in the figure below.

```
Clojure 1.2.0
user=> (+ 1 2 3 4 5)
15
user=> |
```

The Cljr REPL is similar to the stock Clojure REPL, but with additional convenient features as explained at http://github.com/fogus/cljr.

The book won't proceed under the assumption that you're using Cljr but will work regardless of your own personal REPL setup—as long as you're running Clojure version 1.2.

DOWNLOADING CODE EXAMPLES

Source code for all working examples in this book is available for download from the publisher's website at www.manning.com/TheJoyofClojure.

Author Online

Purchase of *The Joy of Clojure* includes free access to a private web forum run by Manning Publications where you can make comments about the book, ask technical questions, and receive help from the authors and from other users. To access the forum and subscribe to it, point your web browser to www.manning.com/TheJoyofClojure. This page provides information on how to get on the forum once you are registered, what kind of help is available, and the rules of conduct on the forum.

Manning's commitment to our readers is to provide a venue where a meaningful dialogue between individual readers and between readers and the authors can take place. It is not a commitment to any specific amount of participation on the part of the authors, whose contribution to the AO remains voluntary (and unpaid). We suggest you try asking the authors some challenging questions lest their interest stray!

The Author Online forum and the archives of previous discussions will be accessible from the publisher's website as long as the book is in print.

About the cover illustration

The figure on the cover of *The Joy of Clojure* is captioned "The Confidence Man," which, in 19th century France, could mean anything from a healer or medicine man to a card shark or money lender or traveling salesman. The illustration is taken from a 19th-century edition of Sylvain Maréchal's four-volume compendium of regional dress customs published in France. Each illustration is finely drawn and colored by hand. The rich variety of Maréchal's collection reminds us vividly of how culturally apart the world's towns and regions were just 200 years ago. Isolated from each other, people spoke different dialects and languages. In the streets or in the countryside, it was easy to identify where they lived and what their trade or station in life was just by their dress.

Dress codes have changed since then and the diversity by region, so rich at the time, has faded away. It is now hard to tell apart the inhabitants of different continents, let alone different towns or regions. Perhaps we have traded cultural diversity for a more varied personal life—certainly for a more varied and fast-paced technological life.

At a time when it is hard to tell one computer book from another, Manning celebrates the inventiveness and initiative of the computer business with book covers based on the rich diversity of regional life of two centuries ago, brought back to life by Maréchal's pictures.

Part 1

Foundations

Even the most elaborate mansion must begin with a firm if humble foundation. We begin here by pouring a foundation of knowledge on which you'll be able to build a solid understanding about Clojure's less familiar ways. This foundation includes, among other things, the philosophy of programming underlying Clojure, sturdy walls of data and functions, and REPLs and nil puns.

Clojure philosophy

This chapter covers

- The Clojure way
- Why a(nother) Lisp?
- Functional programming
- Why Clojure isn't especially object-oriented

Learning a new language generally requires significant investment of thought and effort, and it is only fair that programmers expect each language they consider learning to justify that investment. Clojure was born out of creator Rich Hickey's desire to avoid many of the complications, both inherent and incidental, of managing state using traditional object-oriented techniques. Thanks to a thoughtful design based in rigorous programming language research, coupled with a fervent look toward practicality, Clojure has blossomed into an important programming language playing an undeniably important role in the current state of the art in language design. On one side of the equation, Clojure utilizes Software Transactional Memory (STM), agents, a clear distinction between identity and value types, arbitrary polymorphism, and functional programming to provide an environment conducive to making sense of state in general, and especially in the face of concurrency. On the other side, Clojure shares a symbiotic relationship with the

Java Virtual Machine, thus allowing prospective developers to avoid the costs of maintaining yet another infrastructure while leveraging existing libraries.

In the grand timeline of programming language history, Clojure is an infant; but its colloquialisms (loosely translated as "best practices" or idioms) are rooted[1] in 50 years of Lisp, as well as 15 years of Java history. Additionally, the enthusiastic community that has exploded since its introduction has cultivated its own set of unique idioms. As mentioned in the preface, the idioms of a language help to define succinct representations of more complicated expressions. Although we will certainly cover idiomatic Clojure code, we will also expand into deeper discussions of the "why" of the language itself.

In this chapter, we'll discuss the weaknesses in existing languages that Clojure was designed to address, how it provides strength in those areas, and many of the design decisions Clojure embodies. We'll also look at some of the ways existing languages have influenced Clojure, and define terms that will be used throughout the book.

1.1 The Clojure way

We'll start slowly.

Clojure is an opinionated language—it doesn't try to cover all paradigms or provide every checklist bullet-point feature. Instead it provides the features needed to solve all kinds of real-world problems the Clojure way. To reap the most benefit from Clojure, you'll want to write your code with the same vision as the language itself. As we walk through the language features in the rest of the book, we'll mention not just what a feature does, but why it's there and how best to take advantage of it.

But before we get to that, we'll first take a high-level view of some of Clojure's most important philosophical underpinnings. Figure 1.1 lists some broad goals that Rich Hickey had in mind while designing Clojure and some of the more specific decisions that are built into the language to support these goals.

As the figure illustrates, Clojure's broad goals are formed from a confluence of supporting goals and functionality, which we will touch on in the following subsections.

1.1.1 Simplicity

It's hard to write simple solutions to complex problems. But every experienced programmer has also stumbled on areas where we've made things more complex than necessary, what you might call

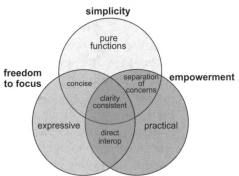

Figure 1.1 Broad goals of Clojure: this figure shows some of the concepts that underlie the Clojure philosophy, and how they intersect.

---

[1] While drawing on the traditions of Lisps (in general) and Java, Clojure in many ways stands as a direct challenge to them for change.

incidental complexity as opposed to complexity that's *essential* to the task at hand (Moseley 2006). Clojure strives to let you tackle complex problems involving a wide variety of data requirements, multiple concurrent threads, independently developed libraries, and so on without adding incidental complexity. It also provides tools reducing what at first glance may seem like essential complexity. The resulting set of features may not always seem simple, especially when they're still unfamiliar, but as you read through this book we think you'll come to see how much complexity Clojure helps strip away.

One example of incidental complexity is the tendency of modern object-oriented languages to require that every piece of runnable code be packaged in layers of class definitions, inheritance, and type declarations. Clojure cuts through all this by championing the *pure function*, which takes a few arguments and produces a return value based solely on those arguments. An enormous amount of Clojure is built from such functions, and most applications can be too, which means that there's less to think about when trying to solve the problem at hand.

1.1.2 Freedom to focus

Writing code is often a constant struggle against distraction, and every time a language requires you to think about syntax, operator precedence, or inheritance hierarchies, it exacerbates the problem. Clojure tries to stay out of your way by keeping things as simple as possible, not requiring you to go through a compile-and-run cycle to explore an idea, not requiring type declarations, and so on. It also gives you tools to mold the language itself so that the vocabulary and grammar available to you fit as well as possible to your problem domain—Clojure is *expressive*. It packs a punch, allowing you to perform highly complicated tasks succinctly without sacrificing comprehensibility.

One key to delivering this freedom is a commitment to dynamic systems. Almost everything defined in a Clojure program can be redefined, even while the program is running: functions, multimethods, types, type hierarchies, and even Java method implementations. Though redefining things on the fly might be scary on a production system, it opens a world of amazing possibilities in how you think about writing programs. It allows for more experimentation and exploration of unfamiliar APIs, and it adds an element of fun that can sometimes be impeded by more static languages and long compilation cycles.

But Clojure's not just about having fun. The fun is a by-product of giving programmers the power to be more productive than they ever thought imaginable.

1.1.3 Empowerment

Some programming languages have been created primarily to demonstrate some nugget of academia or to explore certain theories of computation. Clojure is *not* one of these. Rich Hickey has said on numerous occasions that Clojure has value to the degree that it lets you build interesting and useful applications.

To serve this goal, Clojure strives to be practical—a tool for getting the job done. If a decision about some design point in Clojure had to weigh the trade-offs between the practical solution and a clever, fancy, or theoretically pure solution, usually the practical solution won out. Clojure could try to shield you from Java by inserting a comprehensive API between the programmer and the libraries, but this could make the use of third-party Java libraries more clumsy. So Clojure went the other way: direct, wrapper-free, compiles-to-the-same-bytecode access to Java classes and methods. Clojure strings are Java strings; Clojure function calls are Java method calls—it's simple, direct, and practical.

The decision to use the Java Virtual Machine (JVM) itself is a clear example of this practicality. The JVM has some technical weaknesses such as startup time, memory usage, and lack of *tail-call optimization*[2] (TCO). But it's also an amazingly practical platform—it's mature, fast, and widely deployed. It supports a variety of hardware and operating systems and has a staggering number of libraries and support tools available, all of which Clojure can take advantage of because of this supremely practical decision.

With direct method calls, `proxy`, `gen-class`, `gen-interface` (see chapter 10), `reify`, `definterface`, `deftype`, and `defrecord` (see section 9.3), Clojure works hard to provide a bevy of interoperability options, all in the name of helping you get your job done. Practicality is important to Clojure, but many other languages are practical as well. You'll start to see some ways that Clojure really sets itself apart by looking at how it avoids muddles.

1.1.4   Clarity

When beetles battle beetles in a puddle paddle battle and the beetle battle puddle is a
puddle in a bottle they call this a tweetle beetle bottle puddle paddle battle muddle.

—Dr. Seuss

Consider what might be described as a simple snippet of code in a language like Python:

```
x = [5]
process(x)
x[0] = x[0] + 1
```

After executing this code, what's the value of x? If you assume `process` doesn't change the contents of x at all, it should be `[6]`, right? But how can you make that assumption? Without knowing exactly what `process` does, and whatever function it calls does, and so on, you can't be sure at all.

Even if you're sure `process` doesn't change the contents of x, add multithreading and now you have another whole set of concerns. What if some other thread changes

---

[2] Don't worry if you don't know what tail-call optimization is. Also don't worry if you *do* know what TCO is and think the JVM's lack of it is a critical flaw for a Lisp or functional language such as Clojure. All your concerns will be addressed in section 7.3. Until then, just relax.

x between the first and third lines? Worse yet, what if something is setting x at the moment the third line is doing its assignment—are you sure your platform guarantees an atomic write to that variable, or is it possible that the value will be a corrupted mix of multiple writes? We could continue this thought exercise in hopes of gaining some clarity, but the end result would be the same—what you have ends up not being clear at all, but the opposite: a muddle.

Clojure strives for code clarity by providing tools to ward off several different kinds of muddles. For the one just described, it provides immutable locals and persistent collections, which together eliminate most of the single- and multithreaded issues all at once.

You can find yourself in several other kinds of muddles when the language you're using merges unrelated behavior into a single construct. Clojure fights this by being vigilant about separation of concerns. When things start off separated, it clarifies your thinking and allows you to recombine them only when and to the extent that doing so is useful for a particular problem. Table 1.1 contrasts common approaches that merge concepts together in some other languages with separations of similar concepts in Clojure that will be explained in greater detail throughout this book.

Table 1.1 Separation of concerns in Clojure

Conflated	Separated	Where
Object with mutable fields	Values *from* identities	Chapter 4 and section 5.1
Class acts as namespace for methods	Function namespaces *from* type namespaces	Sections 8.2 and 8.3
Inheritance hierarchy made of classes	Hierarchy of names *from* data and functions	Chapter 8
Data and methods bound together lexically	Data objects *from* functions	Sections 6.1 and 6.2 and chapter 8
Method implementations embedded throughout class inheritance chain	Interface declarations *from* function implementations	Sections 8.2 and 8.3

It can be hard at times to tease apart these concepts in our own minds, but accomplishing it can bring remarkable clarity and a sense of power and flexibility that's worth the effort. With all these different concepts at your disposal, it's important that the code and data you work with express this variety in a consistent way.

1.1.5 Consistency

Clojure works to provide consistency in two specific ways: consistency of syntax and of data structures.

Consistency of syntax is about the similarity in form between related concepts. One simple but powerful example of this is the shared syntax of the `for` and `doseq` macros.

They don't do the same thing—for returns a lazy seq whereas doseq is for generating side effects—but both support the same mini-language of nested iteration, destructuring, and :when and :while guards. The similarities stand out when comparing the following examples:

```
(for [x [:a :b], y (range 5) :when (odd? y)] [x y])
;=> ([:a 1] [:a 3] [:b 1] [:b 3])

(doseq [x [:a :b], y (range 5) :when (odd? y)] (prn x y))
; :a 1
; :a 3
; :b 1
; :b 3
;=> nil
```

The value of this similarity is having to learn only one basic syntax for both situations, as well as the ease with which you can convert any particular usage of one form to the other if that becomes necessary.

Likewise, the consistency of data structures is the deliberate design of all of Clojure's persistent collection types to provide interfaces as similar to each other as possible, as well as to make them as broadly useful as possible. This is actually an extension of the classic Lisp "code is data" philosophy. Clojure data structures aren't used just for holding large amounts of application data, but also to hold the expression elements of the application itself. They're used to describe destructuring forms and to provide named options to various built-in functions. Where other object-oriented languages might encourage applications to define multiple incompatible classes to hold different kinds of application data, Clojure encourages the use of compatible map-like objects.

The benefit of this is that the same set of functions designed to work with Clojure data structures can be applied to all these contexts: large data stores, application code, and application data objects. You can use into to build any of these types, seq to get a lazy seq to walk through them, filter to select elements of any of them that satisfy a particular predicate, and so on. Once you've grown accustomed to having the richness of all these functions available everywhere, dealing with a Java or C++ application's Person or Address class will feel constraining.

Simplicity, freedom to focus, empowerment, consistency, and clarity.

Nearly every element of the Clojure programming language is designed to promote these goals. When writing Clojure code, if you keep in mind the desire to maximize simplicity, empowerment, and the freedom to focus on the real problem at hand, we think you'll find Clojure provides you the tools you need to succeed.

1.2   *Why a(nother) Lisp?*

> *By relieving the brain of all unnecessary work, a good notation sets it free to concentrate on more advanced problems.*
> —Alfred North Whitehead

Go to any open source project hosting site and perform a search for the term "Lisp interpreter." You'll likely get a cyclopean mountain[3] of results from this seemingly innocuous term. The fact of the matter is that the history of computer science is littered (Fogus 2009) with the abandoned husks of Lisp implementations. Well-intentioned Lisps have come and gone and been ridiculed along the way, and still tomorrow the search results will have grown almost without bounds. Bearing in mind this legacy of brutality, why would anyone want to base their brand-new programming language on the Lisp model?

1.2.1 Beauty

Lisp has attracted some of the brightest minds in the history of computer science. But an argument from authority is insufficient, so you shouldn't judge Lisp on this alone. The real value in the Lisp family of languages can be directly observed through the activity of using it to write applications. The Lisp style is one of expressivity and empowerment, and in many cases outright beauty. Joy awaits the Lisp neophyte. The original Lisp language as defined by John McCarthy in his earth-shattering essay "Recursive Functions of Symbolic Expressions and Their Computation by Machine, Part I" (McCarthy 1960) defined the whole language in terms of only seven functions and two special forms: `atom`, `car`, `cdr`, `cond`, `cons`, `eq`, `quote`, `lambda`, and `label`.

Through the composition of those nine forms, McCarthy was able to describe the whole of computation in a way that takes your breath away. Computer programmers are perpetually in search of beauty, and more often than not, this beauty presents itself in the form of simplicity. Seven functions and two special forms. It doesn't get more beautiful than that.

1.2.2 Extreme flexibility

Why has Lisp persevered for more than 50 years while countless other languages have come and gone? There are probably complex reasons, but chief among them is likely the fact that Lisp as a language genotype (Tarver 2008) fosters language flexibility in the extreme. Newcomers to Lisp are sometimes unnerved by its pervasive use of parentheses and prefix notation, which is different than non-Lisp programming languages. The regularity of this behavior not only reduces the number of syntax rules you have to remember, but also makes the writing of macros trivial. We'll look at macros in more detail in chapter 8, but to whet your appetite we'll take a brief look at one now. It's an example that we'll get working on in a moment:

```
(defn query [max]
  (SELECT [a b c]
    (FROM X
      (LEFT-JOIN Y :ON (= X.a Y.b)))
      (WHERE (AND (< a 5) (< b ~max))))))
```

---

[3] ...of madness.

We hope some of those words look familiar to you, because this isn't a book on SQL. Regardless, our point here is that Clojure doesn't have SQL support built in. The words SELECT, FROM, and so forth aren't built-in forms. They're also not regular functions, because if SELECT were, then the use of a, b, and c would be an error, because they haven't been defined yet.

So what does it take to define a domain-specific language (DSL) like this in Clojure? Well, it's not production-ready code and doesn't tie into any real database servers; but with just one macro and the three functions shown in listing 1.1, the preceding query returns these handy values:

```
(query 5)
;=> ["SELECT a, b, c FROM X LEFT JOIN Y ON (X.a = Y.b)
     WHERE ((a < 5) AND (b < ?))"
    [5]]
```

Note that some words such as FROM and ON are taken directly from the input expression, whereas others such as ~max and AND are treated specially. The max that was given the value 5 when the query was called is extracted from the literal SQL string and provided in a separate vector, perfect for using in a prepared query in a way that will guard against SQL-injection attacks. The AND form was converted from the prefix notation of Clojure to the infix notation required by SQL.

Listing 1.1   A domain-specific language for embedding SQL queries in Clojure

```
(ns joy.sql
  (:use [clojure.string :as str :only []]))          ⊲  Use core
                                                         string functions
(defn expand-expr [expr]
  (if (coll? expr)
    (if (= (first expr) `unquote)                  ⊲──── Handle unsafe literals
      "?"
      (let [[op & args] expr]
        (str "(" (str/join (str " " op " ")
                           (map expand-expr args)) ")")))   ⎤ Convert prefix
    expr))                                                  ⎦ to infix

(declare expand-clause)                            ⎤ Support each
                                                   ⎦ kind of clause
(def clause-map
  {'SELECT    (fn [fields & clauses]
                (apply str "SELECT " (str/join ", " fields)
                       (map expand-clause clauses)))
    'FROM      (fn [table & joins]
                (apply str " FROM " table
                       (map expand-clause joins)))
    'LEFT-JOIN (fn [table on expr]
                (str " LEFT JOIN " table
                     " ON " (expand-expr expr)))
    'WHERE     (fn [expr]
                (str " WHERE " (expand-expr expr)))})   ⎤ Call
                                                        ⎥ appropriate
(defn expand-clause [[op & args]]                       ⎦ converter
  (apply (clause-map op) args))
```

```
(defmacro SELECT [& args]
  [(expand-clause (cons 'SELECT args))
   (vec (for [n (tree-seq coll? seq args)
              :when (and (coll? n) (= (first n) `unquote))]
           (second n)))])
```

Provide main entrypoint macro

But the point here isn't that this is a particularly good SQL DSL—more complete ones are available.[4] Our point is that once you have the skill to easily create a DSL like this, you'll recognize opportunities to define your own that solve much narrower, application-specific problems than SQL does. Whether it's a query language for an unusual non-SQL datastore, a way to express functions in some obscure math discipline, or some other application we as authors can't imagine, having the flexibility to extend the base language like this, without losing access to any of the language's own features, is a game-changer.

Although we shouldn't get into too much detail about the implementation, take a brief look at listing 1.1 and follow along as we discuss important aspects of its implementation.

Reading from the bottom up, you'll notice the main entry point, the `SELECT` macro. This returns a vector of two items—the first is generated by calling `expand-clause`, which returns the converted query string, whereas the second is another vector of expressions marked by ~ in the input. The ~ is known as *unquote* and we discuss its more common uses in chapter 8. Also note the use of `tree-seq` here to succinctly extract items of interest from a tree of values, namely the input expression.

The `expand-clause` function takes the first word of a clause, looks it up in the `clause-map`, and calls the appropriate function to do the actual conversion from Clojure s-expression to SQL string. The `clause-map` provides the specific functionality needed for each part of the SQL expression: inserting commas or other SQL syntax, and sometimes recursively calling `expand-clause` when subclauses need to be converted. One of these is the `WHERE` clause, which handles the general conversion of prefix expressions to the infix form required by SQL by delegating to the `expand-expr` function.

Overall, the flexibility of Clojure demonstrated in this example comes largely from the fact that macros accept code forms, such as the SQL DSL example we showed, and can treat them as data—walking trees, converting values, and more. This works not only because code can be treated as data, but because in a Clojure program, code *is* data.

1.2.3 Code is data

The notion of "code is data" is difficult to grasp at first. Implementing a programming language where code shares the same footing as its comprising data structures presupposes a fundamental malleability of the language itself. When your language is represented as the inherent data structures, the language itself can manipulate its own

---

[4] One of note is ClojureQL at http://gitorious.org/clojureql.

structure and behavior (Graham 1995). You may have visions of Ouroboros after reading the previous sentence, and that wouldn't be inappropriate, because Lisp can be likened to a self-licking lollypop—more formally defined as *homoiconicity*. Lisp's homoiconicity takes a great conceptual leap in order to fully grasp, but we'll lead you toward that understanding throughout this book in hopes that you too will come to realize the inherent power.

There's a joy in learning Lisp for the first time, and if that's your experience coming into this book then we welcome you—and envy you.

1.3   *Functional programming*

Quick, what does *functional programming* mean? Wrong answer.

Don't be too discouraged, however—we don't really know the answer either. Functional programming is one of those computing terms[5] that has a nebulous definition. If you ask 100 programmers for their definition, you'll likely receive 100 different answers. Sure, some definitions will be similar, but like snowflakes, no two will be exactly the same. To further muddy the waters, the cognoscenti of computer science will often contradict one another in their own independent definitions. Likewise, the basic structure of any definition of functional programming will be different depending on whether your answer comes from someone who favors writing their programs in Haskell, ML, Factor, Unlambda, Ruby, or Qi. How can *any* person, book, or language claim authority for functional programming? As it turns out, just as the multitudes of unique snowflakes are all made mostly of water, the core of functional programming across all meanings has its core tenets.

1.3.1   *A workable definition of functional programming*

Whether your own definition of functional programming hinges on the lambda calculus, monadic I/O, delegates, or `java.lang.Runnable`, your basic unit of currency is likely to be some form of procedure, function, or method—herein lies the root. Functional programming concerns and facilitates the application and composition of functions. Further, for a language to be considered functional, its notion of function must be *first-class*. The functions of a language must be able to be stored, passed, and returned just like any other piece of data within that language. It's beyond this core concept that the definitions branch toward infinity, but thankfully, it's enough to start. Of course, we'll also present a further definition of Clojure's style of functional programming that includes such topics as purity, immutability, recursion, laziness, and referential transparency, but those will come later in chapter 7.

1.3.2   *The implications of functional programming*

Object-oriented programmers and functional programmers will often see and solve a problem in different ways. Whereas an object-oriented mindset will foster the

---

[5] Quick, what's the definition of combinator? How about cloud computing? Enterprise? SOA? Web 2.0? Real-world? Hacker? Often it seems that the only term with a definitive meaning is "yak shaving."

approach of defining an application domain as a set of nouns (classes), the functional mind will see the solution as the composition or verbs (functions). Though both programmers may in all likelihood generate equivalent results, the functional solution will be more succinct, understandable, and reusable. Grand claims indeed! We hope that by the end of this book you'll agree that functional programming fosters elegance in programming. It takes a shift in mindset to start from thinking in nouns to arrive at thinking in verbs, but the journey will be worthwhile. In any case, we think there's much that you can take from Clojure to apply to your chosen language—if only you approach the subject with an open mind.

1.4 Why Clojure isn't especially object-oriented

Elegance and familiarity are orthogonal.
—Rich Hickey

Clojure was born out of frustration provoked in large part by the complexities of concurrent programming, complicated by the weaknesses of object-oriented programming in facilitating it. This section explores these weaknesses and lays the groundwork for why Clojure is functional and not object-oriented.

1.4.1 Defining terms

Before we begin, it's useful to define terms.[6]

The first important term to define is *time*. Simply put, time refers to the relative moments when events occur. Over time, the properties associated with an entity—both static and changing, singular or composite—will form a concrescence (Whitehead 1929) and be logically deemed its *identity*. It follows from this that at any given time, a snapshot can be taken of an entity's properties defining its *state*. This notion of state is an immutable one because it's not defined as a mutation in the entity itself, but only as a manifestation of its properties at a given moment in time. Imagine a child's flip book, as seen in figure 1.2, to understand the terms fully.

It's important to note that in the canon of object-oriented programming, there's no clear distinction between state and identity. In other words, these two ideas are

Figure 1.2   The Runner: a child's flip book serves to illustrate Clojure's notions of state, time, and identity. The book itself represents the identity. Whenever you wish to show a change in the illustration, you draw another picture and add it to the end of your flip book. The act of flipping the pages therefore represents the states over time of the image within. Stopping at any given page and observing the particular picture represents the state of the Runner at that moment in time.

---

[6]   These terms are also defined and elaborated on in Rich Hickey's presentation, "Are We There Yet?" (Hickey 2009).

Figure 1.3   **The Mutable Runner: modeling state change with mutation requires that you stock up on erasers. Your book becomes a single page, requiring that in order to model changes, you must physically erase and redraw the parts of the picture requiring change. Using this model, you should see that mutation destroys all notion of time, and state and identity become one.**

conflated into what's commonly referred to as *mutable state*. The classical object-oriented model allows unrestrained mutation of object properties without a willingness to preserve historical states. Clojure's implementation attempts to draw a clear separation between an object's state and identity as they relate to time. To state the difference to Clojure's model in terms of the aforementioned flip book, the mutable state model is different, as seen in figure 1.3.

Immutability lies at the cornerstone of Clojure, and much of the implementation ensures that immutability is supported efficiently. By focusing on immutability, Clojure eliminates entirely the notion of *mutable state* (which is an oxymoron) and instead expounds that most of what's meant by objects are instead values. *Value* by definition refers to an object's constant representative[7] amount, magnitude, or epoch. You might ask yourself: what are the implications of the value-based programming semantics of Clojure?

Naturally, by adhering to a strict model of immutability, concurrency suddenly becomes a simpler (although not simple) problem, meaning if you have no fear that an object's state will change, then you can promiscuously share it without fear of concurrent modification. Clojure instead isolates value change to its reference types, as we'll show in chapter 11. Clojure's reference types provide a level of indirection to an identity that can be used to obtain consistent, if not always current, states.

1.4.2   *Imperative "baked in"*

Imperative programming is the dominant programming paradigm today. The most unadulterated definition of an imperative programming language is one where a sequence of statements mutates program state. During the writing of this book (and likely for some time beyond), the preferred flavor of imperative programming is the object-oriented style. This fact isn't inherently bad, because there are countless successful software projects built using object-oriented imperative programming techniques. But from the context of concurrent programming, the object-oriented imperative model is self-cannibalizing. By allowing (and even promoting) unrestrained mutation via *variables*, the imperative model doesn't directly support concurrency. Instead, by allowing a maenadic approach to mutation, there are no guarantees that any variable contains the expected value. Object-oriented programming takes this one step further by aggregating state in object internals. Though individual methods may be thread-safe through locking schemes, there's no way to ensure a consistent

---

[7]   Some entities have no representative value—Pi is an example. But in the realm of computing, where we're ultimately referring to finite things, this is a moot point.

object state across multiple method calls without expanding the scope of potentially complex locking scheme(s). Clojure instead focuses on functional programming, immutability, and the distinction between state, time, and identity. But object-oriented programming isn't a lost cause. In fact, there are many aspects that are conducive to powerful programming practice.

1.4.3 *Most of what OOP gives you, Clojure provides*

It should be made clear that we're not attempting to mark object-oriented programmers as pariahs. Instead, it's important that we identify the shortcomings of object-oriented programming (OOP) if we're ever to improve our craft. In the next few subsections we'll also touch on the powerful aspects of OOP and how they're adopted, and in some cases improved, by Clojure.

POLYMORPHISM AND THE EXPRESSION PROBLEM

Polymorphism is the ability of a function or method to have different definitions depending on the type of the target object. Clojure provides polymorphism via both multimethods and protocols, and both mechanisms are more open and extensible than polymorphism in many languages.

Listing 1.2 Clojure's polymorphic protocols

```
(defprotocol Concatenatable
  (cat [this other]))

(extend-type String
  Concatenatable
  (cat [this other]
    (.concat this other)))

(cat "House" " of Leaves")
;=> "House of Leaves"
```

What we've done in listing 1.2 is to define a *protocol* named `Concatenatable` that groups one or more functions (in this case only one, `cat`) that define the set of functions provided. That means the function `cat` will work for any object that fully satisfies the protocol `Concatenatable`. We then *extend* this protocol to the `String` class and define the specific implementation—a function body that concatenates the argument `other` onto the string `this`. We can also extend this protocol to another type:

```
(extend-type java.util.List
  Concatenatable
  (cat [this other]
    (concat this other)))

(cat [1 2 3] [4 5 6])
;=> (1 2 3 4 5 6)
```

So now the protocol has been extended to two different types, `String` and `java.util.List`, and thus the `cat` function can be called with either type as its first argument—the appropriate implementation will be invoked.

Note that String was already defined (in this case by Java itself) before we defined the protocol, and yet we were still able to successfully extend the new protocol to it. This isn't possible in many languages. For example, Java requires that you define all the method names and their groupings (known as *interfaces*) before you can define a class that implements them, a restriction that's known as the *expression problem*.

> **THE EXPRESSION PROBLEM**   The expression problem refers to the desire to implement an existing set of abstract methods for an existing concrete class without having to change the code that defines either. Object-oriented languages allow you to implement an existing abstract method in a concrete class you control (interface inheritance), but if the concrete class is outside your control, the options for making it implement new or existing abstract methods tend to be sparse. Some dynamic languages such as Ruby and JavaScript provide partial solutions to this problem by allowing you to add methods to an existing concrete object, a feature sometimes known as *monkey-patching*.

A Clojure protocol can be extended to any type where it makes sense, even those that were never anticipated by the original implementor of the type or the original designer of the protocol. We'll dive deeper into Clojure's flavor of polymorphism in chapter 9, but we hope now you have a basic idea of how it works.

SUBTYPING AND INTERFACE-ORIENTED PROGRAMMING

Clojure provides a form of subtyping by allowing the creation of ad-hoc hierarchies. We'll delve into leveraging the ad-hoc hierarchy facility later, in section 9.2. Likewise, Clojure provides a capability similar to Java's interfaces via its protocol mechanism. By defining a logically grouped set of functions, you can begin to define *protocols* to which data-type abstractions must adhere. This *abstraction-oriented programming* model is key in building large-scale applications, as you'll discover in section 9.3 and beyond.

ENCAPSULATION

If Clojure isn't oriented around classes, then how does it provide encapsulation? Imagine that you need a simple function that, given a representation of a chessboard and a coordinate, returns a simple representation of the piece at the given square. To keep the implementation as simple as possible, we'll use a vector containing a set of characters corresponding to the colored chess pieces, as shown next.

Listing 1.3   A simple chessboard representation in Clojure

```
(ns joy.chess)

(defn initial-board []
  [\r \n \b \q \k \b \n \r
   \p \p \p \p \p \p \p \p          ◁——— Lowercase dark
   \- \- \- \- \- \- \- \-
   \- \- \- \- \- \- \- \-
   \- \- \- \- \- \- \- \-
   \- \- \- \- \- \- \- \-
   \P \P \P \P \P \P \P \P          ◁——— Uppercase light
   \R \N \B \Q \K \B \N \R])
```

There's no need to complicate matters with the chessboard representation; chess is hard enough. This data structure in the code corresponds directly to an actual chessboard in the starting position, as shown in figure 1.4.

From the figure, you can gather that the black pieces are lowercase characters and white pieces are uppercase. This kind of structure is likely not optimal, but it's a good start. You can ignore the actual implementation details for now and focus on the client interface to query the board for square occupations. This is a perfect opportunity to enforce encapsulation to avoid drowning the client in board implementation details. Fortunately, programming languages with closures automatically support a form of encapsulation (Crockford 2008) to group functions with their supporting data.[8]

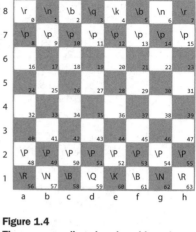

Figure 1.4
The corresponding chessboard layout

The functions in listing 1.4 are self-evident in their intent[9] and are encapsulated at the level of the namespace `joy.chess` through the use of the `defn-` macro that creates namespace private functions. The command for using the `lookup` function in this case would be `(joy.chess/lookup (initial-board) "a1")`.

Listing 1.4   Querying the squares of a chessboard

```
(def *file-key* \a)
(def *rank-key* \0)

(defn- file-component [file]
  (- (int file) (int *file-key*)))          Calculate file
                                            (horizontal) projection

(defn- rank-component [rank]
  (* 8 (- 8 (- (int rank) (int *rank-key*)))))   Calculate rank
                                                  (vertical) projection

(defn- index [file rank]
  (+ (file-component file) (rank-component rank)))
                                            Project ID layout onto
(defn lookup [board pos]                     logical 2D chessboard
  (let [[file rank] pos]
    (board (index file rank))))
```

Clojure's namespace encapsulation is the most prevalent form of encapsulation that you'll encounter when exploring idiomatic source code. But the use of lexical closures provides more options for encapsulation: block-level encapsulation, as shown in listing 1.5, and local encapsulation, both of which effectively aggregate unimportant details within a smaller scope.

---

[8] This form of encapsulation is described as the module pattern. But the module pattern as implemented with JavaScript provides some level of data hiding also, whereas in Clojure—not so much.

[9] And as a nice bonus, these functions can be generalized to project a 2D structure of any size to a 1D representation—which we leave to you as an exercise.

Listing 1.5   Using block-level encapsulation

```
(letfn [(index [file rank]
          (let [f (- (int file) (int \a))
                r (* 8 (- 8 (- (int rank) (int \0))))]
            (+ f r)))]
  (defn lookup [board pos]
    (let [[file rank] pos]
      (board (index file rank)))))
```

It's often a good idea to aggregate relevant data, functions, and macros at their most specific scope. You'd still call `lookup` as before, but now the ancillary functions aren't readily visible to the larger enclosing scope—in this case, the namespace `joy.chess`. In the preceding code, we've taken the `file-component` and `rank-component` functions and the `*file-key*` and `*rank-key*` values out of the namespace proper and rolled them into a block-level `index` function defined with the body of the `letfn` macro. Within this body, we then define the `lookup` function, thus limiting the client exposure to the chessboard API and hiding the implementation specific functions and forms. But we can further limit the scope of the encapsulation, as shown in the next listing, by shrinking the scope even more to a truly function-local context.

Listing 1.6   Local encapsulation

```
(defn lookup2 [board pos]
  (let [[file rank] (map int pos)
        [fc rc]     (map int [\a \0])
        f (- file fc)
        r (* 8 (- 8 (- rank rc)))
        index (+ f r)]
    (board index)))
```

Finally, we've now pulled *all* of the implementation-specific details into the body of the `lookup2` function itself. This localizes the scope of the `index` function and all auxiliary values to only the relevant party—`lookup2`. As a nice bonus, `lookup2` is simple and compact without sacrificing readability. But Clojure eschews the notion of data-hiding encapsulation featured prominently in most object-oriented languages.

NOT EVERYTHING IS AN OBJECT

Finally, another downside to object-oriented programming is the tight coupling between function and data. In fact, the Java programming language forces you to build programs entirely from class hierarchies, restricting all functionality to containing methods in a highly restrictive "Kingdom of Nouns" (Yegge 2006). This environment is so restrictive that programmers are often forced to turn a blind eye to awkward attachments of inappropriately grouped methods and classes. It's because of the proliferation of this stringent object-centric viewpoint that Java code tends toward being verbose and complex (Budd 1995). Clojure functions are data, yet this in no way restricts the decoupling of data and the functions that work upon them. Many of what programmers perceive to be classes are data tables that Clojure provides via maps[10] and records. The final strike against viewing everything as an object is that mathematicians view little (if anything) as objects (Abadi 1996). Instead, mathematics is built on the relationships between one set of elements and another through the application of functions.

1.5 Summary

We've covered a lot of conceptual ground in this chapter, but it was necessary in order to define the terms used throughout the remainder of the book. Likewise, it's important to understand Clojure's underpinnings in order to frame the discussion for the rest of the book. If you've taken in the previous sections and internalized them, then congratulations: you have a solid basis for proceeding to the rest of the book. But if you're still not sure what to make of Clojure, it's okay—we understand that it may be a lot to take in all at once. Understanding will come gradually as we piece together Clojure's story. For those of you coming from a functional programming background, you'll likely have recognized much of the discussion in the previous sections, but perhaps with some surprising twists. Conversely, if your background is more rooted in object-oriented programming, then you may get the feeling that Clojure is very different than you're accustomed to. Though in many ways this is true, in the coming chapters you'll see how Clojure elegantly solves many of the problems that you deal with on a daily basis. Clojure approaches solving software problems from a different angle than classical object-oriented techniques, but it does so having been motivated by their fundamental strengths and shortcomings.

With this conceptual underpinning in place, it's time to make a quick run through Clojure's technical basics and syntax. We'll be moving fairly quickly, but no faster than necessary to get to the deeper topics in following chapters. So hang on to your REPL, here we go...

---

[10] See section 5.6 for more discussion on this idea.

Drinking from the Clojure firehose 2

This chapter provides a quick tour of the bare necessities—the things you'll need to know to understand the rest of this book. If you've been programming with Clojure for a while, this may be a review, but otherwise it should give you everything you need to start writing Clojure code. In most cases throughout this chapter, the examples provided will be perfunctory in order to highlight the immediate point.

Later in the book we'll build on these topics and many more, so don't worry if you don't quite grasp every feature now—you'll get there.

Interaction with Clojure is often performed at the *Read-Eval-Print Loop (REPL)*. When starting a new REPL session, you're presented with a simple prompt:

```
user>
```

The user prompt refers to the top-level namespace of the default REPL. It's at this point that Clojure waits for input expressions. Valid Clojure expressions consist of numbers, symbols, keywords, booleans, characters, functions, function calls, macros, strings, literal maps, vectors, and sets. Some expressions, such as numbers, strings, and keywords, are self-evaluating—when entered, they evaluate to themselves. The Clojure REPL also accepts source comments, which are marked by the semicolon ; and continue to a newline:

```
user> 42     ; numbers evaluate to themselves
;=> 42

user> "The Misfits" ; strings do too
;=> "The Misfits"

user> :pyotr  ; as do keywords
;=> :pyotr
```

Now that we've seen several scalar data types, we'll take a closer look at each of them.

2.1   Scalars

The Clojure language has a rich set of data types. Like most programming languages, it provides scalar types such as integers, strings, and floating-point numbers, each representing a single unit of data. Clojure provides several different categories of scalar data types: integers, floats, rationals, symbols, keywords, strings, characters, booleans, and regex patterns. In this section, we'll address most of these[1] categories in turn, providing examples of each.

2.1.1   Numbers

A number can consist of only the digits 0-9, a decimal point (.), a sign (+ or -), and an optional *e* for numbers written in exponential notation. In addition to these elements, numbers in Clojure can take either octal or hexadecimal form and also include an optional *M*, that flags a number as a decimal requiring arbitrary precision: an important aspect of numbers in Clojure. In many programming languages, the precision[2] of numbers is restricted by the host platform, or in the case of Java and C#, defined by the language specification. Clojure on the other hand uses the host language's primitive numbers when appropriate, but rolls over to the arbitrarily precise versions when needed, or when explicitly specified.

---

[1]   We won't look at regular expression patterns here, but for details on everything regex-related you can flip forward to section 4.6.

[2]   With caveats, as we'll describe in chapter 4.

2.1.2   Integers

Integers comprise the whole number set, both positive and negative. Any number starting with an optional sign or digit followed exclusively by digits is considered and stored as an integer. Integers in Clojure can theoretically take an infinitely large value, although in practice the size is limited by the memory available. The following numbers are recognized by Clojure as integers:

```
42
+9
-107
991778647261948849222819828311491035886734385827028118707676848307166514
```

The following illustrates the use of decimal, hexadecimal, octal, radix-32, and binary literals, respectively, all representing the same number:

```
[127 0x7F 0177 32r3V 2r01111111]
;=> [127 127 127 127 127]
```

The radix notation supports up to base 36. Adding signs to the front of each of the integer literals is also legal.

2.1.3   Floating-point numbers

Floating-point numbers are the decimal expansion of rational numbers. Like Clojure's implementation of integers, the floating-point values are arbitrarily precise.[3] Floating-point numbers can take the traditional form of some number of digits and then a decimal point, followed by some number of digits. But floating-point numbers can also take an exponential form (scientific notation) where a significant part is followed by an exponent part separated by a lower or uppercase *E*. The following numbers are examples of valid floating-point numbers:

```
1.17
+1.22
-2.
366e7
32e-14
10.7e-3
```

Numbers are largely the same across most programming languages, so we'll move on to some scalar types that are more unique to Lisp and Lisp-inspired languages.

2.1.4   Rationals

Clojure provides a rational type in addition to integer and floating-point numbers. Rational numbers offer a more compact and precise representation of a given value over floating-point. Rationals are represented classically by an integer numerator and denominator, and that's exactly how they're represented in Clojure. The following numbers are examples of valid rational numbers:

---

[3]   With some caveats, as we'll discuss in section 4.1.

```
22/7
7/22
1028798300297636767687409028872/88829897008789478784
-103/4
```

Something to note about rational numbers in Clojure is that they'll be simplified if they can—the rational 100/4 will resolve to the integer 25.

2.1.5 Symbols

Symbols in Clojure are objects in their own right, but are often used to represent another value. When a number or a string is evaluated, you get back exactly the same object, but when a symbol is evaluated, you'll get back whatever value that symbol is referring to in the current context. In other words, symbols are typically used to refer to function parameters, local variables, globals, and Java classes.

2.1.6 Keywords

Keywords are similar to symbols, except that they always evaluate to themselves. You're likely to see the use of keywords far more in Clojure than symbols. The form of a keyword's literal syntax is as follows:

```
:chumby
:2
:?
:ThisIsTheNameOfaKeyword
```

Although keywords are prefixed by a colon :, it's only part of the literal syntax and not part of the name itself. We go into further detail about keywords in section 4.3.

2.1.7 Strings

Strings in Clojure are represented similarly to the way they're used in many programming languages: a string is any sequence of characters enclosed within a set of double quotes, including newlines, as shown:

```
"This is a string"
"This is also a
        String"
```

Both will be stored as written, but when printed at the REPL, multiline strings will include escapes for the literal newline characters like `"This is also a\n String"`.

2.1.8 Characters

Clojure characters are written with a literal syntax prefixed with a backslash and are stored as Java Character objects, as shown:

```
\a        ; The character lowercase a
\A        ; The character uppercase A
\u0042    ; The unicode character uppercase B
\\        ; The back-slash character \
\u30DE    ; The unicode katakana character ?
```

And that's it for Clojure's scalar data types. In the next section, we'll discuss Clojure's collection data types, which is where the real fun begins.

2.2   *Putting things together: collections*

We'll cover the collection types in greater detail in chapter 5, but because Clojure programs are made up of various kinds of literal collections, it's helpful to at least glance at the basics of lists, vectors, maps, and sets.

2.2.1   *Lists*

Lists are the classic collection type in List Processing languages, and Clojure is no exception. Literal lists are written with parentheses:

```
(yankee hotel foxtrot)
```

When a list is evaluated, the first item of the list—yankee in this case—will be resolved to a function, macro, or special form. If yankee is a function, the remaining items in the list will be evaluated in order, and the results will be passed to yankee as its parameters.

> **FORMS**   A *form* is any Clojure object meant to be evaluated, including but not limited to lists, vectors, maps, numbers, keywords, and symbols. A *special form* is a form with special syntax or special evaluation rules that are typically not implemented using the base Clojure forms. An example of a special form is the . (dot) operator used for Java interoperability purposes.

If on the other hand yankee is a macro or special form, the remaining items in the list aren't necessarily evaluated, but are processed as defined by the macro or operator.

Lists can contain items of any type, including other collections. Here are some more examples:

```
(1 2 3 4)
()
(:fred ethel)
(1 2 (a b c) 4 5)
```

Note that unlike some Lisps, the empty list in Clojure, written as (), isn't the same as nil.

2.2.2   *Vectors*

Like lists, vectors store a series of values. There are several differences described in section 5.4, but for now only two are important. First, vectors have a literal syntax using square brackets:

```
[1 2 :a :b :c]
```

The other important difference is that when evaluated, vectors simply evaluate each item in order. No function or macro call is performed on the vector itself, though if a list appears within the vector, that list is evaluated following the normal rules for a list. Like lists, vectors are type heterogeneous, and as you might guess, the empty vector [] isn't the same as nil.

2.2.3 *Maps*

Maps store unique keys and one value per key—similar to what some languages and libraries call *dictionaries* or *hashes*. Clojure actually has several types of maps with different properties, but don't worry about that for now. Maps can be written using a literal syntax with alternating keys and values inside curly braces. Commas are frequently used between pairs, but are just whitespace like they are everywhere else in Clojure:

```
{1 "one", 2 "two", 3 "three"}
```

Like vectors, every item in a map literal (each key and each value) is evaluated before the result is stored in the map. Unlike vectors, the order in which they're evaluated isn't guaranteed. Maps can have items of any type for both keys and values, and the empty map {} isn't the same as nil.

2.2.4 *Sets*

Sets are probably the least common collection type that has a literal syntax. Sets store zero or more unique items. They're written using curly braces with a leading hash:

```
#{1 2 "three" :four 0x5}
```

Again, the empty set #{} isn't the same as nil.

That's all for now regarding the basic collection types, but chapter 4 will cover in-depth the idiomatic uses of each, including their relative strengths and weaknesses.

2.3 *Making things happen: functions*

Functions in Clojure are a first-class type, meaning that they can be used the same as any value. Functions can be stored in Vars, held in lists and other collection types, and passed as arguments to and even returned as the result of other functions.

2.3.1 *Calling functions*

Clojure borrows its function calling conventions from Lisp, also known as *prefix notation*:

```
(+ 1 2 3)
;=> 6
```

The immediately obvious advantage of prefix over infix notation used by C-style languages[4] is that the former allows any number of operands per operator, whereas infix allows only two. Another, less obvious advantage to structuring code as prefix notation is that it completely eliminates the problem of operator precedence. Clojure makes no distinction between operator notation and regular function calls—all Clojure constructs, functions, macros, and operators are formed using prefix, or fully parenthesized, notation. This uniform structure forms the basis for the incredible flexibility that Lisp-like languages provide.

---

[4] Of course, Java uses infix notation in only a few instances. The remainder of the language forms tend toward C-style ad hoc debauchery.

2.3.2   *Defining functions*

An anonymous (unnamed) Clojure function can be defined as a special form. A *special form* is a Clojure expression that's part of the core language, but not created in terms of functions, types, or macros.

An example of a function taking two elements that returns a set of those elements would be defined as

```
(fn mk-set [x y] #{x y})
;=> #<user$eval__1$mk_set__2 user$eval__1$mk_set__2@d3576a2>
```

Entering this function definition in a Clojure REPL gives us a seemingly strange result. This is because the REPL is showing its internal name for the function object returned by the `fn` special form. This is far from satisfying, given that now that the function has been defined, there's no apparent way to execute it. It should be noted that the `mk-set` symbol is optional and doesn't correspond to a globally accessible name for the function, but instead to a name internal to the function itself used for self-calls. Recall from the previous section that the function call form is always `(some-function arguments)`:

```
((fn [x y] #{x y}) 1 2)
;=> #{1 2}
```

The second form to define functions allows for arity overloading of the invocations of a function. *Arity* refers to the differences in the argument count that a function will accept. Changing our previous simple set-creating function to accept either one or two arguments would be represented as

```
(fn
  ([x]   #{x})
  ([x y] #{x y}))
```

The difference from the previous form is that we can now have any number of argument/body pairs as long as the arity of the arguments differ. Naturally, the execution of such a function for one argument would be

```
((fn
  ([x]   #{x})
  ([x y] #{x y})) 42)
;=> #{42}
```

As you saw, arguments to functions are bound one-for-one to symbols during the function call, but there is a way for functions to accept a variable[5] number of arguments:

```
((fn arity2 [x y] [x y]) 1 2 3)
;=> java.lang.IllegalArgumentException: Wrong number of args passed
```

Clearly, calling the `arity2` function with three arguments won't work. But what if we wanted it to take any number of arguments? The way to denote variable arguments is to use the `&` symbol followed by a symbol. Every symbol in the arguments list before

---

[5] The implementation details of Clojure prevent the creation of functions with an arity larger than 20, but in practice this should rarely, if ever, be an issue.

the & will still be bound one-for-one to the same number of arguments passed during the function call. But any additional arguments will be aggregated in a sequence bound to the symbol following the & symbol:

```
((fn arity2+ [x y & z] [x y z]) 1 2)
;=> [1 2 nil]

((fn arity2+ [x y & z] [x y z]) 1 2 3 4)
;=> [1 2 (3 4)]

((fn arity2+ [x y & z] [x y z]) 1)
;=> java.lang.IllegalArgumentException: Wrong number of args passed
```

Of course, `arity2+` still requires at least two arguments. But this isn't satisfactory, as it quickly becomes clear that to write programs using only this form would be cumbersome, repetitive, and overly verbose. Thankfully, Clojure provides another, more convenient form to create named functions.

2.3.3 *Simplifying function definitions with def and defn*

The `def` special form is a way to assign a symbolic name to a piece of Clojure data. Clojure functions are first-class; they're equal citizens with data, allowing assignment to Vars, storage in collections, and as arguments to (or returned from) other functions. This is different from programming languages where functions are functions and data are data, and there's a world of capability available to the latter that's incongruous to the former.

Therefore, in order to associate a name with our previous function using `def`, we'd use

```
(def make-a-set
  (fn
    ([x]   #{x})
    ([x y] #{x y})))
```

And we could now call it in a more intuitive way:

```
(make-a-set 1)
;=> #{1}

(make-a-set 1 2)
;=> #{1 2}
```

There's another way to define functions in Clojure using the `defn` macro. While certainly a much nicer way to define and consequently refer to functions by name, using `def` as shown is still cumbersome to use. Instead, the simplest `defn` syntax is a convenient and concise way to create named functions that looks similar to the original `fn` form, and allow an additional documentation string:

```
(defn make-a-set
  "Takes either one or two values and makes a set from them"
  ([x]   #{x})
  ([x y] #{x y}))
```

The function can again be called the same as we saw before.

2.3.4   *In-place functions with #()*

Clojure provides a shorthand notation for creating an anonymous function using the #() reader feature. In a nutshell, *reader features* are analogous to preprocessor directives in that they signify that some given form should be replaced with another at read time. In the case of the #() form, it's effectively replaced with the special form fn. In fact, anywhere that it's appropriate to use #(), it's likewise appropriate for the fn special form.

The #() form can also accept arguments that are implicitly declared through the use of special symbols prefixed with %:

```
(def make-a-list_  #(list %))
(def make-a-list1  #(list %1))
(def make-a-list2  #(list %1 %2))
(def make-a-list3  #(list %1 %2 %3))
(def make-a-list3+ #(list %1 %2 %3 %&))

(make-a-list_ 1)
;=> (1)

(make-a-list3+ 1 2 3 4 5)
;=> (1 2 3 (4 5))
```

The %& argument in make-a-list3+ is used to specify the variable arguments as discussed previously.

2.4   *Vars*

Programmers are typically accustomed to dealing with variables and mutation. Clojure's closest analogy to the variable is the Var. A Var is named by a symbol and holds a single value. Its value can be changed while the program is running, but this is best reserved for the programmer making manual changes. A Var's value can also be shadowed by a thread local value, though this doesn't change its original value or *root binding*.

2.4.1   *Declaring bindings using def*

Using def is the most common way to create Vars in Clojure:

```
(def x 42)
```

Using def to associate the value 42 to the symbol x creates what's known as a *root binding*—a binding that's the same across all threads, unless otherwise rebound relative to specific threads. By default, all threads start with the root binding, which is their associated value in the absence of a thread-bound value.

The trivial case is that the symbol x is bound to the value 42. Because we used def to create the Var's root binding, we should observe that even other threads will view the same root binding by default:

```
(.start (Thread. #(println "Answer: " x)))
; Answer: 42
```

Vars don't require a value; instead we can simply declare them and defer the responsibility of binding their values to individual threads:[6]

```
(def y)
y
;=> java.lang.IllegalStateException: Var user/y is unbound.
```

Functions and vars theoretically provide all you need to implement any algorithm, and some languages leave you with exactly these "atomic" constructs.

2.5 Locals, loops, and blocks

Clojure's function and value binding capabilities provide a basis for much of what a developer needs to start getting operational code, but a large part of the story is missing. Clojure also provides capabilities for creating local value bindings, looping constructs, and aggregating blocks of functionality.

2.5.1 Blocks

Use the do form when you have a series or block of expressions that need to be treated as one. All the expressions will be evaluated, but only the last one will be returned:

```
(do
  6
  (+ 5 4)
  3)
;=> 3
```

The expressions 6 and (+ 5 4) are perfectly valid and legal. The addition in (+ 5 4) is even done, but the value is thrown away—only the final expression 3 is returned. The middle bits of the do form are typically where the side-effects occur.

2.5.2 Locals

Clojure doesn't have local variables, but it does have locals; they just can't vary. Locals are created and their scope defined using a let form, which starts with a vector that defines the bindings, followed by any number of expressions that make up the body. The vector starts with a binding form (usually just a symbol), which is the name of a new local. This is followed by an expression whose value will be bound to this new local for the remainder of the let form. You can continue pairing binding names and expressions to create as many locals as you need. All of them will be available in the body of the let:

```
(let [r         5
      pi        3.1415
      r-squared (* r r)]
  (println "radius is" r)
  (* pi r-squared))
```

---

[6] We'll talk more about per-thread bindings in chapter 11.

The body is sometimes described as an "implicit do" because it follows the same rules: you may include any number of expressions and all will be evaluated, but only the value of the last one is returned.

All of the binding forms in the previous example are simple symbols: r, pi, and r-squared. More complex binding expressions can be used to pull apart expressions that return collections. This feature is called *destructuring*; see section 2.9 for details.

Because they're immutable, locals can't be used to accumulate results; instead, you'd use a high level function or loop/recur form.

2.5.3   *Loops*

The classic way to build a loop in a Lisp is a recursive call, and it's in Clojure as well. Using recursion sometimes requires thinking about your problem in a different way than imperative languages encourage; but recursion from a tail position is in many ways like a structured goto, and has more in common with an imperative loop than it does with other kinds of recursion.

RECUR

Clojure has a special form called recur that's specifically for tail recursion:

```
(defn print-down-from [x]
  (when (pos? x)
    (println x)
    (recur (dec x))))
```

This is nearly identical to how you'd structure a while loop in an imperative language. One significant difference is that the value of x isn't decremented somewhere in the body of the loop. Instead, a new value is calculated as a parameter to recur, which immediately does two things: rebinds x to the new value and returns control to the top of print-down-from.

If the function has multiple arguments, the recur call must as well, just as if you were calling the function by name instead of using the recur special form. And just as with a function call, the expressions in the recur are evaluated in order first and only then bound to the function arguments simultaneously.

The previous example doesn't concern itself with return values; it's just about the println side effects. Here's a similar loop that builds up an accumulator and returns the final result:

```
(defn sum-down-from [sum x]
  (if (pos? x)
    (recur (+ sum x) (dec x))
    sum))
```

The only ways out of the function are recur, which isn't really a way out, and sum. So when x is no longer positive, the function will return the value of sum:

```
(sum-down-from 0 10)
;=> 55
```

You may have noticed that the two preceding functions used different blocks: the first when and the second if. You'll often see one or the other used as a conditional, but it's not always immediately apparent why. In general, the reasons to use when are

- No else-part is associated with the result of a conditional.
- You require an implicit do in order to perform side-effects.

The reasons for the use of if would therefore be the inverse of those listed.

LOOP

Sometimes you want to loop back not to the top of the function, but to somewhere inside. For example, in sum-down-from you might prefer that callers not have to provide an initial value for sum. To help, there's a loop form that acts exactly like let but provides a target for recur to jump to. It's used like this:

```
(defn sum-down-from [initial-x]
  (loop [sum 0, x initial-x]
    (if (pos? x)
      (recur (+ sum x) (dec x))
      sum)))
```

Upon entering the loop form, the locals sum and x are initialized, just as they would be for a let.

A recur always loops back to the closest enclosing loop or fn, so in this case it'll go to the loop. The loop locals are rebound to the values given in recur. The looping and rebinding will continue until finally x is no longer positive. The return value of the whole loop expression is sum, just as it was for the earlier function.

TAIL POSITION

Now that we've looked at a couple examples of how to use recur, we must discuss an important restriction. The recur form can only appear in the tail position of a function or loop. So what's a tail position? Succinctly, a form is in the tail position of an expression when its value may be the return value of the whole expression. Consider this function:

```
(defn absolute-value [x]
  (if (pos? x)
    x           ; "then" clause
    (- x)))     ; "else" clause
```

It takes a single parameter and names it x. If x is already a positive number, then x is returned; otherwise the opposite of x is returned.

The if form is in the function's tail position because whatever it returns, the whole function will return. The x in the "then" clause is also in a tail position of the function. But the x in the "else" clause is *not* in the function's tail position because the value of x is passed to the - function, not returned directly. The else clause as a whole (- x) is in a tail position.

If you try to use the recur form somewhere other than a tail position, Clojure will remind you at compile time:

```
(fn [x] (recur x) (println x))
; java.lang.UnsupportedOperationException:
;    Can only recur from tail position
```

You've seen how Clojure provides core functionality available to most popular programming languages, albeit from a different bent. But in the next section, we'll cover the notion of quoting forms, which are in many ways unique to the Lisp family of languages and may seem alien to programmers coming from classically imperative and/or object-oriented languages.

2.6   Preventing things from happening: quoting

Clojure has two quoting forms: quote and syntax-quote. Both are simple bits of syntax you can put in front of a form in your program. They're the primary ways for including literal scalars and composites in your Clojure program *without* evaluating them as code. But before quoting forms can make sense, you need a solid understanding of how expressions are evaluated.

2.6.1   Evaluation

When a collection is evaluated, each of its contained items is evaluated first:[7]

```
(cons 1 [2 3])
```

If you enter this at the REPL, the form as a whole will be evaluated. In this specific example, the function cons "constructs" a new sequence with its first argument in the front of the sequence provided as its second. Because the form is a list, each of the items will be evaluated first. A symbol, when evaluated, is resolved to a local, a Var, or a Java class name. If a local or a Var, its value will be returned:

```
cons
;=> #<core$cons__3806 clojure.core$cons__3806@24442c76>
```

Literal scalar values evaluate to themselves—evaluating one just returns the same thing:

```
1
;=> 1
```

The evaluation of another kind of collection, a vector, starts again by evaluating the items it contains. Because they're literal scalars, nothing much happens. Once that's done, evaluation of the vector can proceed. Vectors, like scalars and maps, evaluate to themselves:

```
[2 3]
;=> [2 3]
```

Now that all the items of the original list have been evaluated (to a function, the number 1, and the vector [2 3]), evaluation of the whole list can proceed. Lists are

---

[7] ...unless it's a list that starts with the name of a macro or special form. We'll get to that later.

evaluated differently from vectors and maps: they call functions, or trigger special forms, as shown:

```
(cons 1 [2 3])
;=> (1 2 3)
```

Whatever function was at the head of the list, cons in this case, is called with the remaining items of the list as arguments.

2.6.2 Quoting

Using a special form looks like calling a function—a symbol as the first item of a list:

```
(quote tena)
```

Each special form has its own evaluation rules. The quote special form simply prevents its argument from being evaluated at all. Though the symbol tena by itself might evaluate to the value of a Var with the value 9, when it's inside a quote form, it won't:

```
(def tena 9)
(quote tena)
;=> tena
```

Instead, the whole form evaluates to just the symbol itself. This works for arbitrarily complex arguments to quote: nested vectors, maps, even lists that would otherwise be function calls, macro calls, or even more special forms. The whole thing is returned:

```
(quote (cons 1 [2 3]))
;=> (cons 1 [2 3])
```

There are a few reasons you might use the quote form, but by far the most common is so that you can use a literal list as a data collection without having Clojure try to call a function. We've been careful to use vectors in the examples so far in this section because vectors are never themselves function calls. But if we wanted to use a list instead, a naive attempt would fail:

```
(cons 1 (2 3))
; java.lang.ClassCastException:
;     java.lang.Integer cannot be cast to clojure.lang.IFn
```

That's Clojure telling us that an integer (the number 2 here) can't be used as a function. So we have to prevent the form (2 3) from being treated like a function call— exactly what quote is for:

```
(cons 1 (quote (2 3)))
;=> (1 2 3)
```

In other Lisps, this need is so common that they provide a shortcut: a single quote. Although it's used less in Clojure, it's still provided. The previous example can also be written as

```
(cons 1 '(2 3))
;=> (1 2 3)
```

And look at that: one less pair of parens—always welcome in a Lisp. Remember though that quote affects all of its argument, not just the top level. So even though it worked in the preceding examples to replace [] with ' (), this may not always give you the results you want:

```
[1 (+ 2 3)]     ;=> [1 5]
'(1 (+ 2 3))    ;=> (1 (+ 2 3))
```

Finally, note that the empty list () already evaluates to itself; it doesn't need to be quoted. Quoting the empty list isn't idiomatic Clojure.

SYNTAX-QUOTE

Like the quote, syntax-quote prevents its argument and subforms from being evaluated. Unlike quote, it has a few extra features that make it ideal for constructing collections to be used as code.

Syntax-quote is written as a single back-quote:

```
`(1 2 3)
;=> (1 2 3)
```

It doesn't expand to a simple form like quote, but to whatever set of expressions is required to support the following features.[8]

SYMBOL AUTO-QUALIFICATION

A symbol can begin with a namespace and a slash. These can be called *qualified symbols*:

```
clojure.core/map
clojure.set/union
i.just.made.this.up/quux
```

Syntax-quote will automatically qualify all unqualified symbols in its argument:

```
`map
;=> clojure.core/map
`Integer
;=> java.lang.Integer
`(map even? [1 2 3])
;=> (clojure.core/map clojure.core/even? [1 2 3])
```

If the symbol doesn't name a Var or class that exists yet, syntax-quote will use the current namespace:

```
`is-always-right
;=> user/is-always-right
```

This behavior will come in handy in chapter 8, when we discuss macros.

2.6.3   *Unquote*

As you discovered, the quote special form prevents its argument, and all of its subforms, from being evaluated. But there will come a time when you'll want *some* of its

---

[8]   A future version of Clojure is likely to expand the back-quote to syntax-quote at read time and implement the rest of syntax-quote's features as a macro or special form.

constituent forms to be evaluated. The way to accomplish this feat is to use what's known as an *unquote*. An unquote is used to demarcate specific forms as requiring evaluation by prefixing them with the symbol ~ within the body of a syntax-quote:

```
`(+ 10 (* 3 2))
;=> (clojure.core/+ 10 (clojure.core/* 3 2))

`(+ 10 ~(* 3 2))
;=> (clojure.core/+ 10 6)
```

What just happened? The final form uses an unquote to evaluate the subform (* 3 2), which of course performs a multiplication of 3 and 2, thus inserting the result into the outermost syntax-quoted form. The unquote can be used to denote any Clojure expression as requiring evaluation:

```
`(1 2 ~3)
;=> (1 2 3)

(let [x 2]
  `(1 ~x 3))
;=> (1 2 3)

`(1 ~(2 3))
;=> java.lang.ClassCastException: java.lang.Integer
```

Whoops! By using the unquote, we've told Clojure that the marked form should be evaluated. But the marked form here is (2 3), and what happens when Clojure encounters an expression like this? It attempts to evaluate it as a function! Therefore, care needs to be taken with unquote to ensure that the form requiring evaluation is of the form that you expect. The more appropriate way to perform the previous task would thus be

```
(let [x '(2 3)] `(1 ~x))
;=> (1 (2 3))
```

This provides a level of indirection such that the expression being evaluated is no longer (2 3) but x. But this new way breaks the pattern of the previous examples that returned a list of (1 2 3).

2.6.4 Unquote-splicing

Clojure provides a handy feature to solve exactly the problem posed earlier. A variant of unquote called *unquote-splicing* works similarly to unquote, but a little differently:

```
(let [x '(2 3)] `(1 ~@x))
;=> (1 2 3)
```

Note the @ in ~@, which tells Clojure to unpack the sequence x, splicing it into the resulting list rather than inserting it as a nested list.

2.6.5 Auto-gensym

Sometimes you need an unqualified symbol, such as for a parameter or `let` local name. The easiest way to do this inside a syntax-quote is to append a # to the symbol name. This will cause Clojure to generate a new unqualified symbol:

```
`potion#
;=> potion__211__auto__
```

Sometimes even this isn't enough, either because you need to refer to the same symbol in multiple syntax-quotes or because you want to capture a particular unqualified symbol.

Until this point, we've covered many of the basic features making Clojure a unique flavor of Lisp. But one of the main goals that Clojure excels at meeting is that of interoperability with a host language and runtime, namely Java and the Java Virtual Machine.

2.7 Leveraging Java via interop

Clojure is symbiotic with its host,[9] providing its rich and powerful features, while Java provides an object model, libraries, and runtime support. In this section, we'll take a brief look at how Clojure allows you to access Java classes and class members, and how you can create instances and access their members.

2.7.1 Accessing static class members

Clojure provides powerful mechanisms for accessing, creating, and mutating Java classes and instances. The trivial case is accessing static class properties:

```
java.util.Locale/JAPAN
;=> #<Locale ja_JP>
```

Idiomatic Clojure prefers that you access static class members using a syntax like accessing a namespace-qualified Var:

```
(Math/sqrt 9)
;=> 3.0
```

The preceding call is to the `java.lang.Math#sqrt` static method.

2.7.2 Creating Java class instances

Creating Java class instances is likewise a trivial matter with Clojure. The `new` special form closely mirrors the Java model:

```
(new java.util.HashMap {"foo" 42 "bar" 9 "baz" "quux"})
;=> #<HashMap {baz=quux, foo=42, bar=9}>
```

The second, more succinct, Clojure form to create instances is actually the idiomatic form:

---

[9] We'll focus on the Java Virtual Machine throughout this book, but Clojure has also been hosted on the .NET Common Language Runtime (CLR) and JavaScript (http://clojurescript.n01se.net/repl/).

```
(java.util.HashMap. {"foo" 42 "bar" 9 "baz" "quux"})
;=> #<HashMap {baz=quux, foo=42, bar=9}>
```

As you can see, the class name was followed by a dot in order to signify a constructor call.

2.7.3 Accessing Java instance members with the . operator

To access instance properties, precede the property or method name with a dot:

```
(.x (java.awt.Point. 10 20))
;=> 10
```

This returns the value of the field x from the Point instance given.

To access instance methods, the dot form allows an additional argument to be passed to the method:

```
(.divide (java.math.BigDecimal. "42") 2M)
;=> 21M
```

The preceding example calls the #divide method on the class BigDecimal.

2.7.4 Setting Java instance properties

In the absence of mutators in the form setXXX, Java instance properties can be set via the set! function:

```
(let [origin (java.awt.Point. 0 0)]
  (set! (.x origin) 15)
  (str origin))
;=> "java.awt.Point[x=15,y=0]"
```

The first argument to set! is the instance member access form.

2.7.5 The .. macro

When working with Java, it's common practice to chain together a sequence of method calls on the return type of the previous method call:

```
new java.util.Date().toString().endsWith("2010")    /* Java code */
```

Using Clojure's dot special form, the following code is equivalent:

```
(.endsWith (.toString (java.util.Date.)) "2010")    ; Clojure code
;=> true
```

Though correct, the preceding code is difficult to read and will only become more so when we lengthen the chain of method calls. To combat this, Clojure provides the .. macro, which can simplify the call chain as follows:

```
(.. (java.util.Date.) toString (endsWith "2010"))
```

The preceding .. call closely follows the equivalent Java code and is much easier to read. Bear in mind, you might not see .. used often in Clojure code found in the wild outside of the context of macro definitions. Instead, Clojure provides the -> and ->> macros, which can be used similarly to the .. macro but are also useful in non-interop situations, thus making them the preferred method call facilities in most cases. The -> and ->> macros are covered in more depth in the introduction to chapter 8.

2.7.6   *The doto macro*

When working with Java, it's also common to initialize a fresh instance by calling a set of mutators:

```
java.util.HashMap props = new java.util.HashMap();   /* More java code. */
props.put("HOME", "/home/me");                        /* Sorry. */
props.put("SRC",  "src");
props.put("BIN",  "classes");
```

But using this method is overly verbose and can be streamlined using the doto macro, which takes the form

```
(doto (java.util.HashMap.)
  (.put "HOME" "/home/me")
  (.put "SRC"  "src")
  (.put "BIN"  "classes"))

;=> #<HashMap {HOME=/home/me, BIN=classes, SRC=src}>
```

Though these Java and Clojure comparisons are useful, it shouldn't be assumed that their compiled structures are the same.

2.7.7   *Defining classes*

Clojure provides the reify and deftype macros as possible ways to create realizations of Java interfaces, but we'll defer covering them until chapter 9. Additionally, Clojure provides a macro named proxy that can be used to implement interfaces and extend base classes on the fly. Similarly, using the gen-class macro, you can generate statically named classes. More details about proxy and gen-class are available in chapter 10.

2.8   *Exceptional circumstances*

We'll now talk briefly about Clojure's facilities for handling exceptions. Like Java, Clojure provides a couple of forms for throwing and catching runtime exceptions: namely throw and catch, respectively.

2.8.1   *A little pitch and catch*

The mechanism to throw an exception is fairly straightforward:

```
(throw (Exception. "I done throwed"))
;=> java.lang.Exception: I done throwed
```

The syntax for catching exceptions in Clojure is similar to that of Java:

```
(defn throw-catch [f]
  [(try
    (f)
    (catch ArithmeticException e "No dividing by zero!")
    (catch Exception e (str "You are so bad " (.getMessage e)))
```

```
    (finally (println "returning... "))))])
(throw-catch #(/ 10 5))
; returning...
;=> [2]

(throw-catch #(/ 10 0))
; returning...
;=> ["No dividing by zero!"]

(throw-catch #(throw (Exception. "foo")))
; returning...
;=> ["You are so bad foo"]
```

The major difference between the way that Java handles exceptions compared to Clojure is that Clojure doesn't adhere to checked exception requirements. In the next, final section of our introduction to Clojure, we present namespaces, which might look vaguely familiar if you're familiar with Java or Common Lisp.

2.9   *Namespaces*

Clojure's namespaces provide a way to bundle related functions, macros, and values. In this section, we'll briefly talk about how to create namespaces and how to reference and use things from other namespaces.

2.9.1   *Creating namespaces using ns*

To create a new namespace, you can use the ns macro:

```
(ns joy.ch2)
```

Whereupon your REPL prompt will now display as:

```
joy.ch2=>
```

This prompt shows that you're working within the context of the joy.ch2 namespace. Clojure also provides a Var *ns* that holds the value of the current namespace. Any Var created will be a member of the current namespace:

```
(defn hello [] (println "Hello Cleveland!"))
(defn report-ns [] (str "The current namespace is " *ns*))

(report-ns)
;=> "The current namespace is joy.ch2"
```

Entering a symbol within a namespace will cause Clojure to attempt to look up its value within the current namespace:

```
hello
;=> #<ch2$hello joy.ch2$hello@2af8f5>
```

You can create new namespaces at any time:

```
(ns joy.another)
```

Again, you'll notice that your prompt has changed, indicating that the new context is joy.another. Attempting to run report-ns will no longer work:

```
(report-ns)
; java.lang.Exception:
;    Unable to resolve symbol: report-ns in this context
```

This is because `report-ns` exists in the `joy.ch1` namespace and is only accessible via its fully qualified name `joy.ch2/report-ns`. But this will only work for namespaces created locally or those previously loaded, which we'll discuss next.

2.9.2   *Loading other namespaces with :require*

Creating a namespace is straightforward, but how do you load namespaces? Clojure provides a convenience directive `:require` to take care of this task. Observe the following:

```
(ns joy.req
  (:require clojure.set))

(clojure.set/intersection #{1 2 3} #{3 4 5})
;=> #{3}
```

Using `:require` indicates that you want the `clojure.set` namespace loaded, but you don't want the mappings of symbols to functions in the `joy.req` namespace. You can also use the `:as` directive to create an additional alias to `clojure.set`:

```
(ns joy.req-alias
  (:require [clojure.set :as s]))

(s/intersection #{1 2 3} #{3 4 5})
;=> #{3}
```

The qualified namespace form looks the same as a call to a static class method. The difference is that a namespace symbol can only be used as a qualifier, whereas a class symbol can also be referenced independently:

```
clojure.set
; java.lang.ClassNotFoundException: clojure.set

java.lang.Object
;=> java.lang.Object
```

The vagaries of namespace mappings from symbols to Vars both qualified and unqualified have the potential for confusion between class names and static methods in the beginning, but the differences will begin to feel natural as you progress. In addition, idiomatic Clojure code will tend to use `my.Class` and `my.ns` for naming classes and namespaces respectively, to help eliminate potential confusion.

2.9.3   *Loading and creating mappings with :use*

Sometimes you'll want to create mappings from Vars in another namespace to names in your own, in order to avoid calling each function or macro with the qualifying namespace symbol. To create these unqualified mappings, Clojure provides the `:use` directive:

```
(ns joy.use-ex
  (:use [clojure.string :only [capitalize]]))
```

```
(map capitalize ["kilgore" "trout"])
;=> ("Kilgore" "Trout")
```

The :use directive indicates that only the function capitalize should be mapped in the namespace joy.use-ex. Specifying the Vars that you'd like explicit mappings for is good practice in Clojure, as it avoids creating many unnecessary names within a namespace. Unnecessary names increase the odds of names clashes, which you'll see next. A similar directive to :use for managing precise mappings is :exclude

```
(ns joy.exclusion
  (:use [clojure.string :exclude [capitalize]]))

; WARNING: replace already refers to: #'clojure.core/replace in namespace:
;    joy.exclusion, being replaced by: #'clojure.string/replace
; WARNING: reverse already refers to: #'clojure.core/reverse in namespace:
;    joy.exclusion, being replaced by: #'clojure.string/reverse

(map capitalize ["kilgore" "trout"])
; java.lang.Exception: Unable to resolve symbol: capitalize in this context
```

The :exclude directive indicates that we wanted to map names for all of clojure.string's Vars except for capitalize. Indeed, any attempt to use capitalize directly throws an exception. But it's still accessible via clojure.string/capitalize. The reason for this accessibility is because :use implicitly performs a :require directive in addition to creating mappings. As you might've noticed, the creation of the joy.exclusion namespace signaled two warnings. The reason was that the clojure.string namespace defines two functions reverse and replace that are already defined in the clojure.core namespace—which was already loaded by using ns. Therefore, when either of those functions are used, the last Var definition wins:

```
(reverse "abc")
;=> "cba"

(clojure.core/reverse "abc")
(\c \b \a)
```

The clojure.string version of reverse takes precedence over the clojure.core version, which may or may not be what we wanted. You should always strive to eliminate the warnings that Clojure presents in these cases. The most obvious strategy for resolving these particular warnings would be to use the :require directive to create a namespace alias with :as as we showed in the previous section.

2.9.4 *Creating mappings with :refer*

Clojure also provides a :refer directive that works almost exactly like :use except that it only creates mappings for libraries that have already been loaded:

```
(ns joy.yet-another
  (:refer joy.ch1))

(report-ns)
;=> "The current namespace is #<Namespace joy.yet-another>"
```

The use of :refer in this way creates a mapping from the name report-ns to the actual function located in the namespace joy.ch2 so that the function can be called normally. You could also set an alias for the same function using the :rename keyword taking a map, as shown:

```
(ns joy.yet-another
  (:refer joy.ch1 :rename {hello hi}))

(hi)
; Hello Cleveland!
```

Any namespaces referenced must already be loaded implicitly by being previously defined or by being one of Clojure's core namespaces, or explicitly loaded through the use of :require. It should be noted that :rename also works with the :use directive.

2.9.5   *Loading Java classes with :import*

To use unqualified Java classes within any given namespace, they should be imported via the :import directive, as shown:

```
(ns joy.java
  (:import [java.util HashMap]
           [java.util.concurrent.atomic AtomicLong]))

(HashMap. {"happy?" true})
;=> #<HashMap {happy?=true}>

(AtomicLong. 42)
;=> 42
```

As a reminder, any classes in the Java java.lang package are automatically imported when namespaces are created. We'll discuss namespaces in more detail in sections 9.1 and 10.2.

2.10   *Summary*

We named this chapter "Drinking from the Clojure firehose"—and you've made it through! How does it feel? We've only provided an overview of the topics needed to move on to the following chapters instead of a full-featured language tutorial. Don't worry if you don't fully grasp the entirety of Clojure the programming language; understanding will come as you work your way through the book.

In the next chapter, we'll take a step back and delve into some topics that can't be easily categorized, but that deserve attention because of their ubiquity. It'll be short and sweet and give you a chance to take a breath before moving into the deeper discussions on Clojure later in the book.

Dipping our toes in the pool

This chapter covers

- Truthiness
- Nil punning
- Destructuring
- Use the REPL to experiment

Deeper and broader topics will be covered in later chapters, but now's a good time to pick through an eclectic selection of smaller topics. The topics covered in this chapter stand alone but are important. Covering them now will be a fun way to start digging into practical matters of how to use Clojure.

We've covered a lot of conceptual ground in the previous chapter and built our Clojure lexicon. In this chapter, we'll take a bit of a detour into some fundamental underpinnings driving idiomatic Clojure source code. First we'll explore Clojure's straightforward notions of Truthiness,[1] or the distinctions between values

---

[1] As a deviation from the definition coined by Stephen Colbert in his television show *The Colbert Report*. Ours isn't about matters of gut feeling but rather about matters of Clojure's logical truth ideal.

considered logical true and those considered logical false. Much of idiomatic Clojure code is built with matters of Truthiness in mind, and we'll discuss Clojure's extremely simple rules. After this we'll then move on to the notion of nil punning, or treating an empty sequence as `nil`. Those of you coming from a background in Lisp may recognize the term, but Clojure handles nil punning differently. We'll discuss the idioms related to nil punning in Clojure and their rationale. We'll then cover destructuring—a powerful mechanism for pulling apart collection types and binding their constituent parts as individual values. Using destructuring within your own code can often lead to extremely concise and elegant solutions, and we'll provide some examples to illustrate this. Finally, we'll sit down and pair-program together to gain an appreciation for the power of Clojure's Read-Eval-Print Loop (REPL).

3.1   Truthiness

Truthfulness may be an important virtue, but it doesn't come up much in programming. On the other hand, *Truthiness*, or the matter of logical truth values in Clojure, is critical.

Clojure has one Boolean context: the test expression of the `if` form. Other forms that expect Booleans—and, or, when, and so forth—are macros built on top of `if`. It's here that Truthiness matters.

3.1.1   What's truth?

Every value looks like `true` to `if`, except for `false` and `nil`. That means that values which some languages treat as false—zero-length strings, empty lists, the number zero, and so on—are all treated as `true` in Clojure:

```
(if true :truthy :falsey)   ;=> :truthy
(if [] :truthy :falsey)     ;=> :truthy
(if nil :truthy :falsey)    ;=> :falsey
(if false :truthy :falsey)  ;=> :falsey
```

This may feel uncomfortable to you, depending on your background. But because branches in a program's logic are already one of the most likely places for complexity and bugs, Clojure has opted for a simple rule. There's no need to check a class's definition to see if it acts like "false" when you think it should (as is sometimes required in Python, for example). Every object is "true" all the time, unless it's `nil` or `false`.

3.1.2   Don't create Boolean objects

It's possible to create an object that looks a lot like, but isn't actually, `false`.

Java has left a landmine for you here, so take a moment to look at it so that you can step past it gingerly and get on with your life:

```
(def evil-false (Boolean. "false")) ; NEVER do this
```

This creates a new instance of Boolean—and that's already wrong! Because there are only two possible values of Boolean, an instance of each has already been made for you—they're named `true` and `false`.[2] But here you've gone and done it anyway, created a new instance of Boolean and stored it in a Var named `evil-false`. It looks like `false`:

```
evil-false
;=> false
```

Sometimes it even acts like `false`:

```
(= false evil-false)
;=> true
```

But once it gains your trust, it'll show you just how wicked it is by acting like `true`:

```
(if evil-false :truthy :falsey)
;=> :truthy
```

Java's own documentation warns against the creation of this evil thing, and now you've been warned again. If you just want to parse a string, use the Boolean class's static `valueOf` method instead of its constructor. This is the right way:

```
(if (Boolean/valueOf "false") :truthy :falsey)
;=> :falsey
```

3.1.3 *nil versus false*

Rarely do you need to differentiate between the two false values, but if you do, you can use `nil?` and `false?`:

```
(when (nil? nil) "Actually nil, not false")
;=> "Actually nil, not false"
```

Keeping in mind the basic rule that everything in Clojure is truthy unless it's `false` or `nil` is an astonishingly powerful concept, allowing for elegant solutions. Often programming languages have complicated semantics for Truthiness, but Clojure manages to avoid those matters nicely. You'll see this simplicity leveraged throughout this book and in all examples of idiomatic Clojure source code.

Building on that theme, we'll now discuss the matter of *nil punning*, which may or may not surprise you given your background.

3.2 *Nil pun with care*

Because empty collections act like `true` in Boolean contexts, we need an idiom for testing whether there's anything in a collection to process. Thankfully, Clojure provides just such a technique:

```
(seq [1 2 3])
;=> (1 2 3)

(seq [])
;=> nil
```

---

[2] Clojure's `true` and `false` instances are the same as Java's `Boolean/TRUE` and `Boolean/FALSE`, respectively.

The seq function returns a sequence view of a collection, or nil if the collection is empty. In a language like Common Lisp, an empty list acts as a false value and can be used as a *pun* (a term with the same behavior) for such in determining a looping termination. As you saw in section 2.3, Clojure's empty sequences are instead truthy, and therefore to use one as a pun for falsity will lead to heartache and despair. One solution that might come to mind is to use empty? in the test, leading to the awkward phrase (when-not (empty? s) ...). Though it would work, this isn't idiomatic. A better solution would be to use seq as a termination condition, as in the following function print-seq:

```
(defn print-seq [s]
  (when (seq s)
    (prn (first s))
    (recur (rest s))))

(print-seq [1 2])
; 1
; 2
;=> nil

(print-seq [])
;=> nil
```

There are a number of points to take away from this example. First, the use of seq as a terminating condition is the idiomatic way to test whether a sequence is empty. If we tested just s instead of (seq s), then the terminating condition wouldn't occur even for empty collections, leading to an infinite loop.

> **PREFER DOSEQ** An important point not mentioned is that it would be best to use doseq in this case, but that wouldn't allow us to illustrate our overarching points: the Clojure forms named with do at the start (doseq, dotimes, do, and so on) are intended for side-effects in their bodies and generally return nil as their results.

Second, rest is used to consume the sequence on the recursive call, which can return a sequence that's either empty or not empty (has elements). Clojure also provides a next function that returns a seq of the rest, or (seq (rest s)), and thus never returns an empty sequence, but nil instead. But rest is appropriate here because we're using seq explicitly in each subsequent iteration. Finally, print-seq is a template for most functions in Clojure, in that it shows that we should generally not assume seq has been called on our collection arguments, but instead call seq within the function itself and process based on its result. Using this approach fosters a more generic handling of collections, a topic that we explore in great detail in chapter 5. In the meantime, it's important to keep in mind the difference between empty collections and false values; otherwise your attempts at nil punning may cause groans all around.

To top off our trifecta of core Clojure concepts, we next explore the most powerful of the three—destructuring. You'll see just how powerful this mini-language within Clojure can be toward developing elegant and often beautiful solutions.

3.3   *Destructuring*

In the previous section, we briefly described Clojure's destructuring facility as a mini-language embedded within Clojure. *Destructuring* allows us to positionally bind locals based on an expected form for a composite data structure. In this section, we'll explore how destructuring can be used to pull apart composite structures into bindings through the lens of a simple rolodex example project.

> **PATTERN MATCHING**   Destructuring is loosely related to pattern matching found in Haskell, KRC, or Scala, but much more limited in scope. For more full-featured pattern matching in Clojure, consider using http://github.com/dcolthorp/matchure, which may in the future be included in contrib as clojure.core.match.

3.3.1   *Your assignment, should you choose to accept it*

You've heard that the rolodex project has been overdue, but now every developer assigned to it is out sick. The QA team is ready to go, but one function is still missing and it's a show-stopper. You're told to drop everything and write the function ASAP.

The design? Take a vector of length 3 that represents a person's first, middle, and last names and return a string that will sort in the normal way, like "Steele, Guy Lewis". What are you waiting for? Why aren't you done yet?!?!

```
(def guys-whole-name ["Guy" "Lewis" "Steele"])

(str (nth guys-whole-name 2) ", "
     (nth guys-whole-name 0) " "
     (nth guys-whole-name 1)))
;=> "Steele, Guy Lewis"
```

Alas, by the time you've finished typing guys-whole-name for the fourth time, it's too late. The customers have cancelled their orders, and the whole department is bound to be downsized.

If only you'd known about destructuring.

Okay, so you're not likely to lose your job because your function is twice as many lines as it needs to be, but still that's a lot of code repeated in a pretty small function. And using index numbers instead of named locals makes the purpose of the function more obscure than necessary.

Destructuring solves both these problems by allowing you to place a collection of names in a binding form where normally you'd put just a single name. One kind of binding form is the list of parameters given in a function definition.

3.3.2   *Destructuring with a vector*

So let's try that again, but use destructuring with let to create more convenient locals for the parts of Guy's name:

```
(let [[f-name m-name l-name] guys-whole-name]
  (str l-name ", " f-name " " m-name))
```

Positional destructuring

This positional destructuring doesn't work on maps and sets because they're not logically[3] aligned sequentially. Thankfully, positional destructuring will work with Java's `java.util.regex.Matcher` and anything implementing the `CharSequence` and `java.util.RandomAccess` interfaces.

This is the simplest form of destructuring, where you want to pick apart a sequential thing (a vector of strings in this case, though a list or other sequential collection would work as well), giving each item a name.

We don't need it here, but we can also use an ampersand in a destructuring vector to indicate that any remaining values of the input should be collected into a (possibly lazy) seq:

```
(let [[a b c & more] (range 10)]
  (println "a b c are:" a b c)
  (println "more is:" more))
; a b c are: 0 1 2
; more is: (3 4 5 6 7 8 9)
;=> nil
```

Here the locals a, b, and c are created and bound to the first three values of the range. Because the next symbol is an ampersand, the remaining values are made available as a seq bound to more. The name more is pretty common for this purpose, but isn't special—you'll often see etc or xs instead, or some other name that makes sense in a particular context.

The final feature of vector destructuring is :as, which can be used to bind a local to the entire collection. It must be placed after the & local, if there is one, at the end of the destructuring vector:

```
(let [range-vec (vec (range 10))
      [a b c & more :as all] range-vec]
  (println "a b c are:" a b c)
  (println "more is:" more)
  (println "all is:" all))
; a b c are: 0 1 2
; more is: (3 4 5 6 7 8 9)
; all is: [0 1 2 3 4 5 6 7 8 9]
;=> nil
```

We made range-vec a vector in this example, and the directive :as binds the input collection as-is, entirely unmolested, so that the vector stays a vector. This is in contrast to &, which bound more to a seq, not a vector.

---

[3] Technically, positional destructuring might make sense with sorted sets and maps, but alas it doesn't operate as such.

3.3.3 *Destructuring with a map*

Perhaps passing a name as a three-part vector wasn't a good idea in the first place. It might be better stored in a map:

```
(def guys-name-map
  {:f-name "Guy" :m-name "Lewis" :l-name "Steele"})
```

But now we can't use a vector to pick it apart effectively. Instead, we use a map:

```
(let [{f-name :f-name, m-name :m-name, l-name :l-name} guys-name-map]
  (str l-name ", " f-name " " m-name))
```

A couple things about this example may jump out at you. One might be that it still seems repetitive—we'll get to that in a moment.

Another might be that it looks a bit unexpected to have the keywords like :f-name on the right-hand side of each pair even though the input map had keywords on the left. There are a couple reasons for that. The first is to help keep the pattern of the name on the left getting the value specified by the thing on the right. That is, the new local f-name gets the value looked up in the map by the key :f-name, just as the whole map gets its value from guys-name-map in the earlier def form.

The second reason is because it allows us to conjure up other destructuring features by using forms that would otherwise make no sense. Because the item on the left of each pair will be a new local name, it must be a symbol or possibly a nested destructuring form. But one thing it can't be is a keyword, unless the keyword is a specially supported feature such as :keys, :strs, :syms, :as, and :or.

We'll discuss the :keys feature first because it nicely handles the repetitiveness we mentioned earlier. It allows us to rewrite our solution like this:

```
(let [{:keys [f-name m-name l-name]} guys-name-map]
  (str l-name ", " f-name " " m-name))
```

So by using :keys instead of a binding form, we're telling Clojure that the next form will be a vector of names that it should convert to keywords such as :f-name in order to look up their values in the input map. Similarly, if we had used :strs, Clojure would be looking for items in the map with string keys such as "f-name", and :syms would indicate symbol keys.

The directives :keys, :strs, :syms, and regular named bindings can appear in any combination and in any order. But sometimes you'll want to get at the original map—in other words, the keys that you didn't name individually by any of the methods just described. For that, you want :as, which works just like it does with vector destructuring:

```
(let [{f-name :f-name, :as whole-name} guys-name-map]
  whole-name)
;=> {:f-name "Guy", :m-name "Lewis", :l-name "Steele"}
```

If the destructuring map looks up a key that's not in the source map, it's normally bound to nil, but you can provide different defaults with :or:

```
(let [{:keys [title f-name m-name l-name], :or {title "Mr."}} guys-name-map]
  (println title f-name m-name l-name))
; Mr. Guy Lewis Steele
;=> nil
```

ASSOCIATIVE DESTRUCTURING

One final technique worth mentioning is associative destructuring. Using a map to define a number of destructure bindings isn't limited to maps. We can also destructure a vector by providing a map declaring the local name as indices into them, as shown:

```
(let [{first-thing 0, last-thing 3} [1 2 3 4]]
  [first-thing last-thing])
;=> [1 4]
```

We'll explore associative destructuring later in section 6.1 when we discuss Clojure's support for named structures. You've seen the shapes that destructuring takes within the `let` form, but you're not limited to that exclusively, as we'll explore next.

3.3.4   *Destructuring in function parameters*

All the preceding examples use `let` to do their destructuring, but exactly the same features are available in function parameters. Each function parameter can destructure a map or sequence:

```
(defn print-last-name [{:keys [l-name]}]
  (println l-name))

(print-last-name guys-name-map)
; Steele
;=> nil
```

Note that function arguments can include an ampersand as well, but this isn't the same as destructuring. Instead, that's part of their general support for multiple function bodies, each with its own number of parameters.

3.3.5   *Destructuring versus accessor methods*

In many object-oriented languages, you might create new classes to manage your application data objects, each with its own set of getter and setter methods. It's idiomatic in Clojure to instead build your application objects by composing maps and vectors as necessary. This makes destructuring natural and straightforward. So anytime you find that you're calling `nth` on the same collection a few times, or looking up constants in a map, or using `first` or `next`, consider using destructuring instead.

Now that we've made it through the cursory introduction to Clojure, let's take some time to pair-program (Williams 2002). In the next section, we'll take many of the bare necessities that you've just learned and walk through the creation of a couple interesting functions for drawing pretty pictures within Clojure's REPL.

3.4   *Using the REPL to experiment*

Most software development projects include a stage where you're not sure what needs to happen next. Perhaps you need to use a library or part of a library you've never touched before. Or perhaps you know what your input to a particular function will be, and what the output should be, but you aren't sure how to get from one to other. In more static languages, this can be time-consuming and frustrating; but by leveraging the power of the Clojure REPL, the interactive command prompt, it can actually be fun.

3.4.1   *Experimenting with seqs*

Say someone suggests to you that coloring every pixel of a canvas with the xor of its x and y coordinates might produce an interesting image. It shouldn't be too hard, so you can jump right in. You'll need to perform an operation on every x and y in a pair of ranges. Do you know how range works?

```
(range 5)
;=> (0 1 2 3 4)
```

That should do nicely for one coordinate. To nest seqs, for often does the trick. But again, rather than writing code and waiting until you have enough to warrant compiling and testing, you can just try it:

```
(for [x (range 2) y (range 2)] [x y])
;=> ([0 0] [0 1] [1 0] [1 1])
```

There are the coordinates that will form your input. Now you need to xor them:

```
(xor 1 2)
;=> java.lang.Exception: Unable to resolve symbol: xor in this context
```

Bother—no function named xor. Fortunately, Clojure provides find-doc, which searches not just function names but also their doc strings for the given term:

```
(find-doc "xor")
; -------------------------
; clojure.core/bit-xor
; ([x y])
;   Bitwise exclusive or
;=> nil
```

So the function you need is called bit-xor:

```
(bit-xor 1 2)
;=> 3
```

Perfect! Now you want to adjust your earlier for form to return the bit-xor along with the x and y. The easiest way to do this will depend on what tool is hosting your REPL. In many, you can just press the up-arrow key on your keyboard a couple of times to bring back the earlier for form. You're not going to want to retype things to make minor adjustments, so take a moment right now to figure out a method you like that will allow you to make a tweak like this by inserting the bit-xor call:

```
(for [x (range 2) y (range 2)] [x y (bit-xor x y)])
;=> ([0 0 0] [0 1 1] [1 0 1] [1 1 0])
```

That looks about right. Now you're about to shift gears to pursue the graphics side of this problem, so tuck that bit of code away in a function so it'll be easy to use later:

```
(defn xors [max-x max-y] (for [x (range max-x) y (range max-y)] [x y (bit-
    xor x y)]))
(xors 2 2)
;=> ([0 0 0] [0 1 1] [1 0 1] [1 1 0])
```

You might even save that into a .clj file somewhere, if you haven't already.

3.4.2 *Experimenting with graphics*

Clojure's REPL isn't just for playing around; it's also great for experimenting with Java libraries. We believe that there's no better environment for exploring a Java API than Clojure's REPL. To illustrate, poke around with java.awt, starting with a Frame:

```
(def frame (java.awt.Frame.))
;=> #'user/frame
```

That should've created a Frame, but no window appeared. Did it work at all?

```
frame
;=> #<Frame java.awt.Frame[frame0,0,22,0x0,invalid,hidden,...]>
```

Well, you have a Frame object, but perhaps the reason you can't see it is hinted at by the word *hidden* in the #<Frame...> printout. Perhaps the Frame has a method you need to call to make it visible. One way to find out would be to check the Javadoc of the object, but because you're at the REPL already, let's try something else. You've already seen how the for macro works, so maybe you can check a class for which methods it has to see whether one that you can use is available:

```
(for [method (seq (.getMethods java.awt.Frame))
        :let [method-name (.getName method)]
        :when (re-find #"Vis" method-name)]
  method-name)
;=> ("setVisible" "isVisible")
```

The for macro takes a :let flag and bindings vector that works similarly to the let special form that you use to bind the local method-name to the result of calling the method .getName on each method in turn. The :when is used to limit the elements used in its body to only those that return a truthy value in the expression after the directive. Using these directives allows you to iterate through the methods and build a seq of those whose names match a regular expression #"Vis". We'll cover Clojure's regular expression syntax in section 3.5.

> **THE CONTRIB FUNCTION SHOW** The clojure-contrib library also has a function show in the clojure.contrib.repl-utils namespace that allows for more useful printouts of class members than we show using for.

Your query returned two potential methods, so try out each of them:

```
(.isVisible frame)
;=> false
```

That's `false`, as you might've suspected. Will setting it to `true` make any difference?

```
(.setVisible frame true)
;=> nil
```

It did, but it's so tiny! Not to worry, as a `Frame` class also has a `.setSize` method that you can use:

```
(.setSize frame (java.awt.Dimension. 200 200))
;=> nil
```

And up pops a blank window for you to draw on. At this point, we'll guide you through the rest of this section, but keep in mind that Java's official API might be of interest should you choose to extend the example program.

> **THE JAVADOC FUNCTION** As of Clojure 1.2, a `javadoc` function is automatically available at the REPL to query and view official API documentation:
>
> ```
> (javadoc frame)
> ```
>
> This should return a string corresponding to a URL and open a browser window for just the right page of documentation. Prior to Clojure 1.2, this function was in `clojure.contrib.repl-utils`.

What you need to draw into your Frame is its graphics context, which can be fetched as shown:

```
(def gfx (.getGraphics frame))
;=> #'user/gfx
```

Then, to actually draw, you can try out the `fillRect` method of that graphics context. If you're trying this yourself, make sure the blank window is positioned so that it's unobscured while you're typing into your REPL:

```
(.fillRect gfx 100 100 50 75)
```

And just like that, you're drawing on the screen interactively. You should see a single black rectangle in the formerly empty window. Exciting, isn't it? You could be a kid playing with turtle graphics for the first time, it's so much fun. But what it needs now is a dash of color:

```
(.setColor gfx (java.awt.Color. 255 128 0))
(.fillRect gfx 100 150 75 50)
```

Now there should be an orange rectangle as well. Perhaps the coloring would make Martha Stewart cry, but you now have tried out all the basic building blocks you'll need to complete the original task: you have a function that returns a seq of coordinates and their xor values, you have a window you can draw into, and you know how to draw rectangles of different colors. Bear in mind that if you move the actual frame with the mouse, your beautiful graphics will disappear. This is just an artifact of this limited experiment and can be avoided using the full Java Swing capabilities.

3.4.3 *Putting it all together*

What's left to do? Use the graphics functions you just saw to draw the xor values you created earlier:

```
(doseq [[x y xor] (xors 200 200)]
  (.setColor gfx (java.awt.Color. xor xor xor))
  (.fillRect gfx x y 1 1))
```

The xors function you created earlier generates a seq of vectors, if you remember, where each vector has three elements: the x and y for your coordinates and the xor value that goes with them. The first line here uses destructuring to assign each of those three values to new locals x, y, and xor, respectively.

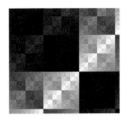

The second line sets the "pen" color to a gray level based on the xor value, and the final line draws a single-pixel rectangle at the current coordinates. The resulting graphic is shown in figure 3.1.

But just because you've succeeded doesn't mean you have to quit. You've built up some knowledge and a bit of a toolbox, so why not play with it a little?

Figure 3.1   Visualization of xor. This is the graphic drawn by the six or so lines of code we've looked at so far—a visual representation of Clojure's bit-xor function.

3.4.4 *When things go wrong*

For example, the pattern appears to cut off in the middle—perhaps you'd like to see a bit more. Re-enter that last expression, but this time try larger limits:

```
(doseq [[x y xor] (xors 500 500)]
  (.setColor gfx (java.awt.Color. xor xor xor))
  (.fillRect gfx x y 1 1))
; java.lang.IllegalArgumentException:
;    Color parameter outside of expected range: Red Green Blue
```

Whoops. Something went wrong, but what exactly? This gives you a perfect opportunity to try out one final REPL tool. When an exception is thrown from something you try at the REPL, the result is stored in a Var named *e. This allows you to get more detail about the expression, such as the stack trace:

```
(.printStackTrace *e)
; java.lang.IllegalArgumentException: Color parameter outside of
;        expected range: Red Green Blue
;    at clojure.lang.Compiler.eval(Compiler.java:4639)
;    at clojure.core$eval__5182.invoke(core.clj:1966)
;    at clojure.main$repl__7283$read_eval_print__7295.invoke(main.clj:180)
; ...skipping a bit here...
; Caused by: java.lang.IllegalArgumentException: Color parameter
;        outside of expected range: Red Green Blue
;    at java.awt.Color.testColorValueRange(Color.java:298)
;    at java.awt.Color.<init>(Color.java:382)
; ...skipping a bit more...
; ... 11 more
;=> nil
```

That's a lot of text, but don't panic. Learning to read Java stack traces will be useful, so let's pick it apart.

The first thing to understand is the overall structure of the trace—there are two "causes." The original or root cause of the exception is listed last—this is the best place to look first.[4] The name and text of the exception there are the same as the REPL printed for us in the first place, though they won't always be. So let's look at that next line:

```
at java.awt.Color.testColorValueRange(Color.java:298)
```

Like most lines in the stack trace, this has four parts: the name of the class, the name of the method, the filename, and finally the line number:

```
at <class>.<method or constructor>(<filename>:<line>)
```

In this case, the function name is `testColorValueRange`, which is defined in Java's own Color.java file. Unless this means more to you than it does to us, let's move on to the next line:

```
at java.awt.Color.<init>(Color.java:382)
```

It appears that it was the Color's constructor (called `<init>` in stack traces) that called that test function you saw earlier. So now the picture is pretty clear—when you constructed a Color instance, it checked the values you passed in, decided they were invalid, and threw an appropriate exception.

If this weren't enough, you could continue walking down the stack trace until the line

```
... 11 more
```

This is your cue to jump up to the cause listed before this one to find out what the next 11 stack frames were.

To fix your invalid Color argument, you can just adjust the `xors` function to return only legal values using the `rem` function, which returns the remainder so you can keep the results under 256:

```
(defn xors [xs ys]
  (for [x (range xs) y (range ys)]
    [x y (rem (bit-xor x y) 256)]))
```

Note that you're redefining an existing function here. This is perfectly acceptable and well-supported behavior. Before moving on, create a function that takes a graphics object and clears it:

```
(defn clear [g] (.clearRect g 0 0 200 200))
```

Calling `(clear gfx)` will clear the `frame`, allowing the `doseq` form you tried before to work perfectly.

---

[4] This is a runtime exception, the most common kind. If you misuse a macro or find a bug in one, you may see compile-time exceptions. The trace will look similar but will have many more references to Compiler.java. For these traces, the most recent exception (listed first) may be the only one that identifies the filename and line number in your code that's at fault.

3.4.5 *Just for fun*

The `bit-xor` function does produce an interesting image, but perhaps you wonder
what other functions might look like. Try adding another parameter to `xors` so that
you can pass in whatever function you'd like to look at. Because it's not just `bit-xor`
anymore, change the name while you're at it:

```
(defn f-values [f xs ys]
  (for [x (range xs) y (range ys)]
    [x y (rem (f x y) 256)]))
```

You might as well wrap your call to `setSize`, `clear`, and the `doseq` form in a function
as well:

```
(defn draw-values [f xs ys]
  (clear gfx)
  (.setSize frame (java.awt.Dimension. xs ys))
  (doseq [[x y v] (f-values f xs ys)]
    (.setColor gfx (java.awt.Color. v v v))
    (.fillRect gfx x y 1 1)))
```

This allows you to try out different functions and ranges quite easily. More nice examples are shown in figure 3.2, resulting from the following:

```
(draw-values bit-and 256 256)
(draw-values + 256 256)
(draw-values * 256 256)
```

If this were the beginning or some awkward middle stage of a large project, you'd
have succeeded in pushing past this troubling point and could now take the functions
you've built and drop them into the larger project.

By trying everything out at the REPL, you're encouraged to try smaller pieces
rather than larger ones. The smaller the piece, the shorter the distance down an
incorrect path you're likely to go. Not only does this reduce the overall development
time, but it provides developers more frequent successes that can help keep morale
and motivation high through even
tough stages of a project. But trial-and-
error exploration isn't enough. An
intuitive basis in Clojure is also
needed to become highly effective.
Throughout this book, we'll help you
to build your intuition in Clojure
through discussions of its idioms and
its motivating factors and rationale.

Figure 3.2 Three possible results from `draw-values`. The `draw-values` function you've written can be used to create a variety of graphics. Here are examples, from left to right, of `bit-and`, `+`, and `*`.

3.5   *Summary*

We started slowly in this chapter in order to take a breather from the sprint that was
chapter 2. Truthiness in Clojure observes a simple rule: every object is true all the
time, unless it's `nil` or `false`. Second, in many Lisp-like languages, the empty list `()`

and the truth value `nil` are analogous—this is known as *nil-punning*—but in Clojure this isn't the case. Instead, idiomatic Clojure employs the `(seq (rest _))` idiom in the form of the `next` function to provide a mechanism fostering "form follows function" and also to eliminate errors associated with falsety/empty-seq disparity. Finally, destructuring provides a powerful mechanism, a mini-language for binding if you will, for partially or entirely pulling apart the constituent components of composite types. Our trek through the REPL illustrated the power in having the whole language (Graham 2001) at your disposal. As a Clojure programmer, you'll spend a lot of time in the REPL, and pretty soon you won't know how you lived without it.

In the next chapter, we'll touch on matters concerning Clojure's seemingly innocent scalar data types. Although in most cases these scalars will expose powerful programming techniques, be forewarned: as you'll see, the picture isn't always rosy.

Part 2

Data types

Clojure has squirreled away interesting tidbits even among its data types. The scalar types include some less common items such as keywords and rational numbers, and the composite types are all immutable. In this part, we'll explore all of them in detail.

On scalars

*It requires a very unusual mind to
undertake the analysis of the obvious.*
—Alfred North Whitehead

This chapter covers
- Understanding precision
- Trying to be rational
- When to use keywords
- Symbolic resolution
- Regular expressions—the second problem

So far, we've covered a somewhat eclectic mix of theoretical and practical concerns. This brings us now to a point where we can dive deeper into a fundamental topic: how Clojure deals with scalar values, including numeric, symbolic, and regular expression values, and how they behave as data and sometimes as code.

A scalar data type is one that can only hold one value at a time of a number, symbol, keyword, string, or character. Most of the use cases for Clojure's scalar data types will be familiar to you. But there are some nuances that should be observed. Clojure's scalar data types exist in an interesting conceptual space. Because of its symbiotic nature, some of the scalar type behaviors walk a conceptual line between pure Clojure semantics and host semantics. This chapter provides a rundown of some of the idiomatic uses of Clojure's scalar data types as well as some pitfalls that you might encounter. In most cases, Clojure will shield you from the quirks of its host, but there are times when they'll demand attention. Clojure's scalar types have the potential to act like Sybil—sweet and kind one moment, vicious and vile the next—requiring some thought to handle properly. We'll also talk about this duality and address its limitations and possible mitigation techniques. Additionally, we'll address the age-old topic of Lisp-1 versus Lisp-2 implementations and how Clojure approaches the matter. Finally, we'll talk briefly about Clojure's regular expression literals and how they're typically used.

We'll first cover matters of numerical precision and how the Java Virtual Machine works to thwart your attempts at mathematical nirvana.

4.1   *Understanding precision*

Numbers in Clojure are by default as precise[1] as they need to be. Given enough memory, you could store the value of Pi accurately up to a billion places and beyond; in practice, values that large are rarely needed. But it's sometimes important to provide perfect accuracy at less-precise values. When dealing with raw Clojure functions and forms, it's a trivial matter to ensure such accuracy; it's handled automatically. Because Clojure encourages interoperability with its host platform, the matter of accuracy becomes less than certain. This section will talk about real matters of precision related to Clojure's support for the Java Virtual Machine. As it pertains to programming languages,[2] numerical precision is proportional to the mechanisms used for storing numerical representations. The Java language specification describes the internal representation of its primitive types thus limiting their precision. Depending on the class of application specialization, a programmer could go an entire career and never be affected by Java's precision limitations. But many industries require perfect accuracy of arbitrarily precise computations, and it's here that Clojure can provide a great boon; but with this power come some pointy edges, as we'll discuss shortly.

4.1.1   *Truncation*

Truncation refers to the limiting of accuracy for a floating-point number based on a deficiency in the corresponding representation. When a number is truncated, its precision is limited such that the maximum number of digits of accuracy is bound by the number of bits that can "fit" into the storage space allowed by its representation. For floating-point values, Clojure truncates by default. Therefore, if high precision is required for your floating-point operations, then explicit typing is required, as seen with the use of the M literal in the following:

---

[1] In a future version of Clojure, this arbitrary precision won't be the default, but will require explicit flagging (with the aforementioned M for decimal numbers and N for longs). Additionally, overflow of primitive numbers will always signal an exception.

[2] As opposed to arithmetic precision.

```
(let [imadeuapi 3.1415926535897932384626433832795028841971693937M]
  (println (class imadeuapi))
  imadeuapi)
; java.math.BigDecimal
;=> 3.1415926535897932384626433832795028841971693937M

(let [butieatedit 3.1415926535897932384626433832795028841971693937]
  (println (class butieatedit))
  butieatedit)
; java.lang.Double
;=> 3.141592653589793
```

As we show, the local `butieatedit` is truncated because the default Java double type is insufficient. On the other hand, `imadeuapi` uses Clojure's literal notation, a suffix character `M`, to declare a value as requiring arbitrary decimal representation. This is one possible way to mitigate truncation for a immensely large range of values, but as we'll explore in section 4.2, it's not a guarantee of perfect precision.

4.1.2   Promotion

Clojure is able to detect when overflow occurs, and will promote the value to a numerical representation that can accommodate larger values. In many cases, promotion results in the usage of a pair of classes used to hold exceptionally large values. This promotion within Clojure is automatic, as the primary focus is first correctness of numerical values, then raw speed. It's important to remember that this promotion *will* occur, as shown in the following listing, and your code should accommodate[3] this certainty.

Listing 4.1   Automatic promotion in Clojure

```
(def clueless 9)
(class clueless)
;=> java.lang.Integer

(class (+ clueless 9000000000000000))
;=> java.lang.Long

(class (+ clueless 90000000000000000000000))
;=> java.math.BigInteger

(class (+ clueless 9.0))
;=> java.lang.Double
```

Java itself has a bevy of contexts under which automatic type conversion will occur, so we advise you to familiarize yourself with those (Lindholm 1999) when dealing with Java native libraries.

---

[3] In the example, it's important to realize that the actual class of the value is changing, so any functions or methods reliant on specific types might not work as expected.

4.1.3   *Overflow*

Integer and long values in Java are subject to overflow errors. When an integer calculation results in a value that's larger than 32 bits of representation will allow, the bits of storage will "wrap" around. When you're operating in Clojure, overflow won't be an issue for most cases, thanks to promotion. But when dealing with numeric operations on primitive types, overflow can occur. Fortunately in these instances an exception will occur rather than propagating inaccuracies:

```
(+ Integer/MAX_VALUE Integer/MAX_VALUE)
;=> java.lang.ArithmeticException: integer overflow
```

Clojure provides a class of unchecked integer and long mathematical operations that assume that their arguments are primitive types. These unchecked operations *will* overflow if given excessively large values:

```
(unchecked-add (Integer/MAX_VALUE) (Integer/MAX_VALUE))
;=> -2
```

You should take care with unchecked operations, because there's no way to detect overflowing values and no reliable way to return from them. Use the unchecked functions only when overflow is desired.

4.1.4   *Underflow*

Underflow is the inverse of overflow, where a number is so small that its value collapses into zero. Simple examples of underflow for float and doubles can be demonstrated:

```
(float 0.0000000000000000000000000000000000000000000001)
;=> 0.0

1.0E-430
;=> 0.0
```

Underflow presents a danger similar to overflow, except that it occurs only with floating-point numbers.

4.1.5   *Rounding errors*

When the representation of a floating-point value isn't sufficient for storing its actual value, then rounding errors will occur (Goldberg 1994). Rounding errors are an especially insidious numerical inaccuracy, as they have a habit of propagating throughout a computation and/or build over time, leading to difficulties in debugging. There's a famous case involving the failure of a Patriot missile caused by a rounding error, resulting in the death of 28 U.S. soldiers in the first Gulf War (Skeel 1992). This occurred due to a rounding error in the representation of a count register's update interval. The timer register was meant to update once every 0.1 seconds, but because the hardware couldn't represent 0.1 directly, an approximation was used instead. Tragically, the approximation used was subject to rounding error. Therefore, over the course of 100 hours, the rounding accumulated into a timing error of approximately 0.34 seconds.

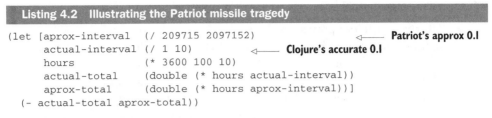

Listing 4.2 Illustrating the Patriot missile tragedy

```
(let [aprox-interval    (/ 209715 2097152)        ◁──── Patriot's approx 0.I
      actual-interval   (/ 1 10)        ◁──── Clojure's accurate 0.I
      hours             (* 3600 100 10)
      actual-total      (double (* hours actual-interval))
      aprox-total       (double (* hours aprox-interval))]
  (- actual-total aprox-total))

;=> 0.34332275390625
```

In the case of the Patriot missile, the deviation of 0.34 seconds was enough to cause a catastrophic software error, resulting in its ineffectiveness. When human lives are at stake, the inaccuracies wrought from rounding errors are unacceptable. For the most part, Clojure will be able to maintain arithmetic accuracies within a certain range, but you shouldn't take for granted that such will be the case when interacting with Java libraries.

One way to contribute to rounding errors is to introduce doubles and floats into an operation. In Clojure, any computation involving even a single double will result in a value that's a double:

```
(+ 0.1M 0.1M 0.1M 0.1 0.1M 0.1M 0.1M 0.1M 0.1M 0.1M)
;=> 0.9999999999999999
```

Can you spot the double?

This discussion was Java-centric, but Clojure's ultimate goal is to be platform-agnostic, and the problem of numerical consistency across platforms is a nontrivial matter. It's still unknown whether the preceding points will be universal across host platforms, so please bear in mind that they should be reexamined when using Clojure outside the context of the JVM. Now that we've identified the root issues when dealing with numbers in Clojure, we'll dive into a successful mitigation technique for dealing with them—rationals.

4.2 Trying to be rational

Clojure provides a data type representing a rational number, and all of its core mathematical functions operate with rational numbers. Clojure's rationals allow for arbitrarily large numerators and denominators. We won't go into depth about the limitations of floating-point operations, but the problem can be summarized simply. Given a finite representation of an infinitely large set, a determination must be made which finite subset *is* represented. In the case of standard floating-point numbers as representations of real numbers, the distribution of represented numbers is logarithmic (Kuki 1973) and not one-for-one. What does this mean in practice? It means that requiring more accuracy in your floating-point operations increases the probability that the corresponding representation won't be available. In these circumstances, you'll have to settle for approximations. But Clojure's rational number type provides a way to retain perfect accuracy when needed.

4.2.1   *Why be rational?*

Of course, Clojure provides a decimal type that's boundless relative to your computer memory, so why wouldn't you just use those? In short, you can, but decimal operations can be easily corrupted, especially when working with existing Java libraries (Kahan 1998) taking and returning primitive types. Additionally, in the case of Java, its underlying `BigDecimal` class is finite in that it uses a 32-bit integer to represent the number of digits to the right of the decimal place. This can represent an extremely large range of values perfectly, but it's still subject to error:

```
1.0E-430000000M
;=> 1.0E-430000000M

1.0E-4300000000M
;=> java.lang.RuntimeException: java.lang.NumberFormatException
```

Even if you manage to ensure that your `BigDecimal` values are free from floating-point corruption, you can never protect them from themselves. At some point or another, a floating-point calculation will encounter a number such as 2/3 that will *always* require rounding, leading to subtle, yet propagating errors. Finally, floating-point arithmetic is neither associative nor distributive, which may lead to the shocking results shown in this listing.

Listing 4.3   Floating-point arithmetic isn't associative or distributive.

```
(def a  1.0e50)
(def b -1.0e50)
(def c 17.0e00)

(+ (+ a b) c)
;=> 17.0                          │ Associativity should
                               ◁─┘ guarantee 17.0 also
(+ a (+ b c))
;=> 0.0

(let [a (float 0.1)
      b (float 0.2)
      c (float 0.3)]
  (=
    (* a (+ b c))                │ Distributive should
    (+ (* a b) (* a c))))     ◁─┘ guarantee equality
;=> false
```

Therefore, for absolutely precise calculations, rationals are the best choice.[4]

4.2.2   *How to be rational*

Aside from the rational data type, Clojure provides functions that can help to maintain your sanity: `ratio?`, `rational?`, and `rationalize`. Additionally, taking apart rationals is also a trivial matter.

---

[4] In the case of irrational numbers like Pi, all bets are off.

The best way to ensure that your calculations remain as accurate as possible is to ensure that they're all done using rational numbers. As shown in the following listing, the shocking results from using floating-point numbers have been eliminated.

Listing 4.4 Being rational preserves associativity and distributive natures.

```
(def a (rationalize 1.0e50))
(def b (rationalize -1.0e50))
(def c (rationalize 17.0e00))

(+ (+ a b) c)
;=> 17

(+ a (+ b c))            ⎤ Associativity
;=> 17                   ⎦ preserved

(let [a (rationalize 0.1)
      b (rationalize 0.2)
      c (rationalize 0.3)]
  (=
    (* a (+ b c))        ⎤ Distributive
    (+ (* a b) (* a c))))) ⎦ nature preserved
;=> true
```

To ensure that your numbers remain rational, you can use `rational?` to check whether a given number is one and then use `rationalize` to convert it to one. There are a few rules of thumb to remember if you want to maintain perfect accuracy in your computations:

1 Never use Java math libraries unless they return results of `BigDecimal`, and even then be suspicious.
2 Don't `rationalize` values that are Java float or double primitives.
3 If you must write your own high-precision calculations, do so with rationals.
4 Only convert to a floating-point representation as a last resort.

Finally, you can extract the constituent parts of a rational using the `numerator` and `denominator` functions:

```
(numerator (/ 123 10))
;=> 123
(denominator (/ 123 10))
;=> 10
```

You might never need perfect accuracy in your calculations. When you do, Clojure provides tools for maintaining sanity, but the responsibility to maintain rigor lies with you.

4.2.3 Caveats of rationality

Like any tool, Clojure's rational type is a double-edged sword. The calculation of rational math, though accurate, isn't nearly as fast as with floats or doubles. Each operation in rational math has an overhead cost (such as finding the least common denominator) that should be accounted for. It does you no good to use rational operations if speed is a primary concern above accuracy.

That covers the numerical scalars, so we'll move on to two data types that you may not be familiar with unless you happen to come from a background in the Lisp family of languages: keywords and symbols.

4.3   When to use keywords

The purpose of Clojure *keywords*, or *symbolic identifiers*, can sometimes lead to confusion for first-time Clojure programmers, because their analogue isn't often found[5] in other languages. This section will attempt to alleviate the confusion and provide some tips for how keywords are typically used.

4.3.1   How are keywords different from symbols?

Keywords *always* refer to themselves. What this means is that the keyword :magma always has the value :magma, whereas the symbol ruins may refer to any legal Clojure value or reference.

AS KEYS

Because keywords are self-evaluating and provide fast equality checks, they're almost always used in the context of map keys. An equally important reason to use keywords as map keys is that they can be used as functions, taking a map as an argument, to perform value lookups:

```
(def population {:zombies 2700, :humans 9})

(:zombies population)
;=> 2700

(println (/ (:zombies population)
            (:humans population))
         "zombies per capita")
; 300 zombies per capita
```

This leads to much more concise code.

AS ENUMERATIONS

Often, Clojure code will use keywords as enumeration values, such as :small, :medium, and :large. This provides a nice visual delineation within the source code.

AS MULTIMETHOD DISPATCH VALUES

Because keywords are used often as enumerations, they're ideal candidates for dispatch values for multimethods, which we'll explore in more detail in section 9.1.

AS DIRECTIVES

Another common use for keywords is to provide a directive to a function, multimethod, or macro. A simple way to illustrate this is to imagine a simple function pour, shown in listing 4.5, that takes two numbers and returns a lazy sequence of the range of those numbers. But there's also a mode for this function that takes a keyword :toujours, which will instead return an infinite lazy range starting with the first number and continuing "forever."

---

[5] Ruby has a symbol type that acts, looks, and is used similarly to Clojure keywords.

Listing 4.5 Using a keyword as a function directive

```
(defn pour [lb ub]
  (cond
    (= ub :toujours) (iterate inc lb)
    :else (range lb ub)))

(pour 1 10)
;=> (1 2 3 4 5 6 7 8 9)

(pour 1 :toujours)
; ... runs forever
```

An illustrative bonus with `pour` is that the macro `cond` itself uses a directive `:else` to mark the default conditional case. In this case, `cond` uses the fact that the keyword `:else` is truthy; any keyword (or truthy value) would've worked just as well.

4.3.2 Qualifying your keywords

Keywords don't belong to any specific namespace, although they may appear to if namespace qualification is used:

```
::not-in-ns
;=> :user/not-in-ns
```

The prefix portion of the keyword marked as `:user/` only looks like it's denoting an owning namespace; in fact, it's a prefix gathered from the current namespace by the Clojure reader. Observe the use of arbitrary prefixing:

```
(ns another)
:user/in-another
;=> :user/in-another

:haunted/name
;=> :haunted/name
```

In the first case, we created a namespace `another` and created a keyword `:user/in-another` that appears to belong to the `user` namespace, but in fact is prefixed. In the second example, we created a keyword `:haunted/name` showing that the prefix doesn't have to belong to a namespace at all, given that one named `haunted` certainly doesn't exist. But the fact that keywords aren't members of any given namespace doesn't mean that namespace-qualifying them is pointless. Instead, it's often more clear to do so, especially when a namespace aggregates a specific functionality and its keywords are meaningful in that context.

> **Separating the plumbing from the domain**
>
> Within a namespace named `crypto`, the keywords `::rsa` and `::blowfish` make sense as being namespace-qualified. Likewise, should we create a namespace `aquarium`, then using `::blowfish` within is contextually meaningful. Likewise, when adding metadata to structures, you should consider using qualified keywords as keys and directives if their intention is domain-oriented. Observe the following code:

(continued)

```
(defn do-blowfish [directive]
  (case directive
    :aquarium/blowfish (println "feed the fish")
    :crypto/blowfish   (println "encode the message")
    :blowfish          (println "not sure what to do")))
(ns crypto)
(user/do-blowfish :blowfish)
; not sure what to do

(user/do-blowfish ::blowfish)
; encode the message
(ns aquarium)
(user/do-blowfish :blowfish)
; not sure what to do

(user/do-blowfish ::blowfish)
; feed the fish
```

When switching to different namespaces using ns, you can use the namespace-qual-ified keyword syntax to ensure that the correct domain-specific code path is executed.

Namespace qualification is especially important when you're creating ad-hoc hierar-chies and defining multimethods, both discussed in section 9.2.

4.4 Symbolic resolution

In the previous section, we covered the differences between symbols and keywords. Whereas keywords were fairly straightforward, symbols abide by a slightly more com-plicated system for lookup resolution.

Symbols in Clojure are roughly analogous to identifiers in many other languages— words that refer to other things. In a nutshell, symbols are primarily used to provide a name for a given value. But in Clojure, symbols can also be referred to directly, by using the symbol or quote function or the ' special operator. Symbols tend to be dis-crete entities from one lexical contour to another, and often even within a single con-tour. Unlike keywords, symbols aren't unique based solely on name alone, as you can see in the following:

```
(identical? 'goat 'goat)
;=> false
```

The reason identical? returns false in this example is because each goat symbol is a discrete object that only happens to share a name and therefore a symbolic represen-tation. But that name is the basis for symbol equality:

```
(= 'goat 'goat)
;=> true

(name 'goat)
"goat"
```

The identical? function in Clojure only ever returns true when the symbols are in fact the same object:

```
(let [x 'goat y x] (identical? x y))
;=> true
```

In the preceding example, x is also a symbol, but when evaluated in the (identical? x x) form it returns the symbol goat, which is actually being stored on the runtime call stack. The question arises: why not make two identically named symbols the same object? The answer lies in metadata, which we discuss next.

4.4.1 Metadata

Clojure allows the attachment of metadata to various objects, but for now we'll focus on attaching metadata to symbols. The with-meta function takes an object and a map and returns another object of the same type with the metadata attached. The reason why equally named symbols are often not the same instance is because each can have its own unique metadata:

```
(let [x (with-meta 'goat {:ornery true})
      y (with-meta 'goat {:ornery false})]
  [(= x y)
   (identical? x y)
   (meta x)
   (meta y)])

;=> [true false {:ornery true} {:ornery false}]
```

The two locals x and y both hold an equal symbol 'goat, but they're different instances, each containing separate metadata maps obtained with the meta function. The implications of this are that symbol equality isn't dependent on metadata or identity. This equality semantic isn't limited to symbols, but is pervasive in Clojure, as we'll demonstrate throughout this book. You'll find that keywords can't hold metadata[6] because any equally named keyword is the same object.

4.4.2 Symbols and namespaces

Like keywords, symbols don't belong to any specific namespace. Take, for example, the following code:

```
(ns where-is)
(def a-symbol 'where-am-i)

a-symbol
;=> where-am-i

(resolve 'a-symbol)
;=> #'where-is/a-symbol

`a-symbol
;=> where-is/a-symbol
```

---

[6] Java class instances, including strings, can't hold metadata either.

The initial evaluation of a-symbol shows the expected value where-am-i. But attempting to resolve the symbol using resolve and using syntax-quote returns what looks like (as printed at the REPL) a namespace-qualified symbol. This is because a symbol's qualification is a characteristic of evaluation and not inherent in the symbol at all. This also applies to symbols qualified with class names. This evaluation behavior will prove beneficial when we discuss macros in chapter 8, but for now we can summarize the overarching idea known as Lisp-1 (Gabriel 2001).

4.4.3 *Lisp-1*

Clojure is what's known as a Lisp-1, which in simple terms means it uses the same name resolution for function and value bindings. In a Lisp-2 programming language like Common Lisp, these name resolutions are performed differently depending on the context of the symbol, be it in a function call position or a function argument position. There are many arguments for and against both Lisp-1 and Lisp-2, but against Lisp-1 one downside bears consideration. Because the same name-resolution scheme is used for functions and their arguments, there's a real possibility of shadowing existing functions with other locals or Vars. Name shadowing isn't necessarily non-idiomatic if done thoughtfully, but if done accidentally it can lead to some unexpected and obscure errors. You should take care when naming locals and defining new functions so that name-shadowing complications can be avoided.

Though name-shadowing errors tend to be rare, the benefit in a simplified mechanism for calling and passing first-class functions far outweighs the negative. Clojure's adoption of a Lisp-1 resolution scheme makes for cleaner implementations and therefore highlights the solution rather than muddying the waters with the nuances of symbolic lookup. For example, the best function highlights this perfectly in the way that it takes the greater-than function > and calls it within its body as f:

```
(defn best [f xs]
  (reduce #(if (f % %2) % %2) xs))

(best > [1 3 4 2 7 5 3])
;=> 7
```

A similar function body using a Lisp-2 language would require the intervention of another function (in this case funcall) responsible for invoking the function explicitly. Likewise, passing any function would require the use of a qualifying tag marking it as a function object, as seen here:

```
(defun best (f xs)
  (reduce #'(lambda (l r)
              (if (funcall f l r) l r))
          xs))

(best #'> '(1 3 4 2 7 5 3))
;=> 7
```

This section isn't intended to champion the cause of Lisp-1 over Lisp-2, only to highlight the differences between the two. Many of the design decisions in Clojure provide succinctness in implementation, and Lisp-1 is no exception. The preference for Lisp-1 versus Lisp-2 typically boils down to matters of style and taste; by all practical measures, they're equivalent.

Having covered the two symbolic scalar types, we now move into a type that you're (for better or worse) likely familiar with: the regular expression.

4.5 Regular expressions—the second problem

> *Some people, when confronted with a problem, think "I know, I'll use regular expressions." Now they have two problems.*
> —Jamie Zawinski

Regular expressions are a powerful and compact way to find specific patterns in text strings. Though we sympathize with Zawinski's attitude and appreciate his wit, sometimes regular expressions are a useful tool to have on hand. Although the full capabilities of regular expressions (or regexes) are well beyond the scope of this section (Friedl 1997), we'll look at some of the ways Clojure leverages Java's regex capabilities.

Java's regular expression engine is reasonably powerful, supporting Unicode and features such as reluctant quantifiers and "look-around" clauses. Clojure doesn't try to reinvent the wheel and instead provides special syntax for literal Java regex patterns plus a few functions to help Java's regex capabilities fit better with the rest of Clojure.

4.5.1 Syntax

A literal regular expression in Clojure looks like this:

```
#"an example pattern"
```

This produces[7] a compiled regex object that can be used either directly with Java interop method calls or with any of the Clojure regex functions described later:

```
(class #"example")
;=> java.util.regex.Pattern
```

Though the pattern is surrounded with double quotes like string literals, the way things are escaped within the quotes isn't the same. This difference is easiest to see in patterns that use backslash-delimited character classes. When compiled as a regex, a string `"\\d"` will match a single digit and is identical to a literal regex without the double backslash. Note that Clojure will even print the pattern back out using the literal syntax:

```
(java.util.regex.Pattern/compile "\\d")
;=> #"\d"
```

In short, the only rules you need to know for embedding unusual literal characters or predefined character classes are listed in the javadoc for Pattern.[8]

---

[7] Literal regex patterns are compiled to java.util.regex.Pattern instances at read-time. This means, for example, if you use a literal regex in a loop, it's *not* recompiled each time through the loop, but just once when the surrounding code is compiled.

[8] See the online reference at http://java.sun.com/j2se/1.5.0/docs/api/java/util/regex/Pattern.html.

Regular expressions accept option flags, shown in table 4.1, that can make a pattern case-insensitive or enable multiline mode, and Clojure's regex literals starting with `(?<flag>)` set the mode for the rest of the pattern.

Table 4.1   Regex flags: these are the flags that can be used within Clojure regular expression patterns, their long name, and a description of what they do. See Java's documentation for the java.util. regex.Pattern class for more details.

Flag	Flag name	Description
d	UNIX_LINES	`.`, `^`, and `$` match only the Unix line terminator `'\n'`.
i	CASE_INSENSITIVE	ASCII characters are matched without regard to upper or lower case.
x	COMMENTS	Whitespace and comments in the pattern are ignored.
m	MULTILINE	`^` and `$` match near line terminators instead of only at the beginning or end of the entire input string.
s	DOTALL	`.` matches any character including the line terminator.
u	UNICODE_CASE	Causes the `i` flag to use Unicode case insensitivity instead of ASCII.

For example, the pattern `#"(?i)yo"` would match the strings "yo", "yO", "Yo", and "YO".

4.5.2   *Functions*

Java's regex Pattern object has several methods that can be used directly, but only `split` is used regularly to split a string into an array[9] of Strings, breaking the original where the pattern matches:

```
(seq (.split #"," "one,two,three"))
;=> ("one" "two" "three")
```

The `re-seq` function is Clojure's regex workhorse. It returns a lazy seq of all matches in a string, which means it can be used to efficiently test whether a string matches at all or to find all matches in a string or a mapped file:

```
(re-seq #"\w+" "one-two/three")
;=> ("one" "two" "three")
```

The preceding regular expression has no capturing groups, so each match in the returned seq is simply a string. A capturing group in the regex causes each returned item to be a vector:

```
(re-seq #"\w*(\w)" "one-two/three")
;=> (["one" "e"] ["two" "o"] ["three" "e"])
```

---

[9] Java arrays don't print very pleasantly at the Clojure REPL, so we used `seq` in this example so you can see the Strings inside.

So where `.split` returns the text between regex matches, `re-seq` returns the matches themselves.[10] Now that we've looked at some nice functions you can use, we'll talk about one object you shouldn't.

4.5.3 *Beware of mutable matchers*

Java's regular expression engine includes a `Matcher` object that mutates in a non-thread-safe way as it walks through a string finding matches. This object is exposed by Clojure via the `re-matcher` function and can be used as an argument to `re-groups` and the single-parameter form of `re-find`. We highly recommend avoiding all of these unless you're certain you know what you're doing. These dangerous functions are used internally by the implementations of some of the recommended functions described earlier, but in each case they're careful to disallow access to the `Matcher` object they use. Use Matchers at your own risk, or better yet don't use them directly[11] at all.

4.6 *Summary*

Clojure's scalar types generally work as expected, but its numerical types have a potential for frustration in certain situations. Though you may rarely encounter issues with numerical precision, keeping in mind the circumstances under which they occur might prove useful in the future. Given its inherent arbitrary-precision big decimal and rational numerics, Clojure provides the tools for perfectly accurate calculations. Keywords in Clojure serve many purposes and are ubiquitous in idiomatic code. When dealing directly with symbols, Clojure's nature as a Lisp-1 defines the nature of how symbolic resolution occurs. Finally, Clojure provides regular expressions as first-class data types, and their usage is encouraged where appropriate.

As you might've speculated, this chapter was nice and short due to the relative simplicity of scalar types. In the following chapter, we'll step it up a notch or 10 when covering Clojure's composite data types. Though scalars are interesting and deeper than expected, the next chapter will start you on your way to understanding Clojure's true goal: providing a sane approach to application state.

---

[10] If you want both at the same time, you may want to look at the `partition` function in the `clojure-contrib` library, found in the `clojure.contrib.string` namespace.

[11] The `clojure.contrib.string` namespace has a bevy of functions useful for leveraging regular expressions.

Composite data types

It is better to have 100 functions operate on one data structure than 10 functions on 10 data structures.

—Alan Perlis

This chapter covers

- Persistence, sequences, and complexity
- Vectors: creating and using them in all their varieties
- Lists: Clojure's code form data structure
- How to use persistent queues
- Persistent sets
- Thinking in maps
- Putting it all together: finding the position of items in a sequence

Clojure provides a rich set of composite data types and we'll cover them all: vectors, lists, queues, sets, and maps. In this chapter, we'll dig into the strengths and weaknesses of each. We'll spend more time on vectors and maps than on the other types, because those two are used in a wider variety of circumstances and warrant the extra discussion. Finally, we'll discuss the design of a simple function to leverage many of the lessons learned in this chapter, and you'll gain specific insight into the preceding quote. By the way, we use the terms *composite types* and *collections* interchangeably, so please bear that in mind as we proceed.

Before we look at the primary collection types individually, we'll discuss the things they have in common. For example, you may have heard of Clojure's *sequence abstraction*—all the persistent collections use it, so we'll examine that as well as some algorithmic complexity concepts we'll be referring to throughout the chapter.

5.1 Persistence, sequences, and complexity

Clojure's composite data types have some unique properties compared to composites in many mainstream languages. Terms such as *persistent* and *sequence* come up, and not always in a way that makes their meaning clear. In this section we'll define their meanings carefully. We'll also briefly examine the topic of algorithmic complexity and Big-O notation as they apply to Clojure collections.

The term *persistent* is particularly problematic because it means something different in other contexts. In the case of Clojure, we believe that a phrase immortalized by Inigo Montoya from the novel and subsequent film *The Princess Bride* summarizes your likely initial reaction...

5.1.1 "You keep using that word. I do not think it means what you think it means."

Although storage to disk may be the more common meaning of *persistent* today, Clojure uses an older meaning of the word having to do with immutable in-memory collections with specific properties. In particular, a persistent collection in Clojure allows you to preserve historical versions (Okasaki 1999) of its state, and promises that all versions will have the same update and lookup complexity guarantees. The specific guarantees depend on the collection type, and we'll cover those details along with each kind of collection.

Here you can see the difference between a persistent data structure and one that's not by using a Java array:

```
(def ds (into-array [:willie :barnabas :adam]))
(seq ds)
;=> (:willie :barnabas :adam)
```

What we've done is create a three-element array of keywords and used seq to produce an object that displays nicely in the REPL. Any change to the array ds happens in-place, thus obliterating any historical version:

```
(aset ds 1 :quentin)
;=> :quentin

(seq ds)
;=> (:willie :quentin :adam)
```

But using one of Clojure's persistent data structures paints a different picture:

```
(def ds [:willie :barnabas :adam])
ds
;=> [:willie :barnabas :adam]

(def ds1 (replace {:barnabas :quentin} ds))
ds
;=> [:willie :barnabas :adam]

ds1
;=> [:willie :quentin :adam]
```

The original vector ds did *not* change on the replacement of the keyword :barnabas but instead created another vector with the changed value. A natural concern when confronted with this picture of persistence is that a naive implementation would copy the whole collection on each change, leading to slow operations and poor use of memory. Clojure's implementations (Bagwell 2001) are instead efficient by sharing structural elements from one version of a persistent structure to another. This may seem magical, but we'll demystify it in the next chapter. For now it's sufficient to understand that each instance of a collection is immutable and efficient. This fact opens numerous possibilities that wouldn't work for standard mutable collections. One of these is the sequence abstraction.

5.1.2 *Sequence terms and what they mean*

> *It is better to have 100 functions operate on one data abstraction than 10 functions on 10 data structures.*
> —Rich Hickey

The words *sequential, sequence,* and *seq* don't sound very different from each other, but they mean specific things in Clojure. We'll start with specific definitions of each term to help you tell them apart, and then go into a bit of detail about how they relate to equality partitions and the sequence abstraction.

TERMS

A *sequential* collection is one that holds a series of values without reordering them. As such it's one of three broad categories of collection types, which we discuss in the next subsection.

A *sequence* is a sequential collection that represents a series of values that may or may not exist yet. They may be values from a concrete collection or values that are computed as necessary. A sequence may also be empty.

Clojure has a simple API called *seq* for navigating collections. It consist of two functions: first and rest. If the collection has anything in it, (first coll) returns the first element; otherwise it returns nil. (rest coll) returns a sequence of the items other than the first. If there are no other items, rest returns an empty sequence and never nil. Functions that promise to return sequences, such as map and filter, work the same way as rest. A *seq* is any object that implements the seq API, thereby supporting the functions first and rest. You might consider it an immutable variant of an enumerator or iterator.

There's also a function called seq that accepts a wide variety of collection-like objects. Some collections, such as lists, implement the seq API directly, so calling seq on them returns the collection itself. More often, calling seq on a collection returns a new seq object for navigating that collection. In either case, if the collection is empty, seq returns nil and never an empty sequence. Functions that promise to return seqs (not sequences), such as next, work the same way.

Clojure's sequence library manipulates collections, strings, arrays, and so on as if they were sequences, using the seq function and seq API.

> **BEWARE TYPE-BASED PREDICATES** Clojure includes a few predicates with names like the words just defined. Though they're not frequently used, it seems worth mentioning that they may not mean exactly what the definitions here might suggest. For example, every object for which sequential? returns true is a sequential collection, but it returns false for some that are also sequential. This is because of implementation details that may be improved sometime after Clojure 1.2.

EQUALITY PARTITIONS

Clojure classifies each composite data type into one of three logical categories or partitions: sequentials, maps, and sets. These divisions draw clear distinctions between the types and help define equality semantics. Specifically, two objects will never be equal if they belong to different partitions. Few composite types are actually *sequences*, though several such as vectors are *sequential*.

If two sequentials have the same values in the same order, = will return true for them, even if their concrete types are different, as shown:

```
(= [1 2 3] '(1 2 3))
;=> true
```

Conversely, even if two collections have the same values in the same order, if one is a sequential collection and the other isn't, = will return false, as shown here:

```
(= [1 2 3] #{1 2 3})
;=> false
```

Examples of things that are sequential include Clojure lists and vectors, and Java lists such as java.util.ArrayList. In fact everything that implements java.util.List is included in the sequential partition.

Generally things that fall into the other partitions include *set* or *map* in their name and so are easy to identify.

THE SEQUENCE ABSTRACTION

Many Lisps build their data types (McCarthy 1962) on the cons-cell abstraction, an elegant two-element structure illustrated in figure 5.1.

Clojure also has a couple of cons-cell-like structures that are covered in section 5.4, but they're not central to Clojure's design. Instead, the conceptual interface fulfilled by the cons-cell has been lifted off the concrete structure illustrated previously and

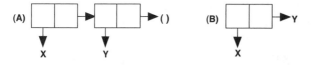

Figure 5.1 Each cons-cell is a simple pair, a `car` and a `cdr`. A. A list with two cells, each of which has a value X and Y as the head (the `car` in Lisp terminology) and a list as the tail (the `cdr`). This is very similar to `first` and `rest` in Clojure sequences. B. A cons-cell with a simple value for both the head and tail. This is called a *dotted pair* but is not supported by any of Clojure's built in types.

been named *sequence*. All an object needs to do to be a sequence is to support the two core functions: `first` and `rest`. This isn't much, but it's all that's required for the bulk of Clojure's powerful library of sequence functions and macros to be able to operate on the collection: `filter`, `map`, `for`, `doseq`, `take`, `partition`, the list goes on.

At the same time, a wide variety of objects satisfy this interface. Every Clojure collection provides at least one kind of seq object for walking through its contents, exposed via the `seq` function. Some collections provide more than one; for example vectors support `rseq` and maps support the functions `keys` and `vals`. All of these functions return a seq, or if the collection is empty, `nil`.

You can see examples of this by looking at the types of objects returned by various expressions. Here's the map class:

```
(class (hash-map :a 1))
;=> clojure.lang.PersistentHashMap
```

Unsurprisingly, the `hash-map` function returns an object of type `PersistentHashMap`. Passing that map object to `seq` returns an entirely new kind of object:

```
(seq (hash-map :a 1))
;=> ([:a 1])

(class (seq (hash-map :a 1)))
;=> clojure.lang.PersistentHashMap$NodeSeq
```

This class name suggests it's a seq of nodes on a hash map. Similarly we can get a seq of keys on the same map:

```
(seq (keys (hash-map :a 1)))
;=> (:a)

(class (keys (hash-map :a 1)))
;=> clojure.lang.APersistentMap$KeySeq
```

Note that these specific class names are an implementation detail that may change in the future, but the concepts they embody are central to Clojure and unlikely to change.

Having laid the foundation for a deeper dive into the sequence abstraction, we now must quickly diverge into a simplified discussion of asymptotic complexity and Big-O notation. If you're already comfortable with these topics then by all means skip forward to section 5.2. If you need a refresher or an overview, then the next section is a minimalist introduction (Cormen 2009) to the topic.

5.1.3   *Big-O*

This book isn't heavily focused on asymptotic complexity but we do mention it a handful of times throughout, so here we'll cover the minimum required for understanding these few mentions. You may have gone your entire career without having to understand Big-O notation, and you may likely go the remainder similarly. But that's no reason not to learn more, and a bit of understanding about Big-O and its implications will go a long way toward helping you in choosing between Clojure collections, as well as to design and analyze algorithms in general.

Algorithmic complexity is a system for describing the *relative* space and time costs for algorithms. Typically the complexity of an algorithm is described using what's known as Big-O notation. For example, you may have heard that finding an element in a linked list is O(n), which is read as "order n." What this means is that if you have a list (:a :b :c) of length 3, then to verify that the keyword :c is in that list requires three comparisons. This highlights the *worst case* of list access because :c is at the end of the list, but we don't worry too much about the worst-case scenario unless that's the only difference between two algorithms. On the other hand, to verify that :a is in the same list is O(1), which is read as constant time. Finding :a represents the *best case* for list access because it's at the front of the list. Rarely do your lists always look exactly like our example, and therefore you shouldn't build your hopes that elements will always be at the front. Therefore, in analyzing algorithms you rarely care about the best-case scenario because it's too rare to matter much. What you really care about when analyzing algorithms is the *expected case*, or what you'd likely see in practice. When looking at a few million runs of verifying that some value is contained in a million different lists, you'd inevitably see that the average number of comparisons required approaches whatever the length of a list was, divided by two. But because doubling the length of the list would also double the number of comparisons done in both the expected and worst case, they're all grouped into the same Big-O category: O(n) also known as *linear time.*

Thus two algorithms that are in the same Big-O category may perform very differently, especially on small work loads. This makes the most difference when there's a large *constant factor*, work that the algorithm has to do up front regardless of the size of the work load.

When the work load is small, an O(1) algorithm with a large constant factor may be more costly than an O(n) algorithm that's without extra costs. But as the work load increases, an O(1) algorithm will *always* overtake the O(n) algorithm as shown in figure 5.2. Big-O doesn't concern itself with these constant factors or small work loads.

When learning about Clojure's persistent data structures, you're likely to hear the term $O(\log_{32} n)$ for those based on the persistent hash trie and $O(\log_2 n)$ for the sorted structures. Accessing an element in a Clojure persistent structure by index is O(log n), or logarithmic. Logarithmic complexity describes a class of algorithms that are effectively immune from large changes in the size of their data. In the case of Clojure's persistent structures, what this means is that there's little difference in "hops" (such as comparisons) between locating an element in a structure containing 100

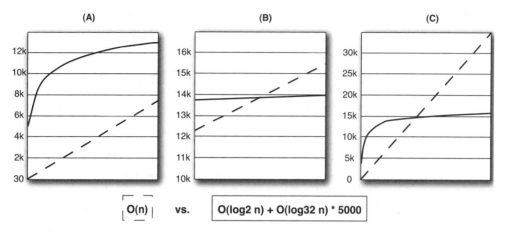

$$\boxed{\text{O}(n)} \quad \text{vs.} \quad \boxed{\text{O}(\log 2 \ n) + \text{O}(\log 32 \ n) * 5000}$$

Figure 5.2   Overtaking the smaller. In Big-O, regardless of the other ancillary costs, the higher order of magnitude will always overtake the lower eventually.

elements or 1 million elements. In practice you may notice some difference because for a billion objects $\text{O}(\log_2 n)$ would require approximately 30 comparisons for a lookup, whereas $\text{O}(\log_{32} n)$ would require only about 6. Given the smaller number of operations required for the $\text{O}(\log_{32} n)$ data structures, they can be viewed as providing a nearly $\text{O}(1)$ lookup and update.

We've covered the basic ideas behind persistence and the sequence abstraction, and even touched on the basics of Big-O notation. Now we'll discuss all of Clojure's primary collection types and how these concepts apply to each, starting with vectors.

5.2   *Vectors: creating and using them in all their varieties*

Vectors store zero or more values sequentially indexed by number, a bit like arrays, but are immutable and persistent. They're versatile and make efficient use of memory and processor resources at both small and large sizes.

Vectors are probably the most frequently used collection type in Clojure code. They're used as literals for argument lists and `let` bindings, for holding large amounts of application data, and as stacks and as map entries. We'll also address the efficiency considerations including growing on the right end, subvectors, and reversals, and finally discuss where vectors aren't an optimal solution.

5.2.1   *Building vectors*

The vector's literal square-bracket syntax is one reason you might choose to use a vector over a list. For example, the `let` form would work perfectly well, and with a nearly identical implementation, if it took a literal *list* of bindings instead of a literal *vector*. But the square brackets are visually different from the round parentheses surrounding the `let` form itself as well as the likely function calls in the body of the `let` form, and this is useful for humans (so we hear). Using vectors to indicate bindings for `let`, `with-open`, `fn`, and such is idiomatic in Clojure and is a pattern you're encouraged to follow in any similar macros you write.

The most common way to create a vector is with the literal syntax described earlier. But in many cases you'll want to create a vector out of the contents of some other kind of collection. For this there's the function vec:

```
(vec (range 10))
;=> [0 1 2 3 4 5 6 7 8 9]
```

If you already have a vector but want to "pour" several values into it, then into is your friend:

```
(let [my-vector [:a :b :c]]
  (into my-vector (range 10)))
;=> [:a :b :c 0 1 2 3 4 5 6 7 8 9]
```

If you want it to return a vector, the first argument to into *must* be a vector. The second arg can be any sequence, such as what range returns, or anything else that works with seq function. You can view the operation of into as similar to a O(n) concatenation based on the size of the second argument.[1] Clojure also provides a vector function to build a vector from its arguments, which is handy for constructs like (map vector a b).

PRIMITIVE VECTORS

Clojure can store primitive types inside of vectors using the vector-of function, which takes any of :int, :long, :float, :double, :byte, :short, :boolean, or :char as its argument and returns an empty vector. This returned vector will act just like any other vector, except that it'll store its contents as primitives internally. All of the normal vector operations still apply, and the new vector will attempt to coerce any additions into its internal type when being added:

```
(into (vector-of :int) [Math/PI 2 1.3])
;=> [3 2 1]
(into (vector-of :char) [100 101 102])
;=> [\d \e \f]
(into (vector-of :int) [1 2 623876371267813267326786327863])
; java.lang.IllegalArgumentException: Value out of range for int:
    -8359803716404783817
```

In addition, all caveats mentioned in section 4.1 regarding overflow, underflow, and so forth also apply to vectors of primitives.

Using vec and into, it's easy to build vectors much larger than are conveniently built using vector literals. But once you have a large vector like that, what are you going to do with it?

5.2.2 *Large vectors*

When collections are small, the performance differences between vectors and lists hardly matters at all. But as both get larger, each becomes dramatically slower at operations the other can still perform efficiently. Vectors are particularly efficient at three things relative to lists: adding or removing things from the right end of the collection,

---

[1] Vectors can't be concatenated any more efficiently than O(n).

accessing or changing items in the interior of the collection by numeric index, and walking in reverse order. Adding and removing from the end is done by treating the vector as a stack—we'll cover that later.

Any item in a vector can be accessed by its index number from 0 up to but not including (count my-vector) in essentially constant time.[2] You can do this using the function nth; the function get, essentially treating the vector like a map; or by invoking the vector itself as a function. Look at each of these as applied to this example vector:

```
(def a-to-j (vec (map char (range 65 75))))
a-to-j
;=> [\A \B \C \D \E \F \G \H \I \J]
```

All three of these do the same work and each returns \E:

```
(nth a-to-j 4)
(get a-to-j 4)
(a-to-j 4)
```

Which to use is a judgment call, but table 5.1 highlights some points you might consider when choosing.

Table 5.1 Vector lookup options: the three ways to look up an item in a vector and how each responds to different exceptional circumstances

	nth	get	Vector as a function
If the vector is nil	Returns nil	Returns nil	Throws an exception
If the index is out of range	Returns "not found" or throws exception	Returns nil	Throws an exception
Supports a "not found" arg	Yes (nth [] 9 :whoops)	Yes (get [] 9 :whoops)	No

Because vectors are indexed, they can be efficiently walked in either direction, left-to-right or right-to-left. The seq and rseq functions return sequences that do exactly that:

```
(seq a-to-j)
;=> (\A \B \C \D \E \F \G \H \I \J)

(rseq a-to-j)
;=> (\J \I \H \G \F \E \D \C \B \A)
```

Any item in a vector can be "changed" using the assoc function. Clojure does this in essentially constant time using structural sharing between the old and new vectors as described at the beginning of this chapter:

```
(assoc a-to-j 4 "no longer E")
;=> [\A \B \C \D "no longer E" \F \G \H \I \J]
```

The assoc function for vectors only works on indices that already exist in the vector, or as a special case, exactly one step past the end. In this case, the returned vector will

---

[2] Several operations on Clojure's persistent data structures are described in this book as "essentially constant time." In all cases these are $O(\log_{32} n)$.

be one item larger than the input vector. More frequently vectors are "grown" using the conj function as you'll see in the next section.

There are a few higher-powered functions provided that use assoc internally. For example, the replace function works on both seqs and vectors, but when given a vector, it uses assoc to fix up and return a new vector:

```
(replace {2 :a, 4 :b} [1 2 3 2 3 4])
;=> [1 :a 3 :a 3 :b]
```

The functions assoc-in and update-in are for working with nested structures of vectors and/or maps, like this one:[3]

```
(def matrix
     [[1 2 3]
      [4 5 6]
      [7 8 9]])
```

All of assoc-in, get-in, and update-in take a series of indices to pick items from each more deeply nested level. For a vector arranged like the earlier matrix example, this amounts to row and column coordinates:

```
(get-in matrix [1 2])
;=> 6

(assoc-in matrix [1 2] 'x)
;=> [[1 2 3] [4 5 x] [7 8 9]]
```

The update-in function works the same way, but instead of taking a value to *overwrite* an existing value, it takes a function to *apply* to an existing value. It'll replace the value at the given coordinates with the return value of the function given:

```
(update-in matrix [1 2] * 100)
;=> [[1 2 3] [4 5 600] [7 8 9]]
```

The coordinates refer to the value 6, and the function given here is * taking an argument 100, so the slot becomes the return value of (* 6 100). There's also a function get-in for retrieving a value in a nested vector. Before exploring its operation, we'll create a function neighbors in listing 5.1 that given a y-x location in an equilateral 2D matrix, returns a sequence of the locations surrounding it.

> **Listing 5.1 A function for finding the neighbors of a spot on a 2D matrix**

```
(defn neighbors
  ([size yx] (neighbors [[-1 0] [1 0] [0 -1] [0 1]] size yx))
  ([deltas size yx]
     (filter (fn [new-yx]
               (every? #(< -1 % size) new-yx))
             (map #(map + yx %) deltas))))
```

---

[3] Nested vectors are far from the most efficient way to store or process matrices, but they're convenient to manipulate in Clojure and so make a good example here. More efficient options include a single vector, arrays, or a library for matrix processing such as Colt or Incanter at http://incanter.org.

The operation of neighbors is fairly straightforward. The deltas local describes that a neighbor can be one spot away, but only along the x or y axis (not diagonal). The function first walks through deltas and builds a vector of each added to the yx point provided. This operation will of course generate illegal point coordinates, so those are then removed using filter, which checks to ensure that the indices lie between -1 and the provided size. You can test this function using get-in as follows:

```
(map #(get-in matrix %) (neighbors 3 [0 0]))
;=> (4 2)
```

For each neighbor coordinate returned from neighbors, we use get-in to retrieve the value at that point. Indeed the position [0 0] corresponding to the value 1 has the neighboring values 4 and 2. We'll use neighbors again before this book comes to an end, but next we'll look at growing and shrinking vectors—treating them like stacks.

5.2.3   *Vectors as stacks*

Classic stacks have at least two operations, *push* and *pop*, and with respect to Clojure vectors these operations are called conj and pop respectively. The conj function adds elements to and pop removes elements from the right side of the stack. Because vectors are immutable, pop returns a new vector with the rightmost item dropped—this is different from many mutable stack APIs, which generally return the dropped item. Consequently, peek becomes more important as the primary way to get an item from the top of the stack:

```
(def my-stack [1 2 3])

(peek my-stack)
;=> 3

(pop my-stack)
;=> [1 2]

(conj my-stack 4)
;=> [1 2 3 4]

(+ (peek my-stack) (peek (pop my-stack)))
;=> 5
```

Each of these operations completes in essentially constant time. Most of the time, a vector that's used as a stack is used that way throughout its life. It's helpful to future readers of your code to keep this is mind and use the stack operations consistently, even when other functions might work. For example, last on a vector returns the same thing as peek, but besides being slower, it leads to unnecessary confusion about how the collection is being used. If the algorithm involved calls for a stack, use conj not assoc for growing the vector, peek not last, and pop not dissoc for shrinking it.

The functions conj, pop, and peek work on any object that implements clojure. lang.IPersistentStack.[4] Besides vectors, Clojure lists also implement this interface,

---

[4] The conj function also works with all of Clojure's other persistent collection types, even if they don't implement clojure.lang.IPersistentStack.

but the functions operate on the left side of lists instead of the right side as with vectors. When operating on either via the stack discipline, it's best to ignore the ordering, because it tends to just add confusion.

5.2.4 *Using vectors instead of reverse*

The ability of vectors to grow efficiently on the right side and then be walked left-to-right produces a noteworthy emergent behavior: idiomatic Clojure code rarely uses the reverse function. This is different from most Lisps and schemes. When processing a list, it's pretty common to want to produce a new list in the same order. But if all you have are classic Lisp lists, often the most natural algorithm[5] leaves you with a backward list that needs to be reversed. Here's an example of a function similar to Clojure's map

```
(defn strict-map1 [f coll]
  (loop [coll coll, acc nil]
    (if (empty? coll)
      (reverse acc)
      (recur (next coll) (cons (f (first coll)) acc)))))

(strict-map1 - (range 5))
;=> (0 -1 -2 -3 -4)
```

This is perfectly good, idiomatic Clojure code, except for that glaring reverse of the final return value. After the entire list has been walked once to produce the desired values, reverse walks it again to get them in the right order. This is both inefficient and nonidiomatic. One way to get rid of the reverse is to use a vector instead of a list as the accumulator:

```
(defn strict-map2 [f coll]
  (loop [coll coll, acc []]
    (if (empty? coll)
      acc
      (recur (next coll) (conj acc (f (first coll)))))))

(strict-map2 - (range 5))
;=> [0 -1 -2 -3 -4]
```

A small change, but the code is now a touch cleaner and a bit faster. It does return a vector instead of a list, but this is rarely a problem, because any client code that wants to treat this as a seq can usually do so automatically.[6]

The examples we've shown so far have all been plain vectors, but we'll turn now to the special features of some other vector types, starting with subvectors.

---

[5] ...the most natural *tail-recursive* algorithm anyway.
[6] Another way to get rid of a reverse is to build a lazy sequence instead of a strict collection; this is how Clojure's own map function is implemented.

5.2.5   *Subvectors*

Although items can't be removed efficiently from a vector (except the rightmost item), subvectors provide a fast way to take a slice of an existing vector based on start and end indices created using the subvec function:

```
(subvec a-to-j 3 6)
;=> [\D \E \F]
```

The first index given to subvec is inclusive (starts *at* index 3) but the second is exclusive (ends *before* index 6). The new subvector internally hangs onto the entire original a-to-j vector, making each lookup performed on the new vector cause the subvector to do a little offset math and then look it up in the original. This makes creating a subvector fast. You can use subvec on any kind of vector and it'll work fine. But there's special logic for taking a subvec of a subvec, in which case the newest subvector keeps a reference to the *original* vector, not the intermediate subvector. This prevents subvectors-of-subvectors from stacking up needlessly, and keeps both the creation and use of the sub-subvecs fast and efficient.

5.2.6   *Vectors as MapEntries*

Clojure's hash map, just like hash tables or dictionaries in many other languages, has a mechanism to iterate through the entire collection. Clojure's solution for this iterator is, unsurprisingly, a seq. Each item of this seq needs to include both the key and the value, so they're wrapped in a MapEntry. When printed, each entry looks like a vector:

```
(first {:width 10, :height 20, :depth 15})
;=> [:width 10]
```

But not only does a MapEntry *look* like a vector, it really is one:

```
(vector? (first {:width 10, :height 20, :depth 15}))
;=> true
```

This means you can use all the regular vector functions on it: conj, get, and so on. It even supports destructuring, which can be handy. For example, the following locals dimension and amount will take on the value of each key/value pair in turn:

```
(doseq [[dimension amount] {:width 10, :height 20, :depth 15}]
  (println (str (name dimension) ":") amount "inches"))
; width: 10 inches
; height: 20 inches
; depth: 15 inches
;=> nil
```

A MapEntry is its own type and has two functions for retrieving its contents: key and val, which do exactly the same thing as (nth my-map 0) and (nth my-map 1), respectively. These are sometimes useful for the clarity they can bring to your code, but frequently destructuring is used instead, because it's so darned handy.

So now you know what vectors are, what specific kinds of vectors are included in Clojure, and some of the things that they're good at doing. To round out your understanding of vectors, we'll conclude with a brief look at things that vectors are *bad* at doing.

5.2.7 *What vectors aren't*

Vectors are versatile, but there are some commonly desired patterns where they might *seem* like a good solution but in fact aren't. Though we prefer to focus on the positive, we hope a few negative examples will help you escape from using the wrong tool for the job.

VECTORS AREN'T SPARSE

If you have a vector of length n, the only position where you can insert a value is at index n—appending to the far right end. You can't skip some indices and insert at a higher index number. If you want a collection indexed by nonsequential numbers, consider a hash map or sorted map. Although you can replace values within a vector, you can't insert or delete items such that indices for the subsequent items would have to be adjusted. Clojure doesn't currently have a native persistent collection that supports this kind of operation, but a possible future addition, finger trees, may help for these use cases.

VECTORS AREN'T QUEUES

Some people have tried to use vectors as queues. One approach would be to push onto the right end of the vector using `conj` and then to pop items off the left using `rest` or `next`. The problem with this is that `rest` and `next` return seqs, not vectors, so subsequent `conj` operations wouldn't behave as desired. Using `into` to convert the seq back into a vector is $O(n)$, which is less than ideal for every `pop`.

Another approach is to use `subvec` as a "pop," leaving off the leftmost item. Because `subvec` does return a vector, subsequent `conj` operations will push onto the right end as desired. But as described earlier, `subvec` maintains a reference to the entire underlying vector, so none of the items being popped this way will ever be garbage collected. Also less than ideal.

So what *would* be the ideal way to do queue operations on a persistent collection? Why, use a PersistentQueue, of course. See section 5.5 for details.

VECTORS AREN'T SETS

If you want to find out whether a vector contains a particular value, you might be tempted to use the `contains?` function, but you'd be disappointed by the results. Clojure's `contains?` is for asking whether a particular *key*, not *value*, is in a collection, which is rarely useful for a vector.

In this section we showed how to create vectors using literal syntax or by building them up programmatically. We looked at how to push them, pop them, and slice them. We also looked at some of the things vectors can't do well. One of these was adding and removing items from the left side; though vectors can't do this, lists can, which we'll discuss next.

5.3   *Lists: Clojure's code form data structure*

Clojure's PersistentLists are by far the simplest of Clojure's persistent collection types. A PersistentList is a singly linked list where each node knows its distance from the end. List elements can only be found by starting with the first element and walking each prior node in order, and can only be added or removed from the left end.

In idiomatic Clojure code, lists are used almost exclusively to represent code forms. They're used literally in code to call functions, macros, and so forth as we'll discuss shortly. Code forms are also built programmatically to then be `evaled` or used as the return value for a macro. If the final usage of a collection isn't as Clojure code, lists rarely offer any value over vectors and are thus rarely used. But lists have rich heritage in Lisps so we'll discuss when they should be used in Clojure, and also when they shouldn't—situations in which there are now better options.

5.3.1   *Lists like Lisps like*

All flavors of Lisp have lists that they like to use, and Clojure lists, already introduced in chapter 2, are similar enough to be familiar. The functions have different names, but what other Lisps call `car` is the same as `first` on a Clojure list. Similarly `cdr` is the same as `next`. But there are substantial differences as well. Perhaps the most surprising is the behavior of `cons`. Both `cons` and `conj` add something to the front of a list, but their arguments in a different order from each other:

```
(cons 1 '(2 3))
;=> (1 2 3)

(conj '(2 3) 1)
;=> (1 2 3)
```

In a departure from classic Lisps, the "right" way to add to the front of a list is with `conj`. For each concrete type, `conj` will add elements in the most efficient way, and for lists this means at the left side. Additionally, a list built using `conj` is homogeneous—all the objects on its `next` chain are guaranteed to be lists, whereas sequences built with `cons` only promise that the result will be some kind of seq. So you can use `cons` to add to the front of a lazy seq, a range, or any other type of seq, but the only way to get a bigger list is to use `conj`.[7] Either way, the `next` part has to be some kind of sequence, which points out another difference from other Lisps: Clojure has no "dotted pair." If you don't know what that is, don't worry about it. All you need to know is that if you want a simple pair in a Clojure program, use a vector of two items.

All seqs print with rounded parentheses, but this does *not* mean they're the same type or will behave the same way. For example many of these seq types don't know their own size the way lists do, so calling `count` on them may be $O(n)$ instead of $O(1)$.[8] An

---

[7] Or to `conj` or `cons` onto `nil`. This is a special case, because `nil` isn't the same as an empty collection of any specific type. Clojure *could* have just left this unsupported, perhaps throwing an exception if you did `(cons 1 nil)`, but instead it provides a reasonable default behavior: building a list one item long.

[8] You can test for this property of being countable in constant time using the `counted?` function. For example `(counted? (range 10))` returns `true` in Clojure 1.0, but `false` in 1.1 because the implementation of range changed between those versions and no longer provided $O(1)$ counting.

unsurprising difference between lists in Clojure versus other Lisps is that they're immutable. At least that had better not be surprising anymore. Changing values within a list is generally discouraged in other Lisps anyway, but in Clojure it's impossible.

5.3.2   Lists as stacks

Lists in all Lisps can be used as stacks, but Clojure goes further by supporting the IPersistentStack interface. This means you can use the functions peek and pop to do roughly the same thing as first and next. Two details are worth noting. One is that next and rest are legal on an empty list, but pop throws an exception. The other is that next on a one-item list returns nil, whereas rest and pop both return an empty list.

When you want a stack, the choice between using a list versus a vector is a somewhat subtle decision. Their memory organization is quite different, so it may be worth testing your usage to see which performs better. Also, the order of values returned by seq on a list is backward compared to seq on a vector, and in rare cases this can point to one or the other as the best solution. In the end, it may come down primarily to personal taste.

5.3.3   What lists aren't

Probably the most common misuse of lists is to hold items that will be looked up by index. Though you can use nth to get the 42nd (or any other) item from a list, Clojure will have to walk the list from the beginning to find it. Don't do that. In fact, this is a practical reason why lists can't be used as functions, as in ((list :a) 0). Vectors are good at looking things up by index, so use one of those instead.

Lists are also not sets. All the reasons we gave in the previous section for why it's a bad idea to frequently search a vector looking for a particular value apply to lists as well. Even moreso since contains? will *always* return false for a list. See the section on sets later in this chapter instead.

Finally, lists aren't queues. You can add items to one end of a list, but you can't remove things from the other end. So what should you use when you need a queue? Funny you should ask...

5.4   How to use persistent queues

We mentioned in section 5.2 that new Clojure developers often attempt to implement simple queues using vectors. Though this is possible, such an implementation leaves much to be desired. Instead, Clojure provides a persistent immutable queue that will serve all your queueing needs. In this section we'll touch on the usage of the PersistentQueue class, where its first-in-first-out (FIFO) queueing discipline (Knuth 1997) is described by conj adding to the rear, pop removing from the front, and peek returning the front element without removal.

Before going further, it's important to point out that Clojure's PersistentQueue is a collection, not a workflow mechanism. Java has classes deriving from the java.util.concurrent.BlockingQueue interface for workflow, which often are useful in Clojure programs, and those aren't these. If you find yourself wanting to repeatedly check a work queue to see if there's an item of work to be popped off, or if you want to use a queue to send a task to another thread, you do *not* want the PersistentQueue discussed in this section.

5.4.1   *A queue about nothing*

Search all you like, but the current implementation of Clojure doesn't provide[9] a core construction function for creating persistent queues. That being the case, how would you go about creating a queue? The answer is that there's a readily available empty queue instance to use, clojure.lang.PersistentQueue/EMPTY. The printed representation for Clojure's queues isn't incredibly informative, but you can change that by providing a method for them on the print-method multimethod, as shown:

```
(defmethod print-method clojure.lang.PersistentQueue
  [q, w]
  (print-method '<- w) (print-method (seq q) w) (print-method '-< w))

clojure.lang.PersistentQueue/EMPTY
;=> <-nil-<
```

Using print-method in this way is a convenient mechanism for printing types in logical ways, as we did earlier with the queue-fish that's not only fun, but indicates an direction of flow for conj and pop.

You might think that popping an empty queue would raise an exception, but the fact is that this action results in just another empty queue. Likewise, peeking an empty queue will return nil. Not breathtaking for sure, but this behavior helps to ensure that queues work in place of other sequences. In fact, the functions first, rest, and next also work on queues and give the results that you might expect, though rest and next return seqs not queues. Therefore, if you're using a queue as a queue, it's best to use the functions designed for this purpose: peek, pop, and conj.

5.4.2   *Putting things on*

The mechanism for adding elements to a queue is conj:

```
(def schedule
  (conj clojure.lang.PersistentQueue/EMPTY
        :wake-up :shower :brush-teeth))
;=> <-(:wake-up :shower :brush-teeth)-<
```

Clojure's persistent queue is implemented internally using two separate collections, the front being a seq and the rear being a vector, as shown in figure 5.3.

All insertions occur in the rear vector and all removals occur in the front seq, taking advantage of each collection's strength. When all the items from the front list have

---

[9]   The Clojure core language grows carefully, tending to incorporate only features that have proven useful. Queues currently stand at the edge of this growth, meaning that there might be more support for them in the future. Unlike the other collections in this chapter, the code you write with queues might be rendered non-idiomatic by future improvements.

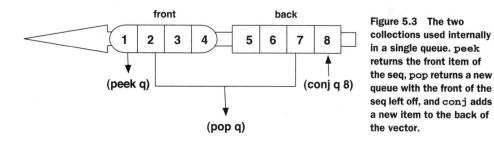

Figure 5.3 The two collections used internally in a single queue. peek returns the front item of the seq, pop returns a new queue with the front of the seq left off, and conj adds a new item to the back of the vector.

been popped, the back vector is wrapped in a seq to become the new front, and an empty vector is used as the new back. Typically, an immutable queue such as this is implemented with the rear as a list in reverse order, because insertion to the front of a list is an efficient operation. But using a Clojure vector eliminates the need for a reversed list.

5.4.3 Getting things

Clojure provides the peek function to get the front element in a queue:

```
(peek schedule)
;=> :wake-up
```

The fact that performing peek doesn't modify the contents of a persistent queue should be no surprise by now.

5.4.4 Taking things off

To "remove" elements from the front of a queue, use the pop function and not rest:

```
(pop schedule)
;=> <-(:shower :brush-teeth)-<

(rest schedule)
;=> (:shower :brush-teeth)
```

Although rest returns something with the same values and even prints the same as what pop returns, the former is a seq not a queue. This is potentially the source of subtle bugs, because subsequent attempts to use conj on it won't preserve the speed guarantees of the queue type and the queue functions pop peek and conj won't behave as expected.

We've talked numerous times in this chapter about the sequence abstraction, and though it's an important consideration, it shouldn't *always* be used. Instead, it's important to know your data structures, their sweet spots, and idiomatic operations. By doing so, you can write code that's specialized in ways that leverage the performance characteristics you need for a given problem space. Clojure's persistent queues illustrate this fact perfectly. To further highlight this point, we'll now explore Clojure's set type.

5.5   *Persistent sets*

Clojure sets work the same as mathematical sets, in that they're collections of unsorted unique elements. In this section we'll cover sets by explaining their strong points, weaknesses, and idioms. We'll also cover some of the functions from the clojure.set namespace.

5.5.1   *Basic properties of Clojure sets*

Sets are functions of their elements that return the matched element or nil:

```
(#{:a :b :c :d} :c)
;=> :c

(#{:a :b :c :d} :e)
;=> nil
```

Set elements can be accessed via the get function, which will return the queried value if it exists in the given set:

```
(get #{:a 1 :b 2} :b)
;=> :b

(get #{:a 1 :b 2} :nothing-doing)
;=> nil
```

As a final point, sets, like all of Clojure's collections, support heterogeneous values.

HOW CLOJURE POPULATES SETS

The key to understanding how Clojure sets determine which elements are discrete lies in one simple statement. Given two elements evaluating as equal, a set will contain only one, independent of concrete types:

> **Finding items in a sequence using a set and some**
>
> This property of sets combines with the some function to provide an extremely useful idiom for searching a seq for any of multiple items. The some function takes a predicate and a sequence. It applies said predicate to each element in turn, returning the first truthy value returned by the predicate or else nil:
>
> ```
> (some #{:b} [:a 1 :b 2])
> ;=> :b
>
> (some #{1 :b} [:a 1 :b 2])
> ;=> 1
> ```
>
> Using a set as the predicate supplied to some allows you to check whether *any* of the truthy values in the set are contained within the given sequence. *This is a frequently used Clojure idiom for searching for containment within a sequence.*

```
#{[] ()}
;=> #{[]}

#{[1 2] (1 2)}
;=> #{[1 2]}

#{[] () #{} {}}
;=> #{#{} {} []}
```

From the first two examples, even though [] and () are of differing types, they're considered equal because their elements are equal or in this case empty. But the last example illustrates nicely that collections within an equality partition will always be equal if their elements are equal, but never across partitions.

5.5.2   *Keeping your sets in order with sorted-set*

There's not much to say about creating sorted sets with the sorted-set function. But there's a simple rule that you should bear in mind:

```
(sorted-set :b :c :a)
;=> #{:a :b :c}

(sorted-set [3 4] [1 2])
;=> #{[1 2] [3 4]}

(sorted-set :b 2 :c :a 3 1)
; java.lang.ClassCastException: clojure.lang.Keyword cannot be cast to
    java.lang.Number
```

As long as the arguments to the `sorted-set` function are mutually comparable, you'll receive a sorted set; otherwise an exception is thrown. This can manifest itself when dealing with sorted sets down stream from their point of creation, leading to potential confusion:

```
(def my-set (sorted-set :a :b))

;; ... some time later
(conj my-set "a")
;=> java.lang.ClassCastException: clojure.lang.Keyword cannot be cast to
    java.lang.String
```

The difficulty in finding the reason for this exception will increase as the distance between the creation of `my-set` and the call to `conj` increases. You can adjust this rule a bit by using `sorted-set-by` instead, and providing your own comparator. This works exactly like the comparator for `sorted-map-by`, which we'll cover in section 6.6.2. Sorted maps and sorted sets are also similar in their support of `subseq` to allow efficiently jumping to a particular key in the collection, and walking through it from there. This is covered in section 5.6.

5.5.3 *contains?*

As we touched on in section 5.2, there's sometimes confusion regarding the usage of Clojure's `contains?` function. Many newcomers to Clojure expect this function to work the same as Java's `java.util.Collection#contains` method; this assumption is false, as shown:

```
(contains? #{1 2 4 3} 4)
;=> true

(contains? [1 2 4 3] 4)
;=> false
```

If you were to draw a false analogy between Java's `.contains` methods and `contains?`, then both of the function calls noted here should've returned true. The official documentation for `contains?` describes it as a function that returns true if a given *key* exists within a collection. When reading the word *key*, the notion of a map springs to mind, but the fact that this function also works on sets hints at their implementation details. Sets are implemented as maps with the same element as the key *and* value,[10] but there's an additional check for containment before insertion.

---

[10] All implementation caveats apply.

5.5.4   *clojure.set*

Mathematical sets form the basis of much of modern mathematical thought, and Clojure's basic set functions in the `clojure.set` namespace are a clear reflection of the classical set operations. In this subsection we'll briefly cover each function and talk about how, when applicable, they differ from the mathematical model. First, we'll start with a simple picture.

Figure 5.4 describes the nature of Clojure's set functions, each of which will be shown presently. Note that Clojure's set functions take an arbitrary number of sets and apply the operation incrementally.

INTERSECTION

Clojure's `clojure.set/intersection` function works as you might expect. Given two sets, `intersection` returns a set of the common elements. Given n sets, it'll incrementally return the intersection of resulting sets and the next set, as seen in the following code:

```
(clojure.set/intersection #{:humans :fruit-bats :zombies}
                          #{:chupacabra :zombies :humans})
;=> #{:zombies :humans}

(clojure.set/intersection #{:pez :gum :dots :skor}
                          #{:pez :skor :pocky}
                          #{:pocky :gum :skor})
;=> #{:skor}
```

In the first example, the resulting set is simply the common elements between the given sets. The second example is the result of the intersection of the first two sets then intersected with the final set.

UNION

There's also likely no surprise when using the `clojure.set/union` function:

```
(clojure.set/union #{:humans :fruit-bats :zombies}
                   #{:chupacabra :zombies :humans})
;=> #{:chupacabra :fruit-bats :zombies :humans}

(clojure.set/union #{:pez :gum :dots :skor}
                   #{:pez :skor :pocky}
                   #{:pocky :gum :skor})
;=> #{:pez :pocky :gum :skor :dots}
```

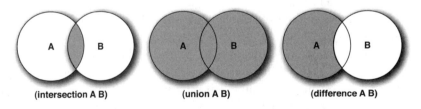

(intersection A B)   (union A B)   (difference A B)

Figure 5.4 Basic set operations. The three Venn diagrams show a graphical representation of Clojure's set functions: intersection, union, and difference.

Given two sets, the resulting set will contain all of the distinct elements from both. In the first example this means :zombies and :humans only show up once each in the return value. Note in the second example that more than two sets may be given to union, but as expected each value given in any of the input sets is included exactly once in the output set.

DIFFERENCE

The only set function that could potentially cause confusion on first glance is clojure.set/difference, which by name implies some sort of opposition to a union operation. Working under this false assumption you might assume that difference would operate thusly:

```
(clojure.set/difference #{1 2 3 4} #{3 4 5 6})
;=> #{1 2 5 6}
```

But if you were to evaluate this expression in your REPL, you'd receive a very different result:

```
(clojure.set/difference #{1 2 3 4} #{3 4 5 6})
;=> #{1 2}
```

The reason for this result is that Clojure's difference function calculates what's known as a *relative complement* (Stewart 1995) between two sets. In other words, difference can be viewed as a set subtraction function "removing" all elements in a set A that are also in another set B.

5.6 *Thinking in maps*

It's difficult to write a program of any significant size without the need for a map of some sort. The use of maps is ubiquitous in writing software because frankly it's difficult to imagine a more robust data structure. But we as programmers tend to view maps as a special case structure outside of the normal realm of data objects and classes. The object-oriented school of thought has relegated the map as a supporting player in favor of the class. We're not going to talk about the merits, or lack thereof, for this relegation here, but in upcoming sections we'll discuss moving away from thinking in classes and instead thinking in the sequence abstraction, maps, protocols, and types. Having said all of that, it need hardly be mentioned that maps should be used to store named values. In this section we talk about the different types of maps and the tradeoffs surrounding each.

5.6.1 *Hash maps*

Arguably, the most ubiquitous[11] form of map found in Clojure programs is the hash map, which provides an unsorted key/value associative structure. In addition to the literal syntax touched on in chapter 2, hash maps can be created using the hash-map function, which likewise takes alternating key/value pairs, with or without commas:

---

[11] Although with the pervasiveness of the map literal, the ubiquity may instead fall to the array map.

```
(hash-map :a 1, :b 2, :c 3, :d 4, :e 5)
;=> {:a 1, :c 3, :b 2, :d 4, :e 5}
```

Clojure hash maps support heterogeneous keys, meaning that they can be of any type and each key can be of a differing type, as this code shows:

```
(let [m {:a 1, 1 :b, [1 2 3] "4 5 6"}]
  [(get m :a) (get m [1 2 3])])
;=> [1 "4 5 6"]
```

As we previously mentioned at the beginning of this chapter, many of Clojure's composite types can be used as functions, and in the case of maps they're functions of their keys. Using maps in this way will act the same as the use of the get function in the previous code sample, as shown when building a vector of two elements:

```
(let [m {:a 1, 1 :b, [1 2 3] "4 5 6"}]
  [(m :a) (m [1 2 3])])
;=> [1 "4 5 6"]
```

Providing a map to the seq function will return a sequence of map entries:

```
(seq {:a 1, :b 2})
;=> ([:a 1] [:b 2])
```

Of course, this sequence appears to be composed of the sets of key/value pairs contained in vectors, and for all practical purposes should be treated as such. In fact, a new hash map can be created idiomatically using this precise structure:

```
(into {} [[:a 1] [:b 2]])
;=> {:a 1, :b 2}
```

Even if your embedded pairs aren't vectors, they can be made to be for building a new map:

```
(into {} (map vec '[(:a 1) (:b 2)]))
;=> {:a 1, :b 2}
```

In fact, your pairs don't have to be explicitly grouped, because you can use apply to create a hash map given that the key/value pairs are laid out in a sequence consecutively:

```
(apply hash-map [:a 1 :b 2])
;=> {:a 1, :b 2}
```

You can also use apply in this way with sorted-map and array-map. Another idiomatic way to build a map is to use zipmap to "zip" together two sequences, the first of which contains the desired keys and the second their corresponding values:

```
(zipmap [:a :b] [1 2])
;=> {:b 2, :a 1}
```

The use of zipmap illustrates nicely the final property of map collections. Hash maps in Clojure have no order guarantees. If you do require ordering, then you should use sorted maps, discussed next.

5.6.2 *Keeping your keys in order with sorted maps*

It's impossible to rely on a specific ordering of the key/value pairs for a standard Clojure map, because there are no order guarantees at all. Using the `sorted-map` and `sorted-map-by` functions, you can construct maps with order assurances. By default, the function `sorted-map` will build a map sorted by the comparison of its keys:

```
(sorted-map :thx 1138 :r2d 2)
;=> {:r2d 2, :thx 1138}
```

You may require an alternative key ordering, or perhaps an ordering for keys that isn't easily comparable. In these cases you must use `sorted-map-by`, which takes an additional comparison function:[12]

```
(sorted-map "bac" 2 "abc" 9)
;=> {"abc" 9, "bac" 2}

(sorted-map-by #(compare (subs %1 1) (subs %2 1)) "bac" 2 "abc" 9)
;=> {"bac" 2, "abc" 9}
```

This means that sorted maps don't generally support heterogeneous keys the same as hash maps, although it depends on the comparison function provided. For example, the preceding one assumes all keys are strings. The default sorted-map comparison function `compare` supports maps whose keys are all mutually comparable with each other. Attempts to use keys that aren't supported by whichever comparison function you're using will generally result in a cast exception:

```
(sorted-map :a 1, "b" 2)
;=> java.lang.ClassCastException: clojure.lang.Keyword cannot be cast to
    java.lang.String
```

One remarkable feature supported by sorted maps (and also sorted sets) is the ability to jump efficiently to a particular key and walk forward or backward from there through the collection. This is done with the `subseq` and `rsubseq` functions for forward and backward respectively. Even if you don't know the exact key you want, these functions can be used to "round up" the next closest key that exists.

Another way that sorted maps and hash maps differ is in their handling of numeric keys. A number of a given magnitude can be represented by many different types; for example 42 can be a long, int, float, and so on. Hash maps would treat each of these different objects as *different*, whereas a sorted map would treat them as the same. You can see the contrast in this example, where the hash map keeps both keys while the sorted map keeps just one:

```
(assoc {1 :int} 1.0 :float)
;=> {1.0 :float, 1 :int}

(assoc (sorted-map 1 :int) 1.0 :float)
;=> {1 :float}
```

---

[12] Note that simple boolean functions like > can be used as comparison functions.

This is because the comparison function used by the sorted map not only determines order by equality, and if two keys compare as equal, only one will be kept. This applies to comparison functions provided to `sorted-map-by` as well as the default comparator shown previously.

Sorted maps will otherwise work just like hash maps and can be used interchangeably. You should use sorted maps if you need to specify or guarantee a specific key ordering. On the other hand, if you need to maintain insertion ordering, then the use of array maps is required as you'll see.

5.6.3   *Keeping your insertions in order with array maps*

If you hope to perform an action under the assumption that a given map is insertion-ordered, then you're setting yourself up for disappointment. But you might already know that Clojure provides a special map that ensures insertion ordering called an array map:

```
(seq (hash-map :a 1, :b 2, :c 3))
;=> ([:a 1] [:c 3] [:b 2])

(seq (array-map :a 1, :b 2, :c 3))
;=> ([:a 1] [:b 2] [:c 3])
```

So when insertion order is important, you should explicitly use an array map. Array maps can be populated quickly by ignoring the form of the key/value pairs and blindly copying them into place. For structures sized below a certain count, the cost associated with map lookup bridges the gap between a linear search through an equally sized array or list. That's not to say that the map will be slower; instead, it allows the map and linear implementations to be comparable. Sometimes your best choice for a map is not a map at all, and like most things in life there are tradeoffs. Thankfully, Clojure takes care of these considerations for you by adjusting the concrete implementations behind the scenes as the size of the map increases. The precise types in play aren't important, because Clojure is careful to document its promises and to leave undefined aspects subject to change and/or improvement. It's usually a bad idea to build your programs around concrete types, and always bad to build around undocumented behaviors. *Clojure handles the underlying efficiency considerations so you don't have to.* But be aware that if ordering is important, you should avoid operations that inadvertently change the underlying map implementation from an array map.

We've covered the basics of Clojure maps in this section, including common usage and construction techniques. Clojure maps, minus some implementation details, shouldn't be surprising to anyone. It'll take a while to grow accustomed to dealing with immutable maps, but in time even this nuance will become second nature.

Now that we've looked at Clojure's primary collection types and their differences in detail, we'll take some time to work through a simple case study. This case study, creating a function named `pos`, will illustrate the thought processes you might consider on your way toward designing an API built on the principles of the sequence abstraction.

5.7 Putting it all together: finding the position of items in a sequence

> *We sometimes underestimate the influence of little things.*
>
> —Charles W. Chesnutt

The case study for this chapter will be to design and implement a simple function to locate the positional index[13] of an element within a sequence. We're going to pool together much of the knowledge that you've gained in this chapter in order to illustrate the steps you might take in designing, writing, and ultimately optimizing a Clojure collection function. Of course, we're going to work against the sequence abstraction and will therefore design the solution accordingly.

The function, named pos, *must*

- Work on any composite type returning indices corresponding to some value
- Return a numerical index for sequential collections or associated key for maps and sets
- Otherwise return nil

5.7.1 Implementation

If we were to address each of the requirements for pos literally and directly, we might come up with a function that looks like the following listing.

Listing 5.2 First cut at our position function

```
(defn pos [e coll]
  (let [cmp (if (map? coll)
              #(= (second %1) %2)          ◁—— Map compare
              #(= %1 %2))]                  ◁—— Default compare
    (loop [s coll idx 0]                    ◁—— Start at beginning
      (when (seq s)
        (if (cmp (first s) e)               ◁—— Compare
          (if (map? coll)
            (first (first s))               ◁—— Map returns key
            idx)                            ◁—— ...Else index
          (recur (next s) (inc idx)))))))

(pos 3 [:a 1 :b 2 :c 3 :d 4])
;=> 5
(pos :foo [:a 1 :b 2 :c 3 :d 4])
;=> nil
(pos 3 {:a 1 :b 2 :c 3 :d 4})
;=> :c
(pos 3 '(:a 1 :b 2 :c 3 :d 4))
;=> 5
(pos \3 ":a 1 :b 2 :c 3 :d 4")
;=> 13
```

---

[13] Stuart Halloway describes a similar function index-of-any in his book *Programming Clojure* that views the problem largely through the lens of reduced complexity. We like his example and this one because it's simple yet powerful and nicely illustrative of the way that Clojure functions should be written.

Pretty hideous right? We think so too. Apart from being overly complicated, it'd likely be more useful if we instead returned a sequence of *all* the indices matching the item, so we'll add that to the requirements. But we've built a heavy load with the first cut at pos and should probably step back a moment to reflect. First of all, it's probably the wrong approach to handle map types and other sequence types differently. The use of the predicate map? to detect the type of the passed collection is incredibly constraining, in that it forces different collections to be processed differently. That's not to say that the use of type-based predicates is strictly prohibited, only that you should try to favor more generic algorithms or at least to minimize their usage.

As chance has it, the exact nature of the problem demands that we view collections as a set of values paired with a given index, be it explicit in the case of maps or implicit in the case of other sequences' positional information. Therefore, imagine how easy this problem would be if all collections were laid out as a sequence of pairs ([index1 value1] [index2 value2] ... [indexn valuen]). Well, there's no reason why they couldn't, as shown next.

Listing 5.3   An index function

```
(defn index [coll]
  (cond
    (map? coll) (seq coll)
    (set? coll) (map vector coll coll)
    :else (map vector (iterate inc 0) coll)))
```

This simple function[14] can generate a uniform representation for indexed collections:

```
(index [:a 1 :b 2 :c 3 :d 4])
;=> ([0 :a] [1 1] [2 :b] [3 2] [4 :c] [5 3] [6 :d] [7 4])

(index {:a 1 :b 2 :c 3 :d 4})
;=> ([:a 1] [:b 2] [:c 3] [:d 4])

(index #{:a 1 :b 2 :c 3 :d 4})
;=> ([1 1] [2 2] [3 3] [4 4] [:a :a] [:c :c] [:b :b] [:d :d])
```

As shown, we're still using type-based predicates, but we've raised the level of abstraction to the equality partitions in order to build contextually relevant indices. Now, the function for finding the positional indices for the desired value is trivial:

```
(defn pos [e coll]
  (for [[i v] (index coll) :when (= e v)] i))

(pos 3 [:a 1 :b 2 :c 3 :d 4])
;=> (5)
(pos 3 {:a 1, :b 2, :c 3, :d 4})
;=> (:c)
(pos 3 [:a 3 :b 3 :c 3 :d 4])
;=> (1 3 5)
(pos 3 {:a 3, :b 3, :c 3, :d 4})
;=> (:a :c :b)
```

---

[14] Clojure has a core function keep-indexed that works similarly but doesn't implicitly build indices along equality partitions. For a vector, you could build the index as (keep-indexed #(-> [% %2]) [:a :b :c :d]).

Much better! But there's one more deficiency with the pos function from a Clojure perspective. Typically in Clojure it's more useful to pass a predicate function in cases such as these, so that instead of pos determining raw equality, it can build its result along any dimension, as shown:

```
(pos #{3 4} {:a 1 :b 2 :c 3 :d 4})
;=> (:c :d)

(pos even? [2 3 6 7])
;=> (0 2)
```

We can modify pos only slightly to achieve the ideal level of flexibility, as shown next.

Listing 5.4   Our final version of pos

```
(defn pos [pred coll]
 (for [[i v] (index coll) :when (pred v)] i))
```

We've vastly simplified the original solution and generated two potentially useful functions (Martin 2002) in the process. By following some simple Clojure principles, we were able to solve the original problem statement in a concise and elegant manner.

5.8   *Summary*

Clojure favors simplicity in the face of growing software complexity. If problems are easily solved by collection abstractions then those abstractions should be used. Most problems can be modeled on such simple types, yet we continue to build monolithic class hierarchies in a fruitless race toward mirroring the "real world"—whatever that means. Perhaps it's time to realize that we no longer need to layer self-imposed complexities on top of software solutions that are already inherently complex. Not only does Clojure provide the sequential, set, and map types useful for pulling ourselves from the doldrums of software complexity, but it's also optimized for dealing with them.

Now that we've discussed each of these types in detail, we're going to take a step back and talk about three important properties of Clojure's collection types that until now we've only touch upon lightly: immutability, persistence, and laziness.

Part 3

Functional programming

In this part of the book, we'll expose some of the underpinnings of Clojure's approach to functional programming, as well as some practical uses of it. Clojure provides mechanisms for immutability, deferred execution, closures, and recursion. We'll show examples of how these can work together to let you create data structures of your own, and find routes through a weighted graph.

Being lazy and
set in your ways

6

This chapter covers

- Immutability
- Designing a persistent toy
- Laziness
- Putting it all together: a lazy quicksort

We've now reached the apex of imperative knowledge and stand at the precipice leading toward functional programming. We mentioned in section 2.3 that the definitions of functional programming are widely disparate, and unfortunately this book won't work to unify them. Instead, we'll start in this chapter to build a basis for Clojure's style of functional programming by digging into its core supporting maxims. In addition, this chapter covers in greater depth the parts of Clojure's composite types that we only touched on.

6.1 On immutability

We've touched on immutability throughout this book, but we've avoided discussing why Clojure has chosen it as a cornerstone principle. Though no panacea, fostering immutability at the language level solves many difficult problems right out of the box, while simplifying many others. Coming from a language background where mutability interwoven with imperative programming methods reign, it often requires a significant conceptual leap to twist your mind to accept and utilize immutability and functional programming. In this section, we'll build a conceptual basis for immutability as it relates to Clojure's underlying philosophy as well as why you should work to foster immutability even when outside the warming confines of Clojure proper.

6.1.1 *Defining immutability*

In many cases, when talking specifically about Clojure's immutable data structures, we could be talking about the broader category of immutable objects without loss of meaning. But we should probably set down some conditions defining just what's meant by immutability.

EVERY DAY IS LIKE SUNDAY

An entire branch of philosophy named *predestination* is devoted to exploring the notion that there's no such thing as free will, but instead, everything that we are or ever will be is determined beforehand. Though this possibility for our own lives may seem bleak, the notion does nicely encapsulate the first principle of immutability: all of the possible properties of immutable objects are defined at the time of their construction and can't be changed thereafter.

IMMUTABILITY THROUGH CONVENTION

Computer systems are in many ways open systems, providing the keys to the vault if you're so inclined to grab them. But in order to foster an air of immutability in your own systems, it's important to create a facade of immutability. Creating immutable classes in Java requires a few steps (Goetz 2006). First, a class itself and all of its fields should be labeled as final. Next, in no way should an object's this reference escape during construction. And finally, any internal mutable objects should originate, either whole-cloth or through a copy, within the class itself and thus never escape. Obviously we're simplifying, because there are finer details to this recipe for Java immutability, but for now these simplified highlights serve to show that by observing convention, even an inherently mutable language such as Java can be made to be immutable. Clojure directly supports immutability as a language feature[1] with its core data structures. By providing immutable data structures as a primary language feature, Clojure separates (Braithwaite 2007) the complexity of working with immutable structures from the complexities of their implementation. By providing immutability either as a core language feature or through convention, you can reap enormous benefit.

---

[1] We're intentionally glossing over Clojure's features that support mutability such as reference types and transients in order to keep this section focused.

6.1.2 *Being set in your ways—immutability*

Clojure's immutable data structures aren't bolted onto the language as an after-thought or as a choice in an a-la-carte menu. Instead, their inclusion in the language runs deep to its philosophical core.

INVARIANTS

Invariant-based programming involves the definition of constraints on classes and functions in order to provide assurances that if instances enter into certain states, assertion errors will arise. Providing invariants within a mutable system requires a fair amount of assertion weaving within the methods of any given class. But by observing a practice of immutability, invariants are defined solely within the construction mechanism and can never be violated thereafter.

REASONING

Because the life of an immutable object is one of predestiny, the matter of reasoning about its possible states is simplified. It follows that the act of testing such a system is simplified, in that the set of possible states and transitions is constrained.

EQUALITY HAS MEANING

Equality in the presence of mutability has no meaning. Equality in the face of mutability and concurrency is utter lunacy. If any two objects resolve as being equal now, then there's no guarantee that they will a moment from now. And if two objects aren't equal forever, then they're technically never equal (Baker 1993). Providing immutable objects once again assigns meaning to equality, in that if two objects are equal now, then they'll always be so.

SHARING IS CHEAP

If you're certain that an object will never change, then sharing said object becomes a simple matter of providing a reference to it. In Java, to do so often requires a lot of defensive copying. Along this vein, because we can freely share references for immutable objects, we can likewise intern them for free.

FLATTENING THE LEVELS OF INDIRECTION

There's a marked difference between a mutable object and a mutable reference. The default in Java is that there are references that might point to mutable data. But in Clojure, there are only mutable references. This may seem like a minor detail, but it certainly works to reduce unnecessary complexities.

IMMUTABILITY FOSTERS CONCURRENT PROGRAMMING

> *Immutable objects are always thread safe.*
>
> —Brian Goetz,
> *Java Concurrency in Practice*

If an object can't change, it can be shared freely between different threads of execution without fear of concurrent modification errors. There can be little debate about this particular point, but that fact doesn't answer the question of how mutation occurs. Without delving into the specifics, you likely already know that Clojure isolates mutation to its reference types while the data wrapped with them is left unchanged. We'll leave this alone for now, becuase we'll devote chapter 11 to this and related topics.

6.2   *Designing a persistent toy*

We won't go into terrible detail about the internals of Clojure's persistent data structures—we'll leave that to others (Krukow 2009). But we do want to explore the notion of structural sharing. Our example will be highly simplified compared to Clojure's implementations, but it should help clarify some of the techniques used.

The simplest shared-structure type is the list. Two different items can be added to the front of the same list, producing two new lists that share their next parts. We'll try this out by creating a base list and then two new lists from that same base:

```
(def baselist (list :barnabas :adam))
(def lst1 (cons :willie baselist))
(def lst2 (cons :phoenix baselist))

lst1
;=> (:willie :barnabas :adam)

lst2
;=> (:phoenix :barnabas :adam)
```

You can think of baselist as a historical version of both lst1 and lst2. But it's also the shared part of both lists. More than being equal, the next parts of both lists are *identical*—the same instance:

```
(= (next lst1) (next lst2))
;=> true

(identical? (next lst1) (next lst2))
;=> true
```

So that's not too complicated, right? But the features supported by lists are also limited. Clojure's vectors and maps also provide structural sharing, while allowing you to change values anywhere in the collection, not just on one end. The key is the structure each of these datatypes uses internally. We'll now build a simple tree to help demonstrate how a tree can allow interior changes and maintain shared structure at the same time.

Each node of our tree will have three fields: a value, a left branch, and a right branch. We'll put them in a map, like this:

```
{:val 5, :L nil, :R nil}
```

That's the simplest possible tree—a single node holding the value 5, with empty left and right branches. This is exactly the kind of tree we want to return when a single item is added to an empty tree. To represent an empty tree, we'll use nil. With the structure decision made, we can write our own conj function xconj to build up our tree, starting with just the code for this initial case:

```
(defn xconj [t v]
  (cond
    (nil? t) {:val v, :L nil, :R nil}))

(xconj nil 5)
;=> {:val 5, :L nil, :R nil}
```

Hey, it works! Not too impressive yet though, so we need to handle the case where an item is being added to a nonempty tree. We keep our tree in order by putting values less than a node's :val in the left branch, and other values in the right branch. That means we need a test like this:

```
(< v (:val t))
```

When that's true, we need the new value v to go into the left branch, (:L t). If this were a mutable tree, we'd *change* the value of :L to be the new node. Instead, we should build a *new* node, copying in the parts of the old node that don't need to change. Something like this:

```
{:val (:val t),
 :L (insert-new-val-here),
 :R (:R t)}
```

This will be the new root node. Now we just need to figure out what to put for insert-new-val-here. If the old value of :L is nil, we simply need a new single-node tree—we even have code for that already, so we could use (xconj nil v). But what if :L isn't nil? In that case, we want to insert v in its proper place within whatever tree :L is pointing to—so (:L t) instead of nil:

```
(defn xconj [t v]
  (cond
    (nil? t)       {:val v, :L nil, :R nil}
    (< v (:val t)) {:val (:val t),
                    :L (xconj (:L t) v),
                    :R (:R t)}))

(def tree1 (xconj nil 5))
tree1
;=> {:val 5, :L nil, :R nil}

(def tree1 (xconj tree1 3))
tree1
;=> {:val 5, :L {:val 3, :L nil, :R nil}, :R nil}

(def tree1 (xconj tree1 2))
tree1
;=> {:val 5, :L {:val 3, :L {:val 2, :L nil, :R nil}, :R nil}, :R nil}
```

There, it's working. At least it seems to be—there's a lot of noise in that output, making it difficult to read. Here's a function to traverse the tree in sorted order, converting it to a seq that will print more succinctly:

```
(defn xseq [t]
  (when t
    (concat (xseq (:L t)) [(:val t)] (xseq (:R t)))))
```

```
(xseq tree1)
;=> (2 3 5)
```

Now we just need a final condition for handling the insertion of values that are *not* less than the node value:

```
(defn xconj [t v]
  (cond
    (nil? t)        {:val v, :L nil, :R nil}
    (< v (:val t))  {:val (:val t),
                     :L (xconj (:L t) v),
                     :R (:R t)}
    :else           {:val (:val t),
                     :L (:L t),
                     :R (xconj (:R t) v)}))
```

Now that we have the thing built, we hope you understand well enough how it's put together that this demonstration of the shared structure will be unsurprising:

```
(def tree2 (xconj tree1 7))
(xseq tree2)
;=> (2 3 5 7)

(identical? (:L tree1) (:L tree2))
;=> true
```

Both `tree1` and `tree2` share a common structure, which is more easily visualized in figure 6.1.

This example demonstrates several features that it has in common with all of Clojure's persistent collections:

- Every "change" creates at least a new root node, plus new nodes as needed in the path through the tree to where the new value is being inserted.
- Values and unchanged branches are never copied, but references to them are copied from nodes in the old tree to nodes in the new one.
- This implementation is completely thread-safe in a way that's easy to check—no object that existed before a call to `xconj` is changed in any way, and newly created nodes are in their final state before being returned. There's no way for any other thread, or even any other functions in the same thread, to see anything in an inconsistent state.

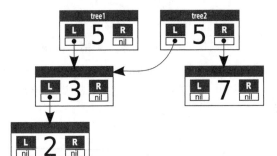

Figure 6.1   Shared structure tree: no matter how big the left side of a tree's root node is, something can be inserted on the right side without copying, changing, or even examining the left side. All those values will be included in the new tree, along with the inserted value.

Our example fails, though, when compared to Clojure's production-quality code:

- It's just a binary tree.[2]
- It can only store numbers.
- It'll overflow the stack if the tree gets too deep.
- It produces (via xseq) a non-lazy seq that will contain a whole copy of the tree.
- It can create unbalanced trees that'll have bad "worst case" algorithmic complexity.[3]

Though structural sharing as described using xconj as a basis example can reduce the memory footprint of persistent data structures, it alone is insufficient. Instead, Clojure leans heavily on the notion of lazy sequences to further reduce its memory footprint, as we'll explore further in the next section.

6.3 *Laziness*

> *Through all the windows I only see infinity.*
>
> —*House of Leaves*
> by Mark Z. Danielewski

Clojure is partially a lazy language. This isn't to say that Clojure vectors lie around the house every day after school playing video games and refusing to get a job. Instead, Clojure is lazy in the way it handles its sequence types—but what does that mean? First, we'll start by defining what it means for a language to be *eager*, or in other words, not lazy. Many programming languages are eager in that arguments to functions are immediately evaluated when passed, and Clojure in most cases follows this pattern as well. Observe the following:

```
(- 13 (+ 2 2))
;=> 9
```

The expression (+ 2 2) is eagerly evaluated, in that its result 4 is passed on to the subtraction function during the actual call, and *not* at the point of need. But a lazy programming language such as Haskell (Hudak 2000) will evaluate a function argument only if that argument is needed in an overarching computation.

In this section we'll discuss how laziness can be used to avoid nontermination, unnecessary calculations, and even combinatorially exploding computations. We'll also discuss the matter of utilizing infinite sequences, a surprisingly powerful technique. Finally, we'll use Clojure's delay and force to build a simple lazy structure. First, we'll start with a simple example of laziness that you may be familiar with from Java.

6.3.1 *Familiar laziness with logical-and*

Laziness isn't limited to the case of the evaluation of function arguments; a common example can be found even in eager programming languages. Take the case of Java's

---

[2] Clojure's sorted collections are binary trees, but its hash maps, hash sets, and vectors all have up to 32 branches per node. This results in dramatically shallower trees, and therefore faster lookups and updates.

[3] Clojure's sorted map and sorted set do use a binary tree internally, but they implement red-black trees to keep the left and right sides nicely balanced.

logical-and operator `&&`. Java implementations optimize this particular operator to avoid performing unnecessary operations should an early subexpression evaluate to `false`. This lazy evaluation in Java allows the following idiom:

```
if (obj != null && obj.isWhatiz()) {
    ...
}
```

For those of you unfamiliar with Java, the preceding code says: "if the object `obj` isn't `null`, then call the method `isWhatiz`." Without a short-circuiting (or lazy, if you will) `&&` operator, the preceding operation would always throw a `java.lang.NullPointer-Exception` whenever `obj` was set to `null`. Though this simple example doesn't qualify Java as a lazy language, it does illustrate the first advantage of lazy evaluation—*laziness allows the avoidance of errors in the evaluation of compound structures.*

Clojure's and operator also works this way, as do a number of other operators, but we won't discuss this type of short-circuiting laziness too deeply. Listing 6.1 illustrates what we mean using the case of a series of nested `if` expressions.

Listing 6.1   Short-circuiting `if` expression

```
(defn if-chain [x y z]
  (if x
    (if y
      (if z
        (do
          (println "Made it!")
          :all-truthy)))))

(if-chain () 42 true)
; Made it!
;=> :all-truthy

(if-chain true true false)
;=> nil
```

The call to `println` is evaluated only in the case of three truthy arguments. But we can perform the equivalent action given only the and macro:

```
(defn and-chain [x y z]
  (and x y z (do (println "Made it!") :all-truthy)))

(and-chain () 42 true)
; Made it!
;=> :all-truthy

(and-chain true false true)
;=> false
```

You may see tricks like this from time to time, but they're not widespread in idiomatic Clojure code. Regardless, we've presented them as a launching point for the rest of the discussion in the section. We'll now proceed to discussing how your own Clojure programs can be made more generally lazy by following an important recipe.

6.3.2 Understanding the lazy-seq recipe

Here's a seemingly simple function `steps` that takes a sequence and makes a deeply nested structure from it:

```
(steps [1 2 3 4])
;=> [1 [2 [3 [4 []]]]]
```

Seems simple enough, no? Your first instinct might be to tackle this problem recursively, as suggested by the form of the desired result:

```
(defn rec-step [[x & xs]]
  (if x
    [x (rec-step xs)]
    []))

(rec-step [1 2 3 4])
;=> [1 [2 [3 [4 []]]]]
```

Things look beautiful at this point; we've created a simple solution to a simple problem. But therein bugbears lurk. What would happen if we ran this same function on a large set?

```
(rec-step (range 200000))
;=> java.lang.StackOverflowError
```

Observing the example, running the same function over a sequence of 200,000 elements[4] causes a stack overflow. How can we fix this problem? Perhaps it's fine to say that you'll never encounter such a large input set in your own programs; such tradeoffs are made all of the time. But Clojure provides lazy sequences to help tackle such problems without significantly complicating your source code. Additionally, idiomatic Clojure code will always strive to deal with, and produce, lazy sequences.

Stepping back a bit, we should examine the lazy-seq recipe for applying laziness to your own functions:

1. Use the `lazy-seq` macro at the outermost level of your lazy sequence producing expression(s).
2. If you happen to be consuming another sequence during your operations, then use `rest` instead of `next`.
3. Prefer higher-order functions when processing sequences.
4. Don't hold onto your head.

These rules of thumb are simple, but they take some practice to utilize to their fullest. For example, #4 is especially subtle in that the trivial case is easy to conceptualize, but it's more complex to implement in large cases. For now we'll gloss over #3, because we'll talk about that approach separately in section 7.1.

So how can you leverage these rules of thumb to ensure laziness?

---

[4] On our machines, 200,000 elements is enough to cause a stack overflow, but your machine may require more or fewer depending on your JVM configuration.

rest versus next

The difference between `rest` and `next` can be seen in the following example:

```
(def very-lazy (-> (iterate #(do (print \.) (inc %)) 1)
                   rest rest rest))
;=> ..#'user/very-lazy

(def less-lazy (-> (iterate #(do (print \.) (inc %)) 1)
                   next next next))
;=> ...#'user/less-lazy
```

When building a lazy seq from another, `rest` doesn't realize any more elements than it needs to; `next` does. In order to determine whether a seq is empty, `next` needs to check whether there's at least one thing in it, thus potentially causing one extra realization. Here's an example:

```
(println (first very-lazy)) ; .4

(println (first less-lazy)) ; 4
```

Grabbing the first element in a lazy seq built with `rest` causes a realization as expected. But the same doesn't happen for a seq built with `next` because it's already been previously realized. Using `next` causes a lazy seq to be one element less lazy, which might not be desired if the cost of realization is expensive. In general, we recommend that you use `next` unless you're specifically trying to write code to be as lazy as possible.

UTILIZING LAZY-SEQ AND REST

In order to be a proper lazy citizen, you should produce lazy sequences using the `lazy-seq` macro:

```
(defn lz-rec-step [s]
  (lazy-seq
    (if (seq s)
      [(first s) (lz-rec-step (rest s))]
      [])))

(lz-rec-step [1 2 3 4])
;=> (1 (2 (3 (4 ()))))

(class (lz-rec-step [1 2 3 4]))
;=> clojure.lang.LazySeq

(dorun (lz-rec-step (range 200000)))
;=> nil
```

There are a few points of note for our new implementation. First, we've eliminated destructuring on the function arguments because the `&` arguments within are implicitly destructured via the `nthnext` function. As we mentioned in our rules of thumb, when consuming a sequence within the body of a `lazy-seq` you'll want to use `rest`, which we did in `lz-rec-step`. Second, we're no longer producing nested vectors as the output of the function, but instead a lazy sequence `LazySeq`, which is the by-product of the `lazy-seq` macro.

With only minor adjustments, we've created a lazy version of the step function while also maintaining simplicity. The first two rules of the lazy sequence recipe can be used in all cases when producing lazy sequences. You'll see this pattern over and over in idiomatic Clojure code.

If what's going on here still doesn't quite make sense to you, consider this even simpler example:

```
(defn simple-range [i limit]
  (lazy-seq
    (when (< i limit)
      (cons i (simple-range (inc i) limit)))))
```

This behaves similarly to Clojure's built-in function `range`, but it's simpler in that it doesn't accept a `step` argument and has no support for producing chunked seqs:[5]

```
(simple-range 0 9)
;=> (0 1 2 3 4 5 6 7 8)
```

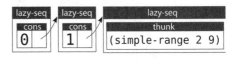

Note that it follows all the lazy-seq recipe rules you've seen so far. Figure 6.2 is a representation of what's in memory when the REPL has printed the first two items in a `simple-range` seq but hasn't yet printed any more than that.

One way in which complications may arise is by accidentally holding onto the head of a lazy sequence. This is addressed by the third rule of lazy sequences.

Figure 6.2   Each step of a lazy seq may be in one of two states. If the step is *unrealized*, it'll contain a function or closure of no arguments (a thunk) that can be called later to realize the step. When this happens, the thunk's return value is cached instead, and the thunk itself is released as pictured in the first two lazy seq boxes, transitioning the step to the *realized* state. Note that although not shown here, a realized lazy seq may simply contain nothing at all, called `nil`, indicating the end of the seq.

6.3.3   *Losing your head*

The primary advantage of laziness in Clojure is that it prevents the full realization of interim results during a calculation. If you manage to hold onto the head of a sequence somewhere within a function, then that sequence will be prevented from being garbage collected. The simplest way to retain the head of a sequence is to bind it to a local. This condition can occur with any type of value bind, be it to a reference type or through the usage of `let` or `binding`:

```
(let [r (range 1e9)] [(first r) (last r)])
;=> [0 999999999]

(let [r (range 1e9)] [(last r) (first r)])
; java.lang.OutOfMemoryError: GC overhead limit exceeded
```

Clojure's compiler can deduce that in the first example, the retention of `r` is no longer needed when the computation of `(last r)` occurs, and therefore aggressively clears it.

---

[5] Chunked seqs are a technique for improving performance that we cover in chapter 12.

But in the second example, the head is needed later in the overall computation and can no longer be safely cleared. Of course, the compiler could perform some rearranging with the order of operations for this case, but it doesn't because in order to do so safely it would have to guarantee that all of the composite functions were pure. It's okay if you're not clear on what a pure function is right now—we'll cover it in section 7.1. In a nutshell, take to heart that Clojure can't rearrange operations, because there's no way to guarantee that order is unimportant. This is one area where a purely functional lazy language such as Haskell (Thompson 1999) really shines by comparison.

6.3.4   *Employing infinite sequences*

Because Clojure's sequences are lazy, they have the potential to be infinitely long. Clojure provides a number of functions for generating and working with infinite sequences:

```
; Run at your own risk
(iterate (fn [n] (/ n 2)) 1)
;=> (1 1/2 1/4 1/8 ...)
```

It sure is a nice trick (although you might not think so had you chosen to ignore our warning), but what could you possibly use infinite sequences for? Working with infinite sequences often fosters more declarative solutions. Take a simple example as a start. Imagine that we have a function that calculates a triangle number for a given integer:

```
(defn triangle [n]
  (/ (* n (+ n 1)) 2))

(triangle 10)
;=> 55
```

The function `triangle` can then be used to build a sequence of the first 10 triangle numbers:

```
(map triangle (range 1 11))
;=> (1 3 6 10 15 21 28 36 45 55)
```

There's nothing wrong with the preceding solution, but it suffers from a lack of flexibility in that it does what it does and that's all. By defining a sequence of *all* of the triangle numbers as in the following listing, you can perform more interesting "queries" in order to retrieve the desired elements.

Listing 6.2   Infinite sequences foster declarative solutions.

```
(def tri-nums (map triangle (iterate inc 1)))

(take 10 tri-nums)                              ◁——— Get first 10
;=> (1 3 6 10 15 21 28 36 45 55)

(take 10 (filter even? tri-nums))
;=> (6 10 28 36 66 78 120 136 190 210)         ◁——— Get first 10 even

(nth tri-nums 99)                ◁——— What Gauss found
```

```
;=> 5050

(double (reduce + (take 1000 (map / tri-nums))))     ⟵——— Converge on 2
;=> 1.998001998001998

(take 2 (drop-while #(< % 10000) tri-nums))          ⟵——— First 2 greater than 10,000
;=> (10011 10153)
;; ...
```

The queries used three ubiquitous Clojure functions: map, reduce, and filter. The map function applies a function to each element in a sequence and returns the resulting sequence. The reduce function applies a function to each value in the sequence *and* the running result to accumulate a final value. Finally, the filter function applies a function to each element in a sequence and returns a new sequence of those elements where said function returned a truthy value. All three of these functions retain the laziness of a given sequence.

Defining the infinite sequence of triangle numbers allows you to take elements from it as needed, only calculating those particular items.

6.3.5   *The delay and force macros*

Although Clojure sequences are largely lazy, Clojure itself isn't. In most cases, expressions in Clojure are evaluated once prior to their being passed into a function rather than at the time of need. But Clojure does provide mechanisms for implementing what are known as *call-by-need semantics*. The most obvious of these mechanisms is its macro facilities, but we'll defer that discussion until chapter 8. The other mechanism for providing what we'll call explicit laziness are Clojure's delay and force. In short, the delay macro is used to defer the evaluation of an expression until explicitly forced using the force function. Using these laziness primitives, we can wrap an expression in a call to delay and use it only if necessary on the callee's side:

```
(defn defer-expensive [cheap expensive]
  (if-let [good-enough (force cheap)]
    good-enough
    (force expensive)))

(defer-expensive (delay :cheap)
                 (delay (do (Thread/sleep 5000) :expensive)))
;=> :cheap

(defer-expensive (delay false)
                 (delay (do (Thread/sleep 5000) :expensive)))
;=> :expensive
```

You can simulate this behavior with the use of anonymous functions, where delay is replaced by (fn [] expr) and force by (delayed-fn), but using delay/force allows you to explicitly check for delayed computations using delay?. Additionally, delay caches its calculation, therefore allowing its wrapped expression to be calculated only once. Of course, you could simulate the same behavior using memoization,[6] but why would you in this case when delay and force solve the problem more succinctly?

---

[6] We'll cover memoization in section 12.4.

if-let and when-let

The `if-let` and `when-let` macros are useful when you'd like to bind the results of an expression based on if it returns a truthy value. This helps to avoid the need to nest `if`/`when` and `let` as shown:

```
(if :truthy-thing
    (let [res :truthy-thing] (println res)))
; :truthy-thing


(if-let [res :truthy-thing] (println res))
; :truthy-thing
```

The latter is much more succinct.

There are more complicated usage patterns for `delay` and `force` besides the simple scheme outlined previously. For example, we can implement a version of the lazy sequence of triangular numbers from a few sections prior using `delay` and `force`:

```
(defn inf-triangles [n]
  {:head (triangle n)
   :tail (delay (inf-triangles (inc n)))})

(defn head  [l]  (:head l))
(defn tail  [l]  (force (:tail l)))
```

The function `inf-triangles` creates a lazy linked-list of nodes. Each node is a map containing a value mapped to `:head` and a link to the remainder of the list keyed as `:tail`. The head of the list is the result of applying the function `triangle` to the incrementing counter passed recursively within the body of `delay`. As you can imagine, the head of a node is always calculated as we walk down the linked-list, even if it's never accessed. This type of lazy structure is known as *head strict* but differs from Clojure's `lazy-seq`, which delays both the head and tail and then realizes them at the same time.

We can now create a structure similar to the original `tri-nums` and start getting at its contained elements:

```
(def tri-nums (inf-triangles 1))

(head tri-nums)
;=> 1
(head (tail tri-nums))
;=> 3
(head (tail (tail tri-nums)))
;=> 6
```

One thing to note about the preceding code is that accessing the values 3 and 6 were deferred calculations only occurring on demand. The structure of the example is shown in figure 6.3.

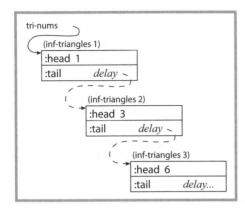

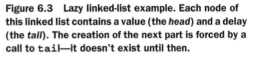

Figure 6.3   Lazy linked-list example. Each node of this linked list contains a value (the *head*) and a delay (the *tail*). The creation of the next part is forced by a call to `tail`—it doesn't exist until then.

Though we can navigate the entire chain of triangular numbers using only `head` and `tail`, it's probably a better idea[7] to use them as primitives for more complicated functions:

```
(defn taker [n l]
  (loop [t n, src l, ret []]
    (if (zero? t)
      ret
      (recur (dec t) (tail src) (conj ret (head src))))))

(defn nthr [l n]
  (if (zero? n)
    (head l)
    (recur (tail l) (dec n))))

(taker 10 tri-nums)
;=> [1 3 6 10 15 21 28 36 45 55]

(nthr tri-nums 99)
;=> 5050
```

Of course, writing programs using `delay` and `force` is an onerous way to go about the problem of laziness, and you'd be better served by using Clojure's lazy sequences to full effect rather than building your own from these basic blocks. But the preceding code, in addition to being simple to understand, harkens back to chapter 5 and the entire sequence "protocol" being built entirely on the functions `first` and `rest`. Pretty cool, right?

6.4   *Putting it all together: a lazy quicksort*

In a time when the landscape of programming languages is rife with new programming languages and pregnant with more, it seems inconceivable that the world would need another quicksort implementation. Inconceivable or not, we won't be deterred from adding yet another to the rich ecosystem of pet problems. Our implementation

---

[7] And as we'll cover in section 9.3, participating in the ISeq protocol is even better.

of quicksort differs from many in a few key ways. First, we'll implement a lazy, tail-recursive version. Second, we'll split the problem such that it can be executed incrementally. Only the calculations required to obtain the part of a sequence desired will be calculated. This will illustrate the fundamental reason for laziness in Clojure: *the avoidance of full realization of interim results.*

THE IMPLEMENTATION

Without further ado, we present our quicksort implementation.[8]

> **Listing 6.3   A lazy, tail-recursive quicksort implementation**

```
(ns joy.q)

(defn nom [n] (take n (repeatedly #(rand-int n))))

(defn sort-parts
  "Lazy, tail-recursive, incremental quicksort.  Works against
   and creates partitions based on the pivot, defined as 'work'."
  [work]
  (lazy-seq                                          Pull
    (loop [[part & parts] work]                   ⤶  apart work
      (if-let [[pivot & xs] (seq part)]                 Define pivot
        (let [smaller? #(< % pivot)]              ⤶     comparison fn
          (recur (list*
                   (filter smaller? xs)    ⟵  Work all < pivot
                   pivot                   ⟵  Work pivot itself
                   (remove smaller? xs)    ⟵  Work all > pivot
                   parts)))               ⟵  Concat parts
        (when-let [[x & parts] parts]
          (cons x (sort-parts parts)))))))     ⟅ Sort rest
                                                   if more parts
(defn qsort [xs]
  (sort-parts (list xs)))
```

The key detail in the code above is that sort-parts works not on a plain sequence of elements but on a carefully constructed list that alternates between lazy seqs and pivots. Every element before each pivot is guaranteed to be less than the pivot and everything after will be greater, but the sequences between the pivots are as yet unsorted. When qsort is given an input sequence of numbers to sort, it creates a new work list consisting of just that input sequence and passes this work to sort-parts. The loop inside sort-parts pulls apart the work, always assuming that the first item, which it binds to part, is an unsorted sequence. It also assumes that if there is a second item, which will be at the head of parts, it is a pivot. It recurs on the sequence at the head of work, splitting out pivots and lazy seqs until the sequence of items less than the most recent pivot is empty, in which case the if-let test is false, and that most recent pivot is returned as the first item in the sorted seq. The rest of the built up list of work

---

[8] This listing uses the list* function, which for some reason is somewhat rarely seen. In cases like this, however, it is exactly what is needed. list* is like list except it expects its last argument to be a list on which to prepend its other arguments. We'll use it again in chapter 8.

held by the returned lazy sequence to be passed into
`sort-parts` again when subsequent sorted items are
needed.

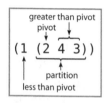

You can see a snapshot of the work list for the
function call `(qsort [2 1 4 3])` in figure 6.4, at an
intermediate point in its process.

The figure includes the characteristics of a standard quicksort implementation, and you can run it
to see that the final sequence is sorted:

```
(qsort [2 1 4 3])
;=> (1 2 3 4)

(qsort (nom 20))
;=> (0 2 3 5 6 7 7 8 9 10 11 11 11 12 12 13 14 16 17 19)
```

**Figure 6.4 The qsort function
shown earlier would use a structure
like this for its work list when
sorting the vector [2 1 4 3]. Note
that all the parts described by a
standard quicksort implementation
are represented here.**

The implementation of the `sort-parts` function works to provide an incremental
solution for lazy quicksort. This incremental approach stands in opposition to a
monolithic approach (Okasaki 1996) defined by its performance of the entire calculation when any segment of the sequence is accessed. For example, grabbing the first
element in a lazy sequence returned from qsort will perform *only* the necessary calculations required to get that first item:

```
(first (qsort (nom 100)))
;=> 1
```

Of course, the number returned here will likely be different in your REPL, but the
underlying structure of the lazy sequence used internally by `sort-parts` will be similar
to that shown in figure 6.5.

The lazy qsort will be able to gather the first element because it only takes some
small subset of comparisons to gather the numbers into left-side smaller and right-side

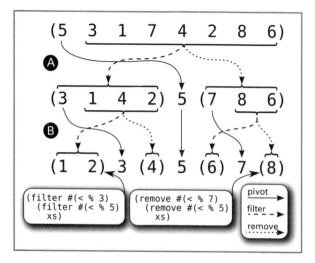

**Figure 6.5 Internal structure of
qsort. Each `filter` and `remove`
lazily returns items from its parent
sequence only as required. So to
return the first two items of the seq
returned by qsort, no `remove` steps
are required from either level A or B.
To generate the sequence `(4)`, a
single `remove` step at level B would
be needed to eliminate everything less
than 3. As more items are forced from
the seq returned by qsort, more of
the internal `filter` and `remove`
steps will be run.**

larger partitions and sort those smaller pieces only. The characteristic of the quicksort algorithm is especially conducive to laziness, because it's fairly cheap to make and shuffle partitions where those with a smaller magnitude can be shuffled first. What then are the benefits of a lazy, tail-recursive, incremental quicksort? The answer is that you can take sorted portions of a large sequence without having to pay the cost of sorting its entirety, as the following command hints:

```
(take 10 (qsort (nom 10000)))
;=> (0 0 0 4 4 7 7 8 9 9)
```

On our machines, this command required roughly 11,000 comparisons, which for all intents and purposes is an $O(n)$ operation—an order of magnitude less than quicksorts's best case. Bear in mind that as the take value gets closer to the number of actual elements, this difference in asymptotic complexity will shrink. But it's an extremely efficient way to determine the smallest n values in a large unsorted (Knuth 1998) sequence.

6.5   *Summary*

We've covered the topics of immutability, persistence, and laziness in this chapter. Clojure's core composite data types are all immutable and persistent by default, and though this fact might presuppose fundamental inefficiencies, we've shown how Clojure addresses them. The implementation of a persistent sorted binary tree demonstrated how structural sharing eliminated the need for full copy-on-write. But structural sharing isn't enough to guarantee memory efficiency, and that's where the benefits of laziness come into the fold. The implementation of a lazy, tail-recursive quicksort demonstrated that laziness guarantees that sequences won't be fully realized in memory at any given step.

In the next chapter, we'll dive into Clojure's notion of functional programming. Along the way, you'll notice that much of the shape of functional implementations in Clojure will be influenced by the topics discussed in this chapter.

Functional
programming

This chapter covers

- Functions in all their forms
- Closures
- Thinking recursively
- Putting it all together: A* pathfinding

At the core of functional programming is a formal system of computation known as the *lambda calculus* (Pierce 2002). Clojure functions, in adherence with the lambda calculus, are first-class—they can be both passed as arguments and returned as results from other functions. This book isn't about the lambda calculus. Instead we'll explore Clojure's particular flavor of functional programming. We'll cover a vast array of useful topics, including function composition, partial evaluation, recursion, lexical closures, pure functions, function constraints, higher-order functions, and first-class functions. We'll use that last item as our starting point.

7.1 Functions in all their forms

In chapter 5, we mentioned that most of Clojure's composite types can be used as functions of their elements. As a refresher, recall that vectors are functions of their indices, so executing ([:a :b] 0) will return :a. But this can be used to greater effect by passing the vector as a function argument:

```
(map [:chthon :phthor :beowulf :grendel] #{0 3})
;=> (:chthon :grendel)
```

In the example, we've used the vector as the function to map over a set of indices, indicating its first and fourth elements by index. Clojure collections offer an interesting juxtaposition, in that not only can Clojure collections act as functions, but Clojure functions can also act as data—an idea known as *first-class functions*.

7.1.1 First-class functions

In a programming language such as Java, there's no notion of a standalone function.[1] Instead, every problem solvable by Java must be performed with the fundamental philosophy that everything is an object. This view on writing programs is therefore rooted in the idea that behaviors within a program must be either modeled as class instances or attached to them—wise or not. Clojure, on the other hand, is a functional programming language and views the problem of software development as the application of functions to data. Likewise, functions in Clojure enjoy equal standing with data—functions are first-class citizens. Before we start, we should define what makes something first-class:

- It can be created on demand.
- It can be stored in a data structure.
- It can be passed as an argument to a function.
- It can be returned as the value of a function.

Those of you coming from a background in Java might find the idea of creating functions on demand analogous to the practice of creating anonymous inner classes to handle Swing events (to name only one use case). Though similar enough to start on the way toward understanding functional programming, it's not a concept likely to bear fruit, so don't draw conclusions from this analogy.

CREATING FUNCTIONS ON DEMAND USING COMPOSITION

Even a cursory glance at Clojure is enough to confirm that its primary unit of computation is the function, be it created or composed of other functions:

```
(def fifth (comp first rest rest rest rest))
(fifth [1 2 3 4 5])
;=> 5
```

---

[1] Although the likely inclusion of closures in some future version of Java should go a long way toward invalidating this. Additionally, for those of you coming from a language such as Python, Scala, or another Lisp, the notion of a first-class function is likely not as foreign as we make it out to be.

The function `fifth` wasn't defined with `fn` or `defn` forms shown before, but instead built from existing parts using the `comp` (compose) function. But it may be more interesting to take the idea one step further by instead proving a way to build arbitrary *nth* functions[2] as shown here:

```
(defn fnth [n]
  (apply comp
         (cons first
               (take (dec n) (repeat rest)))))

((fnth 5) '[a b c d e])
;=> e
```

The function `fnth` builds a list of the function `rest` of the appropriate length with a final `first` consed onto the front. This list is then fed into the `comp` function via `apply`, which takes a function and a sequence of things and effectively calls said function with the list elements as its arguments. At this point, there's no longer any doubt that the function `fnth` builds new functions on the fly based on its arguments. Creating new functions in this way is a powerful technique, but it takes some practice to think in a compositional way. It's relatively rare to see more than one open-parenthesis in a row like this in Clojure, but when you see it, it's almost always because a function (such as `fnth`) is creating and returning a function that's called immediately. A general rule of thumb is that if you need a function that applies a number of functions serially to the return of the former, then composition is a good fit:

```
(map (comp keyword #(.toLowerCase %) name) '(a B C))
;=> (:a :b :c)
```

Splitting functions into smaller, well-defined pieces fosters composability and, as a result, reuse.

CREATING FUNCTIONS ON DEMAND USING PARTIAL FUNCTIONS

There may be times when instead of building a new function from chains of other functions as `comp` allows, you need to build a function from the partial application of another:

```
((partial + 5) 100 200)
;=> 305
```

The function `partial` builds (Tarver 2008) a new function that consists of the partial application of the single argument 5 to the addition function. When the returned partial function is passed the arguments 100 and 200, the result is their summation plus that of the value 5 *captured* by `partial`.

PARTIAL APPLICATION ISN'T CURRYING   The use of `partial` differs from the notion of *currying* in a fundamental way. A function built with `partial` will attempt to evaluate whenever it's given another argument. A curried function

---

[2] We know that Clojure provides an nth function that works slightly differently, but in this case please indulge our obtuseness.

on the other hand will return another curried function until it receives a pre-determined number of arguments—only then will it evaluate. Because Clojure allows functions of variable number of arguments, currying makes little sense.

We'll discuss more about utilizing `partial` later in this section, but as a final point observe that `((partial + 5) 100 200)` is equivalent to `(#(apply + 5 %&) 100 200)`.

REVERSING TRUTH WITH COMPLEMENT

One final function builder discussed here is the `complement` function. Simply put, this function takes a function that returns a truthy value and returns the opposite truthy value:

```
(let [truthiness (fn [v] v)]
  [((complement truthiness) true)
   ((complement truthiness) 42)
   ((complement truthiness) false)
   ((complement truthiness) nil)])

;=> [false false true true]

((complement even?) 2)
;=> false
```

Note that `(complement even?)` is equivalent to `(comp not even?)`.

USING FUNCTIONS AS DATA

First-class functions can not only be treated as data; they *are* data. Because a function is first-class, it can be stored in a container expecting a piece of data, be it a local, a reference, collections, or anything able to store a `java.lang.Object`. This is a significant departure from Java, where methods are part of a class but don't stand alone at run-time (Forman 2004). One particularly useful method for treating functions as data is the way that Clojure's testing framework `clojure.test` stores and validates unit tests in the metadata of a Var holding a function. These unit tests are keyed with the `:test` keyword, laid out as

```
(defn join
  {:test (fn []
           (assert
             (= (join "," [1 2 3]) "1,3,3")))}
  [sep s]
  (apply str (interpose sep s)))
```

We've modified our old friend `join` by attaching some metadata containing a *faulty* unit test. Of course, by that we mean that the attached unit test is meant to fail in this case. The `clojure.test/run-tests` function is useful for running attached unit tests in the current namespace:

```
(use '[clojure.test :as t])
(t/run-tests)
; Testing user
;
; ERROR in (join) (test.clj:646)
; ...
```

```
;    actual: java.lang.AssertionError:
;      Assert failed: (= (join "," [1 2 3]) "1,3,3")
; ...
```

As expected, the faulty unit test for join failed. Unit tests in Clojure only scratch the surface of the boundless spectrum of examples using functions as data, but for now they'll do, as we move into the notion of higher-order functions.

7.1.2 Higher-order functions

A *higher-order function* is a function that does at least one of the following:

- Takes one or more functions as arguments
- Returns a function as a result

A Java programmer might be familiar with the practices of subscriber patterns or schemes using more general-purpose callback objects. There are scenarios such as these where Java treats objects like functions, but as with anything in Java, you're really dealing with objects containing privileged methods.

FUNCTIONS AS ARGUMENTS

In this book, we've used and advocated the use of the sequence functions map, reduce, and filter—all of which expect a function argument that's applied to the elements of the sequence arguments. The use of functions in this way is ubiquitous in Clojure and can make for truly elegant solutions. Let's look at a simple example of a function that takes a sequence of maps and a function working on each, and returns a sequence sorted by the results of the function. The implementation in Clojure is straightforward and clean:

```
(def plays [{:band "Burial",      :plays 979,  :loved 9}
            {:band "Eno",         :plays 2333, :loved 15}
            {:band "Bill Evans",  :plays 979,  :loved 9}
            {:band "Magma",       :plays 2665, :loved 31}])

(def sort-by-loved-ratio (partial sort-by #(/ (:plays %) (:loved %))))
```

The function with the overly descriptive name sort-by-loved-ratio is built from the partial application of the function sort-by and an anonymous function dividing the :plays field by the :loved field. This is a simple solution to the problem presented, and its usage is equally so:

```
(sort-by-loved-ratio plays)
;=> ({:band "Magma",      :plays 2665, :loved 31}
     {:band "Burial",     :plays 979,  :loved 9}
     {:band "Bill Evans", :plays 979,  :loved 9}
     {:band "Eno",        :plays 2333, :loved 15})
```

We intentionally used the additional higher-order function sort-by to avoid reimplementing core functions and instead *build our program from existing parts*. You should strive for the same whenever possible.

FUNCTIONS AS RETURN VALUES

We've already used functions returning functions in this chapter with `comp`, `partial`, and `complement`, but you could build functions that do the same. We'll extend the earlier example to provide a function that sorts rows based on some number of column values. This is similar to the way that spreadsheets operate, in that you can sort on a primary column while falling back on a secondary column to provide the sort order on matching results in the primary. This behavior is typically performed along any number of columns, cascading down from the primary column to the last; each subgroup is sorted appropriately, as the expected result illustrates:

```
(sort-by (columns [:plays :loved :band]) plays)
;=> ({:band "Bill Evans", :plays 979,  :loved 9}
     {:band "Burial",     :plays 979,  :loved 9}
     {:band "Eno",        :plays 2333, :loved 15}
     {:band "Magma",      :plays 2665, :loved 31})
```

This kind of behavior sounds complex on the surface but is shockingly simple[3] in its Clojure implementation:

```
(defn columns [column-names]
  (fn [row]
    (vec (map row column-names))))
```

Running the preceding expression shows that the rows for `Burial` and `Bill Evans` have a tertiary column sorting. The function `columns` returns another function expecting a map. This return function is then supplied to `sort-by` to provide the value on which the `plays` vector would be sorted. Perhaps you see a familiar pattern: we apply the `column-names` vector as a function across a set of indices, building a sequence of its elements *at* those indices. This action will return a sequence of the values of that row for the supplied column names, which is then turned into a vector so that it can then be used as the sorting function,[4] as structured here:

```
(vec (map (plays 0) [:plays :loved :band]))
;=> [979 9 "Burial"]
```

This resulting vector is then used by `sort-by` to provide the final ordering.

Building your programs using first-class functions in concert with higher-order functions will reduce complexities and make your codebase more robust and extensible. In the next subsection, we'll explore pure functions, which all prior functions in this section have been, and explain why your own applications should strive toward purity.

---

[3] Strictly speaking, the implementation of `columns` should use `#(% row)` instead of just `row`, because we can't always assume that the row is implemented as a map (a record might be used instead) and therefore directly usable as a function. Records will be discussed further in chapter 8.

[4] Because `sort-by` is higher-order, it naturally expects a function argument. As mentioned, vectors can also be used as functions. However, as we will discuss in detail in section 10.4, all closure functions implement the `java.util.Comparator` interface, which in this case is the driving force behind the sorting logic behind `sort-by`!

> **Prefer higher-order functions when processing sequences**
>
> We mentioned in section 6.3 that one way to ensure that lazy sequences are never fully realized in memory is to prefer (Hutton 1999) higher-order functions for processing. Most collection processing can be performed with some combination of the following functions:
>
> map, reduce, filter, for, some, repeatedly, sort-by, keep take-while, and drop-while
>
> But higher-order functions aren't a panacea for every solution. Therefore, we'll cover the topic of recursive solutions deeper in section 7.3 for those cases when higher-order functions fail or are less than clear.

7.1.3 *Pure functions*

Simply put, *pure functions* are regular functions that, through convention, conform to the following simple guidelines:

- The function *always* returns the same result, given some expected arguments.
- The function doesn't cause any *observable* side-effects.

Though Clojure is designed to minimize and isolate side-effects, it's by no means a purely functional language. But there are a number of reasons why you'd want to build as much of your system as possible from pure functions, and we'll enumerate a few presently.

REFERENTIAL TRANSPARENCY

If a function of some arguments always results in the same value and changes no other values within the greater system, then it's essentially a constant, or referentially transparent (the reference to the function is transparent to time). Take a look at pure function keys-apply:

```
(defn keys-apply [f ks m]
  "Takes a function, a set of keys, and a map and applies the function
   to the map on the given keys.  A new map of the results of the function
   applied to the keyed entries is returned."
  (let [only (select-keys m ks)]
    (zipmap (keys only) (map f (vals only)))))

(keys-apply #(.toUpperCase %) #{:band} (plays 0))
;=> {:band "BURIAL"}
```

Using another pure function manip-map, we can then manipulate a set of keys based on a given function:

```
(defn manip-map [f ks m]
  "Takes a function, a set of keys, and a map and applies
   the function to the map on the given keys.  A modified
   version of the original map is returned with the results
   of the function applied to each keyed entry."
  (conj m (keys-apply f ks m)))
```

```
(manip-map #(int (/ % 2)) #{:plays :loved} (plays 0))
;=> {:band "Burial", :plays 489, :loved 4}
```

The functions keys-apply and manip-map are both[5] pure functions, illustrated by the fact that you can replace them in the context of a larger program with their expected return values and not change the outcome. Pure functions exist outside the bounds of time. But if you make either keys-apply or manip-map reliant on anything but its arguments or generate a side-effect within, then referential transparency dissolves. We'll add one more function to illustrate this:

```
(defn halve! [ks]
  (map (partial manip-map #(int (/ % 2)) ks) plays))

(halve! [:plays])
;=> ({:band "Burial", :plays 489, :loved 9}
     {:band "Eno", :plays 1166, :loved 15}
     {:band "Bill Evans", :plays 489, :loved 9}
     {:band "Magma", :plays 1332, :loved 31})
```

The function halve! works against the global plays and is no longer limited to generating results solely from its arguments. Because plays could change at any moment, there's no guarantee that halve! would return the same value given any particular argument.

OPTIMIZATION

If a function is referentially transparent, then it can more easily be optimized using techniques such as memoization (discussed in chapter 12) and algebraic manipulations (Wadler 1989).

TESTABILITY

If a function is referentially transparent, then it's easier to reason about and therefore more straightforward to test. Building halve! as an impure function forces the need to test against the possibility that plays could change at any time, complicating matters substantially. Imagine the confusion should you add further impure functions based on further external transient values.

7.1.4   *Named arguments*

Some programming languages allow functions to take named arguments; Python is one such language, as seen here:

```
def slope(p1=(0,0), p2=(1,1)):
    return (float(p2[1] - p1[1])) / (p2[0] - p1[0])

slope((4,15), (3,21))
#=> -6.0

slope(p2=(2,1))
#=> 0.5

slope()
#=> 1.0
```

---

[5]   These functions are based on a similar implementation created by Steven Gilardi.

The Python function `slope` calculates the slope of a line given two tuples defining points on a line. The tuples `p1` and `p2` are defined as named parameters, allowing either or both to be omitted in favor of default values, or passed in any order as a named parameter. Clojure provides a similar feature using its destructuring mechanism coupled with the optional arguments flag `&`. The same function would be written using Clojure's named arguments as in the following listing.

> **Listing 7.1 Named arguments in Clojure functions**

```
(defn slope
  [& {:keys [p1 p2] :or {p1 [0 0] p2 [1 1]}}]
  (float (/ (- (p2 1) (p1 1))
            (- (p2 0) (p1 0))))))

(slope :p1 [4 15] :p2 [3 21])
;=> -6.0

(slope :p2 [2 1])
;=> 0.5

(slope)
;=> 1.0
```

Clojure's named arguments are built on the destructuring mechanism outlined in section 3.3, allowing much richer ways to declare them.

7.1.5 *Constraining functions with pre- and postconditions*

Every function in Clojure can potentially be constrained on its inputs, its output, and some arbitrary relationship between them. These constraints take the form of pre- and postcondition vectors contained in a map defined in the function body. We can simplify the `slope` function to the base case to more clearly illustrate the matter of constraints:

```
(defn slope [p1 p2]
  {:pre [(not= p1 p2) (vector? p1) (vector? p2)]
   :post [(float? %)]}
  (/ (- (p2 1) (p1 1))
     (- (p2 0) (p1 0)))))
```

The constraint map defines two entries: `:pre` constraining the input parameters and `:post` the return value. The function calls in the constraint vectors are all expected to return true for the constraints to pass (via logical and). In the case of the revised `slope` function, the input constraints are that the points must not be equal, and they must both be vectors. In the postcondition, the constraint is that the return result must be a floating-point value. We run through a few scenarios in the following listing to see how the new implementation works.

Listing 7.2   Testing the slope function constraints

```
(slope [10 10] [10 10])                                    ⟵—— Same points
; java.lang.AssertionError: Assert failed: (not= p1 p2)

(slope [10 1] '(1 20))                                     ⟵—— p2 is List
; java.lang.AssertionError: Assert failed: (vector? p2)

(slope [10 1] [1 20])                                      ⟵—— Float not returned
; java.lang.AssertionError: Assert failed: (float? %)

(slope [10.0 1] [1 20])                                    ⟵—— Any/all as floating point
;=> -2.111111111111111
```

Clojure also provides a simple assertion macro that can be used to emulate some pre- and postconditions. Using `assert` instead of `:pre` is typically fairly straightforward. But using `assert` instead of `:post` is cumbersome and awkward. On the contrary, restricting yourself to constraint maps will cover most of the expected cases covered by `assert`, which can be used to fill in the remaining holes (such as loop invariants). In any case, constraint maps provide standard hooks into the assertion machinery of Clojure, while using `assert` is by its nature ad hoc. Yet another advantage for `:pre` and `:post` is that they allow the assertions to come from a different source than the body of the function, which we'll address next.

DECOUPLING ASSERTIONS FROM FUNCTIONS

The implementation of `slope` corresponds to a well-established mathematic property. As a result, it makes perfect sense to tightly couple the constraints and the work to be done to perform the calculation. But not all functions are as well-defined as `slope`, and therefore could benefit from some flexibility in their constraints. Imagine a function that takes a map, puts some keys into it, and returns the new map, defined as

```
(defn put-things [m]
  (into m {:meat "beef" :veggie "broccoli"}))

(put-things {})
;=> {:meat "beef", :veggie "broccoli"}
```

How would you add constraints to `put-things`? You could add them directly to the function definition, but the consumers of the map might have differing requirements for the entries added. Instead, observe how we can abstract the constraints into another function:

```
(defn vegan-constraints [f m]
  {:pre [(:veggie m)]
   :post [(:veggie %) (nil? (:meat %))]}
  (f m))

(vegan-constraints put-things {:veggie "carrot"})
; java.lang.AssertionError: Assert failed: (nil? (:meat %))
```

The `vegan-constraints` function applies specific constraints to an incoming function, stating that the map coming in and going out should have some kind of veggie and should never have meat in the result. The beauty of this scheme is that you can create contextual constraints based on the appropriate expected results, as shown next.

Listing 7.3   Menu constraints

```
(defn balanced-diet [f m]
  {:post [(:meat %) (:veggie %)]}          ◁⌐ Make sure there's
  (f m))                                      meat and veggie

(balanced-diet put-things {})
;=> {:veggie "broccoli", :meat "beef"}

(defn finicky [f m]                          ⌐ Never change
  {:post [(= (:meat %) (:meat m))]}        ◁⌐ the meat
  (f m))

(finicky put-things {:meat "chicken"})
; java.lang.AssertionError: Assert failed: (= (:meat %) (:meat m))
```

By pulling out the assertions into a wrapper function, we've detached some domain-specific requirements from a potentially globally useful function and isolated them in *aspects* (Laddad 2003). By detaching pre- and postconditions from the functions themselves, you can mix in any implementation that you please, knowing that as long as it fulfills the contract (Meyer 1991), its interposition is transparent. This is only the beginning of the power of Clojure's pre- and postconditions, and we'll come back to it a few times more to see how it can be extended and utilized.

Now that we've covered some of the powerful features available via Clojure's functions, we'll take a step further by exploring lexical closures.

7.2   *Closures*

> *On his next walk with Qc Na, Anton attempted to impress his master by saying "Master, I have diligently studied the matter, and now understand that objects are truly a poor man's closures." Qc Na responded by hitting Anton with his stick, saying "When will you learn? Closures are a poor man's object." At that moment, Anton became enlightened.*
>
> —Part of a parable by Anton van Straaten

It took only 30 years, but closures (Sussman 1975) are now a key feature of mainstream programming languages—Perl and Ruby support them, and JavaScript derives much of what power it has from closures. So what's a closure? In a sentence, a *closure* is a function that has access to locals from a larger scope, namely the context in which it was defined:

```
(def times-two
  (let [x 2]
    (fn [y] (* y x))))
```

The `fn` form defines a function and uses `def` to store it in a Var named `times-two`. The `let` forms a lexical scope in which the function was defined, so the function gains access to all the locals in that lexical context. That's what makes this function a closure: it uses the local `x` that was defined *outside* the body of the function, and so the local and its value become a property of the function itself. The function is said to *close over* the local[6] x, as in the following example:

```
(times-two 5)
;=> 10
```

This isn't terribly interesting, but one way to make a more exciting closure is to have it close over something mutable:

```
(def add-and-get
  (let [ai (java.util.concurrent.atomic.AtomicInteger.)]
    (fn [y] (.addAndGet ai y))))

(add-and-get 2)
;=> 2
(add-and-get 2)
;=> 4
(add-and-get 7)
;=> 11
```

The `java.util.concurrent.atomic.AtomicInteger` class simply holds an integer value, and its `.addAndGet` method adds to its value, stores the result, and also returns the result. The function `add-and-get` is holding onto the same instance of `Atomic-Integer`, and each time it's called, the value of that instance is modified. Unlike the earlier `times-two` function, this one can't be rewritten with the local `ai` defined inside the function. If you tried, each time the function was called, it would create a new instance with a default value of 0 to be created and stored in `ai`—clearly not what should happen. A point of note about this technique is that when closing over something mutable, you run the risk of making your functions impure and thus more difficult to test and reason about, especially if the mutable local is shared.

FUNCTIONS RETURNING CLOSURES

Each of the previous examples created a single closure, but by wrapping similar code in another function definition, you can create more closures on demand. For example, we could take the earlier `times-two` example and generalize it to take an argument instead of using 2 directly:

```
(defn times-n [n]
  (let [x n]
    (fn [y] (* y x))))
```

We've covered functions returning functions before, but if you're not already familiar with closures, this may be a stretch. We now have an outer function stored in a Var named `times-n`—note we've used `defn` instead of `def`. When `times-n` is called with an argument, it'll return a new closure created by the `fn` form and closing over the local x. The value of x for this closure will be whatever was passed in to `times-n`. Thus when we call this returned closure with an argument of its own, it'll return the value of y times x, as shown:

---

[6] Locals like x in this example are sometimes called *free variables*. We don't use the term because Clojure locals are immutable.

```
(times-n 4)
;=> #<user$times_n$fn__39 user$times_n$fn__39@427be8c2>
```

Viewing the function form for this closure isn't too useful, so instead we can store it in a Var, allowing us to call it by a friendlier name such as `times-four`:

```
(def times-four (times-n 4))
```

Here we're using `def` again simply to store what `times-n` returns—a closure over the number 4:

```
(times-four 10)
;=> 40
```

Note that when calling the closure stored in `times-four`, it used the local it had closed over as well as the argument in the call.

CLOSING OVER PARAMETERS

In our definition of `times-n`, we created a local x using `let` and closed over that instead of closing over the argument n directly. But this was only to help focus the discussion on other parts of the function. In fact, closures close over parameters of outer functions in exactly the same way as they do over `let` locals. Thus `times-n` could be defined without any `let` at all:

```
(defn times-n [n]
  (fn [y] (* y n)))
```

All of the preceding examples would work exactly the same. Here's another function that creates and returns a closure in a similar way. Note again that the inner function maintains access to the outer parameter even after the outer function has returned:

```
(defn divisible [denom]
  (fn [num]
    (zero? (rem num denom))))
```

We don't have to store a closure in a Var, but can instead create one and call it immediately:

```
((divisible 3) 6)
;=> true

((divisible 3) 7)
;=> false
```

Instead of storing or calling a closure, a particular need is best served by passing a closure along to another function that will use it.

PASSING CLOSURES AS FUNCTIONS

We've shown many examples in previous chapters of higher-order functions built in to Clojure's core libraries. What we've glossed over so far is that anywhere a function is expected, a closure can be used instead. This has dramatic consequences for how powerful these functions can be.

For example, `filter` takes a function (called a *predicate* in this case) and a sequence, applies the predicate to each value of the sequence,[7] and returns a sequence of the just the values for which the predicate returned something truthy. A simple example of its use would be to return only the even numbers from a sequence of numbers:

```
(filter even? (range 10))
;=> (0 2 4 6 8)
```

Note that `filter` only ever passes a single argument to the predicate given it. Without closures, this might be restrictive, but with them we can simply close over the values needed:

```
(filter (divisible 4) (range 10))
;=> (0 4 8)
```

It's common to define a closure right on the spot where it's used, closing over whatever local-context is needed, as shown:

```
(defn filter-divisible [denom s]
  (filter (fn [num] (zero? (rem num denom))) s))

(filter-divisible 4 (range 10))
;=> (0 4 8)
```

This kind of on-the-spot anonymous function definition is desired frequently enough that Clojure spends a little of its small syntax budget on the reader feature to make such cases more succinct. This `#()` form was first introduced in chapter 2, and in this case could be used to write the definition of `filter-divisible` as

```
(defn filter-divisible [denom s]
  (filter #(zero? (rem % denom)) s))

(filter-divisible 5 (range 20))
;=> (0 5 10 15)
```

Though certainly more succinct than the extended anonymous function form and the earlier example using a separate `divisible` function with `filter`, there's a fine line to balance between reuse[8] and clarity. Thankfully, in any case the performance differences among the three choices are nominal.

SHARING CLOSURE CONTEXT

So far, the closures we've shown have stood alone, but it's sometimes useful to have multiple closures closing over the same values. This may take the form of an ad hoc set of closures in a complex lexical environment, such as event callbacks or timer handlers in a nested GUI builder. Or it may be a tidy, specifically designed bundle of values and related functions—something that can be thought of as an object.

---

[7] Please don't construe from this wording that `filter` always iterates through the whole input sequence. Like most of the seq library, it's lazy and only consumes as much of the input sequence as needed to produce the values demanded of it.

[8] By hiding `divisible` as an anonymous function inside `filter-divisible`, we reduce the reusability of this code with no real benefit. Anonymous functions are best reserved for when the lexical context being closed over is more complex or the body of the function too narrow in use to warrant being its own named function.

To demonstrate this, we'll build a robot object that has functions for moving it around a grid based on its current position and bearing. For this we need a list of coordinate deltas for compass bearings, starting with north and going clockwise:

```
(def bearings [{:x  0, :y  1}    ; north
               {:x  1, :y  0}    ; east
               {:x  0, :y -1}    ; south
               {:x -1, :y  0}])  ; west
```

Note that this is on a grid where y increases as you go north and x increases as you go east—mathematical coordinate style rather than spreadsheet cells.

With this in place, it's easy to write a function `forward` that takes a coordinate and a bearing, and returns a new coordinate having moved forward one step in the direction of the bearing:

```
(defn forward [x y bearing-num]
  [(+ x (:x (bearings bearing-num)))
   (+ y (:y (bearings bearing-num)))])
```

Starting with a bearing of 0 (north) at 5,5 and going one step brings the bot to 5,6:

```
(forward 5 5 0)
;=> [5 6]
```

We can also try starting at 5,5 and with bearing 1 (east) or bearing 2 (south) and see the desired results:

```
(forward 5 5 1)
;=> [6 5]
```

```
(forward 5 5 2)
;=> [5 4]
```

But we have no closures yet, so we'll build a bot object that keeps not just its coordinates, but also its bearing. In the process, we'll move this standalone `forward` function into the bot object itself. By making this a closure, we'll also open up possibilities for polymorphism later. So here's a bot that knows how to move itself forward:

```
(defn bot [x y bearing-num]
  {:coords   [x y]
   :bearing ([:north :east :south :west] bearing-num)
   :forward (fn [] (bot (+ x (:x (bearings bearing-num)))
                        (+ y (:y (bearings bearing-num)))
                        bearing-num))})
```

We can create an instance of this bot and query it for its coordinates or its bearing:

```
(:coords (bot 5 5 0))
;=> [5 5]
```

```
(:bearing (bot 5 5 0))
;=> :north
```

But now that we've moved the `forward` function inside, we no longer pass in parameters, because it gets everything it needs to know from the state of the bot that it closes over. Instead, we use `:forward` to fetch the closure from inside the bot object and then use an extra set of parentheses to invoke it with no arguments:

```
(:coords ((:forward (bot 5 5 0))))
;=> [5 6]
```

So now we have a somewhat complicated beastie but still only a single closure in the mix. To make things more interesting, we'll add `turn-left` and `turn-right`[9] functions, and store them right there in the object with `:forward`:

```
(defn bot [x y bearing-num]
  {:coords     [x y]
   :bearing    ([:north :east :south :west] bearing-num)
   :forward    (fn [] (bot (+ x (:x (bearings bearing-num)))
                           (+ y (:y (bearings bearing-num)))
                           bearing-num))
   :turn-right (fn [] (bot x y (mod (+ 1 bearing-num) 4)))
   :turn-left  (fn [] (bot x y (mod (- 1 bearing-num) 4)))})

(:bearing ((:forward ((:forward ((:turn-right (bot 5 5 0)))))))))
;=> :east

(:coords ((:forward ((:forward ((:turn-right (bot 5 5 0)))))))))
;=> [7 5]
```

We won't talk about the verbosity of using the bot object yet, and instead focus on the features leveraged in the definition of `bot` itself. We're freely mixing values computed when a bot is created (such as the `:bearing`) and functions that create values when called later. The functions are in fact closures, and each has full access to the lexical environment. The fact that there are multiple closures sharing the same environment isn't awkward or unnatural and flows easily from the properties of closures already shown.

We'd like to demonstrate one final feature of this pattern for building objects: polymorphism. For example, here's the definition of a bot that supports all of the same usage as earlier, but this one has its wires crossed or perhaps is designed to work sensibly in Alice's Wonderland. When told to go forward it instead reverses, and it turns left instead of right and vice versa:

```
(defn mirror-bot [x y bearing-num]
  {:coords     [x y]
   :bearing    ([:north :east :south :west] bearing-num)
   :forward    (fn [] (mirror-bot (- x (:x (bearings bearing-num)))
                                  (- y (:y (bearings bearing-num)))
                                  bearing-num))
   :turn-right (fn [] (mirror-bot x y (mod (- 1 bearing-num) 4)))
   :turn-left  (fn [] (mirror-bot x y (mod (+ 1 bearing-num) 4)))})
```

---

[9] The `:turn-right` function uses `(+ 1 foo)`, even though in general `(inc foo)` would be more idiomatic. Here it helps highlight to anyone reading the symmetry between `turn-right` and `turn-left`. In this case, using + is more readable than using `inc` and so is preferred.

By bundling the functions that operate on data inside the same structure as the data itself, simple polymorphism is possible. Because each function is a closure, no object state needs to be explicitly passed; instead, each function uses any locals required to do its job.

It's likely you cringed at the number of parentheses required to call these particular object closures, and rightfully so. We encourage you to extrapolate from the closure examples when dealing with your own applications, and see how they can solve a variety of tricky and unusual problems. Although this kind of structure is simple and powerful[10] and may be warranted in some situations, Clojure provides other ways of associating functions with data objects that are more flexible. In fact, the desire to avoid a widespread need for this type of ad hoc implementation has motivated Clojure's `reify` macro, which we'll cover in section 9.3.

COMPILE-TIME VERSUS RUN-TIME

When looking at code that includes a closure, it's not immediately obvious how the work is distributed between compile-time and run-time. In particular, when you see a lot of code or processor-intensive work being done in a closure, you might wonder about the cost of calling the function that creates the closure:

```
(defn do-thing-builder [x y z]
  (fn do-thing [a b]
    ...
    (massive-calculation x y z)
    ...))
```

But you don't need to worry. When this whole expression is compiled, bytecode for the bodies of `do-thing` and `do-thing-builder` are generated and stored in memory.[11] In current versions of Clojure, each function definition gets its own class. But when `do-thing-builder` is called, it doesn't matter how large or slow the body of `do-thing` is—all that's done at run-time is the creation of an *instance* of `do-thing`'s class. This is lightweight and fast. Not until the closure *returned* by `do-thing-builder` is called does the complexity or speed of the body of that inner function matter at all.

In this section, you learned that closures are functions that close over lexical locals, how to create them from inside other functions, how to pass them around and call them, and even how to build lightweight objects using them. Next, we'll take a look at how functions and closures behave when they call themselves, a pattern lovingly known as *recursion*.

7.3 *Thinking recursively*

You're likely already familiar with the basics of recursion, and as a result can take heart that we won't force you to read a beginner's tutorial again. But because recursive

---

[10] ...a fact any sufficiently experienced JavaScript programmer would be able to confirm.

[11] If the code is being compiled ahead of time by the `compile` function, the generated bytecode is also written to disk in .class files.

solutions are prevalent in Clojure code, it's important that we cover it well enough that you can fully understand Clojure's recursive offerings.

Recursion is often viewed as a low-level operation reserved for times when solutions involving higher-order functions either fail or lead to obfuscation. Granted, it's fun to solve problems recursively because even for those of us who've attained some level of acumen with functional programming, finding a recursive solution still injects a bit of magic into our day. Recursion is a perfect building block for creating higher-level looping constructs and functions, which we'll show in this section.

7.3.1 *Mundane recursion*

A classically recursive algorithm is that of calculating some base number raised to an exponent, or the pow function. A straightforward[12] way to solve this problem recursively is to multiply the base by each successively smaller value of the exponent, as implemented in the following listing.

> **Listing 7.4   A version of pow using mundane recursion**

```
(defn pow [base exp]
  (if (zero? exp)
    1
    (* base (pow base (dec exp)))))

(pow 2 10)
;=> 1024
(pow 1.01 925)
;=> 9937.353723241924
```

We say that the recursive call is *mundane*[13] because it's named explicitly rather than through mutual recursion or implicitly with the recur special form. Why is this a problem? The answer lies in what happens when we try to call pow with a large value:

```
(pow 2 10000)
; java.lang.StackOverflowError
```

The implementation of pow is doomed to throw java.lang.StackOverflowError because the recursive call is trapped by the multiplication operation. The ideal solution would be a tail-recursive version that uses the explicit recur form, thus avoiding stack consumption and the resulting exception. One way to remove the mundane recursive call is to perform the multiplication at a different point, thus freeing the recursive call to occur in the tail position, as shown in the next listing.

> **Listing 7.5   A version of pow using tail recursion, accumulator, and helper function**

```
(defn pow [base exp]
  (letfn [(kapow [base exp acc]
```

---

[12] Yes, we're aware of Math/pow.

[13] Typically mundane recursion is referred to as *linear*, or the case where the space requirements needed to perform the recursion is proportional to the magnitude of the input.

```
        (if (zero? exp)
          acc
          (recur base (dec exp) (* base acc)))))]
    (kapow base exp 1)))

(pow 2 10000)
;=> ... A very big number
```

This new version of pow uses two common techniques for converting mundane recursion to tail recursion. First, it uses a helper function kapow that does the majority of the work. Second, kapow itself uses an accumulator acc that holds the result of the multiplication. The exponent exp is no longer used as a multiplicative value but instead functions as a decrementing counter, eliminating a stack explosion.

REGULAR RECURSION IS FUN AGAIN WITH LAZY-SEQ

As mentioned in section 6.3, the lazy-seq recipe rule of thumb #1 states that you should wrap your outer layer function bodies with the lazy-seq macro when generating lazy seqs. The implementation of lz-rec-step used mundane recursion but managed to avoid stack overflow exceptions thanks to the use of lazy-seq. For functions generating sequences, the use of lazy-seq might be a better choice than tail recursion, because often the regular (mundane) recursive definition is the most natural and understandable.

7.3.2 *Tail calls and recur*

In a language such as Clojure, where function locals are immutable, the benefit of tail recursion is especially important for implementing algorithms that require the consumption of a value or the accumulation of a result. Before we get deeper into implementing tail recursion, we'll take a moment to appreciate the historical underpinnings of tail-call recursion and expound on its further role within Clojure.

GENERALIZED TAIL-CALL OPTIMIZATION

In the *Lambda Papers*, Guy L. Steele and Gerald Sussman describe their experiences with the research and implementation of the early versions of the Scheme programming language. The first versions of the interpreter served as a model for Carl Hewitt's Actor model (Hewitt 1973) of concurrent computation, implementing both actors and functions. One day, while eating Ho-Hos,[14] Steele and Sussman noticed that the implementation of control flow within Scheme, implemented using actors, always ended with one actor calling another in its tail position with the return to the callee being deferred. Armed with their intimate knowledge of the Scheme compiler, Steele and Sussman were able to infer that because the underlying architecture dealing with actors and functions was the same, retaining both was redundant. Therefore, actors were removed from the language and functions remained as the more general construct. Thus, generalized tail-call optimization was thrust (Steele 1977) into the world of computer science.

---

[14] This isn't true, but wouldn't it be great if it were?

Generalized tail-call optimization as found in Scheme (Abelson 1996) can be viewed as analogous to object delegation. Hewitt's original actor model was rooted heavily in message delegation of arbitrary depth, with data manipulation occurring at any and all levels along the chain. This is similar to an adapter, except that there's an implicit resource management element involved. In Scheme, any tail call[15] from a function A to a function B results in the deallocation of all of A local resources and the full delegation of execution to B. As a result of this generalized tail-call optimization, the return to the original caller of A is directly from B instead of back down the call chain through A again, as shown in figure 7.1.

Unfortunately for Clojure, neither the Java Virtual Machine nor its bytecode provide generalized tail-call optimization facilities. Clojure does provide a tail call special form recur, but it only optimizes the case of a tail-recursive self-call and not the generalized tail call. In the general case, there's currently no way to reliably optimize (Clinger 1998) tail calls.

TAIL RECURSION

The following function calculates the greatest common denominator of two numbers:

```
(defn gcd [x y]
  (cond
    (> x y) (gcd (- x y) y)
    (< x y) (gcd x (- y x))
    :else x))
```

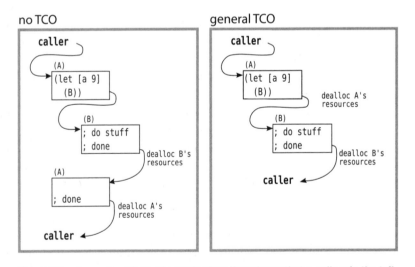

Figure 7.1 Generalized tail-call optimization: if you know that A calls B in the tail position, then you also know that A's resources are no longer needed, allowing Scheme to deallocate them and defer to B for the return call instead.

---

[15] Bear in mind that in this scenario, A and B can be different functions or the same function.

The implementation of gcd is straightforward, but you'll notice that we used mundane recursion instead of tail recursion via recur. In a language such as Scheme containing generalized tail-call optimization, the recursive calls will be optimized automatically. On the other hand, because of the JVM's lack of tail-call optimization, the recur would be needed in order to avoid stack overflow errors.

Using the information in table 7.1, you can replace the mundane recursive calls with the recur form, causing gcd to be optimized by Clojure's compiler.

Table 7.1 Tail positions and recur targets

Form(s)	Tail position	recur target?
fn, defn	(fn [args] expressions *tail*)	Yes
loop	(loop [bindings] expressions *tail*)	Yes
let, letfn, binding	(let [bindings] expressions *tail*)	No
do	(do expressions *tail*)	No
if, if-not	(if test *then tail/else tail*)	No
when, when-not	(when test expressions *tail*)	No
cond	(cond test *test tail* ... :else *else tail*)	No
or, and	(or test test ... *tail*)	No
case	(case const *const tail* ... *default tail*)	No

WHY RECUR?

If you think that you understand why Clojure provides an explicit tail-call optimization form rather than an implicit one, then go ahead and skip to the next section.

There's no technical reason why Clojure couldn't automatically detect and optimize recursive tail calls—Scala does this—but there are valid reasons why Clojure doesn't.

First, because there's no generalized TCO in the JVM, Clojure can only provide a subset of tail-call optimizations: the recursive case and the mutually recursive case (see the next section). By making recur an explicit optimization, Clojure doesn't give the pretense of providing full TCO.

Second, having recur as an explicit form allows the Clojure compiler to detect errors caused by an expected tail call being pushed out of the tail position. If we change gcd to always return an integer, then an exception is thrown because the recur call is pushed out of the tail position:

```
(defn gcd [x y]
  (int
    (cond
      (> x y) (recur (- x y) y)
      (< x y) (recur x (- y x))
      :else x)))

; java.lang.UnsupportedOperationException: Can only recur from tail position
```

With automatic recursive tail-call optimization, the addition of an outer `int` call wouldn't necessarily trigger (Wampler 2009)[16] an error condition. But Clojure enforces that a call to `recur` be in the tail position. This benefit will likely cause `recur` to live on, even should the JVM acquire TCO.

The final benefit of `recur` is that it allows the forms `fn` and `loop` to act as anonymous recursion points.

Why recur indeed.

7.3.3   *Don't forget your trampoline*

We touched briefly on the fact that Clojure can also optimize a mutually recursive function relationship, but like the tail-recursive case, it's done explicitly. Mutually recursive functions are nice for implementing finite state machines (FSA), and in this section we'll show an example of a simple state machine modeling the operation of an elevator (Mozgovoy 2009) for a two-story building. There are only four states that the elevator FSA allows: on the first floor with the doors open or closed and on the second floor with the door open or closed. The elevator can also take four distinct commands: open doors, close doors, go up, and go down. Each command is only valid in a certain context; for example, the close command is only valid when the elevator door is open. Likewise, the elevator can only go up when on the first floor and only down when on the second floor, and the door must be shut in both instances.

We can directly translate these states and transitions into a set of mutually recursive functions by associating the states as a set of functions `ff-open`, `ff-closed`, `sf-closed`, and `sf-open`, and the transitions `:open`, `:close`, `:up`, and `:down`, as conditions for calling the next function. We'd like to create a function `elevator` that starts in the `ff-open` state, takes a sequence of commands, and returns `true` or `false` if they correspond to a legal schedule according to the FSA. For example, the sequence `[:close :open :done]` would be legal, if not pointless, whereas `[:open :open :done]` wouldn't be legal, because an open door can't be reopened. The function `elevator` could be implemented as shown next.

> **Listing 7.6   Using mutually recursive functions to implement a finite state machine**

```
(defn elevator [commands]
  (letfn                              ⊲—— Local functions
    [(ff-open [[cmd & r]]                                  ⊲—— lst floor open
       "When the elevator is open on the 1st floor
        it can either close or be done."
       #(case cmd
          :close (ff-closed r)
          :done  true
          false))
     (ff-closed [[cmd & r]]                                ⊲—— lst floor closed
       "When the elevator is closed on the 1st floor
        it can either open or go up."
```

---

[16] The Scala 2.8 compiler recognizes a `@tailrec` annotation and triggers an error whenever a marked function or method can't be optimized.

```
        #(case cmd
           :open (ff-open r)
           :up   (sf-closed r)
           false))
     (sf-closed [[cmd & r]]                           ⟵— 2nd floor closed
       "When the elevator is closed on the 2nd floor
        it can either go down or open."
       #(case cmd
           :down (ff-closed r)
           :open (sf-open r)
           false))
     (sf-open [[cmd & r]]                              ⟵— 2nd floor open
       "When the elevator is open on the 2nd floor
        it can either close or be done"
       #(case cmd
           :close (sf-closed r)
           :done  true
           false))]
   (trampoline ff-open commands)))                     ⟵— Trampoline call
```

Using letfn in this way allows you to create local functions that reference each other, whereas (let [ff-open #(...)] ...) wouldn't, because it executes its bindings serially. Each state function contains a case macro that dispatches to the next state based on a contextually valid command. For example, the sf-open state will transition to the sf-closed state given a :close command, will return true on a :done command (corresponding to a legal schedule), or will otherwise return false. Each state is similar in that the default case command is to return false indicating an illegal schedule. One other point of note is that each state function returns a function returning a value rather than directly returning the value. This is done so that the trampoline function can manage the stack on the mutually recursive calls, thus avoiding cases where a long schedule would blow the stack. Here's the operation of elevator given a few example schedules:

```
(elevator [:close :open :close :up :open :open :done])
;=> false

(elevator [:close :up :open :close :down :open :done])
;=> true

;; run at your own risk!
(elevator (cycle [:close :open]))
; ... runs forever
```

Like the recur special form, the trampoline for mutual recursion has a definitive syntactic and semantic cost on the structure of your code. But whereas the call to recur could be replaced by mundane recursion without too much effect, save for at the edges, the rules for mutual recursion aren't general. Having said that, the actual rules are simple:

1 Make all of the functions participating in the mutual recursion return a function instead of their normal result. Normally this is as simple as tacking a # onto the front of the outer level of the function body.

2 Invoke the first function in the mutual chain via the trampoline function.

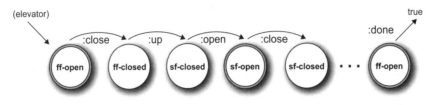

Figure 7.2   Elevator trampoline: the trampoline function explicitly bounces between mutually recursive calls.

The final example won't cause a stack overflow because the `trampoline` function handles the process of the self calls through the placement of the functions within a list where each function is "bounced" back and forth explicitly, as seen in figure 7.2.

The typical use case for mutually recursive functions are state machines, of which the `elevator` FSA is only a simple case.

7.3.4   *Continuation-passing style*

Before wrapping up this chapter, we're going to take time to talk about a style of programming not necessarily prevalent in Clojure, but moreso in the functional tradition: *continuation-passing style.* Continuation-passing style (CPS) is a hybrid between recursion and mutual recursion, but with its own set of idioms. We won't give you a deep survey of CPS, but this subsection should provide a reasonable overview for deeper exploration, should you be so inclined.

The nutshell version of CPS is that it's a way of generalizing a computation (Friedman 2001) by viewing it in terms of up to three functions:

- An accept function that decides when a computation should terminate
- A return continuation that's used to wrap the return values
- A continuation function used to provide the next step in the computation

There's a reason why many sources on CPS will use the factorial function as a base example: because it's exceptionally illustrative, as we show next.

Listing 7.7   Factorial function using continuation-passing style

```
(defn fac-cps [n k]
  (letfn [(cont [v] (k (* v n)))]              ◁───── Next continuation
    (if (zero? n)                              ◁───── Accept function
      (k 1)                  ◁───── Return continuation
      (recur (dec n) cont))))

(defn fac [n]
  (fac-cps n identity))

(fac 10)
;=> 3628800
```

Though this approach is definitely different than the normal functional structure, it's not exactly interesting in and of itself. The power of CPS is that you can extract more generic function builders using CPS. One such builder, shown in the following listing, can be used to make a range of functions that happen to fall into the same mold of a mathematical folding function.

Listing 7.8 Continuation-passing style function generator

```
(defn mk-cps [accept? end-value kend kont]
  (fn [n]
    ((fn [n k]
       (let [cont (fn [v] (k (kont v n)))]          ◁—— Next continuation
         (if (accept? n)                    ◁—— Accept continuation
           (k end-value)                       ◁—— Return continuation
           (recur (dec n) cont))))
     n kend)))

(def fac (mk-cps zero? 1 identity #(* %1 %2)))       ◁—— Factorial fn
(fac 10)
;=> 3628800

(def tri (mk-cps zero? 1 dec #(+ %1 %2)))          ◁—— Triangular fn
(tri 10)
;=> 55
```

Though this is potentially a powerful technique, there are a number of reasons preventing its widespread adoption in Clojure:

- Without generalized tail-call optimization, the number of continuation calls is bounded by the size of the stack. If your own applications can guarantee a bounded execution path for the CPS calls, then this may not be a problem in practice.

- In the case of exception handling, CPS can cause the point of failure to bubble out, especially on deferred computations such as in using delay, future, or promise.[17] In the abstract this may not seem to be a problem, but if your continuation function is supposed to throw the error but an outer layer function is doing so instead, then bugs might be difficult to track down.

- In a language such as Haskell that has ubiquitous lazy evaluation and pure functions, it's often not necessary to impose a strict order of execution. One way to impose a strict order of execution is to design your programs along the continuation-passing style. Though Clojure isn't entirely lazy, the matter of out-of-order execution isn't a factor against CPS. But CPS isn't conducive to parallelization, which is antithetical to Clojure's very nature.

7.4 Putting it all together: A* pathfinding

A* is a best-first pathfinding algorithm that maintains a set of candidate paths through a "world" with the purpose of finding the least difficult (Bratko 2000) path to some goal. The difficulty (or cost) of a path is garnered by the A* algorithm through the use of a function, typically named f, that builds an estimate of the total cost from a

---

[17] Clojure's future and promise will be discussed in detail in chapter 11.

start point to the goal. The application of this cost-estimate function f is used to sort the candidate paths (Hart 1968) in the order most likely to prove least costly.

THE WORLD

To represent the world, we'll again use a simple 2D matrix representation:

```
(def world [[  1   1   1   1   1]
            [999 999 999 999   1]
            [  1   1   1   1   1]
            [  1 999 999 999 999]
            [  1   1   1   1   1]])
```

The world structure is made from the values 1 and 999 respectively, corresponding to flat ground and cyclopean mountains. What would you assume is the optimal path from the upper-left corner [0 0] to the lower-right [4 4]? Clearly the optimal (and only) option is the Z-shaped path around the walls. Implementing an A* algorithm should fit the bill, but first, we'll talk a little bit about how to do so.

NEIGHBORS

For any given spot in the world, we need a way to calculate possible next steps. We can do this brute force for small worlds, but we'd like a more general function. It turns out if we restrict the possible moves to north, south, east, and west, then any given move is +/-1 along the x or y axis. Taking advantage of this fact, we can use the neighbors function from listing 5.1 as shown here:

```
(neighbors 5 [0 0])
;=> ([1 0] [0 1])
```

From the upper-left point, the only next steps are y=0, x=1 or y=1, x=0. So now that we have that, think about how we might estimate the path cost from any given point. A simple cost estimate turns out to be described as, "from the current point, calculate the expected cost by assuming we can travel to the right edge, then down to the lower-right." An implementation of the h function estimate-cost that estimates the remaining path cost is shown next.

Listing 7.9   A straight-line h function to estimate remaining path cost

```
(defn estimate-cost [step-cost-est size y x]
  (* step-cost-est
     (- (+ size size) y x 2)))

(estimate-cost 900 5 0 0)
;=> 7200
(estimate-cost 900 5 4 4)
;=> 0
```

From the y-x point [0 0] the cost of travelling 5 right and 5 down given an estimated single-step cost step-cost-est is 9000. This is a pretty straightforward estimate based on a straight-line path. Likewise, starting at the goal state [4 4] would cost nothing. Still needed is the g function used to calculate the cost of the path so far, named path-cost, which is provided in the following listing.

> **Listing 7.10   A g function used to calculate the cost of the path traversed so far**

```
(defn path-cost [node-cost cheapest-nbr]
  (+ node-cost
     (:cost cheapest-nbr 0)))
```
Add cheapest
neighbor cost,
else 0

```
(path-cost 900 {:cost 1})
;=> 901
```

Now that we've created an estimated cost function and a current cost function, we can implement a simple `total-cost` function for `f`.

> **Listing 7.11   f function to calculate the estimated cost of the path (+ (g ...) (h ...))**

```
(defn total-cost [newcost step-cost-est size y x]
  (+ newcost
     (estimate-cost step-cost-est size y x)))

(total-cost 0 900 5 0 0)
;=> 7200
(total-cost 1000 900 5 3 4)
;=> 1900
```

The second example shows that if we're one step away with a current cost of 1000, then the total estimated cost will be 1900, which is expected. So now we have all of the heuristic pieces in place. You may think that we've simplified the heuristic needs of A*, but in fact this is all that there is to it. The actual implementation is complex, which we'll tackle next.

7.4.1   The A* implementation

Before we show the implementation of A*, we need one more auxiliary function `min-by`, used to retrieve from a collection the minimum value dictated by some function. The implementation of `min-by` would naturally be a straightforward higher-order function, as shown:

```
(defn min-by [f coll]
  (when (seq coll)
    (reduce (fn [min this]
              (if (> (f min) (f this)) this min))
            coll)))

(min-by :cost [{:cost 100} {:cost 36} {:cost 9}])
;=> {:cost 9}
```

This function will come in handy when we want to grab the cheapest path determined by the cost heuristic. We've delayed enough! We'll finally implement the A* algorithm so that we navigate around the `world`. The following listing shows a tail-recursive solution.

Listing 7.12   The main A* algorithm

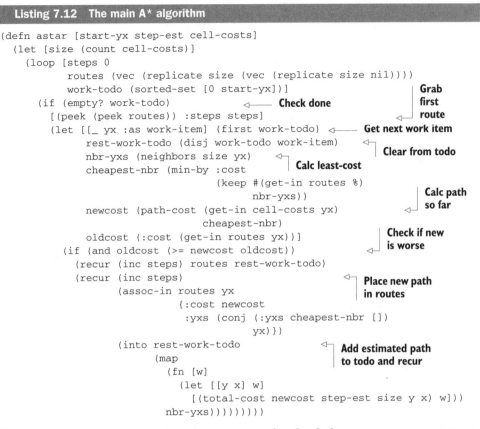

```
(defn astar [start-yx step-est cell-costs]
  (let [size (count cell-costs)]
    (loop [steps 0
           routes (vec (replicate size (vec (replicate size nil))))
           work-todo (sorted-set [0 start-yx])]              Grab
      (if (empty? work-todo)            ◁─── Check done      first
        [(peek (peek routes)) :steps steps]                  route
        (let [[_ yx :as work-item] (first work-todo)  ◁─── Get next work item
              rest-work-todo (disj work-todo work-item)  ◁┐
              nbr-yxs (neighbors size yx)    ◁┐           Clear from todo
              cheapest-nbr (min-by :cost     Calc least-cost
                             (keep #(get-in routes %)
                                   nbr-yxs))             Calc path
              newcost (path-cost (get-in cell-costs yx)  so far
                         cheapest-nbr)
              oldcost (:cost (get-in routes yx))]        Check if new
          (if (and oldcost (>= newcost oldcost))         is worse
            (recur (inc steps) routes rest-work-todo)
            (recur (inc steps)                         Place new path
                   (assoc-in routes yx                 in routes
                     {:cost newcost
                      :yxs (conj (:yxs cheapest-nbr [])
                                 yx)})
                   (into rest-work-todo            Add estimated path
                     (map                          to todo and recur
                       (fn [w]
                         (let [[y x] w]
                           [(total-cost newcost step-est size y x) w]))
                       nbr-yxs)))))))))
```

The main thrust of the astar function occurs at the check that (>= newcost oldcost). Once we've calculated the newcost (the cost so far for the cheapest neighbor) and a cost-so-far oldcost, we perform one of two actions. The first action occurs when the newcost is greater than or equal to the oldcost and is to throw away this new path, because it's clearly a worse alternative. The other action is the core functionality corresponding to the constant sorting of the work-todo, based on the cost of the path as determined by the heuristic function total-cost. The soul of A* is based on the fact that the potential paths stored in work-todo are always sorted and distinct (through the use of a sorted set), based on the estimated path cost function. Each recursive loop through the astar function maintains the sorted routes based on the current cost knowledge of the path, added to the estimated total cost.

The results given by the astar function for the Z-shaped world are shown in the next listing.

Listing 7.13   Running the A* algorithm on the Z World

```
(astar [0 0]
       900
       world)

;=> [{:cost 17,
      :yxs [[0 0] [0 1] [0 2] [0 3] [0 4] [1 4] [2 4]
            [2 3] [2 2] [2 1] [2 0] [3 0] [4 0] [4 1]
            [4 2] [4 3] [4 4]]}
     :steps 94]
```

By following the y-x indices, you'll notice that the astar function traverses the Z World along the path where cost is 1, as seen in figure 7.3.

We can also build another world, as shown next, called Shrubbery World that contains a single weakling shrubbery at position [0 3], represented by the number 2, and see how astar navigates it.

Figure 7.3   A graphical representation of Z World clearly shows the optimal/only path.

Listing 7.14   The Shrubbery World

```
(astar [0 0]
       900
       [[   1    1    1    2    1]          <——— The shrubbery is 2
        [   1    1    1  999    1]
        [   1    1    1  999    1]
        [   1    1    1  999    1]
        [   1    1    1    1    1]])        <——— The clear path

;=> [{:cost 9,
      :yxs [[0 0] [0 1] [0 2] [1 2] [2 2] [3 2]
            [4 2] [4 3] [4 4]]}
     :steps 134]
```

When tracing the best path, you will see that the astar function prefers the nonshrubbery path. But what would happen if we placed a man-eating bunny along the previously safe path, represented by an ominously large number, as shown next?

Listing 7.15   The bunny world

```
(astar [0 0]
       900
       [[   1    1    1    2    1]          The shrubbery
        [   1    1    1  999    1]          looks inviting
        [   1    1    1  999    1]
        [   1    1    1  999    1]          The bunny
        [   1    1    1  666    1]])        lies in wait

;=> [{:cost 10,
      :yxs [[0 0] [0 1] [0 2] [0 3] [0 4] [1 4]
            [2 4] [3 4] [4 4]]}
     :steps 132]
```

As expected, the `astar` function picks the shrubbery path (2) path instead of the evil bunny path to reach the final destination.

7.4.2   *Notes about the A* implementation*

The A* algorithm was implemented as idiomatic Clojure source code. Each of the data structures, from the sorted set to the tail-recursive `astar` function, to the higher-order function `min-by`, was functional in nature and therefore extensible as a result. We encourage you to explore the vast array of possible worlds traversable by our A* implementation and see what happens should you change the heuristic (Dijkstra 1959) functions along the way. Clojure encourages experimentation, and by partitioning the solution this way, we've enabled you to explore different heuristics.

7.5   *Summary*

We've covered a lot about Clojure's flavor of functional programming in this chapter, and you may have noticed that it looks like many others. Clojure favors an approach where immutable data is transformed through the application of functions. Additionally, Clojure prefers that functions be free of side-effects and referentially transparent (pure) in order to reduce the complexities inherent in widespread data mutation. Lexical closures provide a simple yet powerful mechanism for defining functions that carry around with them the value context in which they were created. This allows certain information to exist beyond their lexical context, much like a poor-man's object. Finally, Clojure is built with this in mind, in that its primary form of iteration is through tail recursion as a natural result of its focus on immutability.

In the next chapter, we'll explore the feature most identified with Lisp: macros.

Part 4

Large-scale design

Clojure is a practical language, not an academic one; and in the real world, programs grow large, change over time, and are confronted with shifting requirements. In this part, we'll show how Clojure's Lisp heritage of "code is data" can help address these problems. We'll demonstrate the use of macros, how to create a fluent builder, the benefits of a language that embraces the Java platform, and how Clojure addresses the mutability of the real world.

Macros

If you give someone Fortran, he has Fortran. If you give someone Lisp, he has any language he pleases.

—Guy Steele

This chapter covers

- Data is code is data
- Defining control structures
- Macros combining forms
- Using macros to control symbolic resolution time
- Using macros to manage resources
- Putting it all together: macros returning functions

Macros are where the rubber of "code is data" meets the road of making programs simpler and cleaner. To fully understand macros, you need to understand the different *times* of Clojure, of which macros perform the bulk of their work at compile time. We'll start by looking at what it means for code to be data and data to be used as code. This is the background you'll need to understand that control structures in Clojure are built out of macros, and how you can build your own. The mechanics of macros are relatively simple, and before you're halfway through this chapter you'll have learned all you technically need to write your own. Where macros get complicated is when you try to bring theoretical knowledge of them into the real world, so to help you combat that we'll lead you on a tour of practical applications of macros.

What kinds of problems do macros solve? To start answering that question, consider Clojure's -> and ->> macros that return the result of a number of threaded forms. To understand both versions of the arrow macros, we find it useful to think of them as an arrow indicating the flow of data from one function to another—the form `(-> 25 Math/sqrt int list)` can be read as

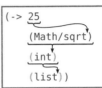

1 Take the value 25.
2 Feed it into the method `Math/sqrt`.
3 Feed that result into the function `int`.
4 Feed that result into the function `list`.

Graphically, this can be viewed as shown in figure 8.1.

It expands into the following expression:

Figure 8.1 Arrow macro: each expression is inserted into the following one at compile time, allowing you to write the whole expression inside-out when that feels more natural.

```
(list (int (Math/sqrt 25)))
```

When viewed this way, the -> macro can be said to *thread* a sequence of forms into each in turn. This threading can be done within any form and is *always* stitched in as the first argument to the outermost expression. On the other hand, the ->> macro will thread the form as the last argument. Observe how the placement of commas[1] works as visual markers for the stitch point:

```
(-> (/ 144 12) (/ ,,, 2 3) str keyword list)
;=> (:2)

(-> (/ 144 12) (* ,,, 4 (/ 2 3)) str keyword (list ,,, :33))
;=> (:32 :33)

(->> a (+ 5 ,,,) (let [a 5] ,,,,))
;=> 10
```

Using the arrows macro is useful when many sequential operations need to be applied to a single object. So this is one potential use case for macros: taking one form of an expression and transforming it into another form. In this chapter, we'll also look at using macros to combine forms, change forms, control evaluation and resolution of arguments, manage resources, and build functions. But first, what does it mean that Clojure code is data, and why should you care?

8.1   *Data is code is data*

You're already familiar with textual representations of data in your programs, at least with strings, lists, vectors, maps, and so on. Clojure, like other Lisps, takes this one step further by having programs be made *entirely* out of data. Function definitions in Clojure programs are also represented using an aggregation of the various data

---

[1] Because commas are considered whitespace. The use here is instructive and not meant as idiomatic.

structures mentioned in the previous chapters. Likewise, the expressions representing the execution of functions and the use of control structures are also data structures! These data representations of functions and their executions represent a concept different from the way other programming languages operate. Typically, there's a sharp distinction between data structures and functions of the language. In fact, most programming languages don't even remotely describe the form of functions in their textual representations. With Clojure, there's no distinction between the textual form and the actual form of a program. When a program is the data that composes the program, then you can write programs to write programs. This may seem like nonsense now, but as you'll see throughout this chapter, it's powerful.

To start with, look at the built-in Clojure function eval, whose purpose is to take a data structure representing a Clojure expression, evaluate it, and return the result. This behavior can be seen in the following examples:

```
(eval 42)
;=> 42

(eval '(list 1 2))
;=> (1 2)

(eval (list 1 2))
; java.lang.ClassCastException: java.lang.Integer cannot be cast to clojure.
    lang.IFn
```

Why did we get an exception for the last example? The answer to that lies in the previous example. The quote in '(list 1 2) causes eval to view it as (list 1 2), which is the function call to create the resulting list. Likewise, for the final example eval received a list of (1 2) and attempted to use 1 as a function, thus failing. Not very exciting, is it? The excitement inherent in eval stems from something that we mentioned[2] earlier—if you provide eval a list in the form expected of a function call, then *something else* should happen. This *something else* would be the evaluation of a function call and not of the data structure itself. Look at what happens when we try evaluating something more complicated:

```
(eval (list (symbol "+") 1 2))
;=> 3
```

In words, the steps involved were as follows:

1 The function symbol received a string + and returned a symbol data type of +.
2 The function list received three arguments: a symbol +, the integer 1, and the integer 2, and returned a list of these elements.
3 The eval function received a list data type of (+ 1 2), recognized it as the function call form, and executed the + function with the arguments 1 and 2, returning the integer 3.

---

[2] All the way back in section 2.5.

8.1.1   *Syntax-quote, unquote, and splicing*

In section 1.5.6, we mentioned quoting and its effects on evaluation, and in this chapter we'll expand on that theme fully as it relates to Clojure's macro facility. But the functionality of the quoting forms is orthogonal to macros, and they can be used independently. As we show[3] in listing 8.1, using quoting and unquoting in a function allows us to create an evaluation function, `contextual-eval`, that takes an explicit context map.

Listing 8.1   An implementation of `eval` taking a local context

```
(defn contextual-eval [ctx expr]
  (eval
    `(let [~@(mapcat (fn [[k v]] [k `'~v]) ctx)]
       ~expr)))
```
⟵ Build let bindings
at compile-time

```
(contextual-eval {'a 1, 'b 2} '(+ a b))
;=> 3

(contextual-eval {'a 1, 'b 2} '(let [b 1000] (+ a b)))
;=> 1001
```

Handling nested syntax-quotes

Dealing with nested syntax-quotes can at times be complicated. But you can visualize the way in which unquoting affects the nested structures as result of repeated evaluations (Steele 1990) relative to its nesting level:

```
(let [x 9, y '(- x)]
  (println `y)
  (println ``y)
  (println ``~y)
  (println ``~~y)
  (contextual-eval {'x 36} ``~~y))
; user/y
; (quote user/y)
; user/y
; (- x)
;=> -36
```

The nesting of the syntax-quotes in the first two `println` calls takes the value of `y` further up the abstraction ladder. But by including a single unquote in the third `println`, we again bring it back down. Finally, by unquoting a second time, we've created a structure that can then be evaluated—and doing so yields the result -36. We had to use `contextual-eval` in the tail because core `eval` doesn't have access to local bindings—only Var bindings. One final note is that had we attempted to unquote one extra time, we'd have seen the exception `java.lang.IllegalStateException: Var clojure.core/unquote is unbound`. The reason for this error is that unquote is the way to "jump" out of a syntax-quote, and to do so more than nesting allows will cause an error. We won't use this technique in this chapter, and in most cases you won't need to utilize it unless you're planning to create macro-defining macros—something we won't do until section 13.1.

---

[3]   Thanks to George Jahad for the implementation on which `contextual-eval` is based.

Rarely will you see the use of syntax-quote outside the body of a macro, but there's nothing preventing it from being used this way—and doing so is powerful. But the maximum power of quoting forms is fully realized when used with macros.

Working from a model where code is data, Clojure is able to manipulate structures into different executable forms at both runtime and compile time. We've already shown how this can be done at runtime using `eval` and `contextual-eval`, but this doesn't serve the purpose of compile-time manipulation. It probably doesn't need saying, but because this is a book about Clojure, we will: macros are the way to achieve this effect.

8.1.2 *Macro rules of thumb*

Before we begin, we should list a few rules of thumb to observe when writing macros:

- Don't write a macro if a function will do. Reserve macros to provide syntactic abstractions or create binding forms.
- Write an example usage.
- Expand your example usage by hand.
- Use `macroexpand`, `macroexpand-1`, and `clojure.walk/macroexpand-all`[4] liberally to understand how your implementation works.
- Experiment at the REPL.
- Break complicated macros into smaller functions whenever possible.

Throughout this chapter, you'll see all of these rules to varying degrees. Obviously, we're trying to balance best practices, teaching, and page counts, so we may not always adhere entirely. Even so, we'll try to highlight those times when we do break from the recommended heuristics. Having said that, we'll talk first about the most ubiquitous use of macros: creating custom control structures.

8.2 *Defining control structures*

Most control structures in Clojure are implemented via macros, so they provide a nice starting point for learning how macros can be useful. Macros can be built with or without using syntax-quote, so we'll show examples of each.

In languages lacking macros, such as Haskell[5] for example, the definition of control structures relies on the use of higher-order functions such as we showed in section 7.1.2. Though this fact in no way limits the ability to create control structures in Haskell, the approach that Lisps take to the problem is different. The most obvious advantage of macros over higher-order functions is that the former manipulate compile-time forms, transforming them into runtime forms. This allows your programs

---

[4] The `macroexpand-all` function is a useful debugging aid, as we'll demonstrate in this chapter. But it's worth knowing that unlike the other `macroexpand` functions, it doesn't use exactly the same logic as the Clojure compiler itself, and thus may in some unusual circumstances produced misleading results.

[5] Although there's a GHC extension named Template Haskell that provides a macro-like capability, this isn't the norm.

to be written in ways natural to your problem domain, while still maintaining runtime efficiency. Clojure already provides a rich set of control structures, including but not limited to doseq, while, if, if-let, and do, but in this section we'll write a few others.

8.2.1 *Defining control structures without syntax-quote*

Because the arguments to defmacro aren't evaluated before being passed to the macro, they can be viewed as pure data structures, and manipulated and analyzed as such. Because of this, amazing things can be done on the raw forms supplied to macros even in the absence of unquoting.

Imagine a macro named do-until that will execute all of its clauses evaluating as true *until* it gets one that is falsey:

```
(do-until
  (even? 2) (println "Even")
  (odd?  3) (println "Odd")
  (zero? 1) (println "You never see me")
  :lollipop (println "Truthy thing"))
; Even
; Odd
;=> nil
```

A good example of this type of macro is Clojure's core macro cond, which with some minor modifications can be made to behave differently:

```
(defmacro do-until [& clauses]
  (when clauses
    (list `when (first clauses)
          (if (next clauses)
            (second clauses)
            (throw (IllegalArgumentException.
                      "do-until requires an even number of forms")))
          (cons 'do-until (nnext clauses)))))
```

The first expansion of do-until illustrates how this macro operates:

```
(macroexpand-1 '(do-until true (prn 1) false (prn 2)))
;=> (when true (prn 1) (do-until false (prn 2)))
```

do-until recursively expands into a series of when calls, which themselves expand into a series of if expressions:

```
(require '[clojure.walk :as walk])
(walk/macroexpand-all '(do-until true (prn 1) false (prn 2)))
;=> (if true (do (prn 1) (if false (do (prn 2) nil))))

(do-until true (prn 1) false (prn 2))
; 1
;=> nil
```

Now you could write out the nested if structure manually and achieve the same result, but the beauty of macros lies in the fact that they can do so on your behalf while presenting a lightweight and intuitive form. In cases where do-until can be used, it removes the need to write and maintain superfluous boilerplate code. This idea can be extended to macros in general and their propensity to reduce unneeded boilerplate for a large category of circumstances, as the programmer desires. One thing to note about do-until is that it's meant to be used only for side effects, because it's designed to always return nil. Macros starting with do tend to act the same.

8.2.2 *Defining control structures using syntax-quote and unquoting*

Not all control structures will be as simple as do-until. Instead, there will be times when you'll want to selectively evaluate macro arguments, structures, or substructures. In this section, we'll explore one such macro named unless, implemented using unquote and unquote-splice.

Ruby provides a control structure named unless that reverses the sense (Olsen 2007) of a when statement, executing the body of a block when a given condition evaluates to false:

```
(unless (even? 3) "Now we see it...")
;=> "Now we see it..."

(unless (even? 2) "Now we don't.")
;=> nil
```

The maverick implementation[6] of unless as demonstrated previously and as shown in the following listing is straightforward.

Listing 8.2 A Clojure implementation of `unless`

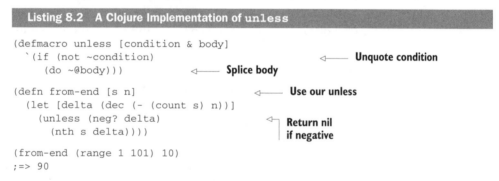

```
(defmacro unless [condition & body]
  `(if (not ~condition)          ⟵── Unquote condition
    (do ~@body)))                 ⟵── Splice body

(defn from-end [s n]             ⟵── Use our unless
  (let [delta (dec (- (count s) n))]
    (unless (neg? delta)          ⟵┐ Return nil
      (nth s delta))))            ⟵┘ if negative

(from-end (range 1 101) 10)
;=> 90
```

The body of the unless implementation uses three features first shown in section 1.5.6: syntax-quote (written as a single back-quote), unquote (written as ~), and unquote-splice (written as ~@). Syntax-quote allows the if form to act as a template for the expression that any use of the macro becomes when expanded. The unquote and splicing-unquote provide the "blanks" where the values for the parameters condition and body will be inserted.

Because unless relies on the result of a condition for its operation, it's imperative that it evaluate the condition part using unquote. If we didn't use unquote in this instance, then instead of evaluating a function (even? 3), it would instead attempt to resolve a namespace Var named condition that may not exist—and if it does exist, it

---

[6] The proper way to define unless is either (defmacro unless [& args] `(when-not ~@args)) or even (clojure.contrib.def/defalias unless when-not)—or just use when-not from the start.

might be arbitrarily truthy at the time of the macro call. Some of the unintended consequences of this mistake are shown in the next listing.

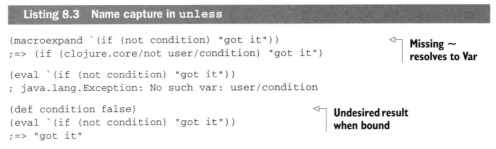

Listing 8.3 Name capture in `unless`

```
(macroexpand `(if (not condition) "got it"))
;=> (if (clojure.core/not user/condition) "got it")    ◁  Missing ~
                                                          resolves to Var

(eval `(if (not condition) "got it"))
; java.lang.Exception: No such var: user/condition

(def condition false)                                  ◁  Undesired result
(eval `(if (not condition) "got it"))                     when bound
;=> "got it"
```

Clearly this isn't the desired behavior. Instead, by unquoting the `condition` local, we ensure that the function call is used instead. It's easy to forget to add an unquote to the body of a macro, and depending on the condition of your runtime environment, the problem may not be immediately obvious.

8.3 *Macros combining forms*

Macros are often used for combining a number of forms and actions into one consistent view. This behavior could be seen in the previous section with the `do-until` macro, but it's more general. In this section, we'll show how macros can be used to combine a number of tasks in order to simplify an API. Clojure's `defn` macro is an instance of this type of macro because it aggregates the processes of creating a function, including

- Creating the corresponding function object using `fn`
- Checking for and attaching a documentation string
- Building the `:arglists` metadata
- Binding the function name to a Var
- Attaching the collected metadata

You could perform all of these steps over and over again every time you wanted to create a new function, but thanks to macros you can instead use the more convenient `defn` form. Regardless of your application domain and its implementation, programming language boilerplate code inevitably occurs. But identifying these repetitive tasks and writing macros to simplify and reduce or eliminate the tedious copy-paste-tweak cycle can work to reduce the incidental complexities inherent in a project. Where macros differ from techniques familiar to proponents of Java's object-oriented style—including hierarchies, frameworks, inversion of control, and the like—is that they're treated no differently by the language itself. Clojure macros work to mold the language into the problem space rather than forcing you to mold the problem space into the constructs of the language. There's a specific term for this, *domain-specific language*, but in Lisp the distinction between DSL and API is thin to the point of transparency.

Envision a scenario where you want to be able to define Vars that call a function whenever their root bindings change. You could do this using the `add-watch` function that allows for the attachment of a *watcher* to a reference type that's called whenever a change occurs within. The add-watch function itself takes three arguments: a reference, a watch function key, and a watch function called whenever a change occurs. You could enforce that every time someone wants to define a new Var, they must follow these steps:

1 Define the Var.
2 Define a function (maybe inline to save a step) that will be the watcher.
3 Call add-watch with the proper values.

A meager three steps isn't too cumbersome a task to remember in a handful of uses, but over the course of a large project it's easy to forget and/or morph one of these steps when the need to perform them many times occurs. Therefore, perhaps a better approach is to define a macro to perform all of these steps for you, as the following definition does:

```
(defmacro def-watched [name & value]
  `(do
     (def ~name ~@value)
     (add-watch (var ~name)
                :re-bind
                (fn [~'key ~'r old# new#]
                  (println old# " -> " new#)))))
```

Ignoring symbol resolution and auto-gensym, which we'll cover in upcoming sections, the macro called as (def-watched x 2) expands into roughly the following:

```
(do (def x 2)
    (add-watch (var x)
               :re-bind
               (fn [key r old new]
                 (println old " -> " new))))
```

The results of def-watched are thus

```
(def-watched x (* 12 12))
x
;=> 144

(def x 0)
; 144 -> 0
```

Lisp programs in general (and Clojure programs specifically) use macros of this sort to vastly reduce the boilerplate needed to perform common tasks. Throughout this chapter, you'll see macros that combine forms, so there's no need to dwell on the matter here. Instead, we'll move on to a macro domain that does just that, with the added bonus of performing some interesting transformations in the process.

8.4 *Using macros to change forms*

One way to design macros is to start by writing out example code that you wish worked—code that has the minimal distance between what you must specify and the specific application domain in which you're working. Then, with the goal of making this code work, you begin writing macros and functions to fill in the missing pieces.

For example, when designing software systems, it's often useful to identify the "things" comprising your given application domain, including their logical groupings. The level of abstraction at this point in the design is best kept high (Rosenberg 2005) and shouldn't include details about implementation. Imagine that you want to describe a simple domain of the ongoing struggle between humans and monsters:

- Man versus monster
  - People
    - Men (humans)
      - Name
      - Have beards?
  - Monsters
    - Chupacabra
      - Eats goats?

Though this is a simple format, it needs work to be programmatically useful. Therefore, the goal of this section is to write macros performing the steps to get from this simple representation to the one more conducive to processing. One such structure is a tree composed of individual generic nodes, each taking a form similar to that shown in the next listing.

Listing 8.4   Domain DSL's underlying form

```
{:tag <node form>,            ⟵——— Domain, grouping
 :attrs {},                                    ⟵——— Name people
 :content [<nodes>]}          ⟵——— Properties
```

You'd never say this is a beautiful format, but it does present practical advantages over the original format—it's a tree, it's composed of simple types, it's regular, and it's recognizable to some existing libraries.

> **CLOJURE APHORISM** Clojure is a design language where the conceptual model is also Clojure.

We'll start with the outer-level element, `domain`:

```
(defmacro domain [name & body]
  `{:tag :domain,
    :attrs {:name (str '~name)},
    :content [~@body]})
```

The body of `domain` is fairly straightforward in that it sets the domain-level tree node and splices the body of the macro into the `:content` slot. After `domain` expands, you'd expect its body to be composed of a number of `grouping` forms, which are then handled by the aptly named macro:

```
(declare handle-things)

(defmacro grouping [name & body]
  `{:tag :grouping,
    :attrs {:name (str '~name)},
    :content [~@(handle-things body)]})
```

Similarly to domain, grouping expands into a node with its body spliced into the :content slot. But grouping differs from domain in that it splices in the result of the call to a function handle-things:

```
(declare grok-attrs grok-props)

(defn handle-things [things]
  (for [t things]
    {:tag :thing,
     :attrs (grok-attrs (take-while (comp not vector?) t))
     :content (if-let [c (grok-props (drop-while (comp not vector?) t))]
                [c]
                [])}))
```

Because the body of a thing is fairly simple and regular, we can simplify the implementation of handle-things by again splitting it into two functions. The first function grok-attrs handles everything within the body of a thing that's not a vector, and the other grok-props handles properties that are. In both cases, these leaf-level functions return specifically formed maps:

```
(defn grok-attrs [attrs]
  (into {:name (str (first attrs))}
        (for [a (rest attrs)]
          (cond
            (list? a) [:isa (str (second a))]
            (string? a) [:comment a]))))
```

The implementation of grok-attrs may seem overly complex, especially given that the example domain model DSL only allows for a comment attribute and an optional isa specification. But by laying out this way, we can easily expand the function to handle a richer set of attributes later. Likewise with grok-props, we provide a more complicated function to pull apart the vector representing a property so that it's more conducive to expansion:

```
(defn grok-props [props]
  (when props
    {:tag :properties, :attrs nil,
     :content (apply vector (for [p props]
                {:tag :property,
                 :attrs {:name (str (first p))},
                 :content nil}))}))
```

Now that we've created the pieces, take a look at the new DSL in action in the following listing.

Listing 8.5   Exploring the domain DSL results

```
(def d
  (domain man-vs-monster
    (grouping people              ◁——— Group of people
      (Human "A stock human")            ◁——— One kind of person

      (Man (isa Human)                   ◁——— Another kind of person
        "A man, baby"
        [name]
        [has-beard?]))
    (grouping monsters            ◁——— Group of monsters
      (Chupacabra                        ◁——— One kind of monster
        "A fierce, yet elusive creature"
        [eats-goats?])))))

(:tag d)
;=> :domain

(:tag (first (:content d)))
;=> :grouping
```

Maybe that's enough to prove to you that we've constructed the promised tree, but probably not. Therefore, we can pass a tree into a function that expects one of that form[7] and see what comes out on the other end:

```
(use '[clojure.xml :as xml])
(xml/emit d)
```

Performing this function call will print out the corresponding XML representation, minus the pretty printing, shown here.

Listing 8.6   An XML transformation of the domain DSL structure

```
<?xml version='1.0' encoding='UTF-8'?>
<domain name='man-vs-monster'>                        ◁——— (Domain ...)
  <grouping name='people'>        ◁——— (Grouping ...)
    <thing name='Human' comment='A stock human'>        ◁——— (Human ...)
      <properties></properties>
    </thing>
    <thing name='Man' isa='Human' comment='A man, baby'>    ◁——— (Man ...)
      <properties>
        <property name='name'/>
        <property name='has-beard?'/>
      </properties>
    </thing>
  </grouping>
  <grouping name='monsters'>                        (Grouping ...)
                                                    ◁—┘
    <thing name='Chupacabra' comment='A fierce, yet elusive creature'>
      <properties>
        <property name='eats-goats?'/>
      </properties>
```

---

[7] The namespace `clojure.contrib.json` in the Clojure contrib library also contains some functions that would be able to handle the domain DSL structure seamlessly. Additionally, Enlive (http://mng.bz/8Hh6) should also recognize the resultant structure.

```
      </thing>
    </grouping>
  </domain>
```

Our approach was to define a single macro entry point domain, intended to build the top-level layers of the output data structure and instead pass the remainder on to auxiliary functions for further processing. In this way, the body of the macro expands into a series of function calls, each taking some subset of the remaining structure and returning some result that's spliced into the final result. This functional composition approach is fairly common when defining macros. The entirety of the domain description could've been written within one monolithic macro, but by splitting the responsibilities, you can more easily extend the representations for the constituent parts.

Macros take data and return data, always. It so happens that in Clojure, code is data and data is code.

8.5 *Using macros to control symbolic resolution time*

Whereas functions accept and return values that are meaningful to your application at runtime, macros accept and return code forms that are meaningful at compile time. Any symbol has some subtleties depending on whether it's fully qualified or not, its resolution time, and its lexical context. These factors can be controlled in any particular case by the appropriate use of quoting and unquoting, which we explore in this section.

Clojure macros are mostly safe from name capture, in that the use of syntax-quote in macros is encouraged and idiomatic, and it'll resolve symbols at macro-expansion time. This strategy reduces complexity by ensuring that symbols refer to those available at a known instance rather than to those unknown in the execution context.

For example, consider one of the simplest possible macros:

```
(defmacro resolution [] `x)
```

Viewing the expansion of this macro is illuminating in understanding how Clojure macros resolve symbols:

```
(macroexpand '(resolution))
;=> user/x
```

The expansion of the macro resolves the namespace of the syntax-quoted symbol x. This behavior is useful in Clojure by helping to avoid free name capturing problems that are possible in a macro system such as that found in Common Lisp.[8] Here's an example that would trip up a lesser implementation of syntax-quote, but which does just what we want in Clojure:

```
(def x 9)
(let [x 109] (resolution))
;=> 9
```

---

[8] Among one of the ways that Common Lisp works to alleviate this kind of problem is the use of gensym. The key difference is that in Common Lisp, you have to be careful to avoid name capturing, whereas Clojure avoids it by default.

The x defined in the let isn't the same as the namespace-qualified user/x referred to by the macro resolution. As you might expect, the macro would've thrown an unbound Var exception had we not first executed the call to def.

Clojure does provide a way to defer symbolic resolution for those instances where it may be useful to resolve it within the execution context, which we'll show now.

8.5.1   *Anaphora*

Anaphora[9] in spoken language is a term used in a sentence referring back to a previously identified subject or object. It helps to reduce repetition in a phrase by replacing "Jim bought 6,000 Christmas lights and hung all of the Christmas lights," with "Jim bought 6,000 Christmas lights and hung *them* all." In this case, the word *them* is the anaphora. Some programming languages use anaphora, or allow for their simple definition. Scala has a rich set of anaphoric (Odersky 2008) patterns primarily focused around its _ operator:

```
Array(1, 2, 3, 4, 5).map(2 * _)
//=> res0: Array[Int] = Array(2, 4, 6, 8, 10)
```

In this Scala example, the underscore serves to refer back to an implicitly passed argument to the map function, which in this case would be each element of the array in succession. The same expression could be written with (x) => 2 * x—the syntax for an anonymous function—in the body of the map call, but that would be unnecessarily verbose.

Anaphora don't nest, and as a result are generally not employed in Clojure. Within a nested structure of anaphoric macros, you can only refer to the most immediate anaphoric binding, and never those from outer lexical contours, as demonstrated in listing 8.7. For example, the Arc programming language (Graham Arc) contains a macro named awhen similar to Clojure's when, save that it implicitly defines a local named it used within its body to refer to the value of the checked expression.

Listing 8.7   An example of anaphora and its weakness

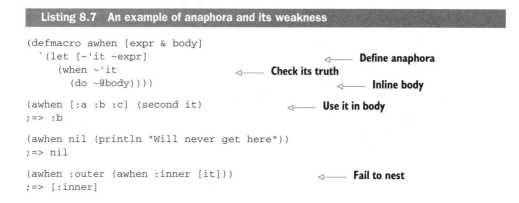

```
(defmacro awhen [expr & body]
  `(let [~'it ~expr]                          <─── Define anaphora
     (when ~'it                               <─── Check its truth
       (do ~@body))))                         <─── Inline body

(awhen [:a :b :c] (second it))                <─── Use it in body
;=> :b

(awhen nil (println "Will never get here"))
;=> nil

(awhen :outer (awhen :inner [it]))            <─── Fail to nest
;=> [:inner]
```

---

[9] Anaphora is pronounced *un-NAF-er-uh.*

Clojure provides similar macros that do nest and replace the need for anaphora: `if-let` and `when-let`. When designing your own macros, it's preferred that you build them along these lines so that the macro itself takes the name to be bound. But just because typical anaphorics are limited, that's not to say that they're entirely useless. Instead, for your own libraries you may find that their usage is intuitive. You'll see the pattern `~'symbol` at times in Clojure macros, because this is the idiomatic way to selectively capture a symbolic name within the body of a macro. The reason for this bit of awkwardness[10] is because Clojure's syntax-quote attempts to resolve symbols in the current context, resulting in fully qualified symbols. Therefore, `~'` avoids that resolution by unquoting a quote.

8.5.2   *(Arguably) useful selective name capturing*

We contend that there's only one case to be made for selective name capturing in Clojure macros—the case when you're forced to embed third-party macros and functions in your macros that rely on the existence of anaphora. One such macro is the `proxy` macro in Clojure's core libraries, which provides an anaphoric symbol named `this` within its body for use therein. We'll cover the `proxy` macro in depth in section 9.1, so there's no need to discuss it here. But bear in mind that should this macro ever be embedded within your own macros, you may be forced to use the `~'this` pattern.

> **HYGIENE**   A *hygienic* macro is one that doesn't cause name capturing at macro expansion time. Clojure macros help to ensure hygiene by namespace-resolving symbols within the body of syntax-quote at macro-definition time. As you saw, symbols are expanded into the form `user/a-symbol` within the body of syntax-quote. To close this hygienic loop, Clojure also disallows the definition of qualified locals within the body of a macro. In order to selectively capture names within Clojure macros, you *must* explicitly do so via the `~'a-symbol` pattern.

Clojure prefers that symbols be either declared or bound at macro-definition time. But using the resolution deferment strategy outlined earlier, you can relax this requirement for those instances where doing so would be useful.

8.6   *Using macros to manage resources*

Managing scarce resources or those with a finite lifetime is often viewed as a sweet spot for macro usage. In Java, such activities are almost always performed using the `try/catch/finally` idiom (Bloch 2008), as shown:

```
try {
    // open the resource
}
catch (Exception e) {
    // handle any errors
```

---

[10] *Awkwardness is good since it's a strong signal to make the user aware he is drifting away from the true path to clojure enlightenment.* —Christophe Grand

```
}
finally {
    // in any case, release the resource
}
```

We showed in section 1.5.8 that Clojure also has a try/catch/finally form that can be used in the same way, but like the Java idiom, you must remember to explicitly close the resource within the finally block. Clojure provides a generic with-open macro, demonstrated in listing 8.8, that when given a "closeable" object bound to a name, will automatically call its .close method (assuming that one exists) within a finally block.

Listing 8.8   An example of with-open

```
(import [java.io BufferedReader InputStreamReader]
        [java.net URL])

(defn joc-www []
  (-> "http://joyofclojure.com/hello" URL.
      .openStream InputStreamReader. BufferedReader.))

(let [stream (joc-www)]
  (with-open [page stream]                    ⟵—— Begin IO block
    (println (.readLine page))
    (print "The stream will now close... "))  ⟵—— Close implicitly
  (println "but let's read from it anyway.")
  (.readLine stream))                         ⟵—— Use illegally after close

; Hello Cleveland
; The stream will now close... but let's read from it anyway.
; java.io.IOException: Stream closed
```

Not all instances of resources in your own programs will be closeable. In these instances, we present a generic template for resource allocating macros that can be used for many cases, shown in the following listing.

Listing 8.9   A more general template for with-open-like macros

```
(defmacro with-resource [binding close-fn & body]
  `(let ~binding
     (try
       (do ~@body)
       (finally
         (~close-fn ~(binding 0))))))

(let [stream (joc-www)]
  (with-resource [page stream]
    #(.close %)
    (.readLine page)))
```

The macro with-resource is generic enough and so generally ubiquitous across differing flavors (Symbolics Inc.[11]) to almost be considered a Lisp design pattern. The

---

[11] The spirit of this section was inspired by a similar discussion of "Writing Macros to Surround Code." If you can get your hands on the original Symbolics manuals, do so—they contain a wealth of information.

macro `with-resource` differs from `with-open` in that it does not assume that its resource is closeable but instead delegates the task of closing the resource to a `close-fn` function taken as an argument. One final point is that `with-resource` avoids the nesting problem of anaphoric macros because it requires that the resource be named explicitly a la `[stream (joc-www)]`. This approach allows for the proper nesting of `with-resource` macros; and in fact, the use of named bindings marked by vectors is ubiquitous and idiomatic in Clojure.

8.7   *Putting it all together: macros returning functions*

In section 7.1, we introduced Clojure's constraint facility that uses pre- and post-condition checks on function arguments and return values respectively to ensure some assertions about said function. In that section, we talked briefly about how separating the constraints from the functions they're constraining allows you to more flexibly apply different assertion templates based on need and context.

> **CLOJURE APHORISM**   Clojure programmers don't write their apps in Clojure. They write the language that they use to write their apps in Clojure.

In this section, we're going to take this idea one step further by introducing a macro named `contract` that implements a simple DSL to describe function constraints. For example, a proposed DSL should be nameable and describe its pre- and post-conditions in an intuitive way, building a higher-order function that will be used to apply its constraints later. The following sketches a contract specifying that a function should take only a positive number and return its value multiplied by 2:

```
(contract doubler
  [x]
  (:require
    (pos? x))
  (:ensure
    (= (* 2 x) %)))
```

The contract's `:require` list (Meyer 2000) refers to preconditions, and the `:ensure` list the postconditions. Given this description, how would you start to implement a macro to realize this sketch? If you haven't already gathered from the section title and the initial problem statement, the macro must return a function, so we'll start there with the following listing.

Listing 8.10   The contract top-level macro

```
(declare collect-bodies)

(defmacro contract [name & forms]
  (list* `fn name (collect-bodies forms)))
```

The `contract` macro calls a function `collect-bodies` that hasn't been written yet, so we had to use `declare` to avoid a compilation error. Hold fast, because we're going to implement that necessary function soon. But first, imagine what the form of the returned function will be when it finally comes out of `contract`:

```
(fn doubler
  ([f x]
     {:post [(= (* 2 x) %)],
      :pre [(pos? x)]}
     (f x)))
```

We also want to allow for the multi-arity function definition form so that the contract can take more than one specification per arity function, each separated by a
vector of symbols. The first step down that path starts with an implementation of
collect-bodies:

```
(declare build-contract)

(defn collect-bodies [forms]
  (for [form (partition 3 forms)]
    (build-contract form)))
```

The primary task of collect-bodies is to build a list of the body portion of the
contract, each partitioned into three segments. These partitions represent the arg-
list, requires, and ensures of the contract, which we'll then pass along to another
function named build-contract, that will build the arity bodies and corresponding
constraint maps. This is shown next.

Listing 8.11   The contract auxiliary function `build-contract`

```
(defn build-contract [c]
  (let [args (first c)]                                          ◁─── Grab args
    (list                                          ◁─── Build list...
      (into '[f] args)                                     ◁─── Include HOF + args
      (apply merge
        (for [con (rest c)]
          (cond (= (first con) :require)                       ◁─── Process requires
              (assoc {} :pre (vec (rest con)))
            (= (first con) :ensure)                          ◁─── Process ensures
              (assoc {} :post (vec (rest con)))
            :else (throw (Exception. (str "Unknown tag " (first con)))))))
      (list* 'f args))))                         ◁─── Build call to f
```

The function build-contract is where the heart of contract construction lies, building the arity bodies that contain constraint maps. The difference is that each body is a
higher-order function that takes an additional function as an argument, which the
arguments are then delegated to. This allows us to compose the contract function
with a constrained function, as shown in the next listing.

Listing 8.12   Composition of contract function and constrained function

```
(def doubler-contract                       ◁─── Define contract
  (contract doubler
    [x]
    (:require
      (pos? x))
    (:ensure
      (= (* 2 x) %))))
```

```
(def times2 (partial doubler-contract #(* 2 %)))          ◁——— Test correct fn
(times2 9)
;=> 18

(def times3 (partial doubler-contract #(* 3 %)))          ◁——— Test incorrect fn
(times3 9)
; java.lang.AssertionError: Assert failed: (= (* 2 x) %)
```

As you might expect, `times2` fulfills the contract, whereas `times3` doesn't. We could extend `doubler-contract` to handle extended arities, as shown here.

Listing 8.13 Contract for multiple-arity functions

```
(def doubler-contract
  (contract doubler
    [x]                              ◁——— Define l-arg contract
      (:require
        (pos? x))
      (:ensure
        (= (* 2 x) %))
    [x y]                            ◁——— Define 2-arg contract
      (:require
        (pos? x)
        (pos? y))
      (:ensure
        (= (* 2 (+ x y)) %))))

((partial doubler-
    contract #(* 2 (+ %1 %2))) 2 3)          ◁——— Test a correct fn
;=> 10

((partial doubler-
    contract #(+ %1 %1 %2 %2)) 2 3)          ◁——— Test another correct fn
;=> 10

((partial doubler-contract #(* 3 (+ %1 %2))) 2 3)    ◁——— Test an incorrect fn
; java.lang.AssertionError:
;     Assert failed: (= (* 2 (+ x y)) %)
```

We could extend the contract to cover any number of expected function arities using `contract`, independent of the functions themselves. This provides a nice separation of the work to be done from the expected work to be done. By using the `contract` macro, we've provided a way to describe the expectations of a function, including but not limited to

- The possible types of its inputs and output
- The relationship of the function output to its inputs
- The expected function arities
- The "shape" of the inputs and output

The `contract` macro could be extended in many complementary ways. For example, Clojure's function constraints are verified using logical and—the implications being that any additional pre- or postcondition works to tighten the requirements. But there may be times when loosening the constraints on the inputs and tightening them on the output makes more sense. In any case, this section isn't about the nuances of contracts programming, and to dig deeper would elude the point that using macros to return functions is an extremely powerful way to extend the capabilities of Clojure itself.

8.8   *Summary*

We've explored various use cases for macros and given examples of each. Though instructive to the point under discussion, we also tried to show how macros can be used to mold Clojure into the language that shortens the gap between your problem space and solution space. In your own unique programs, you should try to do the same. But the most important skill that you can learn on your path toward macro mastery is the ability to recognize when to avoid using them. The general answer of course is whenever, and as often as you can.

In the next chapter, we'll cover various powerful way to organize and categorize data types and functions using Clojure's namespaces, multimethods, types, and protocols.

Combining data and code

9

This chapter covers

- Namespaces
- Exploring Clojure multimethods with the Universal Design Pattern
- Types, protocols, and records
- Putting it all together: a fluent builder for chess moves

Clojure provides powerful features for grouping and partitioning logical units of code and data. Most logical groupings occur within namespaces, Clojure's analogue to Java packages. We explore how to build, manipulate, and reason about them. Also, in this chapter we'll play with Clojure's powerful multimethods that provide polymorphism based on arbitrary dispatch functions. We then uncover recent additions to Clojure supporting *abstraction-oriented programming*—types, protocols, and records. Finally, the chapter concludes with the creation of a fluent chess-move facility, comparing a Java approach to solving the problem with a Clojure approach.

177

9.1   *Namespaces*

Newcomers to Clojure have a propensity to hack away at namespace declarations until they appear to work. This may work sometimes, but it delays the process of learning how to leverage namespaces more effectively.

From a high-level perspective, namespaces can be likened to a two-level mapping, where the first level is a symbol to a namespace containing mappings of symbols to Vars, as shown in figure 9.1. This conceptual model[1] is slightly complicated by the fact that namespaces can be aliased, but even in these circumstances the model holds true.

In the simplest possible terms, qualified symbols of the form joy.ns/authors cause a two-level lookup: a symbol joy.ns used to lookup a namespace map and a symbol authors used to retrieve a Var, as shown in the following listing.

Listing 9.1   Namespace navigation

```
(in-ns 'joy.ns)
(def authors ["Chouser"])

(in-ns 'your.ns)
(clojure.core/refer 'joy.ns)
joy.ns/authors
;=> ["Chouser"]

(in-ns 'joy.ns)
(def authors ["Chouser" "Fogus"])

(in-ns 'your.ns)
joy.ns/authors
;=> ["Chouser" "Fogus"]
```

Because a symbolic name refers to a Var in the current namespace or another, it follows that any referred Var always evaluates to the current value and not the value present at referral time.

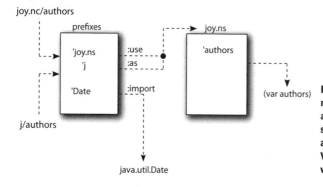

Figure 9.1   The logical layout of namespaces. The process to resolve a Var joy.ns/authors includes a symbolic resolution of the namespace and the Var name. The result is the Var itself. Aliases created with :use work as expected.

---

[1]   As always, we're trying to keep the level of discussion limited to abstractions rather than implementation details.

9.1.1 Creating namespaces

There are a number of ways to create a new namespace; each has its advantages and use cases. The choice of one namespace-creation mechanism over another amounts to choosing the level of control over the default symbolic mappings.

NS

In idiomatic Clojure source code, you'll see the ns macro used almost exclusively. By using the ns macro, you automatically get two sets of symbolic mappings—all classes in the java.lang package and all of the functions, macros, and special forms in the clojure.core namespace:

```
(ns chimp)
(reduce + [1 2 (Integer. 3)])
;=> 6
```

Using the ns macro creates a namespace if it doesn't already exist, and switches to that namespace. The ns macro is intended for use in source code files and not in the REPL, although there's nothing preventing it.

IN-NS

Using the in-ns function also imports the java.lang package like ns; but it doesn't create any mappings for functions or macros in clojure.core. The in-ns function also takes an explicit symbol used as the namespace qualifier, as in

```
(in-ns 'gibbon)

(reduce + [1 2 (Integer. 3)])
; java.lang.Exception: Unable to resolve symbol: reduce in this context

(clojure.core/refer 'clojure.core)
(reduce + [1 2 (Integer. 3)])
;=> 6
```

The in-ns function is more amenable to REPL experimentation when dealing with namespaces than ns.

CREATE-NS

The finest level of control for creating namespaces is provided through the create-ns function, which when called takes a symbol and returns a namespace object:

```
(def b (create-ns 'bonobo))
b
;=> #<Namespace bonobo>

((ns-map b) 'String)
;=> java.lang.String
```

The call to create-ns doesn't switch to the named namespace, but it does create Java class mappings automatically. When given a namespace object (retrieved using the find-ns function also), you can manipulate its bindings programmatically using the functions intern and ns-unmap:

```
(intern b 'x 9)
;=> #'bonobo/x
bonobo/x
;=> 9
```

In the preceding code, we bound the symbol x to the value 9 in the namespace bonobo, and then referenced it directly using its qualified name bonobo/x. We can do the same thing for any type of Var binding:

```
(intern b 'reduce clojure.core/reduce)
;=> #'bonobo/reduce

(intern b '+ clojure.core/+)
;=> #'bonobo/+

(in-ns 'bonobo)
(reduce + [1 2 3 4 5])
;=> 15
```

Because only Java class mappings are created by create-ns, you'll have to intern any Clojure core functions, as we did with + and reduce. You can even inspect the mappings within a namespace programmatically, and likewise remove specific mappings:

```
(in-ns 'user)
(get (ns-map 'bonobo) 'reduce)
;=> #'bonobo/reduce

(ns-unmap 'bonobo 'reduce)   ;=> nil

(get (ns-map 'bonobo) 'reduce)
;=> nil
```

Finally, you can wipe a namespace using remove-ns:

```
(remove-ns 'bonobo)
;=> #<Namespace bonobo>

(all-ns)
;=> (#<Namespace clojure.set> #<Namespace clojure.main>
     #<Namespace clojure.core> #<Namespace clojure.zip>
     #<Namespace chimp> #<Namespace gibbon>
     #<Namespace clojure.xml>)
```

You should be careful when populating namespaces using create-ns and intern, because they cause potentially confusing side-effects to occur. Their use is intended only for advanced techniques, and even then they should be used cautiously.

9.1.2 *Expose only what's needed*

Knowing that namespaces operate as a two-level mapping will only get you so far in creating and using them effectively. You must understand other practical matters to use namespaces to their fullest. For example, for a given namespace joy.contracts, your directory structure could look like that in figure 9.2.

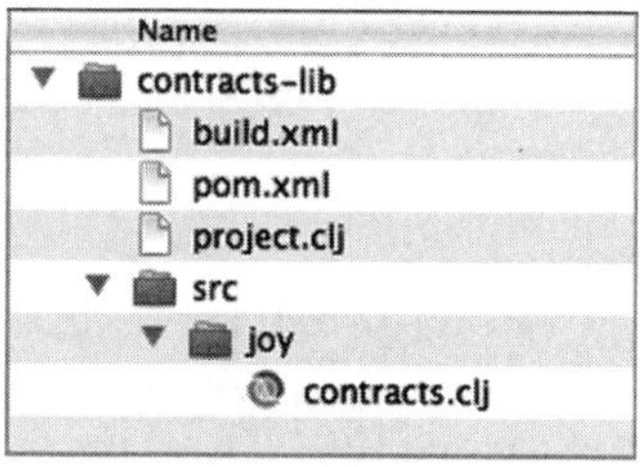

Figure 9.2 Namespace private directories: the directories layout for an illustrative `joy.contracts` namespace

This directory structure is fairly straightforward, but there are a couple items to note. First, though the namespace is named `joy.contracts`, the corresponding Clojure source file is located in the contracts-lib/src/joy directory. This is a common technique in organizing Java and Clojure projects, where the actual source directories and files are located in a common src subdirectory in the main project directory. The additional files build.xml, pom.xml,

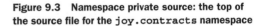

```
(ns joy.contracts)

(defn- build-contract [c]
  (let [args (first c)]
    (list
      (into '[f] args)
      (apply merge
             (for [con (rest c)]
               (cond (= (first con) 'require)
                       (assoc {} :pre (vec (rest con)))
                     (= (first con) 'ensure)
                       (assoc {} :post (vec (rest con)))))
```

Figure 9.3   Namespace private source: the top of the source file for the `joy.contracts` namespace

and project.clj correspond to the build scripts for Apache Ant, Maven, and Leiningen, respectively. These build scripts will know, through either configuration or convention, that the src directory contains the directories and source files for Clojure namespaces and *not* part of the namespace logical layout. If you were to open the contracts.clj file located in contracts-lib/src/joy in your favorite editor, then you might see something like that shown in figure 9.3.

The file contracts.clj defines the namespace `joy.contracts` and defines the function `build-contract` using the `defn-` macro. The use of `defn-` in this way indicates to Clojure that the `build-contract` function is private to the `joy.contracts` namespace. The `defn-` macro is provided for convenience and simply attaches privileged metadata to the Var containing the function. You could attach the same namespace privacy metadata yourself, as shown:

```
(ns hider.ns)

(defn ^{:private true} answer [] 42)

(ns seeker.ns
  (:refer hider.ns))

(answer)
; java.lang.Exception: Unable to resolve symbol: answer in this context
```

The use of `^{:private true}` in this way will also work within a def and a defmacro, and for these cases it's required, because there's no corresponding def- and def-macro- in Clojure's core.

> **HYPHENS/UNDERSCORES** If you decide to name your namespaces with hyphens, à la `my-cool-lib`, then the corresponding source file *must* be named with underscores in place of the hyphens (my_cool_lib.clj).

Because Clojure namespace names are tied to the directory in which they reside, you can also create a certain directory structure conducive to hiding implementation details, as seen in figure 9.4.

By creating another subdirectory to contracts-lib/src/joy named impl, you can effectively hide implementation details for your code. The public-facing API would be located in contracts.clj and the "hidden" implementation details in impl.clj. Your clients would be expected to refer only to the elements in contracts.clj, whereas your library could refer to elements in impl.clj, as shown in figure 9.5.

Of course, nothing's stopping you from also referencing the `joy.contracts.impl` namespace, but you do so at their own peril. There are never any guarantees that implementation details will remain the same shape from one release to the next.

Figure 9.4   Private API directories: using the folder layout to hide namespace implementation details

9.1.3   *Declarative inclusions and exclusions*

When defining namespaces, it's important to include only the references that are likely to be used. Clojure prefers a fine-grained Var mapping via a set of directives on the `ns` macro: `:exclude`, `:only`, `:as`, `:refer-clojure`, `:import`, `:use`, `:load`, and `:require`.

We'll describe a namespace named `joy.ns-ex` first in prose and then using `ns` and its directives. In this namespace, we want to exclude the `defstruct` macro from

```
(ns joy.contracts
  (:use [joy.contracts.impl :only [collect-bodies]]))

(defmacro defcontract
  [& forms]
  (let [name (if (symbol? (first forms))
               (first forms)
               nil)
        body (collect-bodies (if name
                               (rest forms)
                               forms))]
    (list* 'fn name body)))
```
`--:---   contracts.clj   All (13,0)      (Fundamental)-----------------`
```
(ns joy.contracts.impl)

(declare build-contract)

(defn collect-bodies [forms]
  (for [form (partition 3 forms)]
    (build-contract form)))

(defn build-contract [c]
  (let [args (first c)]
    (list
      (into '[f] args)
      (apply merge
             (for [con (rest c)]
               (cond (= (first con) 'require)
                     (assoc {} :pre (vec (rest con)))
                     (= (first con) 'ensure)
```
`--:---   impl.clj      Top (11,23)     (Fundamental)-----------------`

Figure 9.5   Private API source: the client-facing API is located in contracts.clj and the private API in impl.clj.

clojure.core. Next, we want to use everything in clojure.set and clojure.xml without namespace qualification. Likewise, we wish to use only the functions are and is from the clojure.test namespace without qualification. We then want to load the clojure.zip namespace and alias it as z. Finally, we want to import the Java classes java.util.Date and java.io.File. By providing directives, the problem of namespace inclusions and exclusions become a declarative matter, as shown:

```
(ns joy.ns-ex
  (:refer-clojure :exclude [defstruct])
  (:use (clojure set xml))
  (:use [clojure.test :only (are is)])
  (:require (clojure [zip :as z]))
  (:import (java.util Date)
           (java.io File)))
```

We'll touch on further uses of namespaces throughout the rest of the book, with an extensive example explaining their use as JVM class specifications in section 10.3.

> **AVOID NAKED :USE** One point of note that we should mention is that the (:use (clojure set xml)) statement is considered a promiscuous operation and therefore discouraged. The :use directive without the :only option pulls in all of the public Vars in clojure.set and clojure.xml indiscriminately. Though this practice is useful when incrementally building your code, it shouldn't endure into the production environment. When organizing your code along namespaces, it's good practice to export and import *only* those elements needed.

We now turn our focus to Clojure's multimethods, a way of defining polymorphic functions based on the results of arbitrary functions, which will get you halfway toward a system of polymorphic types.

9.2   *Exploring Clojure multimethods with the Universal Design Pattern*

> *The most specific event can serve as a general example of a class of events.*
> —Douglas R. Hofstadter

In Douglas Hofstadter's Pulitzer prize winning work *Gödel, Escher, Bach: An Eternal Golden Braid*, he describes a notion of the *Prototype Principle*—the tendency of the human mind to use specific events as models for similar but different events or things. He presents the idea "that there is generality in the specific" (Hofstadter 1979). Building on this idea, programmer Steve Yegge coined the term *The Universal Design Pattern (UDP)*, extrapolating on Hofstadter's idea (Yegge 2008) and presenting it in terms of prototypal inheritance (Ungar 1987).

The UDP is built on the notion of a map or map-like object. Though not ground-breaking, the flexibility in the UDP derives from the fact that each map contains a reference to a *prototype* map used as a parent link to inherited fields. You might wonder how anyone could model a software problem in this way, but we assure you that countless programmers do so every day when they choose JavaScript (Flanagan 2006). In this section, we'll implement a subset of Yegge's UDP and discuss how it might be used as the basis for abstraction-oriented programming and polymorphism using Clojure's multimethods and ad hoc hierarchies.

9.2.1   *The parts*

In addition to the aforementioned prototype reference, the UDP requires a set of supporting functions to operate: beget, get, put, has?, and forget. The entire UDP is built on these five functions, but we'll need the first three for this section.

BEGET

The beget function performs a simple task. It takes a map and associates its prototype reference to another map, returning a new map:

```
(ns joy.udp
  (:refer-clojure :exclude [get]))

(defn beget [o p] (assoc o ::prototype p))

(beget {:sub 0} {:super 1})
;=> {:joy.udp/prototype {:super 1}, :sub 0}
```

To participate in the UDP, maps must have a :joy.udp/prototype entry.

PUT

The function put takes a key and an associated value and puts them into the supplied map, overwriting any existing key of the same name:

```
(def put assoc)
```

The put function is asymmetric to the functionality of get. The get method retrieves values anywhere along the prototype chain, whereas put only ever inserts at the level of the supplied map.

GET

Because of the presence of the prototype link, get requires more than a simple one-level lookup. Instead, whenever a value isn't found in a given map, the prototype chain is followed until the end:

```
(defn get [m k]
  (when m
    (if-let [[_ v] (find m k)]
      v
      (recur (::prototype m) k))))

(get (beget {:sub 0} {:super 1})
     :super)
;=> 1
```

We don't explicitly handle the case of "removed "properties, but instead treat them like any other associated value. This is fine because the "not found" value of nil is falsey. Most of the time, it's sufficient to rely on the fact that looking up a nonexistent key will return `nil`. But in cases where you want to allow users of your functions to store any value at all, including `nil`, you'll have to be careful to distinguish `nil` from "not found," and the `find` function is the best way to do this.

9.2.2 *Usage*

Using only `beget`, `put`, and `get`, you can leverage the UDP in some simple, yet powerful ways. Assume that at birth cats like dogs and only learn to despise them when goaded. Morris the cat has spent most of his life liking 9-Lives cat food and dogs, until the day comes when a surly Shih Tzu leaves him battered and bruised. We can model this unfortunate story as shown:

```
(def cat {:likes-dogs true, :ocd-bathing true})
(def morris (beget {:likes-9lives true} cat))
(def post-traumatic-morris (beget {:likes-dogs nil} morris))

(get cat :likes-dogs)
;=> true

(get morris :likes-dogs)
;=> true

(get post-traumatic-morris :likes-dogs)
;=> nil
```

The map `post-traumatic-morris` is like the old `morris` in every way except for the fact that he has learned to hate dogs. Modeling cat and dog societal woes is interesting but far from the only use case for the UDP, as you'll see next.

NO NOTION OF SELF

Our implementation of the UDP contains no notion of self-awareness via an implicit `this` or `self` reference. Though adding such a feature would probably be possible, we've intentionally excluded it in order to draw a clear separation between the prototypes and the functions that work on them (Keene 1989). A better solution, and one that follows in line with a deeper Clojure philosophy, would be to access, use, and manipulate these prototypes using Clojure's multimethods.

9.2.3 *Multimethods to the rescue*

Adding behaviors to the UDP can be accomplished easily using Clojure's multimethod facilities. *Multimethods* provide a way to perform function polymorphism based on the result of an arbitrary dispatch function. Coupled with our earlier UDP implementation, we can implement a prototypal object system with differential inheritance similar to (although not as elegant as) that in the Io language (Dekorte Io). First, we'll need to define a multimethod `compiler` that dispatches on a key `:os`:

```
(defmulti  compiler :os)
(defmethod compiler ::unix [m] (get m :c-compiler))
(defmethod compiler ::osx  [m] (get m :c-compiler))
```

The multimethod `compiler` describes a simple scenario: if the function `compiler` is called with a prototype map, then the map is queried for an element `:os`, which has methods defined on the results for either `::unix` or `::osx`. We'll create some prototype maps to exercise `compiler`:

```
(def clone (partial beget {}))
(def unix   {:os ::unix, :c-compiler "cc", :home "/home", :dev "/dev"})
(def osx   (-> (clone unix)
               (put :os ::osx)
               (put :c-compiler "gcc")
               (put :home "/Users")))

(compiler unix)
;=> "cc"

(compiler osx)
;=> "gcc"
```

That's all there is (Foote 2003) to creating behaviors that work against the specific "type" of a prototype map. But a problem of inherited behaviors still persists. Because our implementation of the UDP separates state from behavior, there's seemingly no way to associate inherited behaviors. But as we'll now show, Clojure does provide a way to define ad hoc hierarchies that we can use to simulate inheritance within our model.

9.2.4   *Ad hoc hierarchies for inherited behaviors*

Based on the layout of the `unix` and `osx` prototype maps, the property `:home` is overridden in `osx`. We could again duplicate the use of `get` within each method defined (as in `compiler`), but instead we prefer to say that the lookup of `:home` should be a derived function:

```
(defmulti home :os)
(defmethod home ::unix [m] (get m :home))

(home unix)
;=> "/home"

(home osx)
; java.lang.IllegalArgumentException:
;    No method in multimethod 'home' for dispatch value: :user/osx
```

Clojure allows you to define a relationship stating "`::osx` is a `::unix`" and have the derived function take over the lookup behavior using Clojure's `derive` function:

```
(derive ::osx ::unix)
```

Now the home function works:

```
(home osx)
;=> "/Users"
```

You can query the derivation hierarchy using the functions `parents`, `ancestors`, `descendants`, and `isa?` as shown:

```
(parents ::osx)
;=> #{:user/unix}
```

```
(ancestors ::osx)
;=> #{:user/unix}

(descendants ::unix)
;=> #{:user/osx}

(isa? ::osx ::unix)
;=> true
(isa? ::unix ::osx)
;=> false
```

The result of the isa? function defines how multimethods dispatch. In the absence of a derivation hierarchy, isa? can be likened to pure equality, but with it traverses a derivation graph.

9.2.5   *Resolving conflict in hierarchies*

What if we interject another ancestor into the hierarchy for ::osx and want to again call the home method? Observe the following:

```
(derive ::osx ::bsd)
(defmethod home ::bsd [m] "/home")

(home osx)
; java.lang.IllegalArgumentException: Multiple methods in multimethod
;   'home' match dispatch value: :user/osx -> :user/unix and
;   :user/bsd, and neither is preferred
```

As shown in figure 9.6, ::osx derives from both ::bsd and ::unix, so there's no way to decide which method to dispatch, because they're both at the same level in the derivation hierarchy. Fortunately, Clojure provides a way to assign favor to one method over another using the function prefer-method:

```
(prefer-method home ::unix ::bsd)
(home osx)
;=> "/Users"
```

In this case, we used prefer-method to explicitly state that for the multimethod home, we prefer the method associated with the dispatch value ::unix over the one for ::bsd, as illustrated in figure 9.5. As you'll recall, the home method for ::unix explicitly used get to traverse the prototype chain, which is the preferred behavior.

As you might expect, removing the home method for the ::bsd dispatch value using remove-method will remove the preferential lookup for ::osx:

```
(remove-method home ::bsd)
(home osx)
;=> "/Users"
```

All of these functions manipulate and operate off of the global hierarchy map directly. If you prefer to reduce these potentially confusing side-effects, then you can define a derivation hierarchy using make-hierarchy and derive:

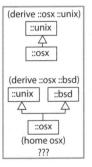

Figure 9.6 Hierarchy conflict: most languages allowing type derivations use a built-in conflict-resolution strategy. In the case of CLOS, it's fully customizable. Clojure requires conflicts to be resolved with prefer-method.

```
(derive (make-hierarchy) ::osx ::unix)
;=> {:parents {:user/osx #{:user/unix}},
     :ancestors {:user/osx #{:user/unix}},
     :descendants {:user/unix #{:user/osx}}}
```

Once you have a separate hierarchy in hand, you can provide it to `defmulti` to specify the derivation context, thus preserving the global hierarchy map.

9.2.6   *Arbitrary dispatch for true maximum power*

Until now, we've only exercised multimethods using a single privileged `:os` property, but this doesn't accentuate their true power. Instead, multimethods are fully open and can dispatch on the result of an arbitrary function, even one that can pull apart and/or combine its inputs into any form:

```
(defmulti  compile-cmd  (juxt :os compiler))

(defmethod compile-cmd [::osx "gcc"] [m]
  (str "/usr/bin/" (get m :c-compiler)))

(defmethod compile-cmd :default [m]
  (str "Unsure where to locate " (get m :c-compiler)))
```

The dispatch values for the new `compile-cmd` methods are vectors composed of the results of looking up the `:os` key and calling the `compiler` function defined earlier. You can now observe what happens when `compile-cmd` is called:

```
(compile-cmd osx)
;=> "/usr/bin/gcc"

(compile-cmd unix)
;=> "Unsure where to locate cc"
```

Using multimethods and the UDP is an interesting way to build abstractions. Multimethods and ad hoc hierarchies are open systems, allowing for polymorphic dispatch based on arbitrary functions. Clojure also provides a simpler model for creating abstractions and gaining the benefits of polymorphism—types, protocols, and records—which we'll cover next.

The handy-dandy juxt function

The `juxt` function is highly useful in defining multimethod dispatch functions. In a nutshell, `juxt` takes a bunch of functions and composes them into a function returning a vector of its argument(s) applied to each given function, as shown:

```
(def each-math (juxt + * - /))
(each-math 2 3)
;=> [5 6 -1 2/3]

((juxt take drop) 3 (range 9))
[(0 1 2) (3 4 5 6 7 8)]
```

Having a convenient and succinct way to build vectors of applied functions is powerful for defining understandable multimethods—although that's not the limit of `juxt`'s usefulness.

9.3 *Types, protocols, and records*

We showed in the previous section that Clojure multimethods provide a way to achieve runtime polymorphism based on arbitrary dispatch functions. Though extremely powerful, multimethods are sometimes less than ideal. Interposing a dispatch function into the polymorphism machinery isn't always conducive to raw speed. Likewise, dispatching on an arbitrary function is often overkill. Therefore, Clojure provides facilities for creating logically grouped polymorphic functions that are both simple and performant—types, records, and protocols. We'll delve into these topics in this section and introduce the concept of abstraction-oriented programming, predicated on the creation of logical groupings. But first, we'll discuss the simplest of the three topics, records, which you might recognize.

9.3.1 *Records*

Using maps as data objects is perfectly acceptable and has several lovely features. Chief among these is that maps require no declaration of any sort: you just use literal syntax to build them right on the spot. We showed this in section 7.2 when we built an object like this:

```
{:val 5, :l nil, :r nil}
```

This is handy but is missing things that are often desirable, the most significant of which is a type of its own. The object constructed here is some kind of map, but it isn't, as far as Clojure is concerned, a TreeNode. That means that when used in its simple form as we did here, there's no clean way[2] to determine whether any particular map is a TreeNode or not.

In such circumstances, records become a compelling[3] solution. You define a record type with a defrecord form. For example, a defrecord for TreeNode looks like this:

```
(defrecord TreeNode [val l r])
```

This creates a new Java class with a constructor that takes a value for each of the fields listed. It also imports that class into your current namespace so you can easily use it to create new instances.

Here's how to create an instance of the TreeNode record:

```
(TreeNode. 5 nil nil)
;=> #:user.TreeNode{:val 5, :l nil, :r nil}
```

---

[2] You could test a map for the existence of the keys :val, :l, and :r, a sort of duck-typing but on fields instead of methods. But because there exists a real possibility than some other kind of object may happen to have these keys but use them in a different way, undesirable complexity and/or unexpected behavior is likely. Fortunately, you can mitigate this risk by using namespace-qualified keywords. Despite the general agreement of experts that ducks are Kosher, we'd definitely classify this particular duck as unclean.

[3] There was a pre-Clojure 1.2 convention of attaching :type metadata to an object, which can be looked up with the type function, but this approach is rarely if ever needed moving forward.

Explicit importing of defrecord and deftype classes

It's important to note that when you define a `defrecord` and `deftype`, corresponding classes are generated. These classes are automatically imported into the same namespace where the `defrecord` and `deftype` declarations occur, but *not* in any other namespace. Instead, you *must explicitly import* `defrecord` and `deftype` classes using the `import` function or `:import` namespace declaration:

```
(ns my-cool-ns
  (:import joy.udp.TreeNode))
```

Loading a namespace via `:require` or `:use` won't be enough to import `defrecord` and `deftype` classes.

The use of `defrecord` buys you several important benefits. First of all, it provides a simple and specific idiom for documenting the expected fields of the object. But it also delivers several important performance improvements. A record will be created more quickly, consume less memory, and look up keys in itself more quickly than the equivalent array map or hash map. Data types can also store primitive values (byte, int, long, and so on), which take up considerably less memory than the equivalent boxed objects (Byte, Integer, Long, and so on) supported by other collection types.

That's a lot of benefit, so what does it cost you? The first cost we already mentioned—you must define the record type before using it. Another is that currently, records aren't printed in a way that the Clojure reader can read, unlike hash maps. This can be a problem if you're using Clojure's print functions to save off or transmit data. Here's what it looks like if we try, successfully, with a literal map and then again, unsuccessfully, with a record:

The downfall of defstructs

Clojure provides a `defstruct` mechanism, which can be viewed as a way to define a map that acts as an ad hoc class mechanism. These structs defined a set of keys that were required to exist in the map and could therefore not be removed via `dissoc`. With the advent of `defrecord`, the need for structs has been nearly eliminated, and therefore structs aren't covered in this book. But if you have a code base reliant on structs, then a record can replace them with minimal code changes, as highlighted here:

```
(defn change-age [p] (assoc p :age 286))

(defstruct person :fname :lname)
(change-age (struct person "Immanuel" "Kant"))
;=> {:fname "Immanuel", :lname "Kant", :age 286}

(defrecord Person [fname lname])
(change-age (Person. "Immanuel" "Kant"))
;=> #:user.Person{:fname "Immanuel", :lname "Kant", :age 286}
```

Note that the `change-age` function works with either structs or records—no change is required. Only the definition and the mechanism of instantiation need to be updated.

```
(read-string (pr-str {:val 5, :l nil, :r nil}))
;=> {:val 5, :l nil, :r nil}

(read-string (pr-str (TreeNode. 5 nil nil)))
; java.lang.RuntimeException: java.lang.Exception: No dispatch macro for:
```

This may change eventually, but there are some tricky problems yet to be worked out before records can be printed and read back in.

Other noteworthy differences between maps and records include

- Records, unlike maps, can't serve as functions.
- Records are never equal to maps with the same key/value mappings.

You still look up values in records by doing (:keyword obj); it's just that if obj is a record, this code will run dramatically faster. By the way, that means destructuring will still work as well. Records support metadata using with-meta and meta just like other Clojure collections, and you can even redefine a record if desired to have different fields giving you the compiled performance of Java dynamically. All of these together mean you can build a lot of code on top of simple hash-map objects and then make minimal changes to switch to using records instead, gaining all the performance benefits we already covered.

You should understand records well enough to be able to reimplement the persistent binary tree from chapter 5 using defrecord instead of maps. This is shown in the following listing. Note that we had to add the defrecord and change the expressions in xconj where objects are created, but the xseq function is defined identically to how it was before.

Listing 9.2 Persistent binary tree built of records

```
(defrecord TreeNode [val l r])                                  ⟵  Define record type

(defn xconj [t v]                          ⟵  Add to tree
  (cond
    (nil? t)        (TreeNode. v nil nil)
    (< v (:val t))  (TreeNode. (:val t) (xconj (:l t) v) (:r t))
    :else           (TreeNode. (:val t) (:l t) (xconj (:r t) v))))

(defn xseq [t]                                               ⟵ Convert trees
  (when t                                                      to seqs
    (concat (xseq (:l t)) [(:val t)] (xseq (:r t)))))

(def sample-tree (reduce xconj nil [3 5 2 4 6]))            ⟵  Try it all out
(xseq sample-tree)
;=> (2 3 4 5 6)
```

You can assoc and dissoc any key you want—adding keys that weren't defined in the defrecord works, though they have the performance of a regular map. Perhaps more surprisingly, dissocing a key given in the record works but returns a regular map rather than a record. In this example, note that the return value is printed as a plain map, not with the #:user.TreeNode prefix of a record:

```
(dissoc (TreeNodePlus 5 nil nil) :l)
;=> {:val 5, :r nil}
```

A final benefit of records is how well they integrate with Clojure protocols. But to fully understand how they relate, we must first explore what protocols are.

9.3.2 *Protocols*

> *The establishment of protocols ... creates an obvious way for two people who are not directly communicating to structure independently developed code so that it works in a manner that remains coherent when such code is later combined.*
>
> —Kent M. Pitman (Pitman 2001)

A *protocol* in Clojure is simply a set of function signatures, each with at least one parameter, that are given a collective name. They fulfill a role somewhat like Java interfaces or C++ pure virtual classes—a class that claims to implement a particular protocol should provide specialized implementations of each of the functions in that protocol. Then, when any of those functions is called, the appropriate implementation is polymorphic on the type of the first parameter, just like Java. In fact, the first parameter to a protocol function corresponds to the target object (the thing to the left of the dot for a method call used in Java source) of a method in object-oriented parlance.

For example, consider what collections such as stacks (First In, Last Out: FILO) and queues (First In, First Out: FIFO) have in common. Each has a simple function for inserting a thing (call it push), a simple function for removing a thing (pop), and usually a function to see what would be removed if you removed a thing (peek). What we just gave you was an informal description of a protocol; all that's missing is the name. We can replace the changing third item of the acronym with an *X* and call objects that provide these functions FIXO. Note that besides stacks and queues, FIXO could include priority queues, pipes, and other critters.

So now let's look at that informal description rewritten as a formal Clojure definition:

```
(defprotocol FIXO
  (fixo-push [fixo value])
  (fixo-pop [fixo])
  (fixo-peek [fixo]))
```

...and that's it. The only reason we prefixed the function names with *fixo-* is so that they don't conflict with Clojure's built-in functions.[4] Besides that, it's hard to imagine how there could be much less ceremony, isn't it?

But in order for a protocol to do any good, something must implement it. Protocols are implemented using one of the *extend* forms: extend, extend-type,[5] or extend-protocol. Each of these does essentially the same thing, but extend-type and

---

[4] It would be better to fix this problem by defining FIXO in a new namespace and excluding from it the similarly named clojure.core functions, except this would be a distraction from the point of this section. We'll discuss interesting interactions between namespaces and protocols later in this chapter.

[5] Records are a specialized kind of data type, so extend-type is used for both. We'll look at data types later in this section.

extend-protocol are convenience macros for when you want to provide multiple functions for a given type. For example, the binary TreeNode from listing 9.2 is a record, so if we want to extend it, extend-type would be most convenient. Because TreeNode already has a function xconj that works just like push should, we'll start by implementing that:

```
(extend-type TreeNode
  FIXO
  (fixo-push [node value]
    (xconj node value)))

(xseq (fixo-push sample-tree 5/2))
;=> (2 5/2 3 4 5 6)
```

The first argument to extend-type is the class or interface that the entire rest of the form will be extending. Following the type name are one or more blocks, each starting with the name of the protocol to be extended and followed by one or more functions from that protocol to implement. So in the preceding example, we're implementing a single function fixo-push for TreeNode objects, and we call the existing xconj function. Got it? The reason this is better than simply defining a regular function named fixo-push is that protocols allow for polymorphism. That same function can have a different implementation for a different kind of object. Clojure vectors can act like stacks by extending FIXO to vectors:

```
(extend-type clojure.lang.IPersistentVector
  FIXO
  (fixo-push [vector value]
    (conj vector value)))

(fixo-push [2 3 4 5 6] 5/2)
;=> [2 3 4 5 6 5/2]
```

Here we're extending FIXO to an interface instead of a concrete class. This means that fixo-push is now defined for all classes that inherit from IPersistentVector. Note that we can now call fixo-push with either a vector or a TreeNode, and the appropriate function implementation is invoked.

> ### Clojure-style mixins
> As you proceed through this section, you'll notice that we extend the FIXO protocol's fixo-push function in isolation. This works fine for our purposes, but you might want to take note of the implications of this approach. Consider the following:
>
> ```
> (use 'clojure.string)
>
> (defprotocol StringOps (rev [s]) (upp [s]))
>
> (extend-type String
>   StringOps
>   (rev [s] (clojure.string/reverse s)))
>
> (rev "Works")
> ;=> "skroW"
> ```

(continued)

Defining the `StringOps` protocol and extending its `rev` function to `String` seems to work fine. But observe what happens when the protocol is again extended to cover the remaining `upp` function:

```
(extend-type String
  StringOps
  (upp [s] (clojure.string/upper-case s)))

(upp "Works")
;=> "WORKS"

(rev "Works?")
; IllegalArgumentException No implementation of method: :rev
;    of protocol: #'user/StringOps found for
;       class: java.lang.String
```

The reason for this exception is that for a protocol to be fully populated (all of its functions callable), it must be extended fully, per individual type. Protocol extension is at the granularity of the entire protocol and not at a per-function basis. This behavior seems antithetical to the common notion of a *mixin*—granules of discrete functionality that can be "mixed into" existing classes, modules, and so on. Clojure too has mixins, but it takes a slightly different approach:

```
(def rev-mixin {:rev clojure.string/reverse})

(def upp-mixin {:upp (fn [this] (.toUpperCase this))})

(def fully-mixed (merge upp-mixin rev-mixin))

(extend String StringOps fully-mixed)

(-> "Works" upp rev)
;=> SKROW
```

Mixins in Clojure refer to the creation of discrete maps containing protocol function implementations that are combined in such a way as to create a complete implementation of a protocol. Once mixed together (as in the Var `fully-mixed`), only then are types extended to protocols. As with many of Clojure's features, mixins and protocol extension are fully open.

What we've just done is impossible with Java interfaces or C++ classes, at least in the order we did it. With either of those languages, the concrete type (such as `TreeNode` or vector) must name *at the time it's defined* all the interfaces or classes it's going to implement. Here we went the other way around—both `TreeNode` and vectors were defined before the `FIXO` protocol even existed, and we easily extended `FIXO` to each of them. This matters in the real world because the concrete types and even the protocol could be provided by third-party libraries—possibly even different third-party libraries—and we could still match them up, provide implementations for the appropriate functions, and get back to work. All this without any adapters, wrappers, monkey-patching, or other incidental complexity getting in the way. In fact, *Clojure polymorphism lives in the protocol functions, not in the classes,* as shown in figure 9.7.

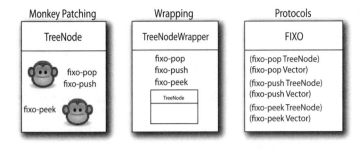

Figure 9.7   As opposed to the notion of monkey-patching and wrapping, the polymorphism in Clojure resides in the functions themselves and not in the classes worked with.

You can even extend a protocol to `nil` itself. You'd be forgiven for not immediately seeing why you'd want to do this; but consider how `TreeNode` implements `fixo-push`, and yet the `sample-tree` we're using was built using `xconj` instead. Trying to build up a tree the same way with `fixo-push` runs into a problem:

```
(reduce fixo-push nil [3 5 2 4 6 0])
; java.lang.IllegalArgumentException:
; No implementation of method: :fixo-push
;   of protocol: #'user/FIXO found for class: nil
```

The `xconj` implementation specifically handled the initial `nil` case, but because protocol methods dispatch on the first argument, we need special support from `extend` to get `fixo-push` to behave similarly. This is done by extending a protocol to the value `nil`, like this:

```
(extend-type nil
  FIXO
  (fixo-push [t v]
    (TreeNode. v nil nil)))

(xseq (reduce fixo-push nil [3 5 2 4 6 0]))
;=> (0 2 3 4 5 6)
```

All the options and arrangements of code allowed by `extend` can be disorienting, but one thing you can keep firmly in mind is that `extend` is always about a protocol. Each method listed in an `extend` form is implementing an intersection between a protocol and something else. That something else can be a concrete class, an interface, a record type, or even `nil`, but it's always being connected to a protocol.

See the following listing for complete implementations of `FIXO` for `TreeNode` and vectors. As mentioned in the sidebar, in order for the `FIXO` protocol to be fully realizable, each of its functions should be mixed in. But you might not always require that a protocol be fully realizable.

Listing 9.3   Complete implementations of `FIXO` for `TreeNode` and vector

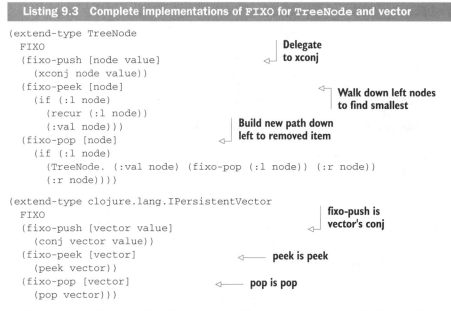

```
(extend-type TreeNode
  FIXO
  (fixo-push [node value]              Delegate
    (xconj node value))                to xconj
  (fixo-peek [node]                        Walk down left nodes
    (if (:l node)                          to find smallest
      (recur (:l node))
      (:val node)))                    Build new path down
  (fixo-pop [node]                     left to removed item
    (if (:l node)
      (TreeNode. (:val node) (fixo-pop (:l node)) (:r node))
      (:r node))))

(extend-type clojure.lang.IPersistentVector
  FIXO
  (fixo-push [vector value]            fixo-push is
    (conj vector value))               vector's conj
  (fixo-peek [vector]                   peek is peek
    (peek vector))
  (fixo-pop [vector]                    pop is pop
    (pop vector)))
```

If you've done six impossible things this morning, why not round it off with breakfast at Milliways, the Restaurant at the End of the Universe?

—Douglas Adams

Each of the function bodies in the previous example have either had no code in common with each other, or called out to another function such as xconj for implementation details that they have in common. These techniques work well when there's a low level of commonality between the methods being implemented, but sometimes you have many methods of a protocol or even whole protocol implementations that you want to extend to multiple classes. In these cases, some languages would encourage you to create a base class that implements some or all of the methods and then inherit from that. Clojure has a different approach.

SHARING METHOD IMPLEMENTATIONS

Clojure doesn't encourage implementation inheritance, so although it's possible to inherit from concrete classes as needed for Java interoperability,[6] there's no way to use extend to provide a concrete implementation and then build another class on top of that. There are important reasons why Clojure intentionally avoids this, but regardless of the reasons, we're left with the question of how best to avoid repeating code when similar objects implement the same protocol method.

The simplest solution is to write a regular function that builds on the protocol's methods. For example, Clojure's own into takes a collection and uses the conj implementation provided by the collection. We can write a similar function for FIXO objects like this:

---

[6] Mechanisms that support something like Java-style implementation inheritance include gen-class, proxy, and extending protocol methods to Java abstract classes and interfaces.

```
(defn fixo-into [c1 c2]
  (reduce fixo-push c1 c2))

(xseq (fixo-into (TreeNode. 5 nil nil) [2 4 6 7]))
;=> (2 4 5 6 7)

(seq (fixo-into [5] [2 4 6 7]))
;=> (5 2 4 6 7)
```

But this is only an option when your function can be defined entirely in terms of the protocol's methods. If this isn't the case, you may need the more nuanced solution provided by the `extend` function. We mentioned it earlier but so far have only given examples of a macro built on top of it, `extend-type`. Though this and `extend-protocol` are frequently the most convenient way to implement protocol methods, they don't provide a natural way to mix in method implementations. The `extend` function takes a map for each protocol you want to implement, and you can build that map however you'd like, including by merging in implementations that are already defined. In the following listing, you should note how a `FIXO` implementation could be defined early using a map and extended to a protocol/record type later (while still maintaining every benefit of using the original map).

Listing 9.4 Using a map to extend `FIXO` to `TreeNode`

```
(def tree-node-fixo                              ◁─┐ Define map of names
  {:fixo-push (fn [node value]                      │ to functions
                (xconj node value))
   :fixo-peek (fn [node]
                (if (:1 node)
                  (recur (:1 node))
                  (:val node)))
   :fixo-pop (fn [node]
               (if (:1 node)
                 (TreeNode. (:val node) (fixo-pop (:1 node)) (:r node))
                 (:r node)))})
                                                  │ Extend protocol
(extend TreeNode FIXO tree-node-fixo)             ◁─┘ using map

(xseq (fixo-into (TreeNode. 5 nil nil) [2 4 6 7]))
;=> (2 4 5 6 7)
```

These record objects and the way protocols can be extended to them result in rather differently shaped code than the objects built out of closures that we showed in section 7.2. Often this ability to define the data and implementation separately is desirable, but you're likely to find yourself occasionally in a circumstance where closures may feel like a better fit than records, and yet you want to extend a protocol or interface, not just provide ad hoc method names as in section 7.2.

REIFY

The `reify` macro brings together all the power of function closures and all the performance and protocol participation of `extend` into a single form. For example, say you want a stack-like `FIXO` that's constrained to a certain fixed size. Any attempt to push items onto one of these fixed-fixos when it's already full will fail, and an unchanged object will be returned. The wrinkle in the requirements that makes `reify` a reasonable option is that you'll want this size limit to be configurable. Thus you'll need a constructor or factory function, shown next, that takes the size limit and returns an object that will obey that limit.

Listing 9.5   Size-limited stack FIXO using `reify`

```
(defn fixed-fixo
  ([limit] (fixed-fixo limit []))
  ([limit vector]
    (reify FIXO
      (fixo-push [this value]
        (if (< (count vector) limit)
          (fixed-fixo limit (conj vector value))
          this))
      (fixo-peek [_]
        (peek vector))
      (fixo-pop [_]
        (pop vector)))))
```

Just like the `extend` forms, `reify` has method arglists that include the object itself. It's idiomatic to use name the argument `this` in methods where you need to use it and `_` in methods where you ignore its value. But both these conventions should only be followed where natural.

NAMESPACED METHODS

A rough analogy can be drawn between protocols and Java interfaces.[7] We've noted some of the differences already, but it can be a useful analogy nonetheless. In such a comparison, where record types are concrete classes, you might see that Java packages and C++ namespaces are each like Clojure namespaces. It's normal in all three of these environments for the interface and the class to each be in a namespace, and not necessarily the same one. For example, probably few readers were surprised to see that when we made the class `IPersistentVector` extend the protocol `user/FIXO`, they were each from a different namespace or package.

One way this analogy breaks down is that methods of the protocol itself are namespaced in a way that Java and C++ interfaces aren't. In those languages, all methods of a class share the same effective namespace, regardless of interfaces they're implementing. In Clojure, the methods always use the same namespace as the protocol itself, which means a record or type can extend (via `extend`, `extend-type`, and so on) identically named methods of two different protocols without any ambiguity. This is a subtle feature, but it allows you to avoid a whole category of issues that can come up when trying to combine third-party libraries into a single codebase.

Note that because the methods share the namespace of their protocol, you can't have identically named methods in two different protocols if those protocols are in the same namespace. Because both are under the control of the same person, it's easy

---

[7]   Those of you familiar with Haskell might recognize analogies to its typeclasses in our discussion.

to resolve this by moving one of the protocols to a different namespace or using more specific method names.

METHOD IMPLEMENTATIONS IN DEFRECORD

We've already shown how both protocols and interfaces can be extended to record types using the various extend forms, but there's another way to achieve similar results. Protocol and interface method implementations can be written directly inside a defrecord form, which ends up looking like the following.

Listing 9.6   Method implementations in `defrecord`

```
(defrecord TreeNode [val l r]
  FIXO                                          ◁┐ Implement FIXO
  (fixo-push [t v]                                │ methods inline
    (if (< v val)
      (TreeNode. val (fixo-push l v) r)
      (TreeNode. val l (fixo-push r v))))
  (fixo-peek [t]
    (if l
      (fixo-peek l)                             ◁┐ Call method instead
      val))                                      │ of using recur
  (fixo-pop [t]
    (if l
      (TreeNode. val (fixo-pop l) r)
      r)))

(def sample-tree2 (reduce fixo-push (TreeNode. 3 nil nil) [5 2 4 6]))
(xseq sample-tree2)
;=> (2 3 4 5 6)
```

This isn't only more convenient in many cases, but it can also produce dramatically faster code. Calling a protocol method like fixo-peek on a record type that implements it inline can be several times faster than calling the same method on an object that implements it via an extend form. Also note that the fields of the object are now available as locals—we use val instead of (:val t).

Polymorphism and recur

Throughout this section, we've implemented the fixo-peek function using different methodologies, but a more subtle difference is worth noting. The first implementation uses recur for its recursive call as shown:

```
(fixo-peek [node]
  (if (:l node)
    (recur (:l node))
    (:val node)))
```

Because of the nature of recur, the first implementation of fixo-peek isn't polymorphic on the recursive call. But the second version of fixo-peek uses a different approach:

(continued)

```
(fixo-peek [t]
  (if l
    (fixo-peek l)
    val))
```

You'll notice that the recursive call in the second implementation is direct (mundane) and as a result is polymorphic. In the course of writing your own programs, this difference will probably not cause issues, but it's worth storing in the back of your mind.

Putting method definitions inside the `defrecord` form also allows you to implement Java interfaces and extend `java.lang.Object`, which isn't possible using any `extend` form. Because interface methods can accept and return primitive values as well as boxed objects, implementations of these in `defrecord` can also support primitives. This is important for interoperability and can provide ultimate performance parity with Java code.

We do need to note one detail of these inline method definitions in relation to `recur`. Specifically, uses of `recur` in these definitions can't provide a new target object: the initial argument will get the same value as the initial (non-recur) call to the method. For example, `fixo-push` takes args `t` and `v`, so if it used `recur`, only a single parameter would be given: the new value for the `v` arg.

9.3.3 *Building from a more primitive base with deftype*

You may have noticed we've been using our own function `xseq` throughout the examples in this section, instead of Clojure's `seq`. This shouldn't be necessary, as Clojure provides an `ISeqable` interface that its `seq` function can use—all we need to do is to have our own type implement `ISeqable`. But an attempt to do this with `defrecord` is doomed:

```
(defrecord InfiniteConstant [i]
  clojure.lang.ISeq
  (seq [this]
    (lazy-seq (cons i (seq this)))))
; java.lang.ClassFormatError: Duplicate method
;    name&signature in class file user/InfiniteConstant
```

This is because record types are maps and implement everything maps should—`seq` along with `assoc`, `dissoc`, `get`, and so forth. Because these are provided for us, we can't implement them again ourselves, and thus the preceding exception. For the rare case where you're building your own data structure instead of just creating application-level record types, Clojure provides a lower-level `deftype` construct that's similar to `defrecord` but doesn't implement anything at all, so implementing `seq` won't conflict with anything:

```
(deftype InfiniteConstant [i]
  clojure.lang.ISeq
  (seq [this]
```

```
      (lazy-seq (cons i (seq this)))))
(take 3 (InfiniteConstant. 5))
;=> (5 5 5)
```

But that also means that keyword lookups, `assoc`, `dissoc`, and so on will remain unimplemented unless we implement them ourselves:

```
(:i (InfiniteConstant. 5))
;=> nil
```

The fields we declared are still public and accessible (although you should try to avoid naming them the same at the methods in `java.lang.Object`); they just require normal Java interop forms to get at them:

```
(.i (InfiniteConstant. 5))
;=> 5
```

With all that in mind, the following listing is a final implementation of `TreeNode` using `deftype`, which lets us implement not only `ISeq` so that we can use `seq` instead of `xseq`, but also `IPersistentStack` so we can use `peek`, `pop`, and `conj` as well as the `fixo-` versions.

Listing 9.7   Implementing map interfaces with `deftype`

```
(deftype TreeNode [val l r]
  FIXO                                        ◁─┐ Implement FIXO
  (fixo-push [_ v]                              │ methods inline
    (if (< v val)
      (TreeNode. val (fixo-push l v) r)
      (TreeNode. val l (fixo-push r v))))
  (fixo-peek [_]
    (if l
      (fixo-peek l)                           ◁─┐ Call method instead
      val))                                     │ of using recur
  (fixo-pop [_]
    (if l
      (TreeNode. val (fixo-pop l) r)
      r))

  clojure.lang.IPersistentStack               ◁──── Implement interfaces
  (cons [this v] (fixo-push this v))
  (peek [this] (fixo-peek this))
  (pop [this] (fixo-pop this))

  clojure.lang.Seqable
  (seq [t]
    (concat (seq l) [val] (seq r))))

(extend-type nil
  FIXO
  (fixo-push [t v]                              │ Redefine to use
    (TreeNode. v nil nil)))                   ◁─┘ new TreeNode

(def sample-tree2 (into (TreeNode. 3 nil nil) [5 2 4 6]))
(seq sample-tree2)
;=> (2 3 4 5 6)
```

One final note about `deftype`—it's the one mechanism by which Clojure lets you create classes with volatile and mutable fields. We won't go into it here because using such classes is almost never the right solution. Only when you've learned how Clojure approaches identity and state, how to use reference types, what it means for a field to be volatile, and all the pitfalls related to that, should you even consider creating classes with mutable fields. By then, you'll have no problem understanding the official docs for `deftype`, and you won't need any help from us.

None of the examples we've shown in this section come close to the flexibility of multimethods. All protocol methods dispatch on just the type of the first argument. This is because that's what Java is good at doing quickly, and in many cases it's all the polymorphism that's needed. Clojure once again takes the practical route and makes the highest-performance mechanisms available via protocols, while providing more dynamic behavior than Java does and leaving multimethods on the table for when ultimate flexibility is required.

9.4   *Putting it all together: a fluent builder for chess moves*

People have been known to say that Java is a verbose programming language. This may be true when compared to the Lisp family of languages, but considerable mind-share has been devoted to devising ways to mitigate its verbosity. One popular technique is known as the *fluent builder* (Fowler 2005) and can be summed up as the chaining of Java methods to form a more readable and agile instance construction technique. In this section, we'll show a simple example of a fluent builder supporting the construction of chess move descriptions. We'll then explain how such a technique is unnecessary within Clojure and instead present an alternative approach that's simpler, concise, and more extensible. We'll leverage Clojure's records in the final solution, illustrating that Java's class-based paradigm is counter to Clojure's basic principles and often overkill for Java programs.

9.4.1   *Java implementation*

We'll start by identifying all of the component parts of a `Move` class including from and to squares, a flag indicating whether the move is a castling move, and also the desired promotion piece if applicable. In order to constrain the discussion, we'll limit our idea of a `Move` to those elements listed. The next step would be to create a simple class with its properties and a set of constructors, each taking some combination of the expected properties. We'd then generate a set of accessors for the properties, but not their corresponding mutators, because it's probably best for the move instances to be immutable.

Having created this simple class and rolled it out to the customers of the chess move API, we begin to notice that our users are sending into the constructor the `to` string before the `from` string, which is sometimes placed after the `promotion`, and so on. After some months of intense design and weeks of development and testing, we release the following elided chess move class:

```
public class FluentMove {
    String from, to, promotion = "";
    boolean castlep;

    public static MoveBuilder desc() { return new MoveBuilder(); }

    public String toString() {
        return "Move " + from +
            " to " + to +
            (castlep ? " castle" : "") +
            (promotion.length() != 0 ? " promote to " + promotion : "");
    }

    public static final class MoveBuilder {
        FluentMove move = new FluentMove();

        public MoveBuilder from(String from) {
            move.from = from; return this;
        }

        public MoveBuilder to(String to) {
            move.to = to; return this;
        }

        public MoveBuilder castle() {
            move.castlep = true; return this;
        }

        public MoveBuilder promoteTo(String promotion) {
            move.promotion = promotion; return this;
        }

        public FluentMove build() { return move; }
    }
}
```

For brevity's sake, our code has a lot of holes, such as missing checks for fence post errors, null, empty strings, assertions, and invariants; it does allow us to illustrate that the code provides a fluent builder given the following main method:

```
public static void main(String[] args) {
    FluentMove move = FluentMove.desc()
        .from("e2")
        .to("e4").build();

    System.out.println(move);

    move = FluentMove.desc()
        .from("a1")
        .to("c1")
        .castle().build();

    System.out.println(move);

    move = FluentMove.desc()
        .from("a7")
        .to("a8")
        .promoteTo("Q").build();

    System.out.println(move);
}
```

```
//   Move e2 to e4
//   Move a1 to c1 castle
//   Move a7 to a8 promote to Q
```

The original constructor ambiguities have disappeared, with the only trade-off being a slight increase in complexity of the implementation and the breaking of the common Java getter/setter idioms—both of which we're willing to live with. But if we'd started the chess move API as a Clojure project, the code would likely be a very different experience for the end user.

9.4.2 *Clojure implementation*

In lieu of Java's class-based approach, Clojure provides a core set of collection types, and as you might guess, its map type is a nice candidate for move representation:

```
{:from "e7", :to "e8", :castle? false, :promotion \Q}
```

Simple, no?

In a language like Java, it's common to represent everything as a class—to do otherwise is either inefficient, non-idiomatic, or outright taboo. Clojure prefers simplification, providing a set of composite types perfect for representing most categories of problems typically handled by class hierarchies. Using Clojure's composite types makes sense for one simple reason: existing functions, built on a sequence abstraction, *just work*:

```
(defn build-move [& pieces]
  (apply hash-map pieces))

(build-move :from "e7" :to "e8" :promotion \Q)

;=> {:from "e7", :to "e8", :promotion \Q}
```

In two lines, we've effectively replaced the Java implementation with an analogous, yet more flexible representation. The term *domain-specific language (DSL)* is often thrown around to describe code such as build-move, but to Clojure (and Lisps in general) the line between DSL and API is blurred. In the original FluentMove class, we required a cornucopia of code in order to ensure the API was agnostic of the ordering of move elements; using a map, we get that for free. Additionally, FluentMove, though relatively concise, was still bound by fundamental Java syntactical and semantic constraints.

There's one major problem with our implementation—it doesn't totally replace the Java solution. If you recall, the Java solution utilized the toString method to print its representative form. The existence of a polymorphic print facility in Java is nice, and it allows a class creator to define a default print representation for an object when sent to any Java print stream. This means that the same representation is used on the console, in log files, and so on. Using raw maps can't give us this same behavior, so how can we solve this problem?

USING RECORDS

If we instead use a record, then the solution is as simple as that shown next.

Listing 9.8   A chess move record

```
(defrecord Move [from to castle? promotion]
  Object
  (toString [this]
    (str "Move " (:from this)
         " to " (:to this)
         (if (:castle? this) " castle"
           (if-let [p (:promotion this)]
             (str " promote to " p)
             ""))))))
```

As we mentioned in the previous section, within the body of a record we can take up to two actions: participate in a protocol, or override any of the methods in the java.lang.Object class. For the Move record, we override toString in order to allow it to participate in Java's overarching polymorphic print facility, as shown:

```
(str (Move. "e2" "e4" nil nil))
;=> "Move e2 to e4"

(.println System/out (Move. "e7" "e8" nil \Q))
; Move e7 to e8 promote to Q
```

We've once again gone back to positional construction using records, but as we'll show, Clojure even has an answer for this.

SEPARATION OF CONCERNS

Both FluentMove and build-move make enormous assumptions about the form of the data supplied to them and do no validation of the input. For FluentMove, object-oriented principles dictate that the validation of a well-formed move (not a legal move, mind you) should be determined by the class itself. There are a number of problems with this approach, the most obvious being that to determine whether a move is well-formed, the class needs information about the rules of chess. We can rewrite FluentMove to throw an exception to prevent illegal moves from being constructed, but the root problem still remains—FluentMove instances are too smart. Perhaps you don't see this as a problem, but if we were to extend our API to include other aspects of the game of chess, then we'll find that bits of overlapping chess knowledge would be scattered throughout the class hierarchy. By viewing the move structure as a value, Clojure code provides some freedom in the implementation of a total solution, as shown:

```
(defn build-move [& {:keys [from to castle? promotion]}]
  {:pre [from to]}
  (Move. from to castle? promotion))

(str (build-move :from "e2" :to "e4"))
;=> "Move e2 to e4"
```

By wrapping the `Move` constructor in a `build-move` function, we put the smarts of constructing moves there instead of in the type itself. In addition, using a precondition, we specified the required fields, and by using Clojure's named parameters and argument destructuring we've again ensured argument order independence. As a final added advantage, Clojure's records are maps and as a result can operate in almost every circumstance where a map would. As author Rich Hickey proclaimed, any new class in general is itself an island, unusable by *any* existing code written by anyone, anywhere. So our point is this: consider throwing the baby out with the bath water.

9.5   *Summary*

Clojure disavows the typical object-oriented model of development. But that's not to say that it completely dismisses all that OOP stands for. Instead, Clojure wholeheartedly touts the virtues of interface-oriented programming (or abstraction-oriented programming, as we've called it), in addition to runtime polymorphism. But in both cases, the way that Clojure presents these familiar topics is quite different from what you might be accustomed to. In almost every circumstance, Clojure's abstraction-oriented facilities will sufficiently represent your problem domain, but there may be times when they simply can't. We'll preach the virtues of abstractions more throughout the rest of the book, but for now we're compelled to take a side path into an explorations of Java interoperability.

Java.next

10

This chapter covers

- Generating objects on the fly with `proxy`
- Clojure `gen-class` and GUI programming
- Clojure's relationship to Java arrays
- All Clojure functions implement...
- Using Clojure data structures in Java APIs
- `definterface`
- Be wary of exceptions

Regardless of your views on the Java language itself, it's difficult to deny that the JVM is a stellar piece of software. The confluence of the just-in-time (JIT) compiler, garbage collection, HotSpot, and the flexible bytecode have created an environment that many programmers have chosen to grow their alternative programming languages. Additionally, the deluge of library options hosted on the JVM further make the JVM the language target of choice. From Clojure to Groovy to Scala to Fantom to Frink to Ioke to Jess to JRuby to Jython, there seems to be no lack of options for the enthusiastic polyglot programmer. We may soon see job listings for "JVM programmers." But where does that leave Java the programming language?

Java the language isn't dead.

The JVM is optimized for running Java bytecode, and only recently[1] have Java.next languages been a consideration. You may ask yourself whether JVM bytecode is equivalent to Java source code, and the answer is no. Instead, languages such as Clojure and Scala compile directly to bytecode and can access Java compiled libraries as needed. Because of their reliance on the JVM as the runtime environment, Clojure and the other Java.next languages will be fundamentally constrained by the limitations of the JVM itself. The limitations of the JVM as defined by the limitations of the Java language specification set the beat by which the Java.next languages dance. Java isn't dead; it's alive and well, and it runs the show.

> **THE JAVA.NEXT MANTRA** The apprentice avoids all use of Java classes. The journeyman embraces Java classes. The master knows which classes to embrace and which to avoid.

An expert understanding of the Java Virtual Machine isn't required for writing powerful applications in Clojure, but it'll help when issues stemming from host limitations arise. Thankfully, Clojure does a good job of mitigating many of the limitations inherent in its host, but some are too deeply embedded in the fibers of the JVM to avoid. Clojure provides a specific set of interoperability tools: gen-class, proxy, definterface, its exceptions facility, and a host of array functions. We'll touch on each of these in turn, but we'll begin with the creation of anonymous objects using proxy.

10.1   *Generating objects on the fly with proxy*

There's a saying within the Clojure community stating (Halloway 2009) that Clojure does Java better than Java. This is a bold statement, but not one without merit, as we'll show throughout this chapter. Java programmers are accustomed to drawing a severe distinction between development time and runtime. Using Clojure's proxy feature allows you to blur this distinction.

> **CLOJURE APHORISM**   Many software projects require a lot of planning because their implementation languages don't foster change. Clojure makes it a lot easier to plan for change.

Clojure's proxy mechanism is meant strictly for interoperability purposes. In section 9.3, we discussed how reify was intended to realize a single instance of a type, protocol, or interface—in other words, abstractions. But when dealing with Java libraries, you're at times required to extend *concrete classes*, and it's in this circumstance where proxy shines. Be aware that by using proxy, you bring a lot of Java's semantics into your Clojure programs. Though extending concrete classes is seen often in Java, doing so in Clojure is considered poor design, leading to fragility, and should therefore be restricted to those instances where interoperability demands it.

---

[1] More details can be found in JSR-000292, "Supporting Dynamically Typed Languages on the Java Platform."

10.1.1 A simple dynamic web service

Using Clojure breaks the ponderous code/compile/run development cycle by adding an element of dynamism into the fold. Take for example a scenario where we want to develop a web service using an existing Java 1.5 API.

Listing 10.1 A simple dynamic web service

```
(ns joy.web
  (:import (com.sun.net.httpserver HttpHandler HttpExchange HttpServer)
           (java.net InetSocketAddress HttpURLConnection)
           (java.io IOException FilterOutputStream)
           (java.util Arrays)))

(defn new-server [port path handler]                    ⟵── Create service
  (doto (HttpServer/create (InetSocketAddress. port) 0)
    (.createContext path handler)
    (.setExecutor nil)
    (.start)))

(defn default-handler [txt]                             ⟵── Print hello message
  (proxy [HttpHandler] []
    (handle [exchange]
      (.sendResponseHeaders exchange HttpURLConnection/HTTP_OK 0)
      (doto (.getResponseBody exchange)
        (.write (.getBytes txt))                        ⟵── Close over txt
        (.close)))))

(def server (new-server 8123
                        "/joy/hello"
                        (default-handler "Hello Cleveland")))
```

After entering the code in listing 10.1, you should see the message "Hello Cleveland" in your web browser at address http://localhost:8123/joy/hello. This is only marginally interesting, especially because the source is organized in a way that doesn't take advantage of Clojure's flexibility.

If we instead organize the code to bind the return of default-handler, we can manipulate the handler independently and update its behavior at runtime, as shown:

```
(.stop server 0)

(def p (default-handler
         "There's no problem that can't be solved
          with another level of indirection"))

(def server (new-server 8123 "/joy/hello" p))
```

At this point, visiting the aforementioned URL will show the new message, making this simple server more compelling. But we can take it one step further by making changes without taking the server instance down in such a clumsy fashion. Ideally, we'd like to be able to call a function to change the message at any time:

```
(change-message p "Our new message")
```

The implementation of change-message is given in the following listing.

Listing 10.2   Convenience functions for changing the web service message

```
(defn make-handler-fn [fltr txt]
  (fn [this exchange]                              ◁——— Name explicit this
    (let [b (.getBytes txt)]
      (-> exchange
          .getResponseHeaders
          (.set "Content-Type" "text/html"))
      (.sendResponseHeaders exchange
                            HttpURLConnection/HTTP_OK
                            0)
      (doto (fltr (.getResponseBody exchange))     ◁——— Pass through filter
        (.write b)
        (.close)))))))

(defn change-message
  "Convenience method to change a proxy's output message"
  ([p txt] (change-message p identity txt))        ◁——— Use identity filter
  ([p fltr txt]
    (update-proxy p
      {"handle" (make-handler-fn fltr txt)}))))
```

We've added a few extras to the implementation that will be useful later, but for now concentrate on the fact that change-message calls the function update-proxy with the proxy object p and a map containing an anonymous function keyed on a string referencing a method name to override. The anonymous function looks similar to the handle method defined in the returned proxy from the original default-handler function, with some extras added for flexibility's sake. You can test this by entering the following function call:

```
(change-message p "Hello Dynamic!")
```

Refreshing your browser will reflect the change made by displaying the string "Hello Dynamic!". If so inclined, you can also inspect the current proxy mappings using the function proxy-mappings. The question remains—how does update-proxy change the behavior of a previously generated proxy class?

IT'S CALLED PROXY FOR A REASON

As we mentioned, the proxy function generates the bytecode for an actual class on demand, but it does so in such a way to provide a more dynamic implementation. Instead of inserting the bytecode for the given function bodies directly into the proxy class, Clojure instead generates a proper proxy in which each method looks up the function implementing a method in a map. This trades highly useful dynamic behavior for some runtime cost, but in many cases this is a fair trade.

Based on the method name, the corresponding function is retrieved from a map and invoked with the this reference and the argument(s).

PROXIES FOR TRUE POWER DYNAMISM

Working from the abstract model in figure 10.1, observe how Clojure updates the mapped functions within a proxy at runtime. This web service is a humble example, but there's a point to take away from this exercise: to perform this same task in Java isn't impossible but would require an enormous amount of scaffolding to implement properly, whereas in Clojure it's built into the language.

PROXIES AS PROPER CITIZENS

In the original `change-message` function, we provided a hook named `fltr` that took the result of the call to the `.getResponseBody` method. Because the result of this method call is a `java.io. OutputStream`, we can use that information to our advantage when creating a filtering function. The use of the `identity` function as the default filter ensures that the usage doesn't break in the default case; but if we're to utilize our own filtering function, we must ensure that we properly wrap the original, which again is a perfect use case for `proxy`. A simple implementation of a `screaming-filter` would be implemented as such:

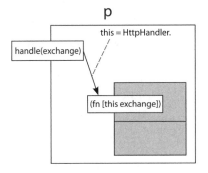

Figure 10.1   Proxy lookup: the instance returned by `proxy` is a proper proxy that does method dispatch to functions in a lookup table. These functions can therefore be swapped out with replacements as needed.

```
(defn screaming-filter [o]
  (proxy [FilterOutputStream] [o]
    (write [b]
      (proxy-super write (.getBytes (str "<strong>"
                                    (.toUpperCase (String. b))
                                    "</strong>")))))))
```

The proxy returned by `screaming-filter` extends the Java class `java.io.Filter-OutputStream` to the superclass constructor (via the `[o]` vector). It passes the argument `o`, which corresponds to the `OutputStream` obtained from the `.getResponseBody` method.

> **ANAPHORIC PROXY**   In section 8.5, we mentioned that it's non-idiomatic to write anaphoric macros, yet you might've noticed that `proxy` is a contradiction of that statement. The use of the anaphora `this` is subject to the same nesting limitations as previously mentioned and is a good candidate for change in later versions of Clojure. You might notice that the `reify` macro, though similar to `proxy`, doesn't use an anaphoric `this` but instead requires that it be named explicitly—the preferred approach for your own, and likely the way forward for all future Clojure core macros.

The call to the `proxy-super` function is similar to Java's `super.method()` semantics. If we now execute the call to `change-message` passing in `screaming-filter`, we'll see the expected filtered message in all caps and bold on a browser refresh:

```
(change-message p screaming-filter "whisper")
```

Note that in a break from almost every other construct in Clojure, `proxy-super` is *not* thread-safe. If some other thread were to call this proxy instance's `write` method while `proxy-super` was still running, the base class's method would be called directly, incorrectly skipping the proxy implementation. So be careful using `proxy-super` and multiple threads in close proximity to each other.

FINAL POINTS ABOUT PROXY

Clojure's proxy capabilities are truly dynamic, allowing you to create fully stubbed proxies using either `construct-proxy`, `get-proxy-class`, or `init-proxy`. In both cases, a partially to fully realized proxy will be constructed, allowing programmatic customization using `update-proxy` and arbitrary mixin maps.

There's a universe of difference between the code outlined in this subsection and systems employing true code hot-loading, but it's a reasonable facsimile. Using `proxy` is powerful, but doing so creates unnamed instances unavailable for later extension. If you instead wish to create named classes then you'll need to use Clojure's `gen-class` mechanism, which we'll discuss next.

10.2   *Clojure gen-class and GUI programming*

In section 9.1, we mentioned that Clojure namespaces can be used as the basis for generating a named class. In this section, we'll address this topic and others related to Clojure's `gen-class` function and `:gen-class` namespace directive in the context of writing a simple graphical user interface (GUI) library.

10.2.1   *Namespaces as class specifications*

Similarly to the `ns` example in section 9.1, the explanation of `gen-class` begs a declarative approach for a namespace defining a class named `joy.gui.DynaFrame`. We'd like this class to extend `javax.swing.JFrame` and declare the Vars providing its overriding method implementations to be prefixed[2] by the symbol `df-`. In addition, we'd like the class to implement the `clojure.lang.IMeta` interface. We'd also like a place to store information about instances of this class in `state` and would like the initialization function called on construction to be named `df-init`. We'd like to define a single constructor, taking a string and passing it onto the superclass constructor also taking a string. We then want to declare two public methods: the first named `display` taking a `java.awt.Container` and returning `void`, and the second static method `version` taking no arguments and returning a string. Finally, we'll declare the required imports needed.

The worded `DynaFrame` class declaration is complex but has the advantage of having a direct code translation, as shown next.

Listing 10.3   The `DynaFrame` class namespace declaration

```
(ns joy.gui.DynaFrame
  (:gen-class
    :name        joy.gui.DynaFrame
    :extends     javax.swing.JFrame        ◁─── Superclass
    :implements  [clojure.lang.IMeta]              ◁┄┄┄┄ Interface
    :prefix      df-
```

---

[2]   If you don't specify a `:prefix`, then the default `-` will be used.

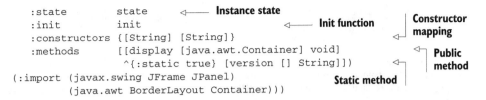

```
    :state          state         <——— Instance state
    :init           init                    <——— Init function
    :constructors {[String] [String]}
    :methods        [[display [java.awt.Container] void]
                     ^{:static true} [version [] String]])
  (:import (javax.swing JFrame JPanel)
           (java.awt BorderLayout Container)))
```

You can compile this namespace by saving it in a directory joy/gui, located on the classpath, in a file named DynaFrame.clj and executing the function (compile 'joy.gui.DynaFrame) in a fresh REPL. This allows a compiled class to be immediately available. But trying to create an instance in the same REPL will prove fruitless:

```
(joy.gui.DynaFrame. "1st")

; java.lang.UnsupportedOperationException:
;   joy.gui.DynaFrame/df-init not defined
```

Clearly we haven't defined the df-init function, so we'll do that now by switching to the joy.gui.DynaFrame namespace, defining it outright:

```
(in-ns 'joy.gui.DynaFrame)

(defn df-init [title]
  [[title] (atom {::title title})])
```

Now run the following in your REPL:

```
(joy.gui.DynaFrame. "2nd")

; java.lang.UnsupportedOperationException:
;   meta (joy.gui.DynaFrame/df-meta not defined?)
```

Because we told the Clojure compiler that the class should implement the IMeta interface, we should've provided a concrete implementation, which you can do at the REPL:

```
(defn df-meta [this] @(.state this))
(defn version [] "1.0")
```

As an added bonus, we implemented the static method version. To see the effects of these functions, execute the following:

```
(meta (joy.gui.DynaFrame. "3rd"))
;=> {:joy.gui.DynaFrame/title "3rd"}

(joy.gui.DynaFrame/version)
;=> "1.0"
```

We've filled in most of the implementation of the DynaFrame class except for the display function, which you can implement as follows:

```
(defn df-display [this pane]
  (doto this
    (-> .getContentPane .removeAll)
    (.setContentPane (doto (JPanel.)
                       (.add pane BorderLayout/CENTER)))
    (.pack)
    (.setVisible true)))
```

Figure 10.2 A simple use of `DynaFrame`: now that you've compiled the `DynaFrame` class, you can start using it to display simple GUIs.

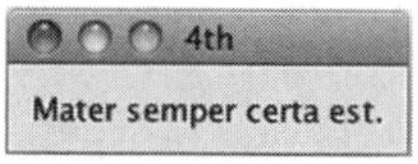

Figure 10.3 A simple dynamic update of `DynaFrame`: we can update the `DynaFrame` on the fly without restarting.

You can see `df-display` in action within the REPL by running the following:

```
(def gui (joy.gui.DynaFrame. "4th"))

(.display gui (doto (javax.swing.JPanel.)
                 (.add (javax.swing.JLabel. "Charlemagne and Pippin"))))
```

This will now display the GUI frame seen in figure 10.2.

And because it's a `DynaFrame` we should be able to change it on the fly, right? Right:

```
(.display gui (doto (javax.swing.JPanel.)
                 (.add (javax.swing.JLabel. "Mater semper certa est." ))))
```

This will change the view to that in figure 10.3.

But now that you have this interesting little frame, what can you do with it? Next, we'll experiment with `DynaFrame` as the foundation for agile GUI prototyping.

THE GUTS OF NAMESPACE COMPILATION

So what exactly does the `:gen-class` directive provide in terms of generated class files? With or without `:gen-class`, Clojure will generate a set of classes corresponding to each function in a namespace. For the function `joy.gui.DynaFrame/df-display`, a class file will be generated on the classpath of `joy.gui.DynaFrame$df_display` containing (at least) a method `invoke`, at the location CLASSPATH/joy/gui/DynaFrame$df_display.class, as shown:

```
package joy.gui;
public class DynaFrame$df_display extends AFunction {
    . . .
    public Object invoke(Object that, Object container) {
        . . . display actions . . .
    }
}
```

Of course, this describes implementation details and shouldn't be considered fact in future version of Clojure. In fact, as shown before, you were able to add implementations for the parts of the `DynaFrame` class at the REPL because Clojure generates a stub that looks up concrete implementations through Vars. But these details are useful for describing the logical product of `:gen-class` and `compile`. The `:gen-class` directive with the argument `:name joy.gui.DynaFrame` creates a class vaguely resembling the following Java source:

```
package joy.gui;

public class DynaFrame extends javax.swing.JFrame {
    public final Object state;
```

```
public DynaFrame(String title) {
    Object r = clojure.lang.RT.var("joy.gui.DynaFrame", "df-init")
                    .invoke(title);
    Object cargs = clojure.lang.RT.nth(r, 0);
    state = clojure.lang.RT.nth(r, 1);
    super((String) clojure.lang.RT.nth(cargs, 0));
}

public static String version() { return "1.0"; }

// Delegate to the display function var
public void display(Object the_this, java.awt.Container c) {
    return clojure.lang.RT.var("joy.gui.DynaFrame", "df-display")
            .invoke(the_this, c);
}

  . . .

}
```

The :gen-class directive creates a class that's a delegate for the Vars (prefixed as specified with df-) located in the corresponding namespace, contains the state, and also holds any static methods. This is a lot of detail to contend with, but understanding it's important when arranging your Clojure projects to take advantage of code compilation.

One final important point when using gen-class is the semantics surrounding the :impl-ns directive. Our example relies on the fact that the gen-class namespace is the same as the implementation namespace (the :impl-ns), meaning that the compilation will transitively compile all of the implementation functions. On the other hand, when your implementation and gen-class namespaces are distinct, you no longer suffer transitive compilation. This provides the benefit of allowing a mixture of compiled (class files) and uncompiled (.clj files) Clojure products.

10.2.2 *Exploring user interface design and development with Clojure*

Before we begin, we'll devise a simple model (_why 2007[3]) for exploring user interface design. We don't have to complicate matters, because the goal is only to get a general idea of how Clojure makes a typically painful task like Java GUI development a joy. To achieve this modest goal, we'll need some simple containers illustrated in figure 10.4: shelves, stacks, and splitters.

Because DynaFrame requires a java.awt. Container as its displayed element, we'll make each container a derivative thereof. This allows the containers to nest, helping to build richer GUIs. Finally, their forms should mirror their graphical layout, within reason. These three containers are implemented in the following listing.

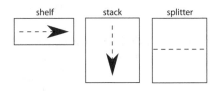

Figure 10.4   Basic GUI containers: using only a handful of rudimentary containers, we can build neato GUI prototypes.

---

[3]   Our GUI model in this section is based loosely on the Ruby framework Shoes created by _why. Thank you sir, wherever you are.

Listing 10.4 Simple GUI containers

```
(ns joy.gui.socks
  (:import
    (joy.gui DynaFrame)
    (javax.swing Box BoxLayout JTextField JPanel
                 JSplitPane JLabel JButton
                 JOptionPane)
    (java.awt BorderLayout Component GridLayout FlowLayout)
    (java.awt.event ActionListener)))

(defn shelf [& components]
  (let [shelf (JPanel.)]
    (.setLayout shelf (FlowLayout.))
    (doseq [c components] (.add shelf c))
    shelf))

(defn stack [& components]
  (let [stack (Box. BoxLayout/PAGE_AXIS)]
    (doseq [c components]
      (.setAlignmentX c Component/CENTER_ALIGNMENT)
      (.add stack c))
    stack))

 (defn splitter [top bottom]
   (doto (JSplitPane.)
     (.setOrientation JSplitPane/VERTICAL_SPLIT)
     (.setLeftComponent top)
     (.setRightComponent bottom)))
```

These simple GUI elements are built on top of the Java Swing library, where each sub-widget in the components argument is added to the properly configured Container-derived parent. These are good as a starting point, but still there's nothing to display unless we dive into the Swing API directly. We can do one better than that by providing a simple base set of widgets: buttons, labels, and text boxes.

Listing 10.5 A set of simple widgets

```
(defn button [text f]
  (doto (JButton. text)
    (.addActionListener
      (proxy [ActionListener] []
        (actionPerformed [_] (f))))))

(defn txt [cols t]
  (doto (JTextField.)
    (.setColumns cols)
    (.setText t)))

(defn label [txt] (JLabel. txt))
```

The button element takes a function executed on a mouse-click, so we'll now provide a JavaScript-like alert function as a simple action:

```
(defn alert
  ([msg] (alert nil msg))
  ([frame msg]
    (javax.swing.JOptionPane/showMessageDialog frame msg)))
```

Figure 10.5 `DynaFrame` alerts: we can create slightly more complex GUIs and attach actions on the fly.

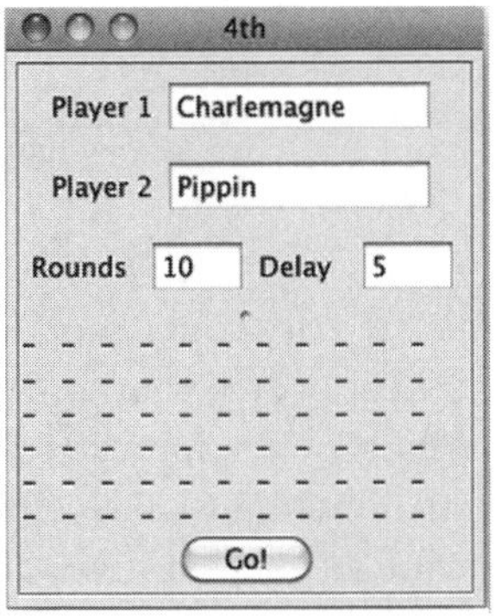

Figure 10.6 A much more elaborate `DynaFrame` GUI: there's no limit to the complexity of this simple GUI model. Go ahead and experiment to your heart's content.

Having built all of these GUI elements, we'll describe the first simple GUI as shown in figure 10.5.

It seems simple, if not pointless. But you might be pleasantly surprised with the concise code used to describe it:

```
(.display gui
  (splitter
    (button "Procrastinate" #(alert "Eat Cheetos"))genclass
    (button "Move It" #(alert "Couch to 5k"))))
```

These widgets are adequate enough to create richer user interfaces, and to illustrate we'll add one more widget builder for grid-like elements:

```
(defn grid [x y f]
  (let [g (doto (JPanel.)
            (.setLayout (GridLayout. x y)))]
    (dotimes [i x]
      (dotimes [j y]
        (.add g (f))))
    g))
```

With a small amount of code, we can build the richer user interface in figure 10.6.

Listing 10.6 A more complex GUI example

```
(.display gui
  (let [g1 (txt 10 "Charlemagne")
        g2 (txt 10 "Pippin")
        r  (txt 3 "10")
        d  (txt 3 "5")]
    (splitter
      (stack
        (shelf (label "Player 1") g1)
        (shelf (label "Player 2") g2)
        (shelf (label "Rounds ") r
               (label "Delay  ") d))
```

```
(stack
  (grid 21 11 #(label "-"))
  (button "Go!" #(alert (str (.getText g1) " vs. "
                             (.getText g2) " for "
                             (.getText r)  " rounds, every "
                             (.getText d)  " seconds.")))))))))
```

Though not perfect, it gives you a good idea how to extend these functions to provide a finer level of control over layout and positioning, as well as ways to provide more functionality to create richer interfaces. How would you go about creating an agile environment for incremental GUI development using plain Java? Clojure allows you to start with a powerful set of primitives and incrementally refine them until they suit your exact needs.

Though this section started as a description of creating a simple dynamic frame using the gen-class facility, we felt it was worthwhile to expand into the realm of dynamic, incremental development. There are times when AOT compilation is absolutely necessary (such as client requirements), but our advice is to avoid it if at all possible. Instead, leverage the dynamic nature of Clojure to its fullest, designing your system to fit into that model.

10.3 Clojure's relationship to Java arrays

In general, the need to delve into arrays should be limited, but such casual dismissal isn't always apropos. In this section, we'll cover some of the uses for Java arrays in Clojure, including but not limited to arrays as multimethod dispatch, primitive versus reference arrays, calling variadic functions and constructors, and multi-dimensional arrays.

10.3.1 Types of arrays: primitive and reference

As mentioned in section 4.1, Clojure numbers are of the boxed variety, but in many cases the Clojure compiler can resolve the correct call for primitive interoperability calls. But it can never resolve the need to pass a primitive array when a reference array is provided instead.

CREATING PRIMITIVE ARRAYS

The Java class java.lang.StringBuilder provides[4] a method .append(char[]) that appends the primitive chars in the passed array to its end. But our first instinct for making this happen in Clojure won't bear fruit:

```
(doto (StringBuilder. "abc")
  (.append (into-array [\x \y \z])))

;=> #<StringBuilder abc[Ljava.lang.Character;@65efb4be>
```

The problem lies in that Clojure's into-array function doesn't return a primitive array of char[], but instead a reference array of Character[], forcing the Clojure

---

[4] When dealing with and manipulating strings, your best options can almost always be found in the core clojure.string namespace or the clojure.contrib.string namespace in the Clojure contrib library.

compiler to resolve the call as to the `StringBuilder.append(Object)` method instead. That the `Array` class is a subclass of `Object` is a constant cause for headache in Java and clearly can be a problem[5] for Clojure as well. What we really want to do is ensure that a primitive array is used as the argument to `.append`, which we do here:

```
(doto (StringBuilder. "abc")
  (.append (char-array [\x \y \z])))

;=> #<StringBuilder abcxyz>
```

Clojure provides a number of primitive array-building functions that work similarly to `char-array`, as summarized in the following list.

- `boolean-array`
- `byte-array`
- `char-array`
- `double-array`
- `float-array`
- `int-array`
- `long-array`
- `object-array`
- `short-array`

You could also use the `make-array` and `into-array` functions to create primitive arrays:

```
(let [ary (make-array Integer/TYPE 3 3)]
  (dotimes [i 3]
    (dotimes [j 3]
      (aset ary i j (+ i j))))
  (map seq ary))

;=> ((0 1 2) (1 2 3) (2 3 4))

(into-array Integer/TYPE [1 2 3])
;=> #<int[] [I@391be9d4>
```

Populating arrays can often be an iterative affair, as seen in the previous snippet, but there are often more concise ways to do so when creating reference arrays.

CREATING REFERENCE ARRAYS

To intentionally create an array of a particular reference type, or of compatible types, use the `into-array` function, passing in a sequence of objects:

```
(into-array ["a" "b" "c"])
;=> #<String[] [Ljava.lang.String;@3c3ac93e>

(into-array [(java.util.Date.) (java.sql.Time. 0)])
;=> #<Date[] [Ljava.util.Date;@178aab40>

(into-array ["a" "b" 1M])
; java.lang.IllegalArgumentException: array element type mismatch

(into-array Number [1 2.0 3M 4/5])
;=> #<Number[] [Ljava.lang.Number;@140b6e46>
```

The function `into-array` determines the type of the resulting array based on the first element of the sequence, and each subsequent element type *must* be compatible (a

---

[5] In this example, it's preferred that a "java.lang.IllegalArgumentException: No matching method found" exception be thrown, because StringBuilder doesn't have a method matching `.append(Character[])` or even `.append(Object[])`.

subclass). To create a heterogeneous array of java.lang.Object, use the to-array or to-array-2d function:

```
(to-array-2d [[1 2 3]
              [4 5 6]])
;=> #<Object[][] [[Ljava.lang.Object;@bdccedd>

(to-array ["a" 1M #(%) (proxy [Object] [])])
;=> #<Object[] [Ljava.lang.Object;@18987a33>

(to-array [1 (int 2)])
;=> #<Object[] [Ljava.lang.Object;@6ad3c65d>
```

Be wary: primitives will be autoboxed when using either to-array or to-array-2d.

10.3.2 *Array mutability*

Because JVM arrays are mutable, you need to be aware that their contents can change at any point. For example:

```
(def ary  (into-array [1 2 3]))
(def sary (seq ary))
sary
;=> (1 2 3)
```

What happens to sary if we change the contents of ary?

```
(aset ary 0 42)
sary
;=> (42 2 3)
```

The seq view of an array is that of the live array and therefore subject to concurrent modification. Be cautious when sharing arrays from one function to the next, and especially across threads. Note that this can be especially disastrous should an array change in the middle of a sequential operation, such as the use of the higher-order array functions amap and areduce, as might be used to define a sum-of-squares function[6] for arrays:

```
(defn asum-sq [xs]
  (let [dbl (amap xs i ret
               (* (aget xs i)
                  (aget xs i)))]
    (areduce dbl i ret 0
      (+ ret (aget dbl i)))))

(asum-sq (float-array [1 2 3 4 5]))
;=> 55.0
```

At any point during the processing of asum-sq, the underlying array could change, causing inaccurate results or worse. You should take great care when using Java's mutable arrays, though sharing only the seq of an array is perfectly safe because there's no way to get at the array when you only have a reference to the seq.

---

[6] This function is fairly clear but slower than it should be. We'll make it faster in sections 12.1 and 12.5.

10.3.3 *That unfortunate naming convention*

You might've noticed (how could you miss?) the ugly names printed by the Clojure REPL whenever an array is evaluated. There's logic to this madness, as part of the jumble is the legal name of the class corresponding to the array—the part formed as [Ljava.lang.String;. For example, the previous name corresponded to a 1D array of strings. The representation for a 2D array of strings is then [[Ljava.lang.String;, and it therefore follows that [[[Ljava.lang.String; is a 3D array of strings. Are you sensing a pattern here? Table 10.1 lays it out.

Using what you know about arrays, the class representation names can be used to do things such as multimethod dispatch:

```
(what-is (into-array ["a" "b"]))
;=> "1d String"

(what-is (to-array-2d [[1 2][3 4]]))
;=> "2d Object"

(what-is (make-array Integer/TYPE 2 2 2 2))
;=> "Primitive 4d int"
```

You can create methods for identifying arrays and returning a descriptive string using the <indexterm><primary>java.lang.Class/forName</primary></indexterm>Class/forName method as shown:

```
(defmulti what-is class)
(defmethod what-is (Class/forName "[Ljava.lang.String;") [a] "1d String")
(defmethod what-is (Class/forName "[[Ljava.lang.Object;") [a] "2d Object")
(defmethod what-is (Class/forName "[[[[I") [a] "Primitive 4d int")
```

Though not the most beautiful task to perform in Clojure, it's easy to understand once you've grasped how the array class names are constructed.

Representation	Array type
[Ljava.lang.Object;	Reference array
[B	Primitive byte array
[I	Primitive int array
[C	Primitive char array
[S	Primitive short array
[F	Primitive float array
[D	Primitive double array
[J	Primitive long array
[Z	Primitive boolean array
Representation	**Dimension**
[	1D
[[	2D
...	and so on...

Table 10.1 Array type class names and dimensions

10.3.4 *Multidimensional arrays*

Observe what happens when the following call is tried:

```
(what-is (into-array [[1.0] [2.0]]))
; java.lang.IllegalArgumentException: No method in multimethod
;  'what-is' for dispatch value: class [Lclojure.lang.PersistentVector;
```

The problem is that the into-array function builds a 1D array of persistent vectors, but we wanted a 2D array of doubles. In order to do this, the array would have to be built differently:

```
(defmethod what-is (Class/forName "[[D") [a] "Primitive 2d double")
(defmethod what-is (Class/forName "[Lclojure.lang.PersistentVector;") [a]
  "1d Persistent Vector")

(what-is (into-array (map double-array [[1.0] [2.0]])))
;=> "Primitive 2d double"

(what-is (into-array [[1.0] [2.0]]))
;=> "1d Persistent Vector"
```

We had to use the map function with double-array on the inner arrays in order to build the properly typed outer array. When working with multidimensional arrays, be sure that you know what your inner elements should be on creation and create them accordingly.

10.3.5 *Variadic method/constructor calls*

There's no such thing as a variadic constructor or method at the bytecode level, although Java provides syntactic sugar at the language level. Instead, variadic methods expect an array as their final argument, and this is how they should be accessed in Clojure interop scenarios. Take, for example, the call to the String/format function:

```
(String/format "An int %d and a String %s" (to-array [99, "luftballons"]))
;=> "An int 99 and a String luftballons"
```

That covers most of the high points regarding arrays in Clojure interoperability. We'll touch on them briefly when we talk about performance considerations in chapter 12, but for now we'll move on to a more interesting topic: the interoperability underpinnings relating to Clojure's implementation.

10.4 *All Clojure functions implement...*

Clojure functions are highly amenable to interoperability. Their underlying classes implement a number of useful interfaces that you can investigate by running (ancestors (class #())). Most of the resulting classes are only applicable to the internals of Clojure itself, but a few interfaces are useful in interop scenarios: java.util.concurrent.Callable, java.util.Comparator, and java.lang.Runnable. In this section, we'll talk briefly about each and also provide simple examples.

10.4.1 *java.util.Comparator*

Simply put, the `java.util.Comparator` interface defines the signature for a single method `.compare` that takes two objects `l` and `r` and returns -1 if `l < r`, 0 if `l == r`, and `> 0` if `l > r`. The static Java method `Collections/sort` provides an implementation that takes a derivative of `java.util.List` and a `Comparator` and destructively sorts the list provided. Using this knowledge, we can provide some basic infrastructure for the remainder of this subsection:

```
(import '[java.util Comparator Collections ArrayList])

(defn gimme [] (ArrayList. [1 3 4 8 2]))

(doto (gimme)
  (Collections/sort (Collections/reverseOrder)))
;=> #<ArrayList [8, 4, 3, 2, 1]>
```

In order to write a simple comparator that provides a reverse-sort `Comparator`, we might naively do so:

```
(doto (gimme)
  (Collections/sort
    (reify Comparator
      (compare [this l r]
        (cond
          (> l r) -1
          (= l r) 0
          :else 1)))))
;=> #<ArrayList [8, 4, 3, 2, 1]>
```

Though this works, Clojure provides a better way by allowing the use of a function as the `Comparator` directly. You can couple this knowledge with the fact that Clojure already provides numerous functions useful for comparison, as shown next.

Listing 10.7 Useful comparison functions

```
(doto (gimme) (Collections/sort #(compare %2 %1)))      ◁——— compare function
;=> #<ArrayList [8, 4, 3, 2, 1]>

(doto (gimme) (Collections/sort >))                     ◁——— Less-than function
;=> #<ArrayList [8, 4, 3, 2, 1]>

(doto (gimme) (Collections/sort <))                     ◁——— Greater-than function
;=> #<ArrayList [1, 2, 3, 4, 8]>

(doto (gimme) (Collections/sort (complement <)))        ◁——— complement function
;=> #<ArrayList [8, 4, 3, 2, 1]>
```

When presented with numerous possible implementation strategies, often the best one in Clojure is the simplest.

10.4.2 *java.lang.Runnable*

Java threads expect an object implementing the `java.lang.Runnable` interface meant for computations returning no value. We won't get into the specifics of threaded computation until the next chapter, but the next two examples are simple enough to require little a priori knowledge on the matter. If you wish to pass a function to another Java thread, it's as simple as providing it as an argument to the `Thread` constructor:

```
(doto (Thread. #(do (Thread/sleep 5000)
                    (println "haikeeba!")))
  .start)
; => #<Thread Thread[Thread-3,5,main]>
; ... 5 seconds later
; haikeeba!
```

This scenario is unlikely to occur often, because Clojure's core concurrency features are often sufficient for most needs. But that's not always the case, and therefore it's nice to know that raw Clojure functions can be used seamlessly in the JVM's concurrency API.

10.4.3 *java.util.concurrent.Callable*

The Java interface `java.util.concurrent.Callable` is specifically meant to be used in a threaded context for computations returning a value. You can use a Clojure function using Java's `java.util.concurrentFutureTask` class representing a "computation to occur later":

```
(import '[java.util.concurrent FutureTask])

(let [f (FutureTask. #(do (Thread/sleep 5000) 42))]
  (.start (Thread. #(.run f)))
  (.get f))
; ... 5 seconds later
;=> 42
```

The call to `FutureTask.get` as the last expression will stop execution (a behavior known as *blocking*) until the function passed to the constructor completes. Because the function in question sleeps for 5 seconds, the call to `.get` must wait.

Clojure's interoperability mechanisms are a two-way street. Not only do they allow Java APIs to work seamlessly within Clojure, but they also provide ways for Clojure functions to work in Java APIs. In the next section, we'll continue on this theme of bidirectional interop with a discussion on the ways that Clojure's collection types can also be used in traditional Java APIs.

10.5   *Using Clojure data structures in Java APIs*

Clojure functions are ready to use in many Java APIs, and as it turns out, so are its collection types. Just as the Clojure collections are separated along three distinct equality partitions[7] (maps, sequences, and sets), so too are its levels of Java collection interoperability support. The Java Collections Framework has a nice high-level design philosophy centered around working against interfaces. These interfaces are additionally cognizant of immutability, in that the mutable parts are optional and the immutable

---

[7] A refresher on equality partitions can be found in section 5.1.2 and throughout the remainder of chapter 5.

parts are clearly demarcated. In this section, we'll give a brief rundown of possible ways that Clojure collections can be used within traditional Java APIs adhering to the immutable collection protocols.

10.5.1 java.util.List

Clojure sequential collections conform to the immutable parts of the `java.util.List` interface, which in turn extends the `java.util.Collection` and `java.lang.Iterable` interfaces. You can see this conformance in action in the following listing.

Listing 10.8 `java.util.List` conformance for sequences and seqs

```
(.get '[a b c] 1)                        <- Vectors
;=> b

(.get (repeat :a) 138)                   <- Lazy seqs
;=> :a

(.containsAll '[a b c] '[b c])           <- Vectors also collections
;=> true

(.add '[a b c] 'd)                       <- Sequences not mutable
; java.lang.UnsupportedOperationException
```

That Clojure sequences and seqs don't provide the mutable API of typical Java collections is obvious. But the implications are that you can't use them in all Java APIs, such as you might attempt when requiring that a vector be sorted destructively with a Java API call:

```
(java.util.Collections/sort [3 4 2 1])
; java.lang.UnsupportedOperationException
```

A better approach is to either use the method used in the previous section using a Clojure function, or even better to use the Clojure's `sort` function instead.

10.5.2 java.lang.Comparable

The interface `java.lang.Comparable` is the cousin of the `Comparator` interface. `Comparator` refers to objects that can compare two other objects, whereas `Comparable` refers to an object that can *compare itself to* another object:

```
(.compareTo [:a] [:a])
;=> 0

(.compareTo [:a :b] [:a])
;=> 1

(.compareTo [:a :b] [:a :b :c])
;=> -1

(sort [[:a :b :c] [:a] [:a :b]])
;=> ([:a] [:a :b] [:a :b :c])
```

One thing to note is that Clojure's vector implementation is currently the only collection type that implements the `java.lang.Comparable` interface providing the

.compareTo method. As a result, attempting to compare a different collection type to a vector leads to a confusing error message:

```
(.compareTo [1 2 3] '(1 2 3))

; java.lang.ClassCastException: clojure.lang.PersistentList
;    cannot be cast to clojure.lang.IPersistentVector
```

Pay no attention to that class-cast exception behind the curtain.

10.5.3 *java.util.RandomAccess*

In general, the java.util.RandomAccess interface is used to indicate that the data type provides constant time indexed access to its elements. This allows for algorithms to follow optimized paths accordingly. This optimization is generally performed by using the .get method for access rather than an iterator:

```
(.get '[a b c] 2)
;=> c
```

Vectors are currently the only Clojure collection type that can make such guarantees.

10.5.4 *java.util.Collection*

The java.util.Collection interface lies at the heart of the Java Collections Framework, and classes implementing it can play in many of Java's core collections APIs. A useful idiom taking advantage of this fact is the use of a Clojure sequence as a model to build a mutable sequence for use in the Java Collections API, as shown:

```
(defn shuffle [coll]
  (seq (doto (java.util.ArrayList. coll)
         java.util.Collections/shuffle)))

(shuffle (range 10))
;=> (3 9 2 5 4 7 8 6 1 0)
```

It's difficult to write a proper sequence-shuffling function, so the shuffle function takes full advantage of an existing Java API that has been tested and used extensively for years. As an added bonus, shuffle is mostly[8] functional, idiomatic, and fast. Clojure favors immutability but doesn't trap you into it when there are practical solutions to be leveraged.

JAVA.UTIL.MAP

Like most of the Clojure collections, its maps are analogous to Java maps in that they can be used in nonmutating contexts. But immutable maps have the added advantage of never requiring defensive copies and will act exactly the same as unmodifiable Java maps:

```
(java.util.Collections/unmodifiableMap
  (doto (java.util.HashMap.) (.put :a 1)))
;=> #<UnmodifiableMap {:a=1}>
```

---

[8] shuffle isn't referentially transparent. Can you see why?

```
(into {} (doto (java.util.HashMap.) (.put :a 1)))
;=> {:a 1}
```

In both cases, any attempt to modify the map entry classes of the maps will throw an exception.

10.5.5 *java.util.Set*

In the case of Java and Clojure sets, the use of mutable objects[9] as elements is highly frowned upon:

```
(def x (java.awt.Point. 0 0))
(def y (java.awt.Point. 0 42))
(def points #{x y})
points
;=> #{#<Point java.awt.Point[x=0,y=0]> #<Point java.awt.Point[x=0,y=42]>}
```

Everything looks peachy at this point, but introducing mutability into the equation has devastating costs:

```
(.setLocation y 0 0)
points
;=> #{#<Point java.awt.Point[x=0,y=0]> #<Point java.awt.Point[x=0,y=0]>}
```

Oh boy. Not only have we confused the set points by modifying its entries out from underneath it, but we've also circumvented Clojure's value-based semantics and the nature of set-ness. Dealing with mutable objects is extremely difficult to reason about, especially when dealing with collections of them. The gates of a mutable class are wide open, and at any point during the execution of your programs this fact can be exploited, willingly or not. But you can't always avoid dealing with mutable nasties in Clojure code because of a strict adherence to fostering interoperability.

We've covered the two-way interop for functions and now collection types, but we have one final path to traverse: the use and benefits of Clojure's definterface macro.

10.6 *definterface*

As we mentioned in section 9.3, Clojure was built on abstractions in the host platform Java. Types and protocols help to provide a foundation for defining your own abstractions in Clojure itself, for use within a Clojure context. But when interoperating with Java code, protocols and types won't always suffice. Therefore, you need to be able to generate interfaces in some interop scenarios, and also for performance in cases involving primitive argument and return types. In this section, we'll talk briefly about generating Java interfaces as the syntax, use cases, and purposes are likely familiar.

10.6.1 *Generating interfaces on the fly*

When you AOT-compile a protocol, you generate a public interface by the same name, with the methods defined. The code in listing 10.9 uses definterface to define an

---

[9] Clojure's mutable reference types used to represent a logical identity are perfectly safe to use in sets. We'll explore the reference types in exquisite detail in the next chapter.

interface ISliceable. This interface is used to define an abstract thing that has the
ability to be sliced using a method slice, which takes start and end indices of type int.
Likewise, the interface defines a method sliceCount that returns an int representing
the number of possible slices.

Listing 10.9   An interface defining a sliceable object

```
(definterface ISliceable
  (slice [^int s ^int e])
  (^int sliceCount []))
;=> user.ISliceable
```

You'll notice the inclusion of the type decoration ^int on the arguments to slice and
the return type of sliceCount. For now you can assume that they operate the same as
a type declaration in most languages providing them. They look similar to type hints
discussed in section 12.1, except that only in definterface are primitive hints supported. Now we can create an instance implementing the user.ISliceable interface,
as shown next.

Listing 10.10   A dummy reified ISliceable

```
(def dumb
  (reify user.ISliceable
    (slice [_ s e] [:empty])
    (sliceCount [_] 42)))

(.slice dumb 1 2)
;=> [:empty]

(.sliceCount dumb)
;=> 42
```

There's nothing terribly surprising about dumb, but you can instead implement it via
deftype, proxy, gen-class, or even a Java class. Note that definterface works even
without AOT compilation.

   We can now take definterface to the next logical step and extend the ISliceable
interface to other types using a well-placed protocol.

Listing 10.11   Using a protocol to extend ISliceable

```
(defprotocol Sliceable
  (slice [this s e])
  (sliceCount [this]))

(extend user.ISliceable
  Sliceable
  {:slice (fn [this s e] (.slice this s e))
   :sliceCount (fn [this] (.sliceCount this))})

(sliceCount dumb)
;=> 42

(slice dumb 0 0)
;=> [:empty]
```

By extending the ISliceable interface along Sliceable, ISliceable is able to participate in the protocol, meaning that you have the possibility for extending other types, even final types such as String, as shown next.

Listing 10.12 Extending strings along the Sliceable protocol

```
(defn calc-slice-count [thing]
  "Calculates the number of possible slices using the formula:
      (n + r - 1)!
      -----------
      r!(n - 1)!
    where n is (count thing) and r is 2"
  (let [! #(reduce * (take % (iterate inc 1)))
        n (count thing)]
    (/ (! (- (+ n 2) 1))
       (* (! 2) (! (- n 1))))))

(extend-type String
  Sliceable
  (slice [this s e] (.substring this s (inc e)))
  (sliceCount [this] (calc-slice-count this)))

(slice "abc" 0 1)
;=> "ab"
(sliceCount "abc")
;=> 6
```

The advantages of using definterface over defprotocol are restricted entirely to the fact that the former allows primitive types for arguments and returns. At some point in the future, the same advantages will likely be extended to the interfaces generated, so use definterface sparingly and prefer protocols unless absolutely necessary.

10.7 *Be wary of exceptions*

There's been much debate on the virtues of checked exceptions in Java, so we won't cover that here. Instead, we'll stick to the facts regarding the nuances the JVM imposes on Clojure's error-handling facilities. Before we begin, consider the following view on the use of exceptions in Clojure source:

> *When writing Clojure code, use errors to mean* can't continue *and exceptions to mean* can or might continue.

We'll attempt to constrain ourselves to the generalities of exception handling in this section. If you desire information on deciphering exception messages, we talked about that in section 3.4. If you're curious about the effects of exceptions on continuation-passing style, then refer back to section 7.3.4. We discussed the behavior of Clojure to attempt to supplant numerical inaccuracies by throwing exceptions in section 4.1.3. If you instead want to learn about the interplay between exceptions and Clojure's reference types, then such matters can be found throughout chapter 11. Finally, if you have no idea what an exception is, then we discuss the basics in section 1.5.8.

10.7.1 *A bit of background regarding exceptions*

The behavior of Clojure's exception features directly spawns from the JVM enforcing the promulgation of checked exceptions. Virtuous or not in the context of Java development, checked exceptions are antithetical to closures and higher-order functions. Checked exceptions require that not only should the thrower and the party responsible for handling them declare interest, but every intermediary is also forced to participate. These intermediaries don't have to actively throw or handle exceptions occurring within, but they must declare that they'll be "passing through." Therefore, by including the call to a Java method throwing a checked exception within a closure, Clojure has two possible alternatives:

- Provide a cumbersome exception declaration mechanism on every single function, including closures.
- By default, declare that all functions throw the root `Exception` or `Runtime-Exception`.

And as you can probably guess, Clojure takes the second approach, which leads to a condition of multilevel wrapping of exceptions as they pass back up the call stack. This is why you see, in almost any `(.printStackTrace *e)` invocation, the point of origin of an error offset by some number of layers of `java.lang.RuntimeException`. Because Java interfaces and classes get to decide what types of problems potential derivative classes and even callers can have, Clojure needs to handle the base `java.lang.Exception` at every level, because it has to preserve dynamism in the face of a closed system. Unless you're directly calling something that throws typed exceptions, your best bet is to catch `Exception` and then see what you have in context.

10.7.2 *Runtime versus compile-time exceptions*

There are two contexts in Clojure where exceptions can be thrown: runtime and compile time. In this section we'll touch on both, explaining how and when to use them.

RUNTIME EXCEPTIONS

The case of runtime exceptions might be the most familiar, because it's likely to have been encountered and utilized in your own code. There are two types of runtime exceptions: errors and exceptions. We can illustrate the difference between the two by showing you the following:

```
(defn explode [] (explode))
(try (explode) (catch Exception e "Stack is blown"))
; java.lang.StackOverflowError
```

So why were we unable to catch the `java.lang.StackOverflowError`? The reason lies in Java's exception class hierarchy and the fact that `StackOverflowError` isn't a derivative of the `Exception` class, but instead of the `Error` class:

```
(try (explode) (catch StackOverflowError e "Stack is blown"))
;=> "Stack is blown"
```

```
(try (explode) (catch Error e "Stack is blown"))
;=> "Stack is blown"

(try (explode) (catch Throwable e "Stack is blown"))
;=> "Stack is blown"

(try (throw (RuntimeException.))
  (catch Throwable e "Catching Throwable is Bad"))
;=> "Catching Throwable is Bad"
```

We started with a catch of the most specific exception type StackOverflowError and gradually decreased specificity until catching Throwable, which as you'll notice also catches a RuntimeException. In Java, catching exceptions at the level of Throwable is considered bad form, and it should generally be viewed the same in Clojure. Therefore, we suggest that you follow the advice stated in the opening to this section and reserve those deriving from Errors for conditions that can't be continued from and those from Exception indicating possible continuation.

COMPILE-TIME EXCEPTIONS

There are a few ways that you might come across compile-time exceptions, the most obvious occurring within the body of a macro:

```
(defmacro do-something [x] `(~x))
(do-something 1)
; java.lang.ClassCastException:
;   java.lang.Integer cannot be cast to clojure.lang.IFn
```

Though the type of the exception is a java.lang.ClassCastException, it was indeed thrown by the compiler, which you'd see if you were to trace the stack using something like (for [e (.getStackTrace *e)] (.getClassName e)).[10] It's perfectly acceptable (and even encouraged) to throw exceptions within your own macros, but it's important to make a distinction between a compile-time and runtime exception.

> **COMPILE-TIME EXCEPTIONS**   Why delay until runtime the reporting of an error that at compile time you know exists?

The way to throw a compile-time exception is to make sure your throw doesn't occur within a syntax-quoted form, as we show in the following listing.

Listing 10.13 Throwing a compile-time exception

```
(defmacro pairs [& args]
  (if (even? (count args))
    `(partition 2 '~args)
    (throw (Exception. (str "pairs requires an even number of args")))))

(pairs 1 2 3)
; java.lang.Exception: pairs requires an even number of args

(pairs 1 2 3 4)
;=> ((1 2) (3 4))
```

---

[10] This is a limited analogy to Groovy's .? operator. Clojure also provides convenience functions for displaying and handling stack traces in the clojure.stacktrace namespace.

Nothing is preventing the exception from being thrown at runtime, but because we know that `pairs` requires an even number of arguments, we instead prefer to fail as early as possible—at compilation time. This difference is clearly demonstrated by repeating the preceding test in a function definition:

```
(fn [] (pairs 1 2 3))
; java.lang.Exception: pairs requires an even number of args
```

A runtime exception wouldn't have been thrown until this function was called, but because the `pairs` macro threw an exception at compile time, users are notified of their error immediately. Though powerful, you should always try to balance the benefits of compile-time error checking with macros and the advantages that implementing as a function provides (the use in higher-order functions, `apply`, and so on).

10.7.3 *Handling exceptions*

There are two ways to handle exceptions and errors, each defined by the way in which the error-handling mechanisms "flow" through the source. Imagine that you want a macro that provides a limited[11] null-safe (Koenig 2007) arrow that catches any occurrence of a `NullPointerException` in a pipeline:

```
(defmacro -?> [& forms]
  `(try (-> ~@forms)
     (catch NullPointerException _# nil)))

(-?> 25 Math/sqrt (+ 100))
;=> 105.0

(-?> 25 Math/sqrt (and nil) (+ 100))
;=> nil
```

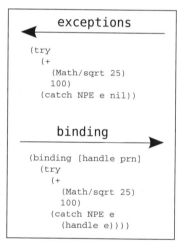

The flow of any occurrence of `NullPointer-Exception` happens from the inner functions of the stitched forms. Conceptually, this flow can be viewed as in figure 10.7, which describes the way that errors can be caught depending on the direction in which data is moving along the stack.

The typical `(try ... (catch ...))` form would therefore be used for the case where the handler catches errors bubbling outward from inner functions and forms, as seen in the `-?>` macro. But if you want to catch errors at their point of origin, you'll need a way to pass handlers up the stack. Fortunately, Clojure provides a way to do this via its dynamic Var feature, which will be discussed in section 13.5.

Figure 10.7   Outside-in and inside-out error handling. There are two ways to handle errors in Clojure. The typical way is to let exceptions flow from the inner forms to the outer. The other way, discussed in section 13.4, uses dynamic bindings to "reach into" the inner forms to handle them immediately.

---

[11] There are much more comprehensive `-?>` and `.?.` macros found in the `clojure.contrib.core` namespace, and those are recommended above the one in this section.

10.7.4 Custom exceptions

If you're inclined to write your own exception and error types, then you'll need to do so using the `gen-class` feature described in section 10.2. JVM exceptions again are a closed system, and it might be better to explore other possibilities (Houser EK) for reporting and handling errors in your Clojure code. But, should you wish to ignore this advice, then bear in mind that it's rare for Clojure core functions to throw exceptions, and even more rarely are they checked exceptions. The idiom is for Clojure to throw derivatives of `RuntimeException` or `Error`, and thus your code should also strive for this when appropriate.

10.8 Summary

Clojure provides an extensive set of data abstractions via its types and protocols. It also provides an extensive interoperability facility through `proxy`, `gen-class`, `definterface`, exception handling, and the implementation of core Java collection interfaces. Though we stress that types and protocols will give you the performant abstractions needed for solving most problems, we realize that not all interop scenarios are solved this way. In these circumstances, you should use the features listed in this chapter to push you the remainder of the way toward your solution. Clojure embraces Java interoperability, but it does so in specific ways, and with a specific set of tools.

In the next chapter, we move on to a rather complex topic, and one that Clojure helps to simplify—shared state concurrency and mutation.

11
Mutation

This chapter covers

- Software transactional memory with multiversion concurrency control and snapshot isolation
- When to use Refs
- When to use Agents
- When to use Atoms
- When to use locks
- When to use futures
- When to use promises
- Parallelism
- Vars and dynamic binding

Clojure's main tenet isn't the facilitation of concurrency. Instead, Clojure at its core is concerned with the sane management of state, and facilitating concurrent programming naturally falls out of that. The JVM operates on a shared-state concurrency model built around juggling fine-grained locks that protect access to shared data. Even if you can keep all of your locks in order, rarely does such a strategy scale well, and even less frequently does it foster reusability. But Clojure's state management is simpler to reason about and promotes reusability.

234

CLOJURE APHORISM A tangled web of mutation means that *any* change to your code potentially occurs in the large.

In this chapter, we'll take the grand tour of the mutation primitives and see how Clojure makes concurrent programming not only possible, but fun. Our journey will take us through Clojure's four major mutable references: Refs, Agents, Atoms, and Vars. When possible and appropriate, we'll also point out the Java facilities for concurrent programming (including locking) and provide information on the trade-offs involved in choosing them. We'll also explore parallelism support in Clojure using futures, promises, and a trio of functions `pmap`, `pvalues`, and `pcalls`.

Before we dive into the details of Clojure's reference types, let's start with a high-level overview of Clojure's *software transactional memory* (STM).

> ## Concurrency vs. parallelism
>
> *Concurrency* refers to the execution of disparate tasks at roughly the same time, each sharing a common resource. The results of concurrent tasks often affect the behavior of other concurrent tasks, and therefore contain an element of nondeterminism. *Parallelism* refers to partitioning a task into multiple parts, each run at the same time. Typically, parallel tasks work toward an aggregate goal and the result of one doesn't affect the behavior of any other parallel task, thus maintaining determinacy.

11.1 Software transactional memory with multiversion concurrency control and snapshot isolation

> *A faster program that doesn't work right is useless.*
>
> —Simon Peyton-Jones
> in "Beautiful Concurrency"

In chapter 1, we defined three important terms:

- *Time*—The relative moments when events occur
- *State*—A snapshot of an entity's properties at a moment in time
- *Identity*—The logical entity identified by a common stream of states occurring over time

These terms form the foundation for Clojure's model of state management and mutation. In Clojure's model, a program must accommodate the fact that when dealing with identities, it's receiving a snapshot of its properties at a moment in time, not necessarily the most recent. Therefore, all decisions must be made in a continuum. This model is a natural one, as humans and animals alike make all decisions based on their current knowledge of an ever-shifting world. Clojure provides the tools for dealing with identity semantics via its *Ref* reference type, the change semantics of which are governed by Clojure's software transactional memory; this ensures state consistency throughout the application timeline, delineated by a *transaction*.

11.1.1 *Transactions*

Within the first few moments of using Clojure's STM, you'll notice something different than you may be accustomed to: no locks. Consequently, because there's no need for ad-hoc locking schemes when using STM, there's no chance of deadlock. Likewise, Clojure's STM doesn't require the use of monitors and as a result is free from lost wakeup conditions. Behind the scenes, Clojure's STM uses *multiversion concurrency control* (MVCC) to ensure *snapshot isolation*. In simpler terms, snapshot isolation means that each transaction gets its own view of the data that it's interested in. This *snapshot* is made up of in-transaction reference values, forming the foundation of MVCC (Ullman 1988). As illustrated in figure 11.1, each transaction merrily chugs along making changes to in-transaction values only, oblivious to and ambivalent about other transactions. At the conclusion of the transaction, the local values are examined against the modification target for conflicts. An example of a simple possible conflict is if another transaction B committed a change to a target reference during the time that transaction A was working, thus causing A to retry. If no conflicts are found, then the in-transaction values are committed and the target references are modified with their updated values. Another advantage that STM provides is that in the case of an exception during a transaction, its in-transaction values are thrown away and the exception propagated outward. In the case of lock-based schemes, exceptions can complicate matters ever more, because in most cases locks need to be released (and in some cases, in the correct order) before an exception can be safely propagated up the call stack.

Because each transaction has its own isolated snapshot, there's no danger in retrying—the data is never modified until a successful commit occurs. STM transactions can easily nest without taking additional measures to facilitate composition. In languages providing explicit locking for concurrency, matters of composability are often difficult, if not impossible. The reasons for this are far-reaching and the mitigating forces (Goetz 2006) complex, but the primary reasons tend to be that lock-based concurrency schemes often hinge on a secret incantation not explicitly understandable through the source itself: for example, the order in which to take and release a set of locks.

11.1.2 *Embedded transactions*

In systems providing embedded transactions, it's often common for transactions to be nested, thus limiting the scope of restarts (Gray 1992). Embedding transactions within Clojure operates differently, as summarized in figure 11.2.

In some database systems, transactions can be used to limit the scope of a restart as shown when transaction `embedded.b` restarts only as far back as its own scope. Clojure has but one transaction per thread, thus causing all subtransactions to be subsumed into the larger transaction. Therefore, when a restart occurs in the (conceptual) subtransaction `clojure.b`, it causes a restart of the larger transaction. Though not shown, some transaction systems provide committal in each subtransaction; in Clojure, commit only occurs at the outermost larger transaction.

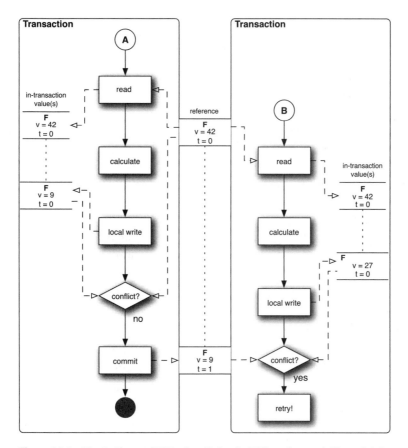

Figure 11.1 Illustrating an STM retry: Clojure's STM works much like a database.

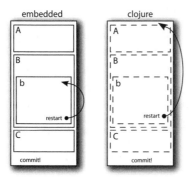

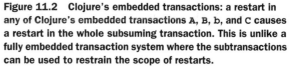

Figure 11.2 Clojure's embedded transactions: a restart in any of Clojure's embedded transactions A, B, b, and C causes a restart in the whole subsuming transaction. This is unlike a fully embedded transaction system where the subtransactions can be used to restrain the scope of restarts.

11.1.3 The things that STM makes easy

The phrase TANSTAAFL, meaning "There ain't no such thing as a free lunch," was popularized in the excellent sci-fi novel *The Moon Is a Harsh Mistress* (Heinlein 1966) and is an apt response to the view that STM is a panacea for concurrency complexities.

As you proceed through this chapter, we urge you to keep this in the back of your mind, because it's important to realize that though Clojure facilitates concurrent programming, it doesn't solve it for you. But there are a few things that Clojure's STM implementation simplifies in solving difficult concurrent problems.

CONSISTENT INFORMATION

The STM allows you to perform arbitrary sets of read/write operations on arbitrary sets of data in a consistent (Papadimitriou 1986) way. By providing these assurances, the STM allows your programs to make decisions given overlapping subsets of information. Likewise, Clojure's STM helps to solve the reporting problem—the problem of getting a consistent view of the world in the face of massive concurrent modification and reading, without stopping (locking).

NO NEED FOR LOCKS

In any sized application, the inclusion of locks for managing concurrent access to shared data adds complexity. There are many factors adding to this complexity, but chief among them are the following:

- You can't use locks without supplying extensive error handling. This is critical in avoiding orphaned locks (locks held by a thread that has died).
- Every application requires that you reinvent a whole new locking scheme.
- Locking schemes often require that you impose a total ordering that's difficult to enforce in client code, frequently leading to a priority inversion scenario.

Locking schemes are difficult to design correctly and become increasingly so as the number of locks grows. Clojure's STM eliminates the need for locking and as a result eliminates dreaded deadlock scenarios. Clojure's STM provides a story for managing state consistently. Adhering to this story will go a long way toward helping you solve software problems effectively. This is true even when concurrent programming isn't a factor in your design.

ACI

In the verbiage of database transactions is a well-known acronym ACID, which refers to the properties ensuring transactional reliability. Clojure's STM provides the first three properties: *atomicity*, *consistency*, and *isolation*. The other, *durability*, is missing due to the fact that Clojure's STM resides in-memory and is therefore subject to data loss in the face of catastrophic system failure. Clojure relegates the problem of maintaining durability to the application developer instead of supplying common strategies by default: database persistence, external application logs, serialization, and so on.

11.1.4 *Potential downsides*

There are two potential problems inherent in STMs in general, which we'll only touch on briefly here.

WRITE SKEW

For the most part, you can write correct programs simply by putting all access and changes to references in appropriately scoped transactions. The one exception to this is *write skew*, which occurs in MVCC systems such as Clojure's. Write skew can occur when one transaction uses the value of a reference to regulate its behavior but doesn't write to that reference. At the same time, another transaction updates the value for that same reference. One way to avoid this would be to do a "dummy write" in the first transaction, but Clojure provides a less costly solution: the ensure function. This scenario is rare in Clojure applications, but possible.

LIVE-LOCK

Live-lock refers to a set of transaction(s) that repeatedly restart one another. Clojure combats live-lock in a couple of ways. First, there are transaction restart limits that will raise an error when breached. Generally this occurs when the units of work within some number of transactions is too large. The second way that Clojure combats live-lock is called *barging*. Barging refers to some careful logic in the STM implementation allowing an older transaction to continue running while younger transactions retry.

11.1.5 *The things that make STM unhappy*

Certain things can rarely (if ever) be safely performed within a transaction, and in this section we'll talk briefly about each.

I/O

Any I/O operation in the body of a transaction is highly discouraged. Due to restarts, the embedded I/O could at best be rendered useless, and cause great harm at worst. It's advised that you employ the io! macro whenever performing I/O operations:

```
(io! (.println System/out "Haikeeba!"))
; Haikeeba!
```

When this same statement is used in a transaction, an exception is thrown:

```
(dosync (io! (.println System/out "Haikeeba!")))
; java.lang.IllegalStateException: I/O in transaction
```

Though it may not be feasible to use io! in every circumstance, it's a good idea to do so whenever possible.

CLASS INSTANCE MUTATION

Unrestrained instance mutation is often not *idempotent*, meaning that running a set of mutating operations multiple times often displays different results.

LARGE TRANSACTIONS

Though the size of transactions is highly subjective, the general rule of thumb when partitioning units of work should always be *get in and get out as quickly as possible.*

Though it's important to understand that transactions will help to simplify the management of state, you should strive to minimize their footprint in your code. The use of I/O and instance mutation is often an essential part of many applications; it's important to work to separate your programs into logical partitions, keeping I/O and its ilk on one side, and transaction processing and mutation on the other. Fortunately for us, Clojure provides a powerful toolset for making the management of mutability sane, but none of the tools provide a shortcut to thinking. Multithreaded programming is a difficult problem, independent of specifics, and Clojure's state-management tools won't solve this problem magically. We'll help to guide you through the proper use of these tools starting with Clojure's Ref type.

11.2 *When to use Refs*

Clojure currently provides four different reference types to aide in concurrent programming: Refs, Agents, Atoms, and Vars. All but Vars are considered shared references and allow for changes to be seen across threads of execution. The most important point to remember about choosing between reference types is that although their features sometimes overlap, each has an ideal use. All the reference types and their primary characteristics are shown in figure 11.3.

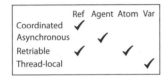

Figure 11.3   Clojure's four reference types are listed across the top, with their features listed down the left. Atoms are for lone synchronous objects. Agents are for asynchronous actions. Vars are for thread-local storage. Refs are for synchronously coordinating multiple objects.

The unique feature of Refs is that they're *coordinated*. This means that reads and writes to multiple refs can be made in a way that guarantees no race conditions. *Asynchronous* means that the request to update is queued to happen in another thread some time later, while the thread that made the request continues immediately. *Retriable* indicates that the work done to update a reference's value is speculative and may have to be repeated. Finally, *thread-local* means that thread safety is achieved by isolating changes to state to a single thread.

Value access via the @ reader feature or the `deref` function provide a uniform client interface, regardless of the reference type used. On the other hand, the write mechanism associated with each reference type is unique by name and specific behavior, but

---

dothreads

To illustrate some major points, we'll use a function `dothreads!` that launches a given number of threads each running a function a number of times:

```
(import '(java.util.concurrent Executors))
(def *pool* (Executors/newFixedThreadPool
              (+ 2 (.availableProcessors (Runtime/getRuntime)))))

(defn dothreads! [f & {thread-count :threads
                       exec-count :times
                       :or {thread-count 1 exec-count 1}}]
  (dotimes [t thread-count]
    (.submit *pool* #(dotimes [_ exec-count] (f)))))
```

The `dothreads!` function is of limited utility—throwing a bunch of threads at a function to see if it breaks.

similar in structure. Each referenced value is changed through the application[1] of a pure function. The result of this function will become the new referenced value. Finally, all reference types allow the association of a validator function via set-validator that will be used as the final gatekeeper on any value change.

11.2.1 *Coordinated, synchronous change using alter*

A Ref is a reference type allowing synchronous, coordinated change to its contained value. What does this mean? By enforcing that any change to a Ref's value occurs in a transaction, Clojure can guarantee that change happens in a way that maintains a consistent view of the referenced value in all threads. But there's a question as to what constitutes coordination. We'll construct a simple vector of Refs to represent a 3 x 3 chess board:

```
(def initial-board
     [[:- :k :-]
      [:- :- :-]
      [:- :K :-]])

(defn board-map [f bd]
  (vec (map #(vec (for [s %] (f s))) bd)))
```

Just as in section 2.4, the lowercase keyword represents a dark king piece and the uppercase a light king piece. We've chosen to represent the board as a 2D vector of Refs (which are created by the board-map function). There are other ways to represent our board, but we've chosen this because it's nicely illustrative—the act of moving a piece would require a *coordinated* change in two reference squares, or else a change to one square in one thread could lead to another thread observing that square as occupied. Likewise, this problem requires synchronous change, because it would be no good for pieces of the same color to move consecutively. Refs are the only game in town to ensure that the necessary coordinated change occurs synchronously. Before you see Refs in action, we need to define auxiliary functions:

```
(defn reset!
  "Resets the board state.  Generally these types of functions are a
   bad idea, but matters of page count force our hand."
  []
  (def board (board-map ref initial-board))
  (def to-move (ref [[:K [2 1]] [:k [0 1]]]))
  (def num-moves (ref 0)))

(def king-moves (partial neighbors
    [[-1 -1] [-1 0] [-1 1] [0 -1] [0 1] [1 -1] [1 0] [1 1]] 3))

(defn good-move? [to enemy-sq]
  (when (not= to enemy-sq) to))

(defn choose-move [[[mover mpos] [_ enemy-pos]]]
  [mover (some #(good-move? % enemy-pos)
               (shuffle (king-moves mpos)))])
```

---

[1] Except for ref-set on Refs, reset! on Atoms, and set! on Vars.

The to-move structure describes the order of moves, so in the base case, it states that the light king :K at y=2,x=1 moves before the dark king :k at y=0,x=1. We reuse the neighbors function from section 7.4 to build a legal-move generator for chess king pieces. We do this by using partial supplied with the kingly position deltas and the board size. The good-move? function states that a move to a square is legal only if the enemy isn't already located there. The function choose-move destructures the to-move vector and chooses a good move from a shuffled sequence of legal moves. The choose-move function can be tested in isolation:

```
(reset!)
(take 5 (repeatedly #(choose-move @to-move)))
;=> ([:K [1 0]] [:K [1 1]] [:K [1 1]] [:K [1 0]] [:K [2 0]])
```

And now we'll create a function to make a random move for the piece at the front of to-move, shown next.

Listing 11.1   Using `alter` to update a Ref

```
(defn place [from to] to)

(defn move-piece [[piece dest] [[_ src] _]]
  (alter (get-in board dest) place piece)        ◁——— Place moving piece
  (alter (get-in board src ) place :-)    ◁——— Empty from square
  (alter num-moves inc))

(defn update-to-move [move]
  (alter to-move #(vector (second %) move)))        ◁——— Swap

(defn make-move []
  (dosync
    (let [move (choose-move @to-move)]
      (move-piece move @to-move)
      (update-to-move move))))
```

The alter function appears four times within the dosync, so that the from and to positions, as well as the to-move Refs, are updated in a coordinated fashion. We're using the place function as the alter function, which states "given a to piece and a from piece, always return the to piece." Observe what occurs when make-move is run once:

```
(make-move)
;=> [[:k [0 1]] [:K [2 0]]]
(board-map deref board)
;=> [[:- :k :-] [:- :- :-] [:K :- :-]]
@num-moves
;=> 1
```

We've successfully made a change to two board squares, the to-move structure, and num-moves using the uniform state change model. By itself, this model of state change is compelling. The semantics are simple to understand: give a reference a function that determines how the value changes. This is the model of sane state change that Clojure preaches. But we can now throw a bunch of threads at this solution and still maintain consistency:

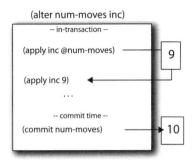

Figure 11.4 Alter path: the in-transaction value 9 for the Ref `num-moves` is retrieved in the body of the transaction and manipulated with the `alter` function `inc`. This resulting value 10 is eventually used for the commit-time value, unless a retry is required.

```
(defn go [move-fn threads times]
  (dothreads! move-fn :threads threads :times times))

(go make-move 100 100)
(board-map #(dosync (deref %)) board)
;=> [[:k :- :-] [:- :- :-] [:K :- :-]]
@to-move
;=> [[:k [0 0]] [:K [2 0]]]
@num-moves
;=> 10001
```

Figure 11.4 shows that at the time of the transaction, the *in-transaction* value of the to square is set to `(apply place @SQUARE-REF PIECE)`. At the end of the transaction, the STM uses this in-transaction value as the commit value. If any other transaction had updated any other coordinated Ref before commit time, then the whole transaction would be retried.

Clojure's retry mechanism guarantees that the Refs in a transaction are always coordinated upon commit because all other transactions line up waiting their turn to commit their coordinated values. Look at what happens should the Ref updates happen in separate transactions:

```
(defn bad-make-move []
  (let [move (choose-move @to-move)]
    (dosync (move-piece move @to-move))
    (dosync (update-to-move move))))

(go bad-make-move 100 100)
(board-map #(dosync (deref %)) board)
;=> [[:- :K :-] [:- :- :-] [:- :K :-]]
```

Clearly something has gone awry, and as we mentioned, the reason lies in splitting the updates of the to and from Refs into different transactions. Being separated into two transactions means that they're (potentially) running on different timelines. Because board and to-move are dependent, their states *must* be coordinated, but we've broken that necessity with bad-make-move. Therefore, somewhere along the line board was updated from two subsequent timelines where it was :K's turn to move!

As shown in figure 11.5, either transaction can commit or be restarted; but because the two Refs are no longer in the same transaction, the occurrences of these conditions become staggered over time, leading to inconsistent values.

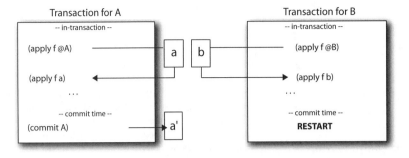

Figure 11.5 Splitting coordinated Refs: if Refs A and B should be coordinated, then splitting their updates across different transactions is dangerous. Value a? is eventually committed to A, but the update for B never commits due to retry and coordination is lost. Another error occurs if B's change depends on A's value and A and B are split across transactions. There are no guarantees that the dependent values refer to the same timeline.

11.2.2 *Commutative change with commute*

Figure 11.4 showed that using alter can cause a transaction to retry if a Ref it depends on is modified and committed while it's running. But there may be circumstances where the value of a Ref within a given transaction isn't important to its completion semantics. For example, the num-moves Ref is a simple counter, and surely its value at any given time is irrelevant for determining how it should be incremented. To handle these loose dependency circumstances, Clojure offers an operation named commute. What if we were to change the make-move function to use the commute function instead of alter?

```
(defn move-piece [[piece dest] [[_ src] _]]
  (commute (get-in board dest) place piece)
  (commute (get-in board src ) place :-)
  (commute num-moves inc))

(reset!)
(go make-move 100 100)
(board-map deref board)
;=> [[:K :- :-] [:- :- :-] [:- :- :k]]
@to-move
;=> [[:K [0 0]] [:k [2 2]]]
```

Everything looks great! But you can't assume that the same will work for update-to-move:

```
(defn update-to-move [move]
  (commute to-move #(vector (second %) move)))

(go make-move 100 100)
(board-map #(dosync (deref %)) board)
;=> [[:- :- :-] [:- :K :-] [:- :- :K]]
@to-move
[[:K [2 2]] [:K [1 1]]]
```

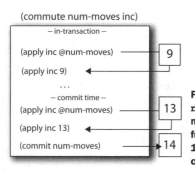

Figure 11.6   **Commute path: the in-transaction value 9 in the num-moves Ref is retrieved in the body of the transaction and manipulated with the commute function. But the commute function inc is again run at commit time with the current value 13 contained in the Ref. The result of this action serves as the committed value 14.**

Thanks to our rash decision, we've once again introduced inconsistency into the system. But why? The reason lies in the fact that the new update-to-move isn't amenable to the semantics of the commute function. commute allows for more concurrency in the STM by devaluing in-transaction value disparity resulting from another transaction's commit. In other words, figure 11.6 shows that the in-transaction value of a Ref is initially set as when using alter, but the *commit time* value is reset just before commute commits.

By retrieving the most current value for a Ref at the time of commit, the values committed might not be those corresponding to the in-transaction state. This leads to a condition of update reordering that your application *must* accommodate. Of course, this new function isn't commutative because vector doesn't give the same answer if its argument order is switched.

Using commute is useful as long as the following conditions aren't problematic:

- The value you see in-transaction may not be the value that gets committed at commit time.
- The function you give to commute will be run at least twice—once to compute the in-transaction value, and again to compute the commit value. It might be run any number of times.

11.2.3 *Vulgar change with ref-set*

The function ref-set is different from alter and commute in that instead of changing a Ref based on a function of its value, it does so given a raw value:

```
(dosync (ref-set to-move '[[:K [2 1]] [:k [0 1]]]))
;=> [[:K [2 1]] [:k [0 1]]]
```

In general, this sort of vulgar change should be avoided. But because the Refs have become out of sync, perhaps you could be forgiven in using ref-set to fix it—just this once.

11.2.4 *Fixing write-skew with ensure*

Snapshot isolation means that within a transaction, all enclosed Ref states represent the *same* moment in time. Any Ref value that you see inside a transaction will *never* change unless *you* change it within that transaction. Your algorithms should be devised so that all you care about is that the values of the references haven't changed before commit (unless your change function is commutative, as mentioned previously). If those values have changed, then the transaction retries, and you try again. Earlier, we talked about write skew, a condition occurring when you make decisions based on the in-transaction value of a Ref that's never written to, which is also changed at the same time. Avoiding write skew is accomplished using Clojure's ensure function, which guarantees a read-only Ref isn't modified by another thread. The make-move function isn't subject to write skew because it has no invariants on read data and in fact never reads a Ref that it doesn't eventually write. This design is ideal because it allows other threads to calculate moves without having to stop them, while any given transaction does the same. But in your own applications, you may be confronted with a true read invariant scenario, and it's in such a scenario that ensure will help.

11.2.5 *Refs under stress*

After you've created your Refs and written your transactions, and simple isolated tests are passing, you may yet run into difficulties in larger integration tests because of how Refs behave under stress from multiple transactions. As a rule of thumb, it's best to avoid having both short- and long-running transactions interacting with the same Ref. Clojure's STM implementation will usually compensate eventually regardless, but you'll soon see some less-than-ideal consequences of ignoring this rule.

To demonstrate this problem, listing 11.2 shows a function designed specifically to over-stress a Ref. It does this by starting a long-running or slow transaction in another thread, where work is simulated by a 200ms sleep, but all it's really doing is reading the Ref in a transaction. This requires the STM to know of a stable value for the Ref for the full 200ms. Meanwhile, the main thread runs quick transactions 500 times in a row, each one incrementing the value in the Ref and thereby frustrating the slow transaction's attempts to see a stable value. The STM works to overcome this frustration by growing the history of values kept for the Ref. But by default this history is limited to 10 entries, and our perverse function can easily saturate that:

```
(stress-ref (ref 0))
;=> :done
; r is: 500, history: 10, after: 26 tries
```

You may see a slightly different number of tries, but the important detail is that the slow transaction is unable to successfully commit and print the value of r until the main thread has finished its frantic looping and returned :done. The Ref's history started at a default of 0 and grew to 10, but this was still insufficient.

Listing 11.2   How to make a Ref squirm

```
(defn stress-ref [r]
  (let [slow-tries (atom 0)]
    (future                              ◁─┐ Long-running
      (dosync                                 transaction
        (swap! slow-tries inc)
        (Thread/sleep 200)
        @r)
```

```
       (println (format "r is: %s, history: %d, after: %d tries"
                         @r (ref-history-count r) @slow-tries)))
    (dotimes [i 500]                              500 very quick
      (Thread/sleep 10)                           transactions
      (dosync (alter r inc)))
    :done))
```

Remember that our real problem here is mixing short- and long-running transactions on the same Ref. But if this is truly unavoidable, Clojure allows us to create a Ref with a more generous cap on the history size:

```
(stress-ref (ref 0 :max-history 30))
; r is: 410, history: 20, after: 21 tries
;=> :done
```

Again, your numbers may be different, but this time the Ref's history grew sufficiently (reaching 20 in this run) to allow the slow transaction to finish first and report about r before all 500 quick transactions completed. In this run, only 410 had finished when the slow transaction committed.

But the slow transaction still had to be retried 20 times, with the history growing one step large each time, before it was able to complete. If our slow transaction were doing real work instead of just sleeping, this could represent a lot of wasted computing effort. If your tests or production environment reveal this type of situation and the underlying transaction size difference can't be resolved, one final Ref option can help. Because you can see that the history will likely need to be 20 anyway, you may as well start it off closer to its goal:

```
(stress-ref (ref 0 :min-history 15 :max-history 30))
; r is: 97, history: 19, after: 5 tries
;=> :done
```

This time the slow transaction finished before even 100 of the quick transactions had finished; and even though the history grew to roughly the same size, starting it off at 15 meant the slow transaction only retried 4 times before succeeding.

The use of Refs to guarantee coordinated change is generally simple for managing state in a synchronous fashion, and tuning with :min-history and :max-history is rarely required. But not all changes in your applications will require coordination, nor will they need to be synchronous. For these circumstances, Clojure also provides another reference type, the Agent, that provides independent asynchronous changes, which we'll discuss next.

11.3   *When to use Agents*

Like all Clojure reference types, an Agent represents an *identity*, a specific thing whose value can change over time. Each Agent has a queue to hold actions that need to be performed on its value, and each action will produce a new value for the Agent to hold and pass to the subsequent action. Thus the state of the Agent advances through time, action after action, and by their nature only one action at a time can be operating on a given Agent. Of course, other actions can be operating on other Agents at the same time, each in its own thread.

You can queue an action on any Agent by using `send` or `send-off`, the minor difference between which we'll discuss later. Agents are integrated with STM transactions, and within a transaction any actions sent are held until the transaction commits or are thrown away if the transaction retries. Thus `send` and `send-off` are *not* considered side-effects in the context of a `dosync`, because they handle retries correctly and gracefully.

11.3.1 *In-process versus distributed concurrency models*

Both Clojure and Erlang are designed (Armstrong 2007) specifically with concurrent programming in mind, and Erlang's process[2] model is similar in some ways to Clojure Agents, so it's fair to briefly compare how they each approach the problem.

Erlang takes a distributed, share-nothing (Armstrong 2007b) approach; Clojure instead promotes shared, immutable data. The key to Clojure's success is the fact that its composite data structures are immutable, because immutable structures can be freely shared among disparate threads. Erlang's composite data structures are also immutable, but because the communication model is distributed, the underlying theme is always one of dislocation. The implications of this are that all knowledge of the world under consideration is provided via messages. But with Clojure's in-process model, data structures are always accessible directly, as illustrated in figure 11.7, whereas Erlang makes copies of the data sent back and forth between processes. This works well for Erlang and allows it to provide its fault recovery guarantees, but many application domains can benefit from the shared-memory model provided by Clojure.

The second difference is that Erlang messages block on reception, opening up the possibility for deadlock. On the other hand, when interacting with Clojure Agents, both sends and derefs proceed immediately and never block or wait on the Agent.

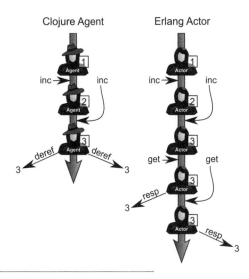

Figure 11.7   Clojure agents versus Erlang processes: each Agent and process starts with the value 1. Both receive an `inc` request simultaneously but can only process one at a time, so more are queued. Requests to the process are queued until a response can be delivered, whereas any number of simultaneous derefs can be done on an Agent. Despite what this illustration may suggest, an Agent is not just an actor with a hat on.

---

[2]   It's interesting that popular opinion has tagged Erlang processes with the "actor" tag although the language implementers rarely, if ever, use that term. Therefore, because the Erlang elite choose not to use that term, we'll avoid doing so also... almost.

Clojure does have an `await` function that can be used to block a thread until a particular Agent has processed a message, but this function is specifically disallowed in Agent threads (and also STM transactions) in order to prevent accidentally creating this sort of deadlock.

The final difference lies in the fact that Agents allow for arbitrary update functions whereas Erlang processes are bound to static pattern-matched message handling routines. In other words, pattern matching couples the data and update logic, whereas the former decouples them. Erlang is an excellent language for solving the extremely difficult problem of distributed computation, but Clojure's concurrency mechanisms service the in-process programming model more flexibly than Erlang allows (Clementson 2008).

11.3.2 *Controlling I/O with an Agent*

One handy use for Agents is to serialize access to a resource, such as an file or other I/O stream. For example, imagine we want to provide a way for multiple threads to report their progress on various tasks, giving each report a unique incrementing number.

Because the state we want to hold is known, we can go ahead and create the Agent:

```
(def log-agent (agent 0))
```

Now we'll supply an action function to send to `log-agent`. All action functions take as their first argument the current state of the Agent and can take any number of other arguments that are sent:

```
(defn do-log [msg-id message]
  (println msg-id ":" message)
  (inc msg-id))
```

Here `msg-id` is the state—the first time `do-log` is sent to the Agent, `msg-id` will be 0. The return value of the action function will be the new Agent state, incrementing it to 1 after that first action.

Now we need to do some work worth logging about, but for this example we'll just pretend:

```
(defn do-step [channel message]
  (Thread/sleep 1)
  (send-off log-agent do-log (str channel message)))

(defn three-step [channel]
  (do-step channel " ready to begin (step 0)")
  (do-step channel " warming up (step 1)")
  (do-step channel " really getting going now (step 2)")
  (do-step channel " done! (step 3)"))
```

To see how `log-agent` will correctly queue and serialize the messages, we need to start a few threads, each yammering away at the Agent, shown next:

```
(defn all-together-now []
  (dothreads! #(three-step "alpha"))
  (dothreads! #(three-step "beta"))
  (dothreads! #(three-step "omega")))
```

```
(all-together-now)
; 0 : alpha ready to being (step 0)
; 1 : omega ready to being (step 0)
; 2 : beta ready to being (step 0)
; 3 : alpha warming up (step 1)
; 4 : alpha really getting going now (step 2)
; 5 : omega warming up (step 1)
; 6 : alpha done! (step 3)
; 7 : omega really getting going now (step 2)
; 8 : omega done! (step 3)
; 9 : beta warming up (step 1)
; 10 : beta really getting going now (step 2)
; 11 : beta done! (step 3)
```

Your output is likely to look different, but one thing that should be exactly the same is the stable, incrementing IDs assigned by the Agent, even while the alpha, beta, and omega threads fight for control.

There are several other possible approaches to solving this problem, and it can be constructive to contrast them. The simplest alternative would be to hold a lock while printing and incrementing. Besides the general risk of deadlocks when a complex program has multiple locks, there are some specific drawbacks even if this would be the only lock in play. For one, each client thread would block anytime there was contention for the lock, and unless some fairness mechanism were used, there'd be at least a slight possibility of one or more threads being "starved" and never having an opportunity to print or proceed with their work. Because Agent actions are queued and don't block waiting for their action to be processed, neither of these is a concern.

Another option would be to use a blocking queue to hold pending log messages. Client threads would be able to add messages to the queue without blocking and with adequate fairness. But you'd generally need to dedicate a thread to popping messages from the queue and printing them, or write code to handle starting and stopping the printing thread as needed. Why write such code when Agents do this for you already? When no actions are queued, the Agent in our example has no thread assigned to it.[3]

Agents have other features that may or may not be useful in any given situation. One is that the current state of an Agent can be observed cheaply. In the previous example, this would allow us to discover the ID of the next message to be written out, as follows:

```
@log-agent
;=> 11
```

Here the Agent is idle—no actions are queued or running, but the same expression would work equally well if the Agent were running.

Other features include the `await` and `await-for` functions, which allow a sending thread to block until all the actions it's sent to a given set of Agents have completed.

---

[3] Using Agents for logging might not be appropriate in all cases. For example, in probing scenarios, the number of log events could be extremely high. Coupling this volume with serialization could make the Agent unable to catch its ever-growing queue.

This could be useful in this logging example if we wanted to be sure a particular message had been written out before proceeding:

```
(do-step "important: " "this must go out")
(await log-agent)
```

The `await-for` function is similar but allows you to specify a number of milliseconds after which to time out, even if the queued actions still haven't completed.

A final feature Agents provide is that the set of actions you can send to an Agent is *open*. You can tell an Agent to do something that wasn't even conceived of at the time the Agent was designed. For example, we could tell the Agent to skip ahead several IDs, and this action would be queued up along with all the `log-message` actions and executed by the Agent when its turn came:

```
(send log-agent (fn [_] 1000))

(do-step "epsilon " "near miss")
; 1000 : epsilon near miss
```

This is another area in which Clojure allows you to extend your design on the fly instead of requiring recompiling or even restarting your app. If you're paying attention, you might wonder why we used `send` in that last example rather than `send-off`.

11.3.3 *The difference between send and send-off*

You can use either `send` or `send-off` with any Agent. When you use `send-off` as we did in most of the examples so far, only a single action queue is involved: the one managed by the individual Agent. Anytime the Agent has a `send-off` action queued, it has a thread assigned to it, working through the queue. With `send`, there's a second queue—actions still go into the Agent's queue, but then the Agent itself queues up waiting for a thread from a fixed-sized pool of threads. The size of this fixed pool is based on the number of processors the JVM is running on, so it's a bad idea to use `send` with any actions that might block, tying up one of these limited number of threads. These differences are illustrated in figure 11.8.

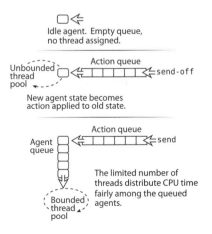

Figure 11.8 Agents using `send` versus `send-off`. When an Agent is idle, no CPU resources are being consumed. Each action is sent to an Agent using either `send` or `send-off`, which determines which thread pool will be used to dequeue and apply the action. Because actions queued with `send` are applied by a limited thread pool, the Agents queue up for access to these threads, a constraint that doesn't apply to actions queued with `send-off`.

We can make this scenario play out if we make a gaggle of Agents and send them actions that sleep for a moment. Here's a little function that does this, using whichever send function we specify, and then waits for all the actions to complete:

```
(defn exercise-agents [send-fn]
  (let [agents (map #(agent %) (range 10))]
    (doseq [a agents]
      (send-fn a (fn [_] (Thread/sleep 1000))))
    (doseq [a agents]
      (await a))))
```

If we use `send-off`, all the agents will begin their one-second wait more or less simultaneously, each in its own thread. So the entire sequence of them will complete in slightly over one second:

```
(time (exercise-agents send-off))
; "Elapsed time: 1008.771296 msecs"
```

Now we can demonstrate why it's a bad idea to mix `send` with actions that block:

```
(time (exercise-agents send))
; "Elapsed time: 3001.555086 msecs"
```

The exact elapsed time you'll see will depend on the number of processors you have, but if you have fewer than eight you'll see this example takes at least two seconds to complete. The threads in the fixed-size pool are all clogged up waiting for `sleep` to finish, so the other Agents queue up waiting for a free thread. Because clearly the computer could complete all 10 actions in about one second using `send-off`, using `send` is a bad idea.

So that's it: `send` is for actions that stay busy using the processor and not blocking on I/O or other threads, whereas `send-off` is for actions that might block, sleep, or otherwise tie up the thread. This is why we used `send-off` for the threads that printed log lines and `send` for the one that did no I/O at all.

11.3.4 *Error handling*

We've been fortunate so far—none of these Agent actions have thrown an exception. But real life is rarely so kind. Most of the other reference types are synchronous and so exceptions thrown while updating their state bubble up the call stack in a normal way, to be caught with a regular `try/catch` in your application (or not). Because Agent actions run in other threads after the sending thread has moved on, we need a different mechanism for handling exceptions that are thrown by Agent actions. As of Clojure 1.2, you can choose between two different error-handling modes for each Agent: `:continue` and `:fail`.

:FAIL

By default, new Agents start out using the `:fail` mode, where an exception thrown by an Agent's action will be captured by the Agent and held so that you can see it later. Meanwhile, the Agent will be considered *failed* or *stopped* and will stop processing its action queue—all the queued actions will have to wait patiently until someone clears up the Agent's error.

One common mistake when dealing with Agents is to forget that your action function *must* take at least one argument for the Agent's current state. For example, we might try to reset the log-agent's current message ID like this:

```
(send log-agent (fn [] 2000))    ; incorrect

@log-agent
;=> 1001
```

At first glance it looks like the action we sent had no effect, or perhaps hasn't been applied yet. But we'd wait in vain for that Agent to do anything ever again without intervention, because it's *stopped*. One way to determine this is with the `agent-error` function:

```
(agent-error log-agent)
;=> #<IllegalArgumentException java.lang.IllegalArgumentException:
;       Wrong number of args passed to: user$eval--509$fn>
```

This returns the error of a stopped Agent, or `nil` if it's still running fine. Another way to see whether an Agent is stopped is to try to send another action to it:

```
(send log-agent (fn [_] 3000))
; java.lang.RuntimeException: Agent is failed, needs restart
```

Even though this action would've worked fine, the Agent has failed and so no further sends are allowed. The state of log-agent remains unchanged:

```
@log-agent
;=> 1001
```

In order to get the Agent back into working order, we need to restart it:

```
(restart-agent log-agent 2500 :clear-actions true)
;=> 2500
```

This resets the value of log-agent to 2500 and deletes all those actions patiently waiting in their queue. If we hadn't included the `:clear-actionstrue` option, those actions would've survived and the Agent would continue processing them. Either way, the Agent is now in good working order again, and so we can again send and sendoff to it:

```
(send-off log-agent do-log "The agent, it lives!")
; 2500 : The agent, it lives!
;=> #<Agent@72898540: 2500>
```

Note that `restart-agent` only makes sense and thus is only allowed when the Agent has failed. If it hasn't failed, any attempt to restart it throws an exception in the thread making the attempt, and the Agent is left undisturbed:

```
(restart-agent log-agent 2500 :clear-actions true)
;=> java.lang.RuntimeException: Agent does not need a restart
```

This mode is perhaps most appropriate for manual intervention. Agents that normally don't have errors but in a running system end up failing can use the :fail mode to keep from doing anything too bad until a human can take things in hand, check to see what happened, choose an appropriate new state for the Agent, and restart it just as we did here.

:CONTINUE

The other error mode that Agents currently support is :continue, where any action that throws an exception is skipped and the Agent proceeds to the next queued action if any. This is most useful when combined with an error handler—if you specify an :error-handler when you create an Agent, that Agent's error mode defaults to :continue. The Agent calls the error handler when an action throws an exception and doesn't proceed to the next action until the handler returns. This gives the handler a chance to report the error in some appropriate way. For example, we could have log-agent handle faulty actions by logging the attempt:

```
(defn handle-log-error [the-agent the-err]
  (println "An action sent to the log-agent threw " the-err))

(set-error-handler! log-agent handle-log-error)

(set-error-mode! log-agent :continue)
```

With the error mode and handler set up, sending faulty actions does cause reports to be printed as we wanted:

```
(send log-agent (fn [x] (/ x 0)))    ; incorrect
; An action sent to the log-
    agent threw java.lang.ArithmeticException: Divide by zero
;=> #<Agent@66200db9: 2501>

(send log-agent (fn [] 0))              ; also incorrect
; An action sent to the log-agent threw java.lang.IllegalArgumentException:
;   Wrong number of args passed to: user$eval--820$fn
;=> #<Agent@66200db9: 2501>
```

And the Agent stays in good shape, always ready for new actions to be sent:

```
(send-off log-agent do-log "Stayin' alive, stayin' alive...")
; 2501 : Stayin' alive, stayin' alive...
```

Note that error handlers can't change the state of the Agent (ours keeps its current message id of 2501 throughout the preceding tests). Error handlers are also supported in the :fail error mode, but handlers can't call restart-agent so they're less often useful for :fail than they are for the :continue error mode.

11.3.5 *When not to use Agents*

It can be tempting to repurpose Agents for any situation requiring the spawning of new threads. Their succinct syntax and "Clojurey" feel often make this temptation strong. But though Agents perform beautifully when each one is representing a real identity in your application, they start to show weaknesses when used a sort of "green thread" abstraction. In cases where you just need a bunch of worker threads banging away on some work, or you have a specific long-running thread polling or blocking on events, or any other kind of situation where it doesn't seem useful that the Agent maintain a value, you'll usually be able to find a better mechanism than Agents. In these cases, there's every reason to consider using a Java `Thread` directly, or a Java executor (as we did with `dothreads!`) to manage a pool of threads, or in some cases perhaps a Clojure future.

Another common temptation is to use Agents when you need state held but you don't actually want the sending thread to proceed until the Agent action you sent is complete. This can be done by using `await`, but it's another form of abuse that should be avoided. For one, because you're not allowed to use `await` in an Agent's action, as you try to use this technique in more and more contexts you're likely to run into a situation where it won't work. But in general, there's probably a reference type that will do a better job of behaving the way you want. Because this is essentially an attempt to use Agents as if they were synchronous, you may have more success with one of the other shared synchronous types. In particular, Atoms are shared and uncoordinated just like Agents, but they're synchronous and so may fit better.

11.4 *When to use Atoms*

Atoms are like Refs in that they're synchronous but are like Agents in that they're independent (uncoordinated). An Atom may seem at first glance similar to a variable, but as we proceed you'll see that any similarities are at best superficial. The use cases for Atoms are similar to those of *compare-and-swap (CAS)* spinning operations. Anywhere you might want to atomically compute a value given an existing value and swap in the new value, an Atom will suffice. Atom updates occur locally to the calling thread, and execution continues after the Atom value has been changed. If another thread B changes the value in an Atom before thread A is successful, then A retries. But these retries are spin-loop and don't occur within the STM, and thus Atom changes can't be coordinated with changes to other reference types. You should take care when embedding changes to Atoms within Clojure's transactions because as you know, transactions can potentially be retried numerous times. Once an Atom's value is set, it's set, and it doesn't roll back when a transaction is retried, so in effect this should be viewed as a side effect. Therefore, use Atoms in transactions only when you're certain that an attempt to update its value, performed numerous times, is idempotent.

Aside from the normal use of @ and `deref` to query an Atom's value, you can also use the mutating functions `swap!`, `compare-and-set!`, and `reset!`.

11.4.1 *Sharing across threads*

As we mentioned, Atoms are thread safe and can be used when you require a lightweight mutable reference to be shared across threads. A simple case is one of a globally accessible incrementing timer created using the `atom` function:

```
(def *time* (atom 0))
(defn tick [] (swap! *time* inc))
(dothreads! tick :threads 1000 :times 100)
```

```
@*time*
;=> 100000
```

Though this will work, Java already provides a concurrent class for just such a purpose, `java.util.concurrent.atomic.AtomicInteger`, which can be used similarly:

```
(def *time* (java.util.concurrent.atomic.AtomicInteger. 0))
(defn tick [] (.getAndIncrement *time*))
(dothreads! tick :threads 1000 :times 100)
*time*
;=> 100000
```

Though the use of `AtomicInteger` is more appropriate in this case, the use of an Atom works to show that it's safe to use across threads.

11.4.2 *Using Atoms in transactions*

Just because we said that Atoms should be used carefully within transactions, that's not to say that they can never be used in that way. In fact, the use of an Atom as the reference holding a function's memoization cache is idempotent on update.

> **MEMOIZATION**   *Memoization* is a way for a function to store calculated values in a cache so that multiple calls to the function can retrieve previously calculated results from the cache, instead of performing potentially expensive calculations every time. Clojure provides a core function `memoize` that can be used on any referentially transparent function.

Individual requirements from memoization are highly personal, and a generic approach isn't always the appropriate solution for every problem. We'll discuss personalized memoization strategies in section 12.4, but for now we'll use an illustrative example appropriate for Atom usage.

ATOMIC MEMOIZATION

The core `memoize` function is great for creating simple function caches, but it has some limitations. First, it doesn't allow for custom caching and expiration strategies. Additionally, `memoize` doesn't allow you to manipulate the cache for the purposes of clearing it in part or wholesale. Therefore, we'll create a function `manipulable-memoize` that allows us to get at the cache and perform operations on it directly. Throughout the book, we've mentioned Clojure's metadata facility, and for this example it will come in handy. We can take in the function to be memoized and attach some metadata[4] with an Atom containing the cache itself for later manipulation.

Listing 11.3   A resettable `memoize` function

```
(defn manipulable-memoize [function]
  (let [cache (atom {})]                    ◁── Store cache
    (with-meta                                   in Atom
      (fn [& args]
```

---

[4] The ability to attach metadata to functions is a recent addition to Clojure version 1.2.

```
      (or (second (find @cache args))           ◁──── Check cache first
          (let [ret (apply function args)]        ◁─┐ Else calculate,
            (swap! cache assoc args ret)            │ store, and return
            ret)))
   {:cache cache}))))        ◁──── Attach metadata
```

As shown in listing 11.3, we've slightly modified the core `memoize` function to attach the Atom to the function being memoized. You can now observe `manipulable-memoize` in action:

```
(def slowly (fn [x] (Thread/sleep 3000) x))
(time [(slowly 9) (slowly 9)])
; "Elapsed time: 6000.63 msecs"
;=> [9 9]

(def sometimes-slowly (manipulable-memoize slowly))
(time [(sometimes-slowly 108) (sometimes-slowly 108)])
; "Elapsed time: 3000.409 msecs"
;=> [108 108]
```

The call to `slowly` is always... well... slow, as you'd expect. But the call to `sometimes-slowly` is only slow on the first call given a certain argument. This too is just as you'd expect. Now we can inspect `sometimes-slowly`'s cache and perform some operations on it:

```
(meta sometimes-slowly)
;=> {:cache #<Atom@e4245: {(108) 108}>}

(let [cache (:cache (meta sometimes-slowly))]
  (swap! cache dissoc '(108)))
;=> {}
```

You may wonder why we used `swap!` to `dissoc` the cached argument 108 instead of using `(reset! cache {})`. There are certainly valid use cases for the wholesale reset of an Atom's value, and this case is arguably one. But it's good practice to set your reference values via the application of a function rather than the in-place value setting. In this way, you can be more selective about the value manipulations being performed. Having said that, here are the consequences our actions had:

```
(meta sometimes-slowly)
;=> {:cache #<Atom@e4245: {}>}

(time (sometimes-slowly 108))
; "Elapsed time: 3000.3 msecs"
;=> 108
```

And yes, you can see that we were able to remove the cached argument value 108 using the metadata map attached to the function `sometimes-slowly`. There are better ways to allow for pointed cache removal than this, but for now you can take heart in that using an Atom, we've allowed for the local mutation of a reference in a thread-safe way. Additionally, because of the nature of memoization, you can use these memoized functions in a transaction without ill effect. Bear in mind that if you do use this in a transaction, then any attempt to remove values from the cache may not be met with the results expected. Depending on the interleaving of your removal and any restarts, the value(s) you remove might be reinserted on the next time through the restart. But even this condition is agreeable if your only concern is reducing total cache size.

11.5   *When to use locks*

Clojure's reference types and parallel primitives cover a vast array of use cases. Additionally, Java's rich set of concurrency classes found in the java.util.concurrent package are readily available. But even with this arsenal of tools at your disposal, there still may be circumstances where explicit locking is the only option available, the common case being the modification of arrays concurrently. We'll start with a simple protocol to describe a concurrent, mutable, *safe array* that holds an internal array instance, allowing you to access it or mutate it safely. A naive implementation can be seen in the following listing.

Listing 11.4   A simple SafeArray protocol

```
(ns joy.locks
  (:refer-clojure :exclude [aget aset count seq])
  (:require [clojure.core :as clj]))

(defprotocol SafeArray                    ◁─┐ Small set
  (aset  [this i f])                         │ of functions
  (aget  [this i])
  (count [this])
  (seq   [this]))

(defn make-dumb-array [t sz]
  (let [a (make-array t sz)]
    (reify
      SafeArray
      (count [_] (clj/count a))
      (seq [_] (clj/seq a))              │ aget and aset
      (aget [_ i] (clj/aget a i))      ◁─┘ are unguarded
      (aset [this i f]
        (clj/aset a i (f (aget this i)))))))
```

If you'll notice, we used the :refer-clojure namespace directive to :exclude the array and sequence functions that the SafeArray protocol overrides. We did this not only because it's important to know how to use :refer-clojure, but also because we're changing the semantics of aset to take a mutating function as its last argument instead of a raw value. We then used the :require directive to alias the Clojure namespace as clj, thus avoiding the need to use the fully qualified function names a la clojure.core/aget.

The dumb array created by make-dumb-array is stored in a closure created by reify, and unguarded access is provided without concern for concurrent matters. Using this implementation across threads is disastrous, as shown:

```
(defn pummel [a]
  (dothreads! #(dotimes [i (count a)] (aset a i inc)) :threads 100))
```

```
(def D (make-dumb-array Integer/TYPE 8))
(pummel D)

;; wait for pummel to terminate

(seq D)
;=> (82 84 65 63 83 65 83 87)
```

This is very wrong—100 threads incrementing concurrently should result in 100 for each array slot. To add insult to injury, Clojure didn't throw a `Concurrent-ModificationException` as you might've expected, but instead just silently went along doing very bad things. Next, we'll talk a little about locking and provide an alternate implementation for `SafeArray` using locking primitives.

11.5.1 Safe mutation through locking

Currently, the only[5] way to safely modify and see consistent values for a mutable object across threads in Clojure is through locking.

REFERENCES AROUND EVIL MUTABLE THINGS

Wrapping a mutable object in a Clojure reference type provides *absolutely no guarantees for safe concurrent modification*. Doing this will at best explode immediately or, worse, provide inaccurate results.

If at all possible, locking should be avoided; but for those times when it's unavoidable, the `locking` macro will help. The `locking` macro takes a single parameter acting as the locking monitor and a body that executes in the monitor context. Any writes and reads to the monitor object are thread safe, and as a bonus the monitor is *always* released at the end of the block. One of the major complexities in concurrent programming using locks is that all errors must be handled fully and appropriately; otherwise you risk orphaned locks, and they spell deadlock. But the `locking` macro will always release the lock, even in the face of exceptions.

Listing 11.5 An implementation of the `SafeArray` protocol using the `locking` macro

```
(defn make-safe-array [t sz]
  (let [a (make-array t sz)]          ◁┐ Array creation
    (reify                             │ is same
      SafeArray
      (count [_] (clj/count a))
      (seq [_] (clj/seq a))
      (aget [_ i]                      ◁── aget is locked
        (locking a
          (clj/aget a i)))
      (aset [this i f]                 ◁── aset is locked
        (locking a
          (clj/aset a i (f (aget this i)))))))))    ◁── aset uses aget

(def A (make-safe-array Integer/TYPE 8))
(pummel A)
```

---

[5] Although a potential future addition to Clojure named *pods* may provide another.

```
;; wait for pummel to terminate

(seq A)
;=> (100 100 100 100 100 100 100 100)
```

We used the `locking` macro on both the `aget` and `aset` functions so that they can both maintain consistency concurrently. Because `aset` calls `aget`, the `locking` macro is called twice. This isn't a problem because `locking` is *reentrant*, or able to be called multiple times in the same thread. Typically, you'd have to manage the releasing of reentrant locking mechanism to match the number of times called, but fortunately `locking` manages that for us.

The `locking` macro is the simplest way to perform primitive locking in Clojure. But the implementation of `make-safe-array` is coarse in that the locks used are guarding the entire array. Any readers or writers wishing to access or update any slot in the array *must* wait their turn, a bottleneck known as *contention*. If you need finer-grained locking, the locking facilities provided by Java will help to gain more control, a topic we cover next.

11.5.2 *Using Java's explicit locks*

Java provides a set of explicit locks in the `java.util.concurrent.locks` package that can also be used as shown in the following listing. One such lock is provided by the `java.util.concurrent.locks.ReentrantLock` class.

Listing 11.6 An implementation of the `SafeArray` protocol using `ReentrantLock`

```
(defn lock-i [target-index num-locks]
  (mod target-index num-locks))

(import 'java.util.concurrent.locks.ReentrantLock)

(defn make-smart-array [t sz]
  (let [a   (make-array t sz)              ⟵——— Array
        Lsz (quot sz 2)
        L   (into-array (take Lsz          ⟵——— Locks
                        (repeatedly #(ReentrantLock.))))]
    (reify
      SafeArray
      (count [_] (clojure.core/count a))
      (seq [_] (clojure.core/seq a))
      (aget [_ i]
        (let [lk (clojure.core/aget L (lock-i (inc i) Lsz))]
          (.lock lk)                       ⟵┐ Explicit
          (try                             │ locking
            (clojure.core/aget a i)                    ┐ Explicit
            (finally (.unlock lk)))))                  │ unlocking
      (aset [this i f]                                 ⟵┘
        (let [lk (clojure.core/aget L (lock-i (inc i) Lsz))]
          (.lock lk)
          (try                                         ┐ Reentrant
            (clojure.core/aset a i (f (aget this i)))  ⟵┘ locking
            (finally (.unlock lk))))))))
```

```
(def S (make-smart-array Integer/TYPE 8))
(pummel S)

;; wait for pummel to terminate

(seq S)
;=> (100 100 100 100 100 100 100 100)
```

The first point of note is that we use a technique (simplified for clarity) called *lock striping* (Herlihy 2008) to reduce the contention of guarding the array as a whole using `locking`. The target array a's slots are guarded by half the number of locks, each chosen using the simple formula (`mod target-index num-locks`). This scheme allows readers and writers to (potentially) act independently when accessing different array slots. It's crucial that we closed over the lock instance array L because for explicit locks to work, each access *must* lock and unlock the *same* instance. Additionally, we're calling the `.unlock` method in the body of a `finally` expression, because failing to do so is a recipe for disaster. Unlike the `locking` macro, the `ReentrantLock` class doesn't manage lock release automatically. Finally, you can also use the `ReentrantLock` in a way equivalent to using the `locking` macro, but using `ReentrantLock` gives you the choice of using `proxy` to provide more complex semantics than `locking` can provide.

One flaw of the `make-smart-array` function is that it uses the same locks for readers and writers. But you can allow for more concurrency if you enable some number of readers to access array slots without blocking at all by using the `java.util.concurrent.locks.ReentrantReadWriteLock` class. The `ReentrantReadWriteLock` class holds two lock instances, one for reads and one for writes, and by adding another lock array you can take advantage of this fact. We won't get into that exercise here, but if you choose to do so then you can use the implementation of `make-smart-array` as a guide.

Using the various locking mechanisms, you can guarantee consistency across threads for mutable objects. But as we showed with explicit locks, there's an expected incantation to unlocking that must be strictly observed. Though not necessarily complex in the `SafeArray` implementations, the conceptual baggage incurred in the semantics of explicit locking scheme doesn't scale well. The `java.util.concurrent` package contains a cacophony of concurrency primitives above and beyond simple locks, but it's not our goal to provide a comprehensive survey herein.

Now that we've covered the matter of guaranteeing coordinated state across disparate threads, we turn our attention to a different topic: parallelization.

11.6   *When to use futures*

Clojure includes two reference types supporting parallelism: *futures* and *promises*. Futures, the subject of this section, are simple yet elegant constructs useful for partitioning a typically sequential operation into discrete parts. These parts can then be asynchronously processed across numerous threads that will block if the enclosed expression hasn't finished. All subsequent dereferencing will return the calculated value. The simplest example of the use of a future is as shown:

```
(time (let [x (future (do (Thread/sleep 5000) (+ 41 1)))]
  [@x @x]))
; "Elapsed time: 5001.682 msecs"
;=> [42 42]
```

The processing time of the do block is only paid for on the first dereference of the future x. Futures represent expressions that have yet to be computed.

11.6.1 *Futures as callbacks*

One nice use case for futures is in the context of a callback mechanism. Normally you might call out to a remote-procedure call (RPC), wait for it to complete, and then proceed with some task depending on the return value. But what happens if you need to make multiple RPC calls? Should you be forced to wait for them all serially? Thanks to futures, the answer is no. In this section, we'll use futures to create an aggregate task that finds the total number of occurrences of a string within a given set of Twitter[6] feeds. This aggregate task will be split into numerous parallel subtasks via futures.

COUNTING WORD OCCURRENCES IN A SET OF TWITTER FEEDS

Upon going to a personal Twitter page such as http://twitter.com/fogus, you can find a link to the RSS 2.0 feed for that user. We'll use this feed as the input to our functions. An RSS 2.0 feed is an XML document used to represent a piece of data that's constantly changing. The layout of a Twitter RSS entry is straightforward:

```
<rss version="2.0">
  <channel>
    <title>Twitter / fogus</title>
    <link>http://twitter.com/fogus</link>
    <item>
      <title>fogus: Thinking about #Clojure futures.</title>
      <link>http://twitter.com/fogus/statuses/12180102647/</link>
    </item>
  </channel>
</rss>
```

There's more to the content of a typical RSS feed, but for our purposes we wish to only retrieve the title element of the item elements (there can be more than one). To do this, we need to first parse the XML and put it into a convenient format. If you recall from section 8.4, we created a domain DSL to create a tree built on a simple node structure of tables with the keys :tag, :attrs, and :content. As mentioned, that structure is leveraged in many Clojure libraries, and we'll take advantage of this fact. Clojure provides some core functions in the clojure.xml and clojure.zip namespaces to help make sense of the feed:

```
(require '(clojure [xml :as xml]))
(require '(clojure [zip :as zip]))

(defmulti rss-children class)
(defmethod rss-children String [uri-str]
```

---

[6] Twitter is online at http://twitter.com.

```
(-> (xml/parse uri-str)
    zip/xml-zip
    zip/down
    zip/children))
```

Using the function clojure.xml/parse, we can retrieve the XML for a Twitter RSS feed and convert it into the familiar tree format. That tree is then passed into a function clojure.zip/xml-zip that converts that structure into another data structure called a *zipper*. The form and semantics of the zipper are beyond the scope of this book (Huet 1997), but using it in this case allows us to easily navigate *down* from the root rss XML node to the channel node, where we then retrieve its children. The child nodes returned from rss-children contain other items besides item nodes (title, link, and so forth) that need to be filtered out. Once we have those item nodes, we then want to retrieve the title text and count the number of occurrences of the target text (case-insensitive). We perform all of these tasks using the function count-tweet-text-task, defined in the following listing.

Listing 11.7 Creating a future task to count word occurrences in a tweet

```
(import '(java.util.regex Pattern))

(defn count-tweet-text-task [txt feed]
  (let [items (rss-children feed)                       ◁——— Get kids
        re    (Pattern/compile (Pattern/quote txt))]
    (count
      (mapcat #(re-seq re (first %))                    ◁——— Get matches
        (for [item (filter (comp #{:item} :tag) items)] ◁——— Filter non-items
          (-> item :content first :content))))))        ◁——— Get title
```

We'll now try to count some text in a Twitter feed to see what happens:

```
(count-tweet-text-task
  "#clojure"
  "http://twitter.com/statuses/user_timeline/46130870.rss")
;=> 7
```

The result you see is highly dependent on when you run this function, because the RSS feeds are ever-changing. But using the count-tweet-text-task function, we can build a sequence of tasks to be performed over some number of Twitter feeds. Before we do that, we'll create a convenience macro as-futures to take said sequence and dispatch the enclosed actions across some futures.

Listing 11.8 A macro to dispatch a sequence of futures

```
(defmacro as-futures [[a args] & body]
  (let [parts          (partition-by #{'=>} body)
        [acts _ [res]] (partition-by #{:as} (first parts))
        [_ _ task]     parts]
    `(let [~res (for [~a ~args] (future ~@acts))]
       ~@task)))
```

The as-futures macro implemented in listing 11.8 names a binding corresponding to the arguments for a given action, which is then dispatched across a number of futures, after which a task is run against the futures sequence. The body of as-futures is segmented so that we can clearly specify the needed parts—the action arguments, the action to be performed for each argument, and the tasks to be run against the resulting sequence of futures:

```
(as-futures [<arg-name> <all-args>]
  <actions-using-args>
  :as <results-name>
 =>
  <actions-using-results>)
```

To simplify the macro implementation, we use the :as keyword and => symbol to clearly delineate its segments. The as-futures body only exits after the task body finishes—as determined by the execution of the futures. We can use as-futures to perform the original task with a new function tweet-occurrences, implemented in the following listing.

Listing 11.9   Counting string occurrences in Twitter feeds fetched in parallel

```
(defn tweet-occurrences [tag & feeds]
  (as-futures [feed feeds]
    (count-tweet-text-task tag feed)
    :as results
   =>
    (reduce (fn [total res] (+ total @res))
            0
            results)))
```

The as-futures macro builds a sequence of futures named results, enclosing the call to count-tweet-text-task across the unique set of Twitter feeds provided. We then sum the counts returned from the dereferencing of the individual futures, as shown:

```
(tweet-occurrences "#Clojure"
  "http://twitter.com/statuses/user_timeline/46130870.rss"
  "http://twitter.com/statuses/user_timeline/14375110.rss"
  "http://twitter.com/statuses/user_timeline/5156041.rss"
  "http://twitter.com/statuses/user_timeline/21439272.rss")
;=> 22
```

And that's that. Using only a handful of functions and macros, plus using the built-in core facilities for XML parsing and navigation, we've created a simple Twitter occurrences counter. Our implementation has some trade-offs made in the name of page count. First, we blindly dereference the future in tweet-occurrences when calculating the sum. If the future's computation freezes, then the dereference would likewise freeze. Using some combination of future-done?, future-cancel, and future-cancelled? in your own programs, you can skip, retry, or eliminate ornery feeds from the calculation. Futures are only one way to perform parallel computation in Clojure, and in the next section we'll talk about another—promises.

11.7 When to use promises

Another tool that Clojure provides for parallel computation is the `promise` and `deliver` mechanisms. Promises are similar to futures, in that they represent a unit of computation to be performed on a separate thread. Likewise, the blocking semantics when dereferencing an unfinished promise are also the same. Whereas futures encapsulate an arbitrary expression that caches its value in the future upon completion, promises are placeholders for values whose construction is fulfilled by another thread via the `deliver` function. A simple example is as follows:

```
(def x (promise))
(def y (promise))
(def z (promise))

(dothreads! #(deliver z (+ @x @y)))

(dothreads!
  #(do (Thread/sleep 2000) (deliver x 52)))

(dothreads!
  #(do (Thread/sleep 4000) (deliver y 86)))

(time @z)
; "Elapsed time: 3995.414 msecs"
;=> 138
```

Promises are write-once; any further attempt to deliver will throw an exception.

11.7.1 Parallel tasks with promises

We can create a macro similar to `as-futures` for handling promises, but because of the more advanced value semantics, the implementation is thus more complicated. We again wish to provide a named set of tasks, but we'd additionally like to name the corresponding promises so that we can then execute over the eventual results, which we do next.

Listing 11.10 A macro to dispatch a sequence of promises across a number of threads

```
(defmacro with-promises [[n tasks _ as] & body]
  (when as
    `(let [tasks# ~tasks
           n# (count tasks#)
           promises# (take n# (repeatedly promise))]
       (dotimes [i# n#]
         (dothreads!
           (fn []
             (deliver (nth promises# i#)
                      ((nth tasks# i#))))))
       (let [~n tasks#
             ~as promises#]
         ~@body))))
```

We could then build a rudimentary parallel testing facility, dispatching tests across disparate threads and summing the results when all of the tests are done:

```
(defrecord TestRun [run passed failed])

(defn pass [] true)
(defn fail [] false)

(defn run-tests [& all-tests]
  (with-promises
    [tests all-tests :as results]
    (into (TestRun. 0 0 0)
          (reduce #(merge-with + %1 %2) {}
            (for [r results]
              (if @r
                {:run 1 :passed 1}
                {:run 1 :failed 1}))))))

(run-tests pass fail fail fail pass)
;=> #:user.TestRun{:run 5, :passed 2, :failed 3}
```

This unit-testing model is simplistic by design in order to illustrate parallelization using promises and not to provide a comprehensive testing framework.

11.7.2 *Callback API to blocking API*

Promises, much like futures, are useful for executing RPC on separate threads. This can be useful if you need to parallelize a group of calls to an RPC service, but there's a converse use case also. Often, RPC APIs take arguments to the service calls and also a callback function to be executed when the call completes. Using the rss-children function from the previous section, we can construct an archetypal RPC function:

```
(defn tweet-items [k feed]
  (k
    (for [item (filter (comp #{:item} :tag) (rss-children feed))]
      (-> item :content first :content))))
```

The tweet-items function is a distillation of the count-tweet-text-task function from the previous chapter, as shown:

```
(tweet-items
  count
  "http://twitter.com/statuses/user_timeline/46130870.rss")
;=> 16
```

The argument k to tweet-items is the callback, or continuation, that's called with the filtered RPC results. This API is fine, but there are times when a blocking call is more appropriate than callback based call. We can use a promise to achieve this blocking behavior with the following:

```
(let [p (promise)]
  (tweet-items #(deliver p (count %))
               "http://twitter.com/statuses/user_timeline/46130870.rss")
  @p)
;=> 16
```

And as you see, the call blocks until the deliver occurs. This is a fine way to transform the callback into a blocking call, but we'd like a way to do this generically. Fortunately, most well-written RPC APIs follow the same form for their callback functions/methods, so we can create a macro to wrap this up nicely in the following listing.

Listing 11.11 A macro for transforming a callback-based function to a blocking call

```
(defmacro cps->fn [f k]
  `(fn [& args#]
     (let [p# (promise)]
       (apply ~f (fn [x#] (deliver p# (~k x#))) args#)
       @p#)))

(def count-items (cps->fn tweet-items count))

(count-items "http://twitter.com/statuses/user_timeline/46130870.rss")
;=> 16
```

This is a simple solution to a common problem that you may have already encountered in your own applications.

11.7.3 *Deterministic deadlocks*

You can cause a deadlock in your applications by never delivering to a promise. One possibly surprising advantage of using promises is that if a promise can deadlock, it'll deadlock deterministically. Because only a single thread can ever deliver on a promise, only that thread will ever cause a deadlock. We can create a cycle in the dependencies between two promises to observe a deadlock using the following code:

```
(def kant (promise))
(def hume (promise))

(dothreads!
  #(do (println "Kant has" @kant) (deliver hume :thinking)))

(dothreads!
  #(do (println "Hume is" @hume) (deliver kant :fork)))
```

The Kant thread is waiting for the delivery of the value for kant from the Hume thread, which in turn is waiting for the value for hume from the Kant thread. Attempting either @kant or @hume in the REPL will cause an immediate deadlock. Furthermore, this deadlock will happen *every* time; it's deterministic rather than dependent on odd thread timings or the like. Deadlocks are never nice, but deterministic deadlocks are better than nondeterministic.[7]

We've only touched the surface for the potential that promises represent. In fact, the pieces that we've assembled in this section represent some of the basic building blocks of dataflow (Van Roy 2004) concurrency. But any attempt to serve justice to dataflow concurrency in a single section would be a futile effort. At its essence,

---

[7] There are experts in concurrent programming who will say that naïve locking schemes are also deterministic. Our simple example is illustrative, but alas it isn't representative of a scheme that you may devise for your own code. In complex designs where promises are created in one place and delivered in a remote locale, determining deadlock will naturally be more complex. Therefore, we'd like to use this space to coin a new phrase: "determinism is relative."

dataflow deals with the process of dynamic changes in values causing dynamic changes in dependent "formulas." This type of processing finds a nice analogy in the way that spreadsheet cells operate, some representing values and others dependent formulas that change as the former also change.

Continuing our survey of Clojure's parallelization primitives, we'll next discuss some of the functions provided in the core library.

11.8 Parallelism

In the previous two sections we built two useful macros as-futures and with-promises, allowing you to parallelize a set of operations across numerous threads. But Clojure has functions in its core library providing similar functionality named pmap, pvalues, and pcalls, which we'll cover briefly in this section.

11.8.1 pvalues

The pvalues macro is analogous to the as-futures macro, in that it executes an arbitrary number of expressions in parallel. Where it differs is that it returns a lazy sequence of the results of all the enclosed expressions, as shown:

```
(pvalues 1 2 (+ 1 2))
;=> (1 2 3)
```

The important point to remember when using pvalues is that the return type is a lazy sequence, meaning that your access costs might not always present themselves as expected:

```
(defn sleeper [s thing] (Thread/sleep (* 1000 s)) thing)
(defn pvs [] (pvalues
                (sleeper 2 :1st)
                (sleeper 3 :2nd)
                (keyword "3rd")))

(-> (pvs) first time)
; "Elapsed time: 2000.309 msecs"
;=> :1st
```

The total time cost of accessing the first value in the result of pvs is only the cost of its own calculation. But accessing any subsequent element costs as much as the most expensive element before it, which you can verify by accessing the last element:

```
(-> (pvs) last time)
; "Elapsed time: 4001.435 msecs"
;=> :3rd
```

This may prove a disadvantage if you want to access the result of a relatively cheap expression that happens to be placed after a more costly expression. More accurately, all seq values within a sliding window [8] are forced, so processing time is limited by the most costly element therein.

---

[8] Currently, the window size is $N+2$, where N is the number of CPU cores. But this is an implementation detail, so it's enough to know only that the sliding window exists.

11.8.2 *pmap*

The pmap function is the parallel version of the core map function. Given a function and a set of sequences, the application of the function to each matching element happens in parallel:

```
(->> [1 2 3]
     (pmap (comp inc (partial sleeper 2)))
     doall
     time)
; "Elapsed time: 2000.811 msecs"
;=> (2 3 4)
```

The total cost of realizing the result of mapping a costly increment function is again limited by the most costly execution time within the aforementioned sliding window. Clearly, in this contrived case, using pmap provides a benefit, so why not just replace every call to map in your programs with a call to pmap? Surely this would lead to faster execution times if the map functions were all applied in parallel, no? The answer is a resounding: it depends. A definite cost is associated with keeping the resulting sequence result coordinated, and to indiscriminately use pmap might actually incur that cost unnecessarily, leading to a performance penalty. But if you're certain that the cost of the function application outweighs the cost of the coordination, then pmap might help to realize performance gains. Only through experimentation will you be able to determine whether pmap is the right choice.

11.8.3 *pcalls*

Finally, Clojure provides a pcalls function that takes an arbitrary number of functions taking no arguments and calls them in parallel, returning a lazy sequence of the results. The use shouldn't be a surprise by now:

```
(-> (pcalls
      #(sleeper 2 :1st)
      #(sleeper 3 :2nd)
      #(keyword "3rd"))
    doall
    time)
; "Elapsed time: 3001.039 msecs"
;=> (:1st :2nd :3rd)
```

The same benefits and trade-offs associated with pvalues and pmap also apply to pcalls and should be considered before use.

Executing costly operations in parallel can be a great boon when used properly, but should by no means be considered a magic potion guaranteeing speed gains. There's currently no magical formula for determining which parts of an application can be parallelized—the onus is on you to determine your application's parallel potential. What Clojure provides is a set of primitives, including futures, promises, pmap, pvalues, and pcalls as the building blocks for your own personalized parallelization needs.

In the next section, we'll cover the ubiquitous Var, but from a different perspective than we have thus far.

11.9 *Vars and dynamic binding*

The last reference type we'll explore is perhaps the most commonly used—the Var. Vars are most often used because of two main features:

- Vars can be named and interned in a namespace.
- Vars can provide thread-local state.

It's through the second feature that Vars contribute most usefully to the reference type landscape. The thread-local value of a Var by definition can only be read from or written to a single thread, and thus provides the thread-safe semantics you've come to expect from a Clojure reference type.

But before you can start experimenting with Vars at the REPL, we to need address some consequences of the first feature. The other reference objects you've looked at aren't themselves named and so are generally *stored* in something with a name. This means that when the name is evaluated, you get the reference object, not the value. To get the object's value, you have to use deref. Named Vars flip this around—evaluating their name gives the value, so if you want the Var object, you need to pass the name to the special operator var.

With this knowledge in hand, you can experiment with an existing Var. Clojure provides a Var named *read-eval*,[9] so you can get its current value by evaluating its name:

```
*read-eval*
;=> true
```

No deref needed, because *read-eval* is a named Var. Now for the Var object itself:

```
(var *read-eval*)
;=> #'clojure.core/*read-eval*
```

That's interesting—when a named Var object is printed, it starts with #' and is then followed by the fully qualified name of the Var. The #' reader feature expands to the Var operator—it means the same thing:

```
#'*read-eval*
;=> #'clojure.core/*read-eval*
```

Now that you've seen how to refer to Var objects, you can look at how they behave. The Var *read-eval* is one of those provided by Clojure that's specifically meant to be given thread-local bindings but by default has only a root binding. You should've seen its root binding when you evaluated it earlier—by default, *read-eval* is bound to true.

---

[9] *read-eval* happens to be a Var that has a default configuration useful for this discussion about Vars—its actual purpose is unimportant here.

11.9.1 *The binding macro*

The root binding of a Var can act as the base of a stack, with each thread's local bindings pushing onto that stack and popping off of it as requested. The most common mechanism for pushing and popping thread-local bindings is the macro `binding`. It takes one or more Var names and a value for each that will initialize the new binding when it's pushed. These bindings remain in effect until control passes out of the `binding` macro, at which point they're popped off the stack.

Here's a simple example of a function that prints the current value of the Var `*read-eval*`, either the root or thread-local value, whichever is currently in effect:

```
(defn print-read-eval []
  (println "*read-eval* is currently" *read-eval*))
```

This function calls `print-read-eval` three times, the first and last of which will print the root binding. The middle time, `binding` is in effect:

```
(defn binding-play []
  (print-read-eval)
  (binding [*read-eval* false]
    (print-read-eval))
  (print-read-eval))
```

This results in the Var temporarily having a thread-local value of `false`:

```
(binding-play)
; *read-eval* is currently true
; *read-eval* is currently false
; *read-eval* is currently true
```

This is a like thread B in figure 11.9, which also shows a simpler scenario than thread A and a more complex one than thread C.

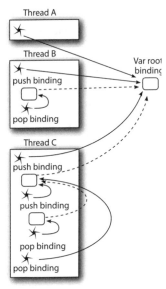

Figure 11.9 Thread-local Var bindings. This illustration depicts a single Var being used from three different threads. Each rounded box is a Var binding, either thread-local or root. Each star is the Var being deref'ed, with the solid arrow pointing to the binding used. The dotted lines point from a thread-local binding to the next binding on the stack.

11.9.2 *Creating a named Var*

Vars are most commonly created with the special operator `def` or one of the many macros that expands to a form that has a `def` inside:

- `defn`—For putting a function in a Var
- `defmacro`—For putting a macro in a Var
- `defonce`—For setting the value of an unbound Var
- `defmulti`—For putting a multimethod in a Var

There are a few others in `clojure.core`[10] and many more in `contrib`. What they have in common is that

---

[10] It's likely that starting with Clojure 1.3 Vars will only have the ability to take on thread-local values when defined using `defdynamic` or marked with metadata like `^{:dynamic true}`. Throughout this book, we will take the latter approach with high confidence that it will just work in 1.3.

each of these will intern a Var in the current namespace. Clojure will search for the named Var in the current namespace. If one is found, it's used; otherwise, a new Var is created and added to the namespace, and that one is used.[11] The Var (specifically the root binding of the Var) is bound to whatever value, function, or macro (and so on) was given. The Var itself is returned:

```
(def favorite-color :green)
#'user/favorite-color
```

When a Var is printed, its fully qualified name is given, along with the namespace where the Var is interned (user) and the Var's name itself (favorite-color). These are preceded by #' because unlike the other reference types, a named Var is automatically dereferenced when its name is evaluated—no explicit @ or call to deref is required:

```
favorite-color
;=> :green
```

So in order to refer to a Var instead of the value it's bound to, you need to use #' or the special form var, which are equivalent:

```
(var favorite-color)
;=> #'user/favorite-color
```

A Var can exist (or *not* exist) in any of four states. The precise state a Var is in can be determined using the functions resolve, bound?, and thread-bound? as shown in Table 11.1.

Table 11.1   Var states

Initialization mechanism	(resolve 'x)	(bound? #'x)	(thread-bound? #'x)
(def x)	#'user/x	false	false
(def x 5)	#'user/x	true	false
(binding [x 7] ...)	#'user/x	true	true
(with-local-vars [x 9] ...)	nil	true (bound? x)	true (thread-bound? x)

The first row of the table shows the results of resolve, bound?, and thread-bound? when a var x is unbound. The remaining rows show how to change x to cause those functions to return the values shown.

11.9.3   *Creating anonymous Vars*

Vars don't always have names, nor do they need to be interned in a namespace. The with-local-vars macro creates Vars and gives them thread-local bindings all at once, but it *won't* intern them. Instead, they're bound to locals, which means that the associated Var isn't implicitly looked up by symbolic name. You need to use deref or var-get to get the current value of the Var. Here's an example of a Var x created and

---

[11] Not all macros starting with def necessarily create or intern Vars. Some that don't: defmethod, defrecord, and deftype.

interned with def, and then a local x that shadows it and is bound to a new var via
with-local-vars:

```
(def x 42)
{:outer-var-value x
 :with-locals (with-local-vars [x 9]
                 {:local-var x
                  :local-var-value (var-get x)})}}

;=> {:outer-var-value 42,
     :with-locals {:local-var #<Var: --unnamed-->,
                   :local-var-value 9}}
```

Within the body of the with-local-vars macro, the bound value can bet set using
(var-set <var> <value>), which will of course only affect the thread-local value. It's
almost stunning how rarely with-local-vars is useful.

11.9.4 *Dynamic scope*

Vars have dynamic scope, which contrasts with the lexical scope of let locals. The most
obvious difference is that with a lexical local, you can easily see where it was initialized
by looking at the nested structure of the code. A Var, on the other hand, may have been
initialized by a binding anywhere earlier in the call stack, not necessarily nearby in the
code at all. This difference can create unexpectedly complex interactions and is one of
the few areas where Clojure does little to help you address such complexity.

An example of this complexity is shown by using the binding macro or any macro
built on top of it, such as with-precision and with-out-str. For example, we can
use the with-precision macro to conveniently set up the *math-context* Var:

```
(with-precision 4
  (/ 1M 3))
;=> 0.3333M
```

We need to use with-precision here because if we don't tell BigDecimal we're okay
with it rounding off the result, it'll refuse to return anything in this case:

```
(/ 1M 3)
; java.lang.ArithmeticException: Non-terminating decimal expansion;
;   no exact representable decimal result.
```

With that in mind, can you see why with-precision isn't doing its job in the next
snippet? The only thing that makes it different from the example that worked earlier
is we're using map to produce a sequence of three numbers instead of just one:

```
(with-precision 4
  (map (fn [x] (/ x 3)) (range 1M 4M)))

; java.lang.ArithmeticException: Non-terminating decimal expansion;
;   no exact representable decimal result.
```

The problem is that map is lazy and therefore doesn't call the function given to it
immediately. Instead, it waits until the REPL tries to print it, and then does the division. Although the map and the function it calls are within the *lexical scope* of with-
binding, and with-binding itself uses a thread-local binding internally, it doesn't care

about lexical scope. When the division operation is performed, we've already left the *dynamic scope* of the with-precision, and it no longer has any effect. The BigDecimal behavior drops back to its default, and it throws an exception.

One way to solve this is to make sure that all the division is done before leaving the dynamic scope. Clojure's doall function is perfect for this:

```
(with-precision 4
  (doall (map (fn [x] (/ x 3)) (range 1M 4M))))
;=> (0.3333M 0.6667M 1M)
```

One drawback is that it completely defeats map's laziness. An alternate solution is to have the function provided to map re-create, when it's run, the dynamic scope in which the function was created. Clojure provides a handy macro bound-fn to do exactly that:

```
(with-precision 4
  (map (bound-fn [x] (/ x 3)) (range 1M 4M)))
;=> (0.3333M 0.6667M 1M)
```

Now the sequence being returned is still lazy, but before each item is computed, the dynamic scope of *math-context* is re-created and the exception is avoided.

This kind of mismatch between a function definition that appears lexically inside a form like with-precision or binding and yet has a different dynamic scope when called doesn't cause problems with lazy sequences alone. You may also see problems with functions sent to Agents as actions or with the body of a future, because these are executed in other threads outside the dynamic scope where they're set up.

Problems related to dynamic scope aren't even exclusive to Vars. The scope of a try/catch is also dynamic and can have similarly unexpected behavior. For example, with-open uses try/finally to close a file automatically when execution leaves its dynamic scope. Failing to account for this can lead to an error when trying to write to a closed file, because the dynamic scope of with-open has been left. Though bound-fn can help make the dynamic scope of a Var borrow from its lexical scope, the only way to deal with try/catch is to make sure everything is executed before leaving its dynamic scope.

11.10 *Summary*

This has been the most complex chapter of the book. State management is a complicated process that can quickly lose all semblance of sanity in the face of concurrent modifications. Clojure's main tenet is not to foster concurrency, but instead to provide the tools for the sane management of state. As a result of this focus, sane concurrency follows. Clojure also provides the building blocks for you to parallelize computations across disparate threads of execution. From the expression-centric future, to the function-centric set-once "variable" promise, to the core functions pcalls, pvalues, and pmap, Clojure gives you the raw materials for your specialized needs. Finally, we talked in depth about Clojure's Var, dynamic binding, and the mechanics of thread-locals.

The next chapter deals with performance considerations and how to make your Clojure programs much faster.

Part 5

Tangential considerations

Some topics are so interesting and important that we must include them, even if they don't fit well in another chapter or warrant a chapter to themselves. In this part, we'll cover several such topics, including transient collections, domain-specific languages, and testing.

Performance

This chapter covers

- Type hints
- Transients
- Chunked sequences
- Memoization
- Understanding coercion

Now that we've spent a book's worth of material learning the why and how of Clojure, it's high time we turned our attention to the subject of performance. There's a meme in programming that can be summarized as follows: make it work first, then make it fast. Throughout this book, we've taught you the ways that Clojure allows you to "make it work," and now we're going to tell how to make it fast.

In many cases, Clojure's compiler will be able to highly optimize idiomatic Clojure source code. But there are times when the form of your functions, especially in interoperability scenarios, will prove to be ambiguous or even outright counter to compiler optimizations. Therefore, we'll lead you through optimization techniques such as type hints, transients, chunked sequences, memoization, and coercion. Using some combination of these techniques will help you approach, and sometimes exceed, the performance of Java itself.

The most obvious place to start, and the one you're most likely encounter, is type hinting—so this is where we'll begin.

12.1   *Type hints*

The path of least resistance in Clojure often produces the fastest and most efficient compiled code, but not always. The beauty of Clojure is that this path of least resistance allows simple techniques for gaining speed via type hints. The first thing to know about type hints is that they're used to indicate that an object is an instance of some class—never a primitive.

> **THE RULE OF TYPE HINTING**   Write your code so that it's first and foremost correct; then add type-hint adornment to gain speed. Don't trade the efficiency of the program for the efficiency of the programmer.

12.1.1   *Advantages of type adornment*

There are epic debates about the virtues of static versus dynamic type systems; we won't engage in those arguments here. But there are a few advantages to a dynamic type system like Clojure's that also allows type hinting to occur after the bulk of development. One such advantage is that in a static type system, the cost of changing argument lists is extended to all of the callers, whereas in Clojure the cost is deferred until adornment time or even outright avoided.[1] This scenario isn't limited to the case of function arguments in Clojure nor to statically typed languages, but instead to any typed element. This dynamic type system provides an agile experience in general to Clojure, which can later be optimized when there's a need.

12.1.2   *Type-hinting arguments and returns*

If you recall from section 10.3, we created a function asum-sq that took an array of floats and performed a sum of squares on its contents. Unfortunately, asum-sq wasn't as fast as it could've been. We can illuminate the cause of its inefficiency using a REPL flag named *warn-on-reflection*, which by default is set to false:

```
(set! *warn-on-reflection* true)
;=> true
```

What this seemingly innocuous statement does is to signal to the REPL to report when the compiler encounters a condition where it can't infer the type of an object and must use reflection to garner it at runtime. You'll see a reflection warning by entering asum-sq into the REPL:

```
(defn asum-sq [xs]
  (let [dbl (amap xs i ret
              (* (aget xs i)
                 (aget xs i)))]
    (areduce dbl i ret 0
      (+ ret (aget dbl i)))))

; Reflection warning - call to aclone can't be resolved.
; ...
```

---

[1]   Aside from the case where type hints don't require client changes, the use of keyword arguments as seen in section 7.1 can help to localize additional function requirements to only the callers needing them.

Though not terribly informative in and of itself, the fact that a reflection warning occurs is portentous. Running the call to asum-sq in a tight loop verifies that something is amiss:

```
(time (dotimes [_ 10000] (asum-sq (float-array [1 2 3 4 5]))))
; "Elapsed time: 410.539 msecs"
;=> nil
```

Though the reflection warning didn't point to the precise inefficiency, you can infer where it could be given that Clojure deals with the java.lang.Object class across function boundaries. Therefore, you can assume that the problem lies in the argument xs coming into the function as something unexpected. Adding two type hints to xs and dbl (because it's built from xs) might do the trick:

```
(defn asum-sq [ ^floats xs]
  (let [^floats dbl (amap xs i ret
  ...
```

Rerunning the tight loop verifies that the assumption was correct:

```
(time (dotimes [_ 10000] (asum-sq (float-array [1 2 3 4 5]))))
; "Elapsed time: 17.087 msecs"
;=> nil
```

This is a dramatic increase in speed using a simple type hint that casts the incoming array xs to one containing primitive floats. The whole range of array type hints is shown next:

- objects
- ints
- longs
- floats
- doubles
- chars
- shorts
- bytes
- booleans

The problems might still not be solved, especially if you want to do something with the return value of asum-sq, as shown:

```
(.intValue (asum-sq (float-array [1 2 3 4 5])))
; Reflection warning, reference to field intValue can't be resolved.
;=> 55
```

This is because the compiler can't garner the type of the return value and must therefore use reflection to do so. By hinting the return type of asum-sq, the problem goes away:

```
(defn ^Float asum-sq [ ^floats xs]
  ...

(.intValue (asum-sq (float-array [1 2 3 4 5])))
;=> 55
```

With minor decoration on the asum-sq function, we've managed to increase its speed as well as potentially increasing the speed of expressions downstream.

12.1.3 Type-hinting objects

In addition to allowing for the hinting of function arguments and return values, you can also hint arbitrary objects. If you didn't have control over the source to `asum-sq`, then these reflection problem would be insurmountable when executing `(.intValue (asum-sq (float-array [1 2 3 4 5])))`. But you can instead hint at the point of usage and gain the same advantage as if `asum-sq` had been hinted all along:

```
(.intValue ^Float (asum-sq (float-array [1 2 3 4 5])))
;=> 55
```

All isn't lost when you don't own a piece of code causing performance problems, because Clojure is flexible in the placement of type hints.

12.2 Transients

We've harped on you for this entire book about the virtues of persistent data structures and how wonderful they are. In this section, we'll present an optimization technique provided by Clojure called *transients*, which offer a mutable view of a collection. It seems like blasphemy, but we assure you there's a good reason for their existence, which we'll discuss currently.

12.2.1 Ephemeral garbage

The design of Clojure is such that it presumes that the JVM is extremely efficient at garbage collection of ephemeral (or short-lived) objects, and in fact it is. But as you can imagine based on what you've learned so far, Clojure does create a lot of young objects that are never again accessed, shown (in spirit) here:

```
(reduce merge [{1 3} {1 2} {3 4} {3 5}])
;=> {1 2, 3 5}
```

A naive implementation[2] of `reduce` would build intermediate maps corresponding to the different phases of accumulation. The accumulation of these short-lived instances can in some circumstances cause inefficiencies, which transients are meant to address.

> **THE RULE OF TRANSIENTS**   Write your code so that it's first and foremost correct using the immutable collections and operations; then, make changes to use transients for gaining speed. But you might be better served by writing idiomatic and correct code and letting the natural progression of speed enhancements introduced in new versions of Clojure take over. Spot optimizations often quickly become counter-optimizations by preventing the language/libraries from doing something better.

We'll explore how you can use transients in the next section.

---

[2] The actual implementation of `reduce` follows a reduce protocol that delegates to a smart "internal reduce" mechanism that's meant for data structures that know the most efficient way to reduce themselves.

12.2.2 *Transients compare in efficiency to mutable collections*

Mutable objects generally don't make new allocations during intermediate phases of an operation on a single collection type, and comparing persistent data structures against that measure assumes a lesser memory efficiency. But you can use transients to provide not only efficiency of allocation, but often of execution as well. Take a function zencat, intended to work similarly to Clojure's concat, but with vectors exclusively:

```
(defn zencat1 [x y]
  (loop [src y, ret x]
    (if (seq src)
      (recur (next src) (conj ret (first src)))
      ret)))

(zencat1 [1 2 3] [4 5 6])
;=> [1 2 3 4 5 6]

(time (dotimes [_ 1000000] (zencat1 [1 2 3] [4 5 6])))
; "Elapsed time: 486.408 msecs"
;=> nil
```

The implementation is simple enough, but it's not all that it could be. The effects of using transients is shown next.

Listing 12.1 A concatenation function using transients

```
(defn zencat2 [x y]
  (loop [src y, ret (transient x)]        ◁──── Create transient
    (if (seq src)
      (recur (next src) (conj! ret (first src)))    ◁──── Use transient conj!
      (persistent! ret))))                ◁──── Return persistent

(zencat2 [1 2 3] [4 5 6])
;=> [1 2 3 4 5 6]

(time (dotimes [_ 1000000] (zencat2 [1 2 3] [4 5 6])))
; "Elapsed time: 846.258 msecs"
;=> nil
```

Wait, what? It seems that by using transients, we've actually made things worse—but have we? The answer lies in the question, "what am I actually measuring?" The timing code is executing zencat2 in a tight loop. This type of timing isn't likely representative of actual use, and instead highlights an important consideration: the use of persistent! and transient, though constant time, aren't free. By measuring the use of transients in a tight loop, we've introduced a confounding measure, with the disparate cost of using transients compared to the cost of concatenating two small vectors. A better benchmark would instead be to measure the concatenation of larger vectors, therefore minimizing the size-relative cost of transients:

```
(def bv (vec (range 1e6)))

(first (time (zencat1 bv bv)))
; "Elapsed time: 181.988 msecs"
```

```
;=> 0

(first (time (zencat2 bv bv)))
;  "Elapsed time: 39.353 msecs"
;=> 0
```

In the case of concatenating large vectors, the use of transients is ~4.5 times faster than the purely functional approach. Be careful how you use transients in your own applications, because as you saw, they're an incredible boon in some cases, and quite the opposite in others. Likewise, be careful designing performance measurements, because they might not always measure what you think.

Because transients are a mutable view of a collection, you should take care when exposing outside of localized contexts. Fortunately, Clojure doesn't allow a transient to be modified across threads and will throw an exception if attempted. But it's easy enough to forget that you're dealing with a transient and return it from a function. That's not to say that you couldn't return a transient from a function—it can be useful to build a pipeline of functions that work in concert against a transient structure. Instead, we ask that you remain mindful when doing so.

The use of transients can help to gain speed in many circumstances. But be mindful of the trade-offs when using them, because they're not cost-free operations.

12.3 *Chunked sequences*

With the release of Clojure 1.1, the granularity of Clojure's laziness was changed from a one-at-a-time model to a chunk-at-a-time model. Instead of walking through a sequence one node at a time, chunked sequences provide a windowed view (Boncz 2005) on sequences some number of elements wide, as illustrated here:

```
(def gimme #(do (print \.) %))

(take 1 (map gimme (range 32)))
```

You might expect that this snippet would print (.0) because we're only grabbing the first element, and if you're running Clojure 1.0, that's exactly what you'd see. But in later versions, the picture is different:

```
;=> (...............................0)
```

If you count the dots, you'll see exactly 32, which is what you'd expect given the statement from the first paragraph. Expanding a bit further, if you increase the argument to range to be 33 instead, you'll see the following:

```
(take 1 (map gimme (range 33)))
;=> (...............................0)
```

Again you can count 32 dots. Moving the chunky window to the right is as simple as obtaining the 33rd element:

```
(take 1 (drop 32 (map gimme (range 64))))
;=> (........................................................32)
```

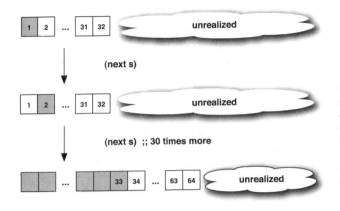

Figure 12.1 Clojure's chunked sequences allow a windowed view of a sequence. This model is more efficient, in that it allows for larger swaths of memory to be reclaimed by the garbage collector and better cache locality in general. There's a cost to total laziness, but often the benefit gained is worth the cost.

As we showed in chapter 5, Clojure's sequences are implemented as trees fanning out at increments of 32 elements per node. Therefore, chunks of size 32 are a natural fit, allowing for the garbage collection of larger chunks of memory as seen in figure 12.1.

You might be worried that chunked sequences have squashed the entire point of lazy sequences, and for small sequences this would be correct. But the benefits of lazy sequences are striking when dealing with cyclopean magnitudes or sequences larger than memory. Chunked sequences in the extreme cases are an incredible boon because not only do they make sequence functions more efficient overall, they still fulfill the promise of lazy sequences: avoiding full realization of interim results.

12.3.1 *Regaining one-at-a-time laziness*

There are legitimate concerns about this chunked model, and one such concern is the desire for a one-at-a-time model to avoid exploding computations. Assuming that you have such a requirement, one counterpoint against chunked sequences is that of building an infinite sequence of Mersenne primes.[3] Implicit realization of the first 32 Mersenne primes through chunked sequences will finish long after the Sun has died.

But you can use `lazy-seq` to create a function `seq1` that can be used to restrict (or dechunkify, if you will) a lazy sequence and enforce the one-at-a-time model, as in the following listing.

Listing 12.2 A dechunkifying `seq1` function

```
(defn seq1 [s]
  (lazy-seq
    (when-let [[x] (seq s)]
      (cons x (seq1 (rest s))))))

(take 1 (map gimme (seq1 (range 32))))
;=> (.0)

(take 1 (drop 32 (map gimme (seq1 (range 64)))))
;=> (.............................32)
```

---

[3] See http://en.wikipedia.org/wiki/Mersenne_Primes.

You can again safely generate your lazy, infinite sequence of Mersenne primes. The world rejoices. But `seq1` eliminates the garbage-collection efficiencies of the chunked model and again regressed back to that shown in figure 12.2.

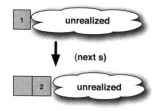

Clojure may one day provide an official API for one-at-a-time lazy sequence granularity, but for now `seq1` will suffice. We advise that you instead stick to the chunked model, because you'll probably never notice its effects during normal usage.

Figure 12.2 Using `seq1`, you can again reclaim the one-at-a-time sequence model. Though not as efficient as the chunked model, it does again provide total sequence laziness.

12.4 *Memoization*

As we mentioned briefly in section 11.4, memoization (Michie 1968) refers to storing a cache of values local to a function so that its arguments can be retrieved rather than calculated on every call. The cache is a simple mapping of a given set of arguments to a previously calculated result. In order for this to work, the memoized function *must* be referentially transparent, which we discussed in section 7.1. Clojure comes with a `memoize` function that can be used to build a memoized version of any referentially transparent function, as shown:

```
(def gcd (memoize
          (fn [x y]
            (cond
              (> x y) (recur (- x y) y)
              (< x y) (recur x (- y x))
              :else x))))
(gcd 1000645475 56130776629010010)
;=> 215
```

Defining a "greatest common denominator" function using `memoize` helps to speed subsequent calculations using the arguments `1000645475` and `56130776629010010`. The function `memoize` wraps another function[4] in a cache lookup pass-through function and returns it. This allows you to use `memoize` on literally any referentially transparent function. The operation of the `memoize` is analogous to, but not exactly the operation of Clojure's lazy sequences that cache the results of their realized portions. This general technique can be useful, but the indiscriminate storage provided by `memoize` might not always be appropriate. Therefore, we'll take a step back and devise a way to generalize the operation of memoization into useful abstractions and build a framework for employing caching strategies more appropriate to the domain at hand.

---

[4] You might've noticed that we explicitly bound the Var `gcd` to the memoization of an anonymous function but then used `recur` for implementing the function body. This approach suffers from the inability to cache the intermediate results (Norvig 1991) of `gcd`. We leave the solution to this short-coming as an exercise for the reader.

Similar to Haskell's typeclasses, Clojure's protocols define a set of signatures providing a framework of adherence to a given set of features. This section serves a three-fold goal:

- Discussion of memoization
- Discussion of protocol design
- Discussion of abstraction-oriented programming

12.4.1 Re-examining memoization

As mentioned in section 11.4, memoization is a personal affair, requiring a certain domain knowledge to perform efficiently and correctly. That's not to say that the core `memoize` function is useless, only that the base case doesn't cover all cases. In this section, we'll define a memoization protocol in terms of the primitive operations: `lookup`, `has?`, `hit`, and `miss`. Instead of providing a memoization facility that allows the removal of individual cache items, it's a better idea to provide one that allows for dynamic cache-handling strategies.[5]

12.4.2 A memoization protocol

The protocol for a general-purpose cache feature is provided in the following listing.

Listing 12.3 A protocol for caching

```
(defprotocol CacheProtocol
  (lookup  [cache e])
  (has?    [cache e] )
  (hit     [cache e])
  (miss    [cache e ret]))
```

The function `lookup` retrieves the item in the cache if it exists. The function `has?` will check for a cached value. The function `hit` is called when an item is found in the cache, and `miss` is called when it's *not*. If you're familiar with creating Java interfaces, the process of creating a protocol should be familiar. Moving on, we next implement the core `memoize` functionality.

Listing 12.4 A basic cache type

```
(deftype BasicCache [cache]
  CacheProtocol
  (lookup [_ item]
    (get cache item))
  (has? [_ item]
    (contains? cache item))
  (hit [this item] this)
  (miss [_ item result]
    (BasicCache. (assoc cache item result)))))
```

---

[5] This section is motivated by the fantastic work of the brilliant Clojurians Meikel Brandmeyer, Christophe Grand, and Eugen Dück summarized at http://kotka.de/blog/2010/03/memoize_done_right.html.

The `BasicCache` takes a cache on construction used for its internal operations. Testing the basic caching protocol in isolation shows:

```
(def cache (BasicCache. {}))

(lookup (miss cache '(servo) :robot) '(servo))
;=> :robot
```

In the case of a miss, the item to be cached is added and a new instance of `BasicCache` (with the cached entry added) is returned for retrieval using `lookup`. This is a simple model for a basic caching protocol, but not terribly useful in isolation. We can go further by creating an auxiliary function `through`, meaning in effect, "pass an element through the cache and return its value":

```
(defn through [cache f item]
  (if (has? cache item)
    (hit cache item)
    (miss cache item (delay (apply f item)))))
```

With `through`, the value corresponding to a cache `item` (function arguments in this case) would either be retrieved from the cache via the `hit` function, or calculated and stored via `miss`. You'll notice that the calculation (apply f item) is wrapped in a `delay` call instead of performed outright or lazily through an ad hoc initialization mechanism. The use of an explicit delay in this way helps to ensure that the value is calculated only on first retrieval. With these pieces in place, we can then create a `PluggableMemoization` type, as shown next.

Listing 12.5   A type implementing pluggable memoization

```
(deftype PluggableMemoization [f cache]
  CacheProtocol
  (has? [_ item] (has? cache item))
  (hit  [this item] this)
  (miss [_ item result]
    (PluggableMemoization. f (miss cache item result)))
  (lookup [_ item]
    (lookup cache item)))
```

The purpose of the `PluggableMemoization` type is to act as a delegate to an underlying implementation of a `CacheProtocol` occurring in the implementations for `hit`, `miss`, and `lookup`. Likewise, the `PluggableMemoization` delegation is interposed at the protocol points to ensure that when utilizing the `CacheProtocol`, the `Pluggable-Memoization` type is used and not the `BasicCache`. We've made a clear distinction between a caching protocol fulfilled by `BasicCache` and a concretized memoization fulfilled by `PluggableMemoization` and `through`. With the creation of separate abstractions, you can use the appropriate concrete realization in its proper context. Clojure programs will be composed of various abstractions. In fact, the term *abstraction-oriented programming* is used to describe Clojure's specific philosophy of design.

The original `manipulable-memoize` function from section 11.4 is modified in the following listing to conform to our memoization cache realization.

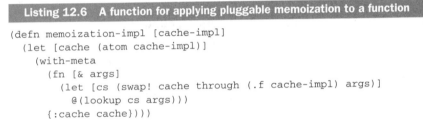

Listing 12.6 A function for applying pluggable memoization to a function

```
(defn memoization-impl [cache-impl]
  (let [cache (atom cache-impl)]
    (with-meta
      (fn [& args]
        (let [cs (swap! cache through (.f cache-impl) args)]
          @(lookup cs args)))
      {:cache cache})))
```

If you'll recall from the implementation of the through function, we stored delay objects in the cache requiring they be deferenced when looked up. Returning to our old friend the slowly function, we can exercise the new memoization technique as shown:

```
(def slowly (fn [x] (Thread/sleep 3000) x))
(def sometimes-slowly (memoization-impl
                        (PluggableMemoization.
                          slowly
                          (BasicCache. {})))))

(time [(sometimes-slowly 108) (sometimes-slowly 108)])
; "Elapsed time: 3001.611 msecs"
;=> [108 108]

(time [(sometimes-slowly 108) (sometimes-slowly 108)])
; "Elapsed time: 0.049 msecs"
;=> [108 108]
```

You can now fulfill your personalized memoization needs by implementing pointed realizations of CacheProtocol, plugging them into instances of PluggableMemoization, and applying them as needed via function redefinition, higher-order functions, or dynamic binding. Countless caching strategies can be used to better support your needs, each displaying different characteristics, or if needed your problem may call for something wholly new.

We've only scratched the surface of memoization in this section in favor of providing a more generic substrate on which to build your own memoization strategies. Using Clojure's abstraction-oriented programming techniques, your own programs will likewise be more generic and be built largely from reusable parts.

12.5 *Understanding coercion*

Although Clojure is a dynamically typed language, it does provide mechanisms for specifying value types. The first of these mechanisms, type hints, was covered in section 12.1. The second, *coercion*, is the subject of this section. Although the nature of type hints and coercion are similar, their intended purposes are quite different. In the case of coercion, its purpose is to get at the primitive data type for a value, which we'll show next.

12.5.1 *First rule of coercion: don't*

Clojure's compiler is sophisticated enough that in many ways it'll be unnecessary to coerce values into primitives. It's often better to start with a function or code block devoid of coercions. Unless your specific application requires the utmost speed in execution, it's better to stick with the version that favors simplicity over the alternative. But should you decide that coercion might be the choice for you, then this section will provide guidance.

12.5.2 *Corollary: you're probably not doing it right*

If you've determined that coercion can help, then it's worth stressing that you have to be careful when going down that road. In many cases with coercion, the act of adding it can actually *slow* your functions. The reason lies in the nature of Clojure. Functional composition leads to passing arguments back and forth between pieces, and in the circumstance of coercion you're just boxing and unboxing[6] from one call to the next. This particular circumstance is especially devious within the body of a loop, and follows the same performance degradations observed with Java. Clojure's unboxing is an explicit[7] operation performed using the coercion functions, so there's a speck of light there. Unfortunately, autoboxing is still a danger and should be avoided if speed is a concern, as we'll explore now:

```
(defn occur-count [words]
  (let [res (atom {})]
    (doseq [w words] (swap! res assoc w (+ 1 (@res w 0))))
    @res))

(defn roll [n d]
  (reduce + (take n (repeatedly #(inc (rand-int d))))))

(time (dorun (occur-count (take 1000000 (repeatedly #(roll 3 6))))))
; "Elapsed time: 4055.505 msecs"
```

The function `occur-count` will return a map of the occurrence counts[8] found in a given sequence. This fairly straightforward implementation uses the function `roll` to populate a sequence with a million simulated rolls of three six-sided dice. But four seconds seems like a long time to wait, so perhaps we can speed things up by using coercions. An initial attempt to gain speed may be to pull out the stored count from the table and coerce it into an `int`:

```
(defn occur-count [words]
  (let [res (atom {})]
    (doseq [w words]
      (let [v (int (@res w 0))]
        (swap! res assoc w (+ 1 v))))
    @res))
```

---

[6] Autoboxing is the automatic conversion the Java compiler makes between the primitive types and their corresponding object wrapper classes.

[7] Except when directly or indirectly (via inlining or a macro body) calling a method.

[8] Clojure has a function `frequencies` that does this, so we provide `occur-count` for illustrative purposes only.

```
(time (dorun (occur-count (take 1000000 (repeatedly #(roll 3 6))))))
; "Elapsed time: 4385.8 msecs"
```

Well, that didn't work. The reason for a decrease in speed is that although we're specifying the type at the outer loop, we haven't reduced the need to box and unbox that value further downstream in the roll function. We might then be led to try and optimize the roll function too:

```
(defn roll [n d]
  (let [p (int d)]
    (reduce + (take n (repeatedly #(inc (rand-int p)))))))

(time (dorun (occur-count (take 1000000 (repeatedly #(roll 3 6))))))
; "Elapsed time: 4456.393 msecs"
;=> nil
```

Again we've made matters worse and have spread the problems over the surface of the entire code. Being adventurous, we grasp for straws and attempt to force integer arithmetic with roll by using the unchecked-inc function:

```
(defn roll [n d]
  (let [p (int d)]
    (reduce + (take n (repeatedly #(unchecked-inc (rand-int p)))))))

(time (dorun (occur-count (take 1000000 (repeatedly #(roll 3 6))))))
```

Go ahead and run that in the REPL, then go get some coffee and a bagel. Toast the bagel. Eat the bagel. Drink the coffee. By that time, you might've received a result.

So what happened? In an attempt to be clever, we've confused the Clojure compiler into near unconsciousness. Instead of making direct calls to Clojure's math functions, we're now making calls indirectly via Java reflection! You can observe this by setting *warn-on-reflection* to true and reentering roll.

How can we speed things up? The problem isn't with coercion itself, but instead with the implementations of roll and occur-count. You can observe significant speed-ups by rethinking your original implementations *first* and then resorting to coercion second. The use of coercion should *always* be preceded by a reevaluation of your implementation, because often by doing so you can eliminate the need for coercion altogether, as shown next.

Listing 12.7   Using coercion to gain speed

```
(defn roll [n d]
  (loop [n (int n), sum 0]                          ⟵── Coerce n to int
    (if (zero? n)
      sum
      (recur (dec n) (+ sum (inc (rand-int d)))))))

(defn occur-count [words]
  (reduce #(assoc %1 %2 (inc (%1 %2 0))) {} words))

(time (dorun (occur-count (take 1000000 (repeatedly #(roll 3 6))))))
; "Elapsed time: 937.346 msecs"
;=> nil
```

By refactoring the original functions, we've gained a five-fold increase in speed and yet used only a single coercion. Additionally, we've managed to make the new implementation faster while also maintaining clarity. This should be a general goal when writing your Clojure code, and when forced to make a trade between the two, it might be a good idea to favor clarity.

12.5.3   *Second rule of coercion:* don't

In the previous example, there's too much noise in collection and sequence operations for primitive coercion to help much. This goes to show that it's important to remember that the Clojure compiler will often do a better job at optimization than you.

12.5.4   *Third rule of coercion:* coerce a stable local

When coercing a local to a primitive type, it's tempting to do so at the point of use, but this practice should be avoided. A good rule of thumb for coercion is to coerce only within a local context via `let`, `binding`, or `loop`. This provides a stable value point for the primitive, allowing you to reuse that same local elsewhere in the same function without having to again coerce at different points of use. This can be illustrated by the following:

```
(defn mean
  "Takes a sequence of integers and returns their mean value"
  [sq]
  (let [length (int (count sq))]
    (if (zero? length)
      0
      (/ (int (reduce + sq)) length))))
```

The `length` value has been bound in the `let`, allowing it to be reused twice within the body of the function. This allows for a cleaner implementation than the alternative, which coerces the results of `(count sq)` in multiple places. Using this advice and the fact that Clojure provides lexical scope by default, you can also avoid the need to define a name-mangled local by instead using `let` to rebind original argument names to coerced values `(defn [x] (let [x (int x)] ...))`.

12.5.5   *Fourth rule of coercion:* watch your sizes

Primitive type coercions in Clojure act the same as type truncation in Java. If a given value is coerced into a type that can't hold a value of its magnitude, then data loss will occur, and in the case of integer overflow, exceptions will be thrown.

12.5.6   *Fifth rule of coercion:* truncate only as a goal

By default, Clojure doesn't limit the accuracy of mathematical operations, but this can occur when using coercion. There will be many instances in your own projects when speed is more important than accuracy in mathematical operations. Likewise, there will also be times when truncation is necessary, especially when dealing with Java library methods that take primitive types:

```
(Math/round 1.23897398798929929872987890030893796768727987138M)
; java.lang.IllegalArgumentException:
;    No matching method found: round
```

When a method or function isn't overloaded, the Clojure compiler can determine whether an argument can be coerced to a primitive type and will do so if able. The preceding issue exception arises from the fact that Math/round is overloaded, taking either a float or double typed argument. Therefore, you have to explicitly use coercion to truncate the argument:

```
(Math/round (float 1.23897398798929929872987890030893796768727987138M))
;=> 1
```

Our goal in using the truncating operation float was to get a result that we knew wouldn't be affected by truncation. But many instances will arise when truncation will affect your results and will often do so to your detriment. Therefore, it's best to be wary when using coercion, because it propagates inaccuracies. It's best to limit its usage when truncation is desired and document vigorously when it's absolutely needed for speed.

Coercion can be an effective tool in your Clojure applications, but take care to be sure you understand the caveats. If you take away one lesson from this section, let it be this: *do not rush to coercion.*

12.6 Summary

Clojure provides numerous ways to gain speed in your applications. Using some combination of type hints, transients, chunked sequences, memoization, and coercion, you should be able to achieve noticeable performance gains. Like any powerful tool, these performance techniques should be used cautiously and thoughtfully. But once you've determined that performance can be gained, their use is minimally intrusive and often natural to the unadorned implementation.

In the final chapter, we'll cover a number of ways that the Clojure way of thinking might be different from what you're accustomed to. The discussion therein, when explored with an open mind, will change the way that you write software.

13

Clojure changes the way you think

This chapter covers

- DSLs
- Testing
- A lack of design patterns
- Error handling and debugging
- Fare thee well

In this final chapter, we cover some tangential topics that you might already be familiar with, but perhaps not from a Clojure perspective. Our discussion will start with domain-specific languages (DSLs) and the unique way that Clojure applications are built from a layering of unique application-specific DSLs. Next, you're unlikely to be ignorant of the general push toward a test-driven development (TDD) philosophy, with a special focus on unit testing. We'll explore why Clojure is especially conducive to unit testing and why it's often unnecessary. Next, whether you agree with the cult of design patterns or not, it's inarguable that patterns have changed the way that object-oriented software is designed and developed. The classical design patterns are often invisible, or at times outright nonexistent in Clojure code, which we'll discuss in this chapter. As we'll then show, error handling in Clojure flows in two directions: from inner functions to outer via exceptions, and from outer functions in via dynamic bindings. Finally, we'll explore how having the entire language at your disposal can help to change the way that your debugging occurs. We hope that by the time you've finished this chapter, you'll agree—Clojure changes the way you think about programming.

13.1 DSLs

Lisp is not the right language for any particular problem. Rather, Lisp encourages one to attack a new problem by implementing new languages tailored to that problem.
        —"Lisp: A Language for Stratified Design" (Abelson 1988)

In chapter 8, we explored the notion of a domain-specific language for describing domains. This meta-circularity, while playful, was meant to make a subtle point: Clojure blurs, and often obliterates, the line between DSL and API. When a language is built from the same data structures that the language itself manipulates, it's known as *homoiconic* (Mooers 1965). When a programming language is homoiconic, it's simple to mold the language into a form that bridges the gap between the problem and solution domains. When designing DSLs in Clojure, it's important to determine when the existing language facilities will suffice (Raymond 2003) and when it's appropriate to create one from whole cloth (Ghosh 2010). In this section we'll do both and provide a little discussion about each.

13.1.1 A ubiquitous DSL

The declarative language SQL is among the most widespread DSLs in use today. In section 1.2 we showed a simple Clojure DSL, which provided a simple subset of the SELECT statement that created a representational SQL string. Though that particular example was meant to be instructive, Clojure provides a comprehensive library for relational algebra, on which SQL is based (Date 2009). Imagine a dataset of the following:

```
(def artists
  #{{:artist "Burial"  :genre-id 1}
    {:artist "Magma"   :genre-id 2}
    {:artist "Can"     :genre-id 3}
    {:artist "Faust"   :genre-id 3}
    {:artist "Ikonika" :genre-id 1}
    {:artist "Grouper"}})

(def genres
  #{{:genre-id 1 :genre-name "Dubstep"}
    {:genre-id 2 :genre-name "Zeuhl"}
    {:genre-id 3 :genre-name "Prog"}
    {:genre-id 4 :genre-name "Drone"}})
```

You can try Clojure's relational functions by entering the examples shown in the following listing.

Listing 13.1   Examples of Clojure's relational algebra functions

```
(require '[clojure.set :as ra])
(def ALL identity)

(ra/select ALL genres)
;=> #{{:genre-id 4, :genre-name "Drone"}
      {:genre-id 3, :genre-name "Prog"}
      {:genre-id 2, :genre-name "Zeuhl"}
      {:genre-id 1, :genre-name "Dubstep"}}

(ra/select #(#{1 3} (:genre-id %)) genres)
;=> #{{:genre-id 3, :genre-name "Prog"}
      {:genre-id 1, :genre-name "Dubstep"}}

(take 2 (ra/select ALL (ra/join artists genres)))
;=> #{{:artist "Burial",   :genre-id 1, :genre-name "Dubstep"}
      {:artist "Magma",    :genre-id 2, :genre-name "Zeuhl"}}
```

The relational functions in `clojure.set` are a perfect example of the way that Clojure blurs the line between API and DSL. No macro tricks are involved, but through the process of functional composition, the library provides a highly expressive syntax matching closely (Abiteboul 1995) that of SQL itself. Though you might be tempted to create a custom query language for your own application(s), there are times when the relational functions are exactly what you need. Your time might be better spent solving actual problems, one of which we'll cover in the following section.

13.1.2 *Putting parentheses around the specification*

Many applications deal in measurements of differing units. For example, it's widely known that the U.S. works almost exclusively in English units of measure, whereas most of the rest of the planet works in SI, or metric units. To convert[1] from one to the other isn't an arduous task and can be handled easily with a set of functions of this general form:

```
(defn meters->feet [m] (* m 3.28083989501312))
(defn meters->miles [m] (* m 0.000621))

(meters->feet 1609.344)
;=> 5279.9999999999945

(meters->miles 1609.344)
;=> 0.999402624
```

This approach will certainly work if only a few functions define the extent of your conversion needs. But if your applications are like ours, then you probably need to convert to and from differing units of measure of many different magnitudes. You may also need to convert back and forth between units of time, dimension, orientation, and a host of others. Therefore it'd be nice to be able to write a specification of unit conversions (Hoyte 2008) as a Clojure DSL and use its results as a low-level layer

---

[1] A spectacular general-purpose JVM language named Frink excels at conversions of many different units. We highly advocate exploring Frink at your next available opportunity: http://futureboy.us/frinkdocs/.

for high-layer application specifics. This is precisely the nature of Lisp development in general—each level in an application provides the primitive abstractions for the levels above it.

In this section, we're going to create a small specification and then convert it into a Clojure DSL using a technique coined by Rainer Joswig as "putting parentheses around the specification."

DEFUNITS

An ideal representation for a unit-conversion specification language would be simple:

> *Our base unit of distance is the meter. There are 1,000 meters in a kilometer. There are 100 centimeters in a meter. There are 10 millimeters in a centimeter. There are 3.28083 feet in a meter. And finally, there are 5,280 feet in a mile.*

Of course, to make sense of free text is a huge task in any language, so it behooves us to change it so that it's easier to reason about programmatically, but not so much that it's cumbersome for someone attempting to describe unit conversions. As a first pass, we'll try to group the most obvious parts using some Clojure syntactical elements:

```
(Our base unit of distance is the :meter
   [There are 1000 :meters in a :kilometer]
   [There are 100 :centimeters in a :meter]
   [There are 10 :millimeters in a :centimeter]
   [There are 3.28083 :feet in a :meter]
   [There are 5280 :feet in a :mile])
```

This specification is starting to look a little like Clojure code, but it would still be difficult to parse this into a usable form. Likewise, it'll be difficult for the person writing the specification to use the correct terms, avoid spelling mistakes, properly punctuate, and so forth. In a word, this form is still not useful. It'd be ideal if we could make this into a form that's still recognizable to both Clojure *and* a conversion expert. We'll try one more time:

```
(define unit of distance
  {:m 1,
   :km 1000,
   :cm 1/100,
   :mm [1/10 of a :cm],
   :ft 0.3048,
   :mile [is 5280 :ft]})
```

This *almost* looks like Clojure source code, except for a few minor details. We've changed the measure of feet from an "in a" relationship to a relative one with regard to the meter base unit. Also, a vector indicates the use of a different relative unit, keeping the DSL regular in its meaning between one conversion and the next and providing a way to describe intermediate relative units of measure. Those definitions look like a map, so we should write a utility function that takes a unit and a map like the preceding one and returns the number of units it takes to compose the base unit.

Listing 13.2   A function for calculating compositional units of a base unit

```
(defn relative-units [u units]
  (let [spec (u units)]                          ⟵──── Look up unit spec
    (if (nil? spec)
      (throw (Exception. (str "Undefined unit " u)))
      (if (vector? spec)
        (let [[conv to] spec]                     ⟵──── Deconstruct relative spec
          (* conv                          ⟵──── Multiply relative units
             (relative-units to units)))
        spec))))
```

The function `relative-units` goes through the map `units` looking up units and multiplying their compositional values. When it finds an indirect specification (such as
millimeters defined in terms of centimeters), it traverse the chain of indirect references multiplying the factors along the way, as shown:

```
(relative-units :m {:m 1 :cm 100 :mm [10 :cm]})
;=> 1

(relative-units :cm {:m 1 :cm 100 :mm [10 :cm]})
;=> 100

(relative-units :mm {:m 1 :cm 100 :mm [10 :cm]})
;=> 1000
```

We changed the unit conversions map to remove the natural language phrase "in a,"
because English isn't good for a DSL. Natural language often lacks the precision that a
simple yet regular form has. Now that we have the auxiliary function created, we'd like
to create a macro to interpret the unit specification as shown:

```
(defunits-of distance :m
  :km 1000
  :cm 1/100
  :mm [1/10 :cm]
  :ft 0.3048
  :mile [5280 :ft])
```

This is a simplification versus the original verbal form of the conversion specification.
This final form is indubitably more conducive to parsing, yet doesn't appreciably sacri-
fice readability. The implementation of the `defunits-of` macro is presented in the
following listing.

Listing 13.3   A defunits-of macro

```
(defmacro defunits-of [name base-unit & conversions]
  (let [magnitude (gensym)
        unit (gensym)                                    ⎤  Create
        units-map (into `{~base-unit 1}                  ⎦  units map
                        (map vec (partition 2 conversions)))]
    `(defmacro ~(symbol (str "unit-of-" name))
       [~magnitude ~unit]
       `(* ~~magnitude                          ⎤  Multiply magnitude
           ~(case ~unit                         ⎦  by target unit
```

```
~@(mapcat
    (fn [[u# & r#]
      `[~u# ~(relative-units u# units-map)])
    units-map))))))
```

Unroll unit conversions into case lookup

The macro `defunits-of` is different than any macro that you've seen thus far, but it's typical for macros that expand into another macro definition. In this book you've yet to see a macro that builds another macro and uses multiple levels of nested[2] syntax-quotes. You won't likely see macros of this complexity often, but in this case we use nested syntax-quotes so that we can feed structures from the inner layers of the nested macros to the outer layers, processing each fully before proceeding. At this point, we can now run a call to the `defunits-of` macro with the simplified metric to English units conversion specification to define a new macro named `unit-of-distance`:

```
(unit-of-distance 1 :m)
;=> 1

(unit-of-distance 1 :mm)
;=> 1/1000

(unit-of-distance 1 :ft)
;=> 0.3048

(unit-of-distance 1 :mile)
;=> 1609.344
```

Perfect! Everything is relative to the base unit `:m`, just as we'd like (read as "how many meters are in a _"). The generated macro `unit-of-distance` allows you to work in your given system of measures relative to a standard system without loss of precision or the need for a bevy of awkward conversion functions. To calculate the distance a home run hit by the Orioles' Matt Wieters travels in Canada is a simple call to `(unit-of-distance 441 :ft)` away. The expansion of the `distance` specification given as `(defunits-of distance :m ...)` looks approximately like the following:

```
(defmacro unit-of-distance [G__43 G__44]
  `(* ~G__43
    (case ~G__44
      :mile 1609.344
      :km 1000
      :cm 1/100
      :m 1
      :mm 1/1000
      :ft 0.3048)))
```

The `defunits-of` macro is an interpreter of the unit-conversion DSL, which generates another macro `unit-of-distance` that performs a straightforward lookup of relative unit values. Amazingly, the expansion given by `(macroexpand '(unit-of-distance 1 :cm))` is that of a simple multiplication `(* 1 1/100)`. This is an awe-inspiring revelation. What we've managed to achieve is to fuse the notion of compilation and evalua-

---

[2] We talked briefly about making sense out of nested syntax-quotes in section 8.1. However, you're not likely to need them very often.

tion by writing a relative units of measure "mini-language" that's interpreted into a simple multiplication at compile time!

This is nothing new; Lisp programmers have known about this technique for decades, but it never ceases to amaze. There's one downside to our implementation—it allows for circular conversion specifications (seconds defined in terms of minutes, which are then defined in terms of seconds), but this can be identified and handled in `relative-units` if you're so inclined.

13.1.3 *A note about Clojure's approach to DSLs*

DSLs and control structures implemented as macros in Common Lisp tend to be written in a style more conducive to macro writers. But Clojure macros such as `defunit-of`, `cond`, and `case` are idiomatic in their minimalism; their component parts are paired and meant to be grouped through proper spacing. Clojure macro writers should understand that the proliferation and placement of parentheses are legitimate concerns for some, and as a result you should strive to reduce the number whenever possible. Why would you explicitly group your expressions when their groupings are only a call to `partition` away?

> **CLOJURE APHORISM**   If a project elicits a sense of being lost, then start from the bottom up.

DSLs are an important part of a Clojure programmer's toolset and stem from a long Lisp tradition. When Paul Graham talks about "bottom-up programming" in his perennial work *On Lisp*, this is what he's referring to. In Clojure, it's common practice to start by defining and implementing a low-level language specifically for the levels above. Creating complex software systems is hard, but using this approach, you can build the complicated parts out of smaller, simpler pieces.

Clojure changes the way that you think.

13.2 *Testing*

Object-oriented programs can be highly complicated beasts to test properly, thanks to mutating state coupled with the need to test across class hierarchies. Programs are a vast tapestry of interweaving execution paths, and to test each path comprehensively is difficult, if not impossible. In the face of unrestrained mutation, the execution paths are overlaid with mutation paths, further adding to the chaos. Conversely, Clojure programs tend to be compositions of pure functions with isolated pools of mutation. The result of this approach helps to foster an environment conducive to unit testing. But though the layers of an application are composed of numerous functions, each individually and compositionally tested, the layers themselves and the wiring between them must also be tested.

Test-driven development (Beck 2002) has conquered the software world, and at its core it preaches that test development should drive the architecture of the overall application. Unfortunately, this approach isn't likely to bear fruit in your Clojure programs. Instead, Clojure provides the foundation for a contracts-based program specification that's more amenable for writing correct programs. But before we discuss contracts, we'll touch on the ways Clojure facilitates one part of TDD, unit testing.

13.2.1 *Some useful techniques*

We don't want to disparage test-driven development, because its goals are virtuous and testing in general is essential. Because Clojure programs are organized using namespaces, and they are themselves aggregations of functions, often pure, the act of devising a unit-test suite at the namespace boundary is often mechanical in its directness. From a larger perspective, devising comprehensive test strategies is the subject of numerous volumes and therefore outside of the scope of this book; but there are a few Clojure-specific techniques that we wish to discuss.

USING WITH-VAR-ROOT TO STUB

Stubbing (Fowler 2007) is the act of supplying an imitation implementation of a function for testing purposes. One mechanism that can perform this stubbing is the `with-redefs` macro implemented in the following listing. Though this exact macro will likely be included in future versions of Clojure, it's not in Clojure 1.2, so a definition is provided.

Listing 13.4   Macro to aid in mocking

```
(defn with-redefs-fn [binding-map func & args]
  (let [root-bind (fn [m]
                     (doseq [[a-var a-val] m] (.bindRoot a-var a-val)))
        old-vals (zipmap (keys binding-map)
                         (map deref (keys binding-map)))]
    (try
      (root-bind binding-map)
      (apply func args)
      (finally
        (root-bind old-vals)))))

(defmacro with-redefs [bindings & body]
  `(with-redefs-fn ~(zipmap (map #(list `var %) (take-nth 2 bindings))
                            (take-nth 2 (next bindings)))
     (fn [] ~@body)))
```

The function `rss-children` from section 11.6 parses a Twitter RSS2 feed, returning a sequence of the top-level feed elements. Testing functions that rely on `rss-children` is futile against live Twitter feeds, so a stubbed implementation returning a known sequence would be more prudent, as shown next.

Listing 13.5   Using `with-redefs` to create stubs

```
(defn tweetless-rss-children [s]                          ⟵── Create stub
  '({:tag :title, :attrs nil, :content ["Stub"]}))

(defn count-rss2-children [s]
  (count (rss-children s)))
```

```
(with-redefs [rss-children tweetless-rss-children]
  (count-rss2-children "dummy"))
;=> 1
```

**Dynamically
bind with stub**

The `tweetless-rss-children` function returns a sequence of some canned data. Therefore, when testing the `count-rss2-children` function we temporarily change the value of `rss-children` so that it resolves to `tweetless-rss-children` instead. This change is made at the root of the `rss-children` Var and so is visible to all threads. As long as all the test calls to it are made before control leaves the `with-redefs` form, the stub will be invoked every time. Because `tweet-occurrences` doesn't return until it collects results from all the futures it creates, it will use the redef given by `with-redefs`:

```
(with-redefs [rss-children tweetless-rss-children]
  (tweet-occurrences "dummy" "test-url"))
;=> 0
```

Another option that is sometimes suggested is to use binding in place of `with-redefs`. This would push a thread-local binding for `rss-children`, which might seem attractive in that it could allow other threads to bind the same Var to a different stub function, potentially for simultaneously running different tests. But because `tweet-occurrences` uses futures, the other threads will be calling `rss-children` and will see the root binding rather than the stub,[3] causing an error:

```
(binding [rss-children tweetless-rss-children]
  (tweet-occurrences "dummy" "test-url"))

; java.util.concurrent.ExecutionException:
;   java.io.FileNotFoundException: test-url
```

When the root binding of `rss-children` runs, it tries to actually load "test-url" and fails, instead of calling our stub and succeeding. The `with-redefs` macro is a better solution for mocking.

CLOJURE.TEST AS SPECIFICATION

Clojure ships with a testing library in the `clojure.test` namespace used to create test suites that can further serve as partial system specifications. We won't provide a comprehensive survey of the `clojure.test` functionality, but you should get a feel for how it works. Unit-test specifications in Clojure are declarative in nature, as shown next.

> **Listing 13.6   clojure.test as a partial specification**

```
(require '[clojure.test :as test])

(test/deftest feed-tests
  (with-redefs [rss-children tweetless-rss-children]
    (test/testing "RSS2 Child Counting"
      (test/is (= 1000 (count-rss2-children "dummy"))))))
```

---

[3]   Alpha versions for Clojure 1.3 handle binding's interaction with `future` and Agent send differently, passing dynamic bindings through to code executed in these other thread contexts. But because these are not the only kinds of threads that can be spawned, `with-redefs` (which may be included in Clojure 1.3) is still recommended for mocking out functions during tests.

```
      (test/testing "Twitter Occurrence Counting"
        (test/is (= 0 (count-tweet-text-task "#clojure" "")))))))
(defn test-ns-hook []
  (feed-tests))
```

Clojure's test library provides a DSL for describing unit test cases. If you'll notice, we added a failing test to the RSS2 Child Counting test so that when run, the test will fail as expected:

```
(test/run-tests 'user)
; Testing user
;
;   FAIL in (feed-tests) (NO_SOURCE_FILE:101)
;   RSS2 Child Counting
;   expected: (= 1000 (count-rss2-children "dummy"))
;     actual: (not (= 1000 1))
;
;   Ran 1 tests containing 2 assertions.
;   1 failures, 0 errors.
;=> {:type :summary, :test 1, :pass 1, :fail 1, :error 0}
```

Though tests are a good way to find *some* errors, they make few guarantees that the system works properly. The ideal approach is the design and implementation of a framework corresponding closely with the domain of the application itself. This framework would ideally take the literal form of a domain DSL built incrementally through an interaction with domain experts and *must* come before testing begins. No amount of testing can substitute for thoroughly thinking through the fundamental design details. That's not to say that the domain DSLs should be fully realized from the start; instead, the form of the DSL and its constituent parts should be reflective of the actual domain. In our experience, there are no languages comparable to Clojure for this kind of domain modeling, save for perhaps Haskell, Factor, and Scala. Having said that, the domain isn't simply defined by the shape of its language; it also includes its expectations, which we'll discuss presently.

13.2.2 *Contracts programming*

Test-driven development is in many ways a heuristic affair. People tend to only test the error conditions and expectations that they can conceptualize. Surely there's no such thing as an exhaustive test suite, but in many cases test suites tend toward a local maxima. There's a better way to define semantic expectations within your application: using Clojure pre- and postconditions.

REVISITING PRE- AND POSTCONDITIONS

In section 7.1, we explored Clojure's pre- and postcondition facility. Function constraint specification is a conceptually simple model for declaring the expectations for any given function. Function constraints can cover the full range of expected conditions imposed on the function's inputs, its outputs, and their relative natures. The beauty of specifying constraints is that they can augment a testing regimen with the application of random values. The reason this works is that you can effectively throw out the values that fail the preconditions and instead focus on the values that cause error in the postconditions. We'll try this approach for a simple function to square a number:

```
(def sqr (partial
  (contract sqr-contract
    [n]
    (require (number? n))
    (ensure (pos? %)))
  #(* % %)))

[(sqr 10) (sqr -9)]
;=> [100 81]
```

The contract for sqr states simply: require a number and ensure that its return is positive. Now we can create a simple test driver[4] that throws many random values at it to see if it breaks:

```
(doseq [n (range Short/MIN_VALUE Short/MAX_VALUE)]
  (try
    (sqr n)
    (catch AssertionError e
      (println "Error on input" n)
      (throw e))))

; Error on input 0
;=> java.lang.AssertionError: Assert failed: (pos? %)
```

Even when adhering to the tenets of the preconditions, we've uncovered an error in the sqr function at the postcondition end. Postconditions should be viewed as the guarantee of the return value given that the preconditions are met. The reason for the postcondition error is that the function's contract doesn't specify that the number n should be nonzero. By adding a check for zero (not= 0 n) in the preconditions, we can guarantee that the sqr function acts as expected. To perform this same verification using unit testing is trivial in this case, but what if the edge condition wasn't as obvious? In such a case, it's probable that the error might not be caught until it's too late. Of course, there's no guarantee that your contracts are comprehensive, but that's why domain expertise is often critical when defining them.

ADVANTAGES OF PRE- AND POSTCONDITIONS

Function constraints aren't code. They take the form of code, but that fact is only a matter of representation. Instead, constraints should be viewed as a specification language describing expectations and result assurances. On the other hand, unit tests are code, and code has bugs. Contracts, on the other hand, are essential semantic coupling.

Another potential advantage of contracts over tests is that in some cases, tests can be generated from the contracts themselves. Also, pre- and postconditions are amenable to being expressed as an overall description of the system itself, which can thus be

---

[4] For the sake of highlighting this technique, we've simplified our test driver. Testing a limited range of input values might not be an appropriate approach in all circumstances.

fed into a rule base for query and verification. Both of these cases are outside of the scope of this book, but you shouldn't be surprised if they make their way into future versions of Clojure. There's tremendous potential in Clojure's pre- and postconditions. Though they're currently low-level constructs, they can be used to express full-blown design by contract facilities for your own applications.

Clojure changes the way that you think.

13.3 A lack of design patterns

> *Any sufficiently complicated C or Fortran program contains an ad hoc, informally-specified, bug-ridden, slow implementation of half of Common Lisp.*
>
> —Greenspun's Tenth Rule

The book *Design Patterns: Elements of Reusable Object-Oriented Software* (Gamma et al 1995) was a seminal work of software design and development. You'd be hard pressed to find a software programmer in this day and age who's not familiar with this work. The book describes 24 software best practices encountered throughout the course of experience in developing software projects of varying sizes.

Design patterns have obtained a bad reputation in some circles, whereas in others they're considered indispensable. From our perspective, design patterns are a way to express software best practices in a language-neutral way. But where patterns fall short is that they don't represent pure abstraction. Instead, design patterns have come to be viewed as goals in and of themselves, which is likely the source of the antagonism aimed at them. The ability to think in abstractions is an invaluable skill for a software programmer to strengthen. In this section, we'll attempt to dissuade you from viewing Clojure features as design patterns (Norvig 1998) and instead as an inherent nameless quality.

13.3.1 Clojure's first-class design patterns

Most if not all of the patterns listed in the book are applicable to functional programming languages in general, and to Clojure in particular. But at its most pragmatic, the patterns described are aimed at patching deficiencies in popular object-oriented programming languages. This practical view of design patterns isn't directly relevant to Clojure, because in many ways the patterns are ever-present and are first-class citizens of the language itself. We won't provide a comprehensive survey of the ways that Clojure implements or eliminates popular design patterns but will provide enough to make our point.

OBSERVER

Clojure's `add-watch` and `remove-watch` functions provide the underpinnings of an observer (publisher/subscriber) capability based on reference types. We can illustrate this through the implementation of the simple `defformula` macro shown in listing 13.7.

Listing 13.7 A macro to create spreadsheet-cell-like formulas

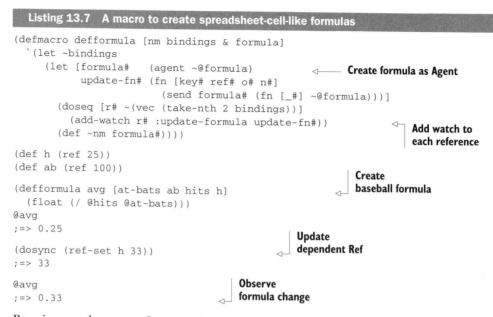

```
(defmacro defformula [nm bindings & formula]
  `(let ~bindings
     (let [formula#   (agent ~@formula)                    Create formula as Agent
           update-fn# (fn [key# ref# o# n#]
                        (send formula# (fn [_#] ~@formula)))]
       (doseq [r# ~(vec (take-nth 2 bindings))]
         (add-watch r# :update-formula update-fn#))        Add watch to
       (def ~nm formula#)))))                              each reference

(def h (ref 25))
(def ab (ref 100))
                                                           Create
(defformula avg [at-bats ab hits h]                        baseball formula
  (float (/ @hits @at-bats)))
@avg
;=> 0.25
                                                           Update
(dosync (ref-set h 33))                                    dependent Ref
;=> 33

@avg                                                       Observe
;=> 0.33                                                   formula change
```

By using watchers on references, you can use `defformula` to provide an abstract value that changes when any of its parts change. A more traditional Lisp approach is to provide predefined hooks (Glickstein 1997) that are called at certain times within the execution cycle. In addition, using `proxy` or `gen-class` to extend `java.util. Observable` is the most straightforward way to wire into existing source code using the Observer pattern.

STRATEGY

Algorithm strategies selected at runtime are common practice in Clojure, and there are a number of ways to implement them. One such way is via continuation-passing style, as we explored in section 7.3. A more general solution is to pass the desired function as an argument to a higher-order function, such as you'd see in the ubiquitous `map`, `reduce`, and `filter` functions. Further, we'll provide a case of dynamic error functions in the next section illustrating how Clojure's multimethods are a more powerful substitute for the classic strategy pattern.

VISITOR

The Visitor pattern is designed to describe a way to decouple operations on a structure from the structure itself. Even casual observers will see the parallel to Clojure's multimethods, protocols, types, proxies, and reify features.

ABSTRACT FACTORY

The Abstract Factory pattern is used to describe a way to create related objects without having to name explicit types at the point of creation. Clojure's types avoid the creation of explicit hierarchies (although ad hoc hierarchies can be created, as seen in section 9.2). Therefore, in Clojure this particular usage scenario is relegated to use within Java interoperability contexts. But the use of factory functions to abstract the call to the constructors of types and records is idiomatic and in fact actively promoted. The reasons for a Clojure-style factory are to simplify the importing requirements of a type or record, and also to add additional project-specific functionality to the constructor (keyword arguments, default values, and so on).

INTERPRETER

The Interpreter pattern is in every way Greenspun's Tenth Rule formalized. Many projects of sufficient size can be well served by the inclusion of a specialized grammar describing parts of the system itself. Clojure macros make the matter of creating specialized grammars a first-class member of the language.

BUILDER

The creation of complex structures from representation is central to Clojure programming, although it's viewed differently from a similar object-oriented approach—the Builder pattern. In section 8.4, we used a simple data representation as the input to Clojure's `clojure.xml/emit` function to produce an analogous XML representation. If you preferred a different output representation, then you could write another conversion function. If you preferred finer control over the constituent parts, then you could write functions or multimethods for each and specialize at runtime.

FAÇADE

The use of Clojure namespaces, as seen in section 9.1, is the most obvious way to provide a simplified façade for a more complex API. You can also use the varying levels of encapsulation (as outlined in section 2.4) for more localized façades.

ITERATOR

Iteration in Clojure is defined through an adherence to the seq protocol, as outlined in section 5.1 and later elaborated on in sections 9.3 about types and protocols.

DEPENDENCY INJECTION

Though not a classical pattern in the *Design Patterns* sense, dependency injection has become a de facto pattern for object-oriented languages that don't allow overridable class constructors. This condition requires that separate factory methods and/or classes create concrete instances conforming to a given interface. In forsaking the ability to define classes, Clojure completely avoids the problem that DI solves. Instead, Clojure's closest analogue to this "pattern" is the use of functions returning closures that are specialized based on the original arguments. Likewise, you could use partial application and composition similarly.

We could go further with this survey, but to do so would belabor the point: most of what are known as design patterns are either invisible or trivial to implement in Clojure. But what about the Prototype pattern, you ask? We implemented the UDP in section 9.2. Decorators or chain of responsibility? Why not use a macro that returns a function built from a list of forms spliced into the `->` or `->>` macro? Proxies would likely be implemented as closures and so would commands. The list goes on and on, and in the end you must face the inevitable—Clojure changes the way that you think.

13.4   *Error handling and debugging*

Our goal throughout this book was to show the proper way to write Clojure code, with mostly deferral and hand-waving regarding error handling and debugging. In this section, we'll cover these topics with what you might view as a unique twist, depending on your programming background.

13.4.1   *Error handling*

As we showed in figure 10.7, there are two directions for handling errors. The first, and likely most familiar, refers to the passive handling of exceptions bubbling outward from inner functions. But built on Clojure's dynamic Var binding is a more active mode of error handling, where handlers are pushed into inner functions. In section 11.10, we mentioned that the `binding` form is used to create thread-local bindings, but its utility isn't limited to this use case. In its purest form, dynamic scope is a structured form of a side effect (Steele 1978). You can use it to push Vars down a call stack from the outer layers of a function nesting into the inner layers, a technique that we'll demonstrate next.

DYNAMIC TREE TRAVERSAL

In section 8.4, we built a simple tree structure for a domain model where each node was of this form:

```
{:tag <node form>, :attrs {}, :content [<nodes>]}
```

As it turns out, the traversal of a tree built from such nodes is straightforward using mundane recursion, as shown:

```
(defn traverse [node f]
  (when node
    (f node)
    (doseq [child (:content node)]
      (traverse child f))))
```

For each node in the tree, the function f is called with the node itself, and then each of the node's children is traversed in turn. Observe how `traverse` works for a single root node:

```
(traverse {:tag :flower :attrs {:name "Tanpopo"} :content []}
          println)
; {:tag :flower, :attrs {:name Tanpopo}, :content []}
```

But it's much more interesting if we traverse trees larger than a single node. Therefore, we can build a quick tree from an XML representation using Clojure's `clojure.xml/parse` function:

```
(use '[clojure.xml :as xml])

(def DB
  (-> "<zoo>
        <pongo>
          <animal>orangutan</animal>
```

```
      </pongo>
      <panthera>
        <animal>Spot</animal>
        <animal>lion</animal>
        <animal>Lopshire</animal>
      </panthera>
    </zoo>"
  .getBytes
  (java.io.ByteArrayInputStream.)
  xml/parse))
```

The DB Var contains an animal listing for a small zoo. Note that two of the animals listed have the elements Spot and Lopshire; both are seemingly out of order for a zoo. Therefore, we can write a function to handle these nefarious intruders.

> **Listing 13.8 Handling nefarious tree nodes with exceptions**

```
(defn ^{:dynamic true} handle-weird-animal
  [{[name] :content}]                              ←── Define error handler
  (throw (Exception. (str name " must be 'dealt with'"))))

(defmulti visit :tag)

(defmethod visit :animal [{[name] :content :as animal}]
  (case name
    "Spot"     (handle-weird-animal animal)
    "Lopshire" (handle-weird-animal animal)
    (println name)))

(defmethod visit :default [node] nil)
```

The multimethod visit can be used as the input function to the traverse function and will only trigger when a node with the :tag attribute of :animal is encountered. When the method triggered on :animal is executed, the node :content is destructured and checked against the offending Spot and Lopshire values. When found, the devious node is then passed along to an error handler handle-weird-animal for reporting.[5] By default, the error handler throws an exception. This model of error handling is the inside-out model of exceptions. But handling errors in this way stops the processing:

```
(traverse DB visit)
; orangutan
; java.lang.Exception: Spot must be 'dealt with'
```

We've managed to identify Spot, but the equally repugnant Lopshire escapes our grasp. It'd be nice to instead use a different version of handle-weird-animal that allows us to both identify and deal with every such weird creature. We could pass handle-weird-animal along as an argument to be used as an error continuation,[6] but

---

[5] The metadata {:dynamic true} attached to handle-weird-animal isn't really used in Clojure 1.2, but it may be required in future versions of Clojure starting with 1.3 to allow the dynamic binding we're about to demonstrate.

[6] See section 7.3 for more information on continuation-passing style.

that pollutes the argument list of every function along the way. Likewise, we could inject `catch` blocks at a point further down the call chain, say within `visit`, but we might not be able to change the source, and if we could it makes for a more insidious pollution. Instead, using a dynamic binding is a perfect solution, because it allows us to attach specific error handlers at any depth in the stack according to their appropriate context:

```
(defmulti handle-weird  (fn [{[name] :content}] name))

(defmethod handle-weird "Spot" [_]
  (println "Transporting Spot to the circus."))

(defmethod handle-weird "Lopshire" [_]
  (println "Signing Lopshire to a book deal."))

(binding [handle-weird-animal handle-weird]
  (traverse DB visit))

; orangutan
; Transporting Spot to the circus.
; lion
; Signing Lopshire to a book deal.
```

As you might expect, this approach works across threads to allow for thread-specific handlers:

```
(def _ (future
          (binding [handle-weird-animal #(println (:content %))]
            (traverse DB visit))))
; orangutan
; [Spot]
; lion
; [Lopshire]
```

What we've outlined here is a simplistic model for a grander error-handling scheme. Using dynamic scope via `binding` is the preferred way to handle recoverable errors in a context-sensitive manner.

13.4.2 Debugging

The natural progression of debugging techniques as discovered by a newcomer to Clojure follows a fairly standard progression:

1. `(println)`
2. A macro to make `(println)` inclusion simpler
3. Some variation on debugging as discussed in this section
4. IDEs, monitoring, and profiling tools

Many Clojure programmers stay at step 1, because it's simple to understand and also highly useful, but there are better ways. After all, you're dealing with Clojure—a highly dynamic programming environment. Observe the following function:

```
(defn div [n d] (int (/ n d)))
```

The function `div` simply divides two numbers and returns an integer value. You can break `div` in a number of ways, but the most obvious is to call it with zero as the denominator: `(div 10 0)`. Such an example would likely not give you cause for concern should it fail, because the conditions under which it fails are fairly limited, well known, and easily identified. But not all errors are this simple, and the use of `println` is fairly limited. Instead, a better tool would likely be a generic breakpoint[7] that could be inserted at will and used to provide a debug console for the current valid execution context. Imagine it would work as follows:

```
(defn div [n d] (break) (int (/ n d)))
(div 10 0)
debug=>
```

At this prompt, you can query the current lexical environment, experiment with different code, and then resume the previous execution as before. As it turns out, such a tool is within your grasp.

A BREAKPOINT MACRO

We hope that by the end of this section, you'll understand that Lisps in general, and Clojure in particular, provide an environment where the whole of the language truly is "always available" (Graham 1993). First of all, an interesting fact to note is that the Clojure REPL is available and extensible via the Clojure REPL itself, via the `clojure.main/repl` function. By accessing the REPL implementation directly, you can customize it as you see fit for application-specific tasks.

Typing `(clojure.main/repl)` at the REPL seemingly does nothing, but rest assured you've started a sub-REPL. What use is this? To start, the `repl` function takes a number of named parameters, each used to customize the launched REPL in different ways. We'll utilize three such hooks—`:prompt`, `:eval`, and `:read`—to fulfill a breakpoint functionality.

OVERRIDING THE REPL'S READER

The `repl` function's `:read` hook takes a function of two arguments: the first corresponding to a desired display prompt, and the second to a desired exit form. We want the debug console to provide convenience functions—we'd like it to show all of the available lexical bindings and also to resume execution. It also needs to be able to read valid Clojure forms, but because that's too complex a task, we'll instead farm that functionality out to Clojure's default REPL reader.

Listing 13.9   A modest debug console reader

```
(defn readr [prompt exit-code]
  (let [input (clojure.main/repl-read prompt exit-code)]
    (if (= input ::t1)
      exit-code
      input)))
```

---

[7] The code in this section is based on `debug-repl` created by the amazing George Jahad, extended by Alex Osborne, and integrated into Swank-Clojure by Hugo Duncan.

We can start testing the reader immediately:

```
(readr #(print "invisible=> ") ::exit)
[1 2 3]
;=> [1 2 3]

(readr #(print "invisible=> ") ::exit)
::tl
;=> :user/exit
```

The prompt that we specified was of course not printed, and typing `::tl` at the prompt did nothing because the `readr` function isn't yet provided to the `repl` as its `:read` hook. But before we do that, we need to provide a function for the `:eval` hook. Needless to say, this is a more complex task.

OVERRIDING THE REPL'S EVALUATOR

In order to evaluate things in context, we first need a function cab to garner the bindings in the current context. Fortunately for us, Clojure macros provide an implicit argument `&env` that's a map of the local bindings available at macro-expansion time. We can then extract from `&env` the values associated with the bindings and zip them up with their names into a map for the local context, as shown next.

Listing 13.10   Creating a map of the local context using `&env`

```
(defmacro local-context []
  (let [symbols (keys &env)]
    (zipmap (map (fn [sym] `(quote ~sym)) symbols) symbols)))

(local-context)
;=> {}

(let [a 1, b 2, c 3]
  (let [b 200]
    (local-context)))
;=> {a 1, b 200, c 3}
```

The `local-context` macro provides a map to the most immediate lexical bindings, which is what we want. But what we really want to do is to provide a way to evaluate expressions with this contextual bindings map. Wouldn't you know it, the `contextual-eval` function from section 8.1 fits the bill. So now that we have the bulk of the implementation complete, we'll now hook into the `repl` function to provide a breakpoint facility.

PUTTING IT ALL TOGETHER

The hard parts are done, so to wire them into a usable debugging console is relatively easy, as shown next.

Listing 13.11   The implementation of a breakpoint macro

```
(defmacro break []
  `(clojure.main/repl
    :prompt #(print "debug=> ")
    :read readr
    :eval (partial contextual-eval (local-context))))
```

Using this macro, we can now debug the original `div` function:

```
(defn div [n d] (break) (int (/ n d)))
(div 10 0)
debug=>
```

Querying locals to find the "problem" is simple:

```
debug=> n
;=> 10
debug=> d
;=> 0
debug=> (local-context)
;=> {div #<user$div__155 user$div__155@51e67ac>, n 10, d 0}
debug=> ::tl
; java.lang.ArithmeticException: Divide by zero
```

So there's the problem! We passed in a zero as the denominator. We should fix that.

MULTIPLE BREAKPOINTS AND BREAKPOINTS IN MACROS

What would be the point if you couldn't set multiple breakpoints? Fortunately, you can, as we show in the following listing.

Listing 13.12 Using multiple breakpoints in function `keys-apply`

```
(defn keys-apply [f ks m]
  (break)
  (let [only (select-keys m ks)]
    (break)
    (zipmap (keys only) (map f (vals only)))))

(keys-apply inc [:a :b] {:a 1, :b 2, :c 3})

debug=> only
; java.lang.Exception: Unable to resolve symbol: only in this context
debug=> ks
;=> [:a :b]
debug=> m
;=> {:a 1, :b 2, :c 3}
debug=> ::tl
debug=> only
;=> {:b 2, :a 1}
debug=> ::tl
;=> {:a 2, :b 3}
```

And finally, you can use breakpoints within the body of a macro (in its expansion, not its logic), as shown next.

Listing 13.13 Using a breakpoint in a macro `awhen`

```
(defmacro awhen [expr & body]
  (break)
  `(let [~'it ~expr]
     (if ~'it
       (do (break) ~@body))))

(awhen [1 2 3] (it 2))
```

```
debug=> it
; java.lang.Exception: Unable to resolve symbol: it in this context
debug=> expr
;=> [1 2 3]
debug=> body
;=> ((it 2))
debug=> ::tl
debug=> it
;=> [1 2 3]
debug=> (it 1)
;=>  2
debug=> ::tl
;=> 3
```

There's much room for improvement, but we believe that the point has been made. Having access to the underpinnings of the language allows you to create a powerful debugging environment with little code. We've run out of ideas by now, so we'll say our credo only once more, and we hope by now you believe us.

Clojure changes the way that you think.

13.5 *Fare thee well*

This book possess many lacunae, but it's this way by design. In many cases, we've skipped approaches to solving problems via a certain route to avoid presenting non-idiomatic code. In many examples, we've left exposed wiring. For example, the defcontract macro requires that you partially apply the contract to the function under constraint instead of providing a comprehensive contract overlay façade. It was our goal to leave wiring exposed because exposed wiring can be explored, tampered with, and ultimately enhanced—which we hope you'll find the motivation to do. We've worked hard to provide a vast array of relevant references should you choose to further enhance your understanding of the workings and motivations for Clojure. But it's likely that we've missed some excellent resources, and we hope that you instead are able to uncover them in time. Finally, this wasn't a survey of Clojure, and many of the functions available to you weren't used in this book. We provide some pointers in the resource list, but there's no way that we could do justice to the libraries and applications mentioned and those unmentioned. We implore you to look deeper into the functionality of not only Clojure, but the rich ecology of libraries and applications that have sprung up in its relatively short life span.

Thank you for taking the time to read this book; we hope it was as much a pleasure to read as it was for us to write. Likewise, we hope that you'll continue your journey with Clojure. Should you choose to diverge from this path, then we hope that some of what you've learned has helped you to view the art of programming in a new light. Clojure is an opinionated language, but it and most of its community believe that these opinions can work to enhance the overall state of affairs in our software industry. The onus is on us to make our software robust, performant, and extensible. We believe that the path toward these goals lies with Clojure.

Do you?

—FOGUS AND HOUSER 2010

resources

Miscellaneous resources

Abadi, Martin, and Luca Cardelli. 1996. *A Theory of Objects.* New York: Springer. Although not a mathematical concept, object-oriented programming has obtained rigor with this gem.

Abelson, Harold, and Gerald Jay Sussman. 1988. "Lisp: A Language for Stratified Design." *AI Memo* (MIT) 986.

———. 1996. *Structure and Interpretation of Computer Programs.* Cambridge, MA: MIT Press. There is no better book for learning Scheme and the fine art of programming.

Abiteboul, Serge, Richard Hull, and Victor Vianu. 1995. *Foundations of Databases.* Boston: Addison-Wesley. Clojure's `clojure.set` namespace is actually modeled more on the named conjunctive algebra, for which this book provides a great reference.

Armstrong, Joe. 2007. *Programming Erlang.* Raleigh, NC: Pragmatic Bookshelf.

———. 2007. "A History of Erlang." *Proceedings of the Third ACM SIGPLAN Conference on History of Programming Languages.*

Bagwell, Phil. 2001. *Ideal Hash Trees.* Technical report. Clojure's persistent data structures owe a lot to Phil Bagwell's paper.

Baker, Henry. 1993. "Equal Rights for Functional Objects or, The More Things Change, The More They Are the Same." ACM SIGPLAN OOPS *Messenger* 4, no. 4.

Beck, Kent. 2002. *Test Driven Development: By Example.* Boston: Addison-Wesley.

Bloch, Joshua. 2008. *Effective Java.* Upper Saddle River, NJ: Addison-Wesley.

Boncz, Peter, Zukowski Marcin, and Niels Nes. 2005. "MonetDB/X100: Hyper-Pipelining Query Execution." *Proceedings of the CIDR Conference.* This paper motivated the implementation of chunked sequences.

Bratko, Ivan. 2000. *PROLOG: Programming for Artificial Intelligence.* New York: Addison Wesley.

Budd, Timothy. 1995. *Multiparadigm Programming in Leda.* Reading, MA: Addison-Wesley. This is an expanded discussion of the complexities wrought from a mono-paradigm approach to software development.

Clinger, William. 1998. "Proper Tail Recursion and Space Efficiency." *Proceedings of the ACM SIGPLAN 1998 Conference on Programming Language Design and Implementation.*

Cormen, Thomas, Charles Leiserson, Ronald Rivest, and Clifford Stein. 2009. *Introduction to Algorithms.* Cambridge, MA: MIT Press. This is a great reference on algorithmic complexity and Big-O, and as an added bonus, you could use it to stop a charging rhinoceros.

Crockford, Douglas. 2008. *JavaScript: The Good Parts*. Yahoo Press.

Date, C.J. 2009. *SQL and Relational Theory: How to Write Accurate SQL Code*. Sebastopol, CA: O'Reilly.

Dijkstra, Edsger Wijbe. 1959. "A Note on Two Problems in Connexion with Graphs." *Numerische Mathematik* 1, no. 1. You could change the h function in listing 7.9 to (defn dijkstra-estimate-cost [step-cost-est sz y x] 0) to conform to the ideal presented in this paper.

Flanagan, David. 2006. *JavaScript: The Definitive Guide*. Sebastopol, CA: O'Reilly.

Forman, Ira, and Nate Forman. 2004. *Java Reflection in Action*. Greenwich, CT: Manning. Although reflection provides some meta-level manipulation, it's quite apart from the notion of functions as data.

Friedl, Jeffrey. 1997. *Mastering Regular Expressions*. Sebastopol, CA: O'Reilly.

Friedman, Daniel, Mitchell Wand, and Christopher T. Haynes. 2001. *Essentials of Programming Languages*. Cambridge, MA: MIT Press.

Gabriel, Richard, and Kent Pitman. 2001. "Technical Issues of Separation in Function Cells and Value Cells." This is a more thorough examination of the differences between Lisp-1 and Lisp-2.

Gamma, Erich, Richard Helm, Ralph Johnson, and John Vlissides. 1995. *Design Patterns: Elements of Reusable Object-Oriented Software*. Reading, MA: Addison-Wesley.

Ghosh, Debasish. 2010. *DSLs in Action*. Greenwich, CT: Manning. There is a much finer level of distinction determining what constitutes whole cloth, including that between internal and external DSLs. In this book, we focus on the classical Lisp model of internal DSLs, but *DSLs in Action* provides a survey of many DSL-creation techniques.

Glickstein, Bob. 1997. *Writing GNU Emacs Extensions*. Sebastopol, CA: O'Reilly.

Goetz, Brian. 2006. *Java Concurrency in Practice*. Upper Saddle River, NJ: Addison-Wesley. Why haven't you read this yet?

Goldberg, David. 1991. "What Every Computer Scientist Should Know About Floating-Point Arithmetic." *Computing Surveys* (March).

Graham, Paul. 1993. *On Lisp*. Englewood Cliffs, NJ: Prentice Hall. Is there any book or any author more influential to the current generation of dynamic programmers than Graham and *On Lisp*?

———. 1995. *ANSI Common Lisp*. Englewood Cliffs, NJ: Prentice Hall.

Gray, Jim, and Andreas Reuter. 1992. *Transaction Processing: Concepts and Techniques*. San Mateo, CA: Morgan Kaufmann Publishers.

Halloway, Stuart. 2009. "Clojure is a better Java than Java." Presented at the Greater Atlanta Software Symposium, Atlanta. The origin of the phrase "Java.next" most likely stems from this talk by Halloway.

Hart, Peter, Nils Nilsson, and Bertram Raphael. 1968. "A Formal Basis for the Heuristic Determination of Minimum Cost Paths." *IEEE Transactions on Systems Science and Cybernetics In Systems Science and Cybernetics* 4, no. 2.

Hewitt, Carl, Peter Bishop, and Richard Steiger. 1973. "A Universal Modular ACTOR Formalism for Artificial Intelligence." *Proceedings of the Third International Joint Conference on Artificial Intelligence*.

Heinlein, Robert. 1966. *The Moon Is a Harsh Mistress*. New York: Putnam. We had considered offering an implementation of Mike as an appendix, but we ran over our page count.

Herlihy, Maurice, and Nir Shavit. 2008. *The Art of Multiprocessor Programming*. Amsterdam; Boston: Elsevier/Morgan Kaufmann.

Hickey, Rich. 2009. "Are We There Yet?" Presented at JVM Languages Summit. This wonderful presentation made firm the popular view of Rich as Philosopher Programmer.

Hofstadter, Douglas. 1979. *Gödel, Escher, Bach: An Eternal Golden Braid*. New York: Basic Books. See the sections "Classes and Instances," "The Prototype Principle," and "The Splitting-off of Instances from Classes" for more detail of the topics in section 9.2.

Hoyte, Doug. 2008. *Let Over Lambda.* Lulu.com. This is an amazing look into the mind-bending power of Common Lisp macros that provided the motivation for the DSLs section of this book. It will blow your mind—in a good way.

Hudak, Paul. 2000. *The Haskell School of Expression: Learning Functional Programming Through Multimedia.* New York: Cambridge University Press.

Huet, Gerard. 1997. "Functional Pearl: The Zipper." *Journal of Functional Programming.*

Hutton, Graham. 1999. "A Tutorial on the Universality and Expressiveness of fold." *Journal of Functional Programming* 9, no. 4.

Kahan, William, and Joseph Darcy. 1998. "How Java's Floating-Point Hurts Everyone Everywhere." Presented at the ACM Workshop on Java for High-Performance Network Computing. This paper provides more information on the cyclopian nightmares awaiting you in Java floating point.

Keene, Sonya. 1989. *Object-Oriented Programming in Common Lisp: A Programmer's Guide to CLOS.* Boston: Addison-Wesley. The best book on CLOS ever written.

Knuth, Donald. 1997. *The Art of Computer Programming: Volume 1 - Fundamental Algorithms.* Reading, MA: Addison-Wesley. This book goes into exquisite detail about the primary characteristics of FIFO queues and is highly recommended reading.

———. 1998. *The Art of Computer Programming, Vol. 3: Sorting and Searching.* Reading, MA: Addison-Wesley. Running quick-sort on a sorted sequence is an $O(n^2)$ operation, which for our implementation in chapter 6 completely defeats its laziness.

Koenig, Dierk, Andrew Glover, Paul King, Guilaume LaForge, and Jon Skeet. 2007. *Groovy in Action.* Greenwich, CT: Manning.

Kuki, Hirondo, and William James Cody. 1973. "A Statistical Study of the Accuracy of Floating Point Number Systems." *Communications of the ACM* 1973 16, no. 4.

Laddad, Ramnivas. 2003. *AspectJ in Action: Practical Aspect-Oriented Programming.* Greenwich, CT: Manning. We do not do justice to the notion of aspects—so read this instead.

Martin, Robert. 2002. *Agile Software Development: Principles, Patterns, and Practices.* Upper Saddle River, NJ: Prentice Hall.

McCarthy, John. 1960. "Recursive Functions of Symbolic Expressions and Their Computation by Machine, Part I." *Communications of the ACM.* This is the essay that started it all.

———. 1962. *LISP 1.5 Programmer's Manual.* Cambridge, MA: MIT Press. Lisp had an array type at least as early as 1962. Sadly, this fact is little known.

McConnell, Steve. 2004. *Code Complete: A Practical Handbook of Software Construction.* Redmond, WA: Microsoft Press.

Meyer, Bertrand. 1991. *Eiffel: The Language.* New York: Prentice Hall. The programming language Eiffel relies heavily on contract-based programming methodologies, a cornerstone element of Fogus's philosophy of Apperception-Driven Development.

———. 2000. *Object-Oriented Software Construction.* Upper Saddle River, NJ: Prentice Hall.

Michie, Donald. 1968. "Memo Functions and Machine Learning." *Nature 218.*

Mooers, Calvin, and Peter Deutsch. 1965. "TRAC, A Text-Handling Language."

Moseley, Ben, and Peter Marks. 2006. "Out of the Tar Pit." Presented at SPA2006.

Mozgovoy, Maxim. 2009. *Algorithms, Languages, Automata, and Compilers: A Practical Approach.* Sudbury, MA: Jones and Bartlett Publishers.

Noble, James, and Brian Foote. 2003. "Attack of the Clones." *Proceedings of the 2002 Conference on Pattern Languages of Programs 13.* The clone function is inspired by this paper.

Norvig, Peter. 1991. *Paradigms of Artificial Intelligence Programming: Case Studies in Common Lisp.* San Francisco: Morgan Kaufman Publishers.

Odersky, Martin, Lex Spoon, and Bill Venners. 2008. *Programming in Scala: A Comprehensive Step-by-step Guide.* Mountain View, CA: Artima.

Okasaki, Chris. 1996. "The Role of Lazy Evaluation in Amortized Data Structures." Presented at the International Conference on Functional Programming. This is a much more thorough discussion of incremental vs. monolithic computation.

———. 1999. *Purely Functional Datastructures.* Cambridge University Press. Chris Okasaki to the rescue again! Clojure's persistent queue implementation is based on Okasaki's batched queue from this seminal work.

Olsen, Russ. 2007. *Design Patterns in Ruby.* Upper Saddle River, NJ: Addison-Wesley

Papadimitriou, Christos. 1986. *Theory of Database Concurrency Control.* New York: Computer Science Press, Inc.

Pierce, Benjamin. 2002. *Types and Programming Languages.* Cambridge, MA: MIT Press. Fun fact: Representing numbers using lambda calculus is known as *church encoding*. The church-encoded number 9 would be represented as `(fn [f] (fn [x] (f (f (f (f (f (f (f (f (f x))))))))))` in Clojure.

Raymond, Eric. 2003. *The Art of Unix Programming.* Reading, MA: Addison-Wesley Professional.

Rosenberg, Doug, Mark Collins-Cope, and Matt Stephens. 2005. *Agile Development with ICONIX Process: People, Process, and Pragmatism.* Berkeley, CA: Apress.

Skeel, Robert. 1992. "Roundoff Error and the Patriot Missile." *SIAM News* 25, no. 4: 11.

Steele, Guy L. 1977. "Lambda: the Ultimate GOTO." *ACM Conference Proceedings.*

———. 1990. *Common LISP: The Language.* Bedford, MA: Digital Press. This is a very witty book in addition to being packed with information.

Steele, Guy L., and Gerald Sussman. 1978. "The Art of the Interpreter." *AI Memo* (MIT) 453.

Stewart, Ian. 1995. *Concepts of Modern Mathematics.* New York: Dover. These Dover math books are often true gems. It would be great to see an adventurous publisher print a similar series revolving around C.S.-relevant topics—monads, category theory, lambda calculus, and so on.

Sussman, Gerald, and Guy L. Steele. 1975. "Scheme: An Interpreter for the Extended Lambda Calculus." *Higher-Order and Symbolic Computation* 11, no. 4. This is a discussion of Scheme's early implementation of lexical closures.

Symbolics Inc. 1986. *Reference Guide to Symbolics Common Lisp: Language Concepts.* Symbolics Release 7 Document Set.

Thompson, Simon. 1999. *Haskell: The Craft of Functional Programming.* Reading, MA: Addison-Wesley.

Ullman, Jeffrey. 1988. *Principles of Database & Knowledge-Base Systems Vol. 1: Classical Database Systems.* Rockville, MD: Computer Science Press.

Ungar, David, and Randal Smith. 1987. "SELF: The power of simplicity." Presented at the Conference on Object-Oriented Programming Systems, Languages, and Applications (OOPSLA), Orlando. The Self programming language is likely the greatest influence on prototypal inheritance.

Van Roy, Peter, and Seif Haridi. 2004. *Concepts, Techniques, and Models of Computer Programming.* Cambridge, MA: MIT Press.

Wadler, Philip. 1989. "Theorems for Free!" Presented at the fourth International Conference on Functional Programming and Computer Architecture.

Wampler, Dean, and Alex Payne. 2009. *Programming Scala.* Sebastopol, CA: O'Reilly.

Whitehead, Alfred North. 1929. *Process and Reality: An Essay in Cosmology.* Cambridge University Press. For a general overview of Whitehead, see *The Wit And Wisdom of Alfred North Whitehead* by A.H. Johnson (Boston, Beacon Press, 1947).

Williams, Laurie. 2002. *Pair Programming Illuminated.* Boston: Addison-Wesley Professional. The limitations of the book format only shadow the idealistic model of pair programming.

Online resources

Braithwaite, Reginald. 2007. "Why Why Functional Programming Matters Matters." http://mng.bz/2pZP. This column discusses a language-level separation of concerns.

Clementson, Bill. 2008. "Clojure could be to Concurrency-Oriented Programming what Java was to OOP." http://bc.tech.coop/blog/081201.html. A much deeper discussion concerning Erlang actors and Clojure agents.

Dekorte, Steve. Io. http://iolanguage.com.

Fogus, Michael. Lithp. http://github.com/fogus/lithp.

Fowler, Martin. 2005. "Fluent Interface." http://mng.bz/e2r5.

———. 2007. "Mocks Aren't Stubs." http://mng.bz/mq95.

Graham, Paul. Arc. www.paulgraham.com/arc.html.

———. 2001. "What Made Lisp Different." www.paulgraham.com/diff.html. As Paul Graham states, "The whole language always available" appears as a theme throughout this book and as a finale in section 13.5.

Houser, Chris. error-kit API. http://mng.bz/07FF. The `clojure.contrib.error-kit` namespace contains an open error system similar to CL conditions that don't require recompilation when defining new error types.

Krukow, Karl. 2009. "Understanding Clojure's PersistentVector Implementation." http://mng.bz/tmjv.

Lindholm, Tim, and Frank Yellin. 1999. Java Virtual Machine Specification. http://java.sun.com/docs/books/jvms/.

Peter. 1998. "Design Patterns in Dynamic Programming." http://norvig.com/design-patterns/. The section on design patterns was inspired by this presentation.

Tarver Mark. 2008. *Functional Programming in Qi.* www.lambdassociates.org/Book/page000.htm. Some programming languages perform partial application automatically when a function is supplied with fewer than the expected number of arguments. One such language is Qi.

———. 2009. "The Next Lisp: Back to the Future." http://mng.bz/8wA9. The notion of Lisp as a programming language genotype is explored.

_why. Shoes. http://github.com/shoes/shoes.

Yegge, Steve. 2006. "Execution in the Kingdom of Nouns." http://mng.bz/9ApS.

———. 2008. "The Universal Design Pattern." http://mng.bz/6531. Like many programmers of our generation, we were in many ways inspired and influenced by Steve Yegge's work—which is why we asked him to write this book's foreword.

index